A Dictionary of All Religions and Religious Denominations

THE AMERICAN ACADEMY OF RELIGION
CLASSICS IN RELIGIOUS STUDIES

Carl A. Raschke, Editor

Classics in Religious Studies, No. 8

A Dictionary of All Religions
and Religious Denominations

by

Hannah Adams

Introduction by

Thomas A. Tweed

A DICTIONARY OF ALL RELIGIONS AND RELIGIOUS DENOMINATIONS

JEWISH, HEATHEN, MAHOMETAN, CHRISTIAN, ANCIENT AND MODERN

by
Hannah Adams

Introduction by
Thomas A. Tweed

Scholars Press
Atlanta, Georgia

THE AMERICAN ACADEMY OF RELIGION
CLASSICS IN RELIGIOUS STUDIES

A Dictionary of All Religions and Religious Denominations

Library of Congress Cataloging-in-Publication Data

Adams, Hannah, 1755-1831.
A dictionary of all religions and religious denominations : Jewish heathen, Mahometan, Christian, ancient, and modern / by Hannah Adams ; introduction by Thomas A. Tweed.
p. cm. — (Classics in religious studies ; no. 8)
Originally published: 4th ed. Boston : Cummings and Hilliard, 1817. With new introd.
Includes bibliographical references.
ISBN 1-55540-727-7 (alk. paper). — ISBN 1-55540-728-5 (pbk. : alk. paper)
1. Religion—Dictionaries. 2. Religions—Dictionaries.
I. Tweed, Thomas A. II. Title. III. Series.
BL31.A3 1992
291'.03—dc20 92-15133
CIP

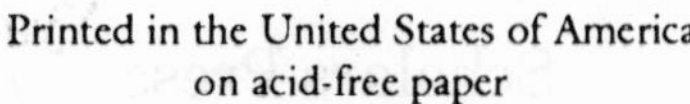

Printed in the United States of America
on acid-free paper

CONTENTS

Introduction by Thomas A. Tweed vii

Key Entries xxxv

A Note on the Text xxxix

A DICTIONARY OF ALL RELIGIONS AND RELIGIOUS DENOMINATIONS by Hannah Adams 1

INTRODUCTION
Hannah Adams's Survey of the Religious Landscape*

Thomas A. Tweed

Hannah Adams (1755-1831) began writing the first edition of her groundbreaking survey of religions in her house in Medfield, Massachusetts, in 1778. As she penned that book, Adams looked out on the broad pastures and cultivated fields of "South Plain," the name the locals gave to that area of the town that lies about twenty miles southwest of Boston. Like her contemporaries, she might have illuminated the page by following the sunlight around the house, moving her chair and table from window to window. From any vantage point Adams encountered only the natural landscape since she had no close neighbors at the time. She might have seen an occasional tall tree, left there so that cows could shade themselves in summer. But from any window the land looked flat. As you walked it, however, the view changed. Adams, who reported that she loved nature, might have noticed on her walks, for instance, that the west end of the pasture sloped slightly toward the river or that the ground swelled near that large oak.[1]

---

*The author gratefully acknowleges the support of the National Endowment for the Humanities (#FE-26028-91). A grant from the NEH allowed him to finish research for this introduction.

[1] On the starting date of Adams's research and writing see the informal autobiographical account she provided at the request of William S. Shaw, one of her friends and benefactors. Hannah Adams to William Shaw, 28 Aug. 1805, Hannah Adams Papers, Massachusetts Historical Society, Boston, Massachusetts. On Adams's love of nature see Hannah Adams, *A Memoir of Miss Hannah Adams, Written by Herself with Additional Notices by a Friend* (Boston: Gray and Bowen, 1832): 5, 51.

The same happened, it seems, as Adams—out of financial need and raging curiosity—began to survey the religious landscape. At first it seemed flat. Yet the more she explored, the more textured, the more irregular, it got. Adams had been raised in Medfield, an old New England town of Puritan heritage. She quickly discovered, however, that there was much beyond the established Congregational Church which had been gathering in the town meeting house since 1653. The religious ground included not only Baptists, the only "dissenting" group in Medfield during her lifetime, but also Swedenborgians and Moravians, Zoroastrians and Buddhists. At least at first, Adams wandered that broad religious plain disoriented by its vastness, surprised by its variability, and, as she acknowledged, disquieted. Adams was disturbed by the competing claims of Christian groups. "As I read controversy," she recalled, "I suffered extremely from mental indecision, while persuing the various and contradictory arguments adduced by men of piety and learning in defence of their respective religious systems. Sometimes my mind was so strongly excited, that extreme feeling obliged me for a time to lay aside my employment." She also was worried by "this great and painful truth"—that "heathens" and Muslims greatly outnumbered Christians. Vast numbers remained beyond the boundaries of Christendom.[2]

Adams also was unsettled by the vast terrain, in part, because she felt unprepared for the task of mapping it. Sometimes she hinted that her handicaps arose from fixed factors such as disposition or gender. For example, she traced the "mental indecision" she experienced as she confronted competing religious claims to inherited characteristics. Her mind, she explained, was "*naturally* wanting in firmness and decision." Most often she blamed her lack of formal education or her unwise reading habits. "Stimulated by an ardent curiosity," she recalled years later, " I entered the vast field of religious controversy, for which my reading had ill prepared me." She had been too ill to attend school regularly; and, as one of her friends pointed out, the schools in rural communities in the 1760s and 1770s were not particularly good anyway. Adams had one important

2 On her motives for writing her book, see Adams, *Memoirs*, 12-13. On the history of Medfield, see William S. Tilden, *History of the Town of Medfield, Massachusetts, 1650-1886* (Boston: George H. Ellis, 1887) and *Medfield Reflections* (Medfield: The 325th Anniversary and Special Bicentennial Committee for the Town of Medfield, Massachusetts, 1976). She described her "mental indecision" in Adams, *Memoirs*, 14. She noted the "great and painful truth" about the religious world in the edition reprinted here: Hannah Adams, *A Dictionary of All Religions and Religious Denominations, Jewish, Heathen, Mahometan, and Christian, Ancient and Modern* (Boston: Cummings and Hilliard, 1817), 375.

advantage: her bookish father encouraged her learning and guided her reading. Yet, like other women of the age, Adams complained that she had been hampered by reading too much "women's literature," which stimulated the sentiments, not the reason. She had been, to use her own words, "debilitated by reading Romances and novels, which are addressed to the fancy and the imagination." If only she had read works of theology like the young men training for the ministry at Harvard, Adams believed, she might have been better prepared to adjudicate the disputes she encountered as she surveyed the contradictory claims of Christian groups and world religions.[3]

Yet she overcame the obstacles—sexism, shyness, and poverty as well as religious doubt, limited education, and "debilitating" reading. She finished her survey, and it was published in 1784 as *Alphabetical Compendium of the Various Sects Which Have Appeared from the Beginning of the Christian Era to the Present Day*. By 1817, when the version of the book that is reprinted here was issued as *A Dictionary of All Religions and Religious Denominations*, it had changed its title twice and had appeared in three previous American editions and two British editions.[4]

"A Mere Woman"

Of all the obstacles Adams faced as she set out to describe the religious landscape, the internal and external effects of sexism might have been the greatest. With the publication of her *Alphabetical Compendium*, and the eight books and pamphlets that followed, Adams became the first woman in America to earn her living by writing. Even more than the next generation of liberal New England female authors such as Lydia Maria Child (1802-80) and Catharine Maria Sedgwick (1789-1867), then, Adams

---

[3] Adams, *Memoirs*, 14, 12, 14-15.

[4] For bibliographical information on the four editions, see my "Note on the Text" in this reprint edition. Unless otherwise noted, all references in this introduction are to the fourth and final American edition of Adams's survey, the one reprinted here. Adams's survey was published in England with a preface and additions by the Reverend Andrew Fuller, the Baptist theologian and missionary advocate. It also appeared there in another form. Thomas Williams, the Calvinist preacher, edited that version. See Hannah Adams, *A View of Religions, in three parts...A new edition, with corrections and additions. To which is prefixed, An essay on truth, by Andrew Fuller* (London: W. Button & Son, 1805) and Hannah Adams, *A Dictionary of All Religions and Religious Denominations...; including the substance of Mrs. [sic] H. Adams's View of Religions, reduced to one alphabet, with 150 additional articles, the whole carefully corrected and revised by Thomas Williams.... To the whole is prefixed An Essay on Truth, by Andrew Fuller* (London: Printed by T. Smith for Button and Son, 1815).

had to struggle with the most basic issue: Is it proper, even possible, for women to earn a living by writing? Child and Sedgwick, at least, had the advantage of her example and that of others. Adams had to find her own way. For her, the inhibiting pressures of sexism were both internal and external. On the one hand, she fought self-deprecating impulses all her life. Those impulses arose from her conviction that she had been poorly trained for her profession and from an awkwardness bred by the seclusion of her sickly childhood. Yet, no doubt, they also were rooted in socially constructed notions of gender identity. Reflecting the ethos of her age, at times Adams called herself "a mere woman." She was not a feminist—if we define feminism as explicit and unambiguous verbal support for women's equality in the public sphere. In fact, it is difficult to say whether Adams would have had the courage to publish if she had not been driven to it by the force of poverty. She tried publishing because her father had failed miserably in business, and she needed to support herself and her sister. She did show uncommon boldness when it was in the line of professional duty: Adams felt free to ask prominent strangers to help her with her research. For example, she wrote to the busy John Carroll (1735-1815), the first American Catholic bishop, to request information on Catholics. After her first book she also allowed herself some self-congratulation. Adams began to sense that books could be more than a way to survive. They might be useful. She might be useful. "It was poverty not ambition, or vanity, that first induced me to become an author...but now I formed the flattering idea, that I might not only help myself, but benefit the public." Encouraged and advised by members of the Boston elite, she also mustered the courage to squabble publicly with a prominent Congregationalist minister, Jedidiah Morse (1761-1826), over the rights to the publication of a textbook on New England history. Yet she felt most at home alone with her books or in the company of a small group of female friends. Most other times, observers agreed, she seemed unsure of herself.[5]

---

[5] John Carroll to Hannah Adams, n.d. [c.1791?], Hannah Adams Papers, New England Historic Genealogical Society, Boston, Massachusetts. Adams, *Memoirs*, 22. For Adams view of the conflict with Jedidiah Morse, with "notices" in her support by friends, see Hannah Adams, *Narrative of the Controversy Between the Rev. Jedidiah Morse, D.D. and the Author* (Boston: John Eliot Printer; sold by Cummings and Hilliard and Read, Cornhill and Isaiah Thomas, Jr., 1814). See also the letters regarding the incident, especially those between Adams and Morse, in the Massachusetts Historical Society. For example, see Jedidiah Morse to Hannah Adams, 26 Sept. 1804, Massachusetts Historical Society. Adams's first, and longer, history of New England appeared as Hannah Adams, *A Summary History of New England, From the First Settlement at Plymouth, to the Acceptance of the Federal*

Adams, then, dipped her toes into the waters of the male public sphere cautiously and tentatively; and once she took the plunge, she found that the currents ran both warm and cold. In some ways her gender, and the prevailing sexism, worked in her favor. Partly out of respect for her erudition and sympathy for her poverty, yet also apparently from a condescending chivalry, a number of prominent Boston professionals befriended her. Men at the Boston Athenaeum and the Massachusetts Historical Society allowed her access to their forbidden halls. The Reverend Joseph Stevens Buckminster (1784-1812), the young but influential Unitarian preacher, and President John Adams, a distant relative, invited her to browse their personal libraries so that she no longer would have to squat in bookseller's shops copying information for hours. Local professionals wrote letters on her behalf. They negotiated with publishers and helped sell her books. They vigorously defended her in the public debate with Morse. They even arranged to pay her an annual stipend so that she would not have to worry about money. If being a woman was a main portion of her problem, it also helped attract aid—sincere and condescending—from the elite.[6]

In most ways, however, her gender was yet another handicap. Adams acknowledged this in her typically cautious and self-deprecating way. In her *Memoir*, she quoted a passage from a biography of the British poet and novelist, Charlotte Smith (1749-1806), in which the biographer complained that the "penalties and discouragements attending authors in general fall upon woman with double weight." Adams then added a qualified endorsement of this assessment: "Though I have been too insignificant, and treated with too much candor, fully to realize the above remarks, yet I have been in a situation deeply to feel the trials which attend literary pursuits." Lydia Child, who had met the elderly Adams, was less hesitant to point out the negative effects of sexism for Adams and other female authors of the previous generation. Child wrote of Adams sixty

---

Constitution (Dedham: H. Mann and J. H. Adams, 1799). The abridged edition intended for classroom use, which was the center of the controversy with Morse, had a different title: Hannah Adams, *An Abridgment of the History of New England, for the Use of Young Persons* (1801; Boston: B. and J. Homans, and John West, A. Newell, printer, 1805).

6 On Adams's use of bookseller shops see Adams, *Memoir*, 28. For her use of the personal libraries of John Adams and Joseph Buckminster and for her account of William Shaw's role in allowing her to use the library of the Boston Athenaeum, see Adams, *Memoir*, 38, 74-75. The Unitarian minister, James Freeman, negotiated with publishers for her after her father no longer was able to do so. On this, see Adams, *Memoir*, 27. On her annual stipend see Adams, *Memoir*, 36-37.

years after the first edition of her *Dictionary of Religions* had appeared that "the prejudice against literary women was then much stronger than now." To illustrate, Child relayed a story, one of many that circulated about the learned but idiosyncratic Adams: "Someone happened to remark that they wondered Hannah Adams had never been married, for she was really a very sensible and pleasant woman. 'Marry Hannah Adams!,' exclaimed a gentleman who was present; 'why I should as soon think of marrying my Greek Grammar.'" Child felt compelled to reassure the reader that Adams had not been a textbook. In Adams's day, and Child's too, many remained uncomfortable with learning when it was found in a woman. It seemed incompatible with femininity.[7]

A few men seemed able to acknowledge her intellectual accomplishments without reference to gender, but not many. Ezra Stiles (1727-1795), the erudite and pious president of Yale, recorded this generous assessment in his diary for 25 September 1793: "Visited Miss Hannah Adams at 36 at Medfield and detained with her one day by NE Storm. She is an Authoress, & has read more than most psons [*sic*] of her age." Note that Stiles' qualification concerned age, not gender. He did not say that she had read rather widely for a woman. But most of those who admired her accomplishments could not see beyond the barrier of gender. Adams had dedicated the second edition of her compendium of religions to President John Adams. In return, he later praised her in one letter by saying that her writing had "done honor to your sex." As in this informal assessment, there often was a note of surprise, and perhaps even a touch of condescension, in the adulation that Adams received.[8]

Adams's Method: The Principles of Cartography

Even if many of Adams's early readers emphasized her singularity as a female writer—always the qualification—she herself was able to look beyond gender to the issues that confronted all those who had tried to map the religious world. She did not claim originality in that task. In fact,

---

7 Adams, *Memoir*, 34, 35. L[ydia] Maria Child, *Letters from New York*, Second Series, 11th ed. (New York: C. S. Francis; Boston: J. H. Francis, 1852): 133-34. Child's letter was dated 15 May, 1844. Adams's friend, Hannah Farnham Sawyer Lee, who wrote the "Additional Notices" affixed to Adams's posthumously published autobiography, also acknowledged that some contemporaries had thought of her as "a walking dictionary." See Adams, *Memoir*, 49.

8 Franklin Bowditch Dexter, ed., *Extracts from the Itineraries and Other Miscellanies of Ezra Stiles, D.D., LL.D., 1755-1794* (New Haven: Yale University Press, 1916), 507. John Adams to Hannah Adams, 27 August 1800, Adams Family Papers, Massachusetts Historical Society.

Adams described herself—here again the self-deprecating impulse—as a "compiler" rather than an author. Yet she boasted that her approach to the task was novel. She outlined her self-imposed guidelines in the "Advertisement" printed at the front of each edition. Adams vowed to be faithful to the self-understanding of those she described, using their own words wherever possible. She promised to offer a comprehensive and balanced view of the group's history, worldview, and practices and not focus on isolated or unflattering incidents. Adams wanted to be fair to secondary sources—even when she felt compelled to alter their accounts because the authors had violated her most important methodological principle, scholarly disinterestedness. She aimed, most of all, "to avoid giving the least preference of one denomination above another." Placing herself among the earliest Western students of religion to hold herself to such standards, Adams strove to avoid denigrating labels and withhold dismissive judgments.[9]

In fact, she claimed that she had been driven to write her first book, in part, by outrage at other biased accounts. To earn money, her father took in young male boarders. One of them taught her Latin and Greek. He also brought into the house a survey of religions authored by Thomas Broughton (1704-1774), a British clergyman of the Church of England. That book, *An Historical Dictionary of All Religions from the Creation of the World to the Present,* changed her life. She was so annoyed by its hostile treatment of dissenting Christian sects and various non-Christian religions that she began to read everything she could find on religious history. Adams discovered that other writers were little better, and so she resolved to write a more tolerant and accurate account. "I soon became disgusted with the want of candor in the authors I consulted, in giving the most unfavorable descriptions of the denominations they disliked, and applying to them the names of heretics, fanatics, enthusiasts, &. I therefore made a plan for myself, made a blank book, and wrote rules for transcribing, and adding to, my compilation."[10]

The View from Adams's Window: Mapping the Terrain

For Adams, the problem with Broughton's book, and others like it, began with the scheme for classifying religions. It was bivalent. Religions could be divided into two groups—true and false. Although Judaism was a bit

---

[9] Adams, *Memoir*, 22. Adams, "Advertisement," *Dictionary*.

[10] Thomas Broughton, *An Historical Dictionary of All Religions from the Creation of the World to This Perfect Time* (London: Printed for C. Davis and T. Harris, 1742). Adams, *Memoir*, 11.

closer to the true religion than the others since it was of divine origin, all other non-Christian traditions were dismissed as wholly and unambiguously false. The diversity that any student of religion encounters, even using eighteenth-century sources, was, finally, dissolved. "The first general division of Religion is into True and False," Broughton wrote. "That infinite variety, therefore, in the doctrines and modes of worship, which have prevailed in the world (one only scheme excepted) are but so many deviations from the truth, so many False Religions." Broughton did distinguish "four grand religions of the world"—"Pagan, Jewish, Christian, and Mohammedan." He also sometimes distinguished religions chronologically into "antient" and "modern." But these distinctions remained unimportant for Broughton. For him the religious landscape appeared rather limited in scope—and not especially forbidding or unsettling.[11]

If Adams had been able to accept Broughton's classification, her initial disorientation at the vastness of the religious field might have been reduced or eliminated. What diversity? Which competing claims? But, of course, she could not accept that bivalent scheme. Even though Adams clearly favored Christianity, she did not merely separate religions and sects into the true and the false. For the most part, as promised, she also avoided negative labels. But, as a person of her age who was restricted by her sources, Adams also did not alter significantly the basic map of the religious world that she inherited. In fact, the most basic contours of that map had changed little since the voyages of discovery. New peoples and religions were added here. New boundaries were drawn there. But until approximately the second quarter of the nineteenth century the religious world still was populated by Christians, Jews, Muslims, and "Pagans" or "Heathens." Christians, as those following the revealed religion, stood in the highest position. Jews were second best. Muslims, because they shared a monotheistic faith and some common heritage, stood next in the hierarchy. For Adams and most of her contemporaries, the final category, "Heathens" or "Pagans," included an extremely wide range of groups and peoples. In the entry under "Pagans" in her *Dictionary*, for instance, Adams listed four subgroups of those who stand outside the traditions of the monotheistic West. The first two included the religions of various ancient peoples (Greeks and Romans as well as "Chaldeans, Phenicians, and Sabians, etc..."). Next came the major Asian religions ("The Chinese,

---

11 Broughton, *Historical Dictionary*, 1.

Hindoos, Japanese, &"). Finally, Adams listed the religions of non-literate peoples (the "barbarians" of the Americas, the South Seas, and Africa).[12]

Adams's map of the religious world might seem distorted and crude by late-twentieth century standards; yet it was an advance over Broughton's sketch, and that of many others. She not only avoided a bivalent classification that undercut all subsequent distinctions and overvalued one tradition, but her subdivision and coverage of "heathen" religions was both more judicious and more comprehensive. The dictionary format itself—instead of Broughton's thematic organization—also added to the reader's sense of the vastness and variability of the terrain. Open Adams's *Dictionary* almost anywhere, and the reader encounters variety. A typical two-page selection might include, for instance, entries on a Christian sect, a Christian "heresy," a non-literate religion, and an Asian religion.[13]

But Adams's volume can be somewhat inaccessible for modern readers. Who are the "Bezpopoftschins" or the "Cerdonians"? Are they important? Look at the entries on Asian religions. The Buddhist "Birmins" are described as worshippers of "Boodh" while the Chinese Buddhists are described as worshippers of "Foe." Adams used different terms for Buddhism's founder, as her sources did; and she did not seem to understand that the object of veneration, the Buddha, and the tradition, Buddhism, were the same in the various Asian lands. Her labels and categories can be confusing. To offer another example, try to find Adams's treatment of Zoroastrianism. The reader could search all day for the entry if s/he did not know to look under "Gaurs." To add to the confusion, minor Christian sects or "heresies" receive disproportionate coverage in this book while some major religions receive only passing notice. To guide the reader, then, at the end of this introduction I include a list of key entries, with potentially confusing terms translated according to modern usage. Below I also place Adams's coverage of Western religions, Eastern

---

[12] For example, the classification scheme used by Thomas Jefferson, the Deist; Joseph Tuckerman, the Unitarian; Ezra Stiles, the Trinitarian Congregationalist; and David Benedict, the Baptist, were basically the same. Ezra Stiles, *The United States Elevated to Glory and Honour...*, 2nd ed. (1783; Worcester, Mass.: Isaiah Thomas, 1785), 132. John S. Pancake, ed., *Thomas Jefferson: Revolutionary Philosopher: A Selection of Writings* (Woodbury, N.J.: Barron's 1976), 326, 334. [Joseph Tuckerman], "On the Causes by which Unitarians Have Been Withheld from Exertions in the Cause of Foreign Missions," *Christian Examiner* 1 (May-June 1824): 183. David Benedict, *History of All Religions, As Divided into Paganism, Mahometism, Judaism, and Christianity* (Providence: John Miller, 1824), 1-51.

[13] See, for example, pages forty-six and forty-seven or pages fifty-four and fifty-five.

religions, and the religions of non-literate peoples in a wider context. I conclude with an assessment of Adams's place in the history of the study of religion.

Christianity, Judaism, and Islam

Once you begin to read through the entries you find that Adams did cover most of the religious world in one way or another, but Christianity received disproportionate attention. In fact, more than eighty-five percent of the more than seven hundred entries deal with "orthodox" or "heretical" Christian groups or ideas. This is not surprising since Adams was a committed Christian of Congregational heritage and Unitarian inclinations who wrote decades before the formal rise of the field of "comparative religion" or "the science of religions." But, to a large extent, she managed to set aside her heritage and inclinations as she composed her accounts of Christian sects. Adams wrote those accounts by sifting through primary and secondary sources for relevant information and then modifying the received interpretation according to her particular purposes and methodological principles. With few exceptions, the secondary sources that she found most helpful were travel accounts, sermons, histories, or encyclopedia entries written by Christians who were not afraid to reveal their evaluations of the groups they described. Two of her most often cited sources, for instance, were Broughton's Dictionary (the book that had annoyed her so much) and Johann Lorenz von Mosheim's (1694-1755) *An Ecclesiastical History, Antient and Modern, from the Birth of Christ to the Present Century*. The latter, a multi-volume work written by the influential German Lutheran church historian, was no more gentle with opposing views than Broughton's survey. In dealing with these secondary sources, Adams usually did what she promised: she omitted deprecatory labels and adjectives as she recorded information. Her treatment of the Anabaptists, that group of Protestants who often suffered persecution in Europe because of their unconventional beliefs, is typical. Mosheim had minced no words as he described "the frenzy of their disordered brains and the madness of their pretensions and projects." He called them "fanatical" and "outrageous." Only a hint of Mosheim's condemnation survives in Adam's account, however. In a much abbreviated description, she portrayed them as "a sect which arose in the time of Luther's Reformation in Germany, and excited various insurrections, under pretence of erecting the kingdom of Christ on earth." That word "pretence" is a bit loaded. By using it Adams implied that their claims were false. Yet overall, as with most accounts of Christian groups, the entry on Anabaptists in Adams's *Dictionary* was much less dismissive than that found in her sources.[14]

Of the many Christian groups that Adams described, most of them were as controversial as the Anabaptists. Many of them, in fact, were more controversial. She paid a great deal of attention to groups and ideas that lost in the battle for Christian orthodoxy. Of course, most of the traditional Christian groups and positions also are represented in her book. There are, for example, the expected depictions of "Protestants," "Roman Catholics," "Lutherans," and "Calvinists." Yet most of the entries on Christian topics concern dissenting viewpoints. Various Gnostic groups and positions—including Manichaeism, which was viewed as a Christian heresy—receive a surprising amount of coverage. Arians, Pelagians, and many other interpreters of doctrine who had been stamped as "heretical" by some official church body found their way into her overview too.

Adams's text also provides an excellent angle of vision from which to view the increasing diversity and shifting contours of American religion from the Revolution through the Second Great Awakening. As with surveys of American religion into the twentieth century, Adams underemphasized Native Americans everywhere, ignored African Americans living in the former colonies, and passed by Hispanic and French Catholics residing beyond the formal boundaries of the United States. Yet she read everything that she could find and continually asked

---

[14] Adams's other works on Christianity offer a glimpse of her religious views. See Hannah Adams, *The Truth and Excellence of the Christian Religion* (Boston: John West, 1804) and Hannah Adams, *Letters on the Gospels* (Cambridge: Hilliard and Metcalf, 1824). She explicitly sided with the Unitarians in her *Memoirs* (43). Besides being friends with important early Unitarian ministers such as James Freeman and Joseph Buckminster she also apparently went to hear the most famous and important Unitarian preacher of her day, William Ellery Channing (1780-1842). The membership records of Channing's church in Boston, Federal Street Church, do not include her name (Unitarian-Universalist Archives, Special Collections, Andover-Harvard Library, Harvard Divinity School, Cambridge, Massachusetts). Yet other evidence suggests that Adams regularly heard Channing preach. "She attended Dr. Channing's church," Lydia Child recalled, "and had great personal respect for him." Child, *Letters from New York,* 132. There are different ways to date the opening of the field of the "science of religions" or "comparative religions." I follow William Clebsch, who argued that the field formally arose in 1870, when Friedrich Max Müller in London and Émile Louis Burnouf in Paris independently and simultaneously called for a "scientific" study of religions. William A. Clebsch, "Apples, Oranges, and Manna: Comparative Religion Revisited," *Journal of the American Academy of Religion* 49 (Mar. 1981): 6. John Laurence Mosheim, *An Ecclesiastical History, Antient and Modern, From the Birth of Christ to the Present Century*, trans. by Archibald MacLaine, 5 vols., 2nd ed., (London: Printed for A. Millar and sold by T. Cadell, 1758), 3: 363, 4: 129-64.

her correspondents for more information. And she managed to provide a relatively comprehensive and representative view of the religious situation in the United States during this interesting transitional period. During the years she wrote, there were only a handful of synagogues in America, and a native Catholic church only officially emerged in 1790, when John Carroll was consecrated bishop of Baltimore. American religion looked mostly Protestant, but it was hardly homogeneous. It was a time of change, and most of the changes meant more rather than less pluralism. The older British Protestant sects, Congregationalists and Episcopalians, were losing some hold in New England and elsewhere. Dissenting denominations, Methodists and Baptists, were ascending. Her coverage reflected these, and other, changes. For example, she included the expected entries on "Puritans," "Congregationalists," and the "English Church." Yet, at the same time, the entry on the Methodists expanded in the second edition (1791). Reflecting other religious shifts underway, in that same edition a nine-page account of "Unitarianism" appeared for the first time too. Unitarians would not formally become a denomination until the middle of the nineteenth century, but many Congregational churches in eastern Massachusetts, began to embrace a more liberal faith during her adult years. After much thinking, she sided with the most traditional Unitarians, those who did not slide toward the view that Jesus was indistinguishable from other humans. "I deeply felt the difficulty upon both sides of the question," she revealed in her *Memoirs*, "yet prevailingly give the preference to that class of Unitarians, who adopt the highest idea of the greatness and dignity of the Son of God."[15]

In her *Dictionary*, Adams also provided a glimpse of other dissenting groups and new sects in America. She offered an extremely long account (ten and a half pages) of the Universalists, a denomination that began to emerge in the late-eighteenth century. She sneered at Deism, the view that emphasized natural and not supernatural sources of religious knowledge and was embraced by a small but influential collection of intellectuals. She described Moravians ("Unitas Fratrum"), Swedenborgians ("New Jerusalem Church"), and the Church of the Brethren ("Dunkers"). Adams also provided especially interesting views of the Shakers and the Universal Friends, two new communitarian sects that emerged from the revival, or "New Light Stir," that swept across rural New England in the

[15] Adams, *Memoir*, 43. More information about American religion was included in the appendix added to the fourth edition. There Adams reprinted Thomas Williams' overview of American Christian denominations.

late-eighteenth-century. Adding to the significance of these new groups for readers then and now, both sects were founded by women. The Shakers, or The United Society of Believers in Christ's Second Coming, were brought to America from England in 1774 when Ann Lee Stanley (1736-84) emigrated with eight followers. The Universal Friends, which was established by Jemima Wilkinson (1752-1819), flourished in Rhode Island and Connecticut from 1776 to 1789 (see "Jemima Wilkinson"). Adherents of both communities held a number of unconventional views; but they, like all other dissenters that Adams described, claimed to be orthodox Christians.[16]

The cumulative effect of Adams's treatment of Christianity, in America and elsewhere, was to highlight conflict and variety. Adams, perhaps only after she finished the first draft, realized this. In fact, a good deal of the anxiety that she experienced arose, no doubt, as she read and recorded accounts of the many versions of "orthodox" Christianity and the countless "heretical" ones. In the appendix to her book she tried to deal with the psychological discomfort and theological problems such a treatment might create. There she, first, bluntly acknowledged that "the diversity of sentiment among Christians has been exhibited in the preceding pages." She went on, however, to reassure her readers that this need not challenge their faith. "The candid mind," Adams continued, "will not consider those various opinions as an argument against divine revelation. The truth of the sacred writings is attested by the strongest evidence...." She then listed the evidence. Miracles and prophecies safeguarded the authority of revealed religion. So did the coherence of the scriptures, the rapid spread of the gospel, the purity of Christian precepts, and the "benevolent" impulse of Christian social ethics. Further, the dizzying diversity need not be so disorienting, she implied, since Christians—true Christians—have agreed on several fundamental doctrinal matters. Modifying slightly the famous summary of Edward Herbert of Cherbury (1583-1648), Adams claimed that all agree that (1) there is a supreme being; (2) this being is worthy of worship; (3) that Jesus is the appointed representative of this being; (4) that there will be some

---

16 On Shakers, Universal Friends, and the "New Light Stir" see Stephen A. Marini, *Radical Sects of Revolutionary New England* (Cambridge: Harvard University Press, 1982).

sort of resurrection of the dead; and (5) that virtue will be rewarded and vice punished in a future life.[17]

Whether or not she and her readers found the Christian apologetic affixed to her dictionary reassuring, there were other theological problems on the horizon. What do we make of the Jews? Scriptures prophesied, Adams believed, that the Jews would turn to Christianity before the end of the world and Christ's reappearance. Yet they remained unconverted. What, she asked herself, is the Christian's obligation in this context? She had an answer: it is to help bring Jews to the true faith and, so, fulfill Biblical prophecy and culminate sacred history. The entry on Adams in the *Encyclopedia of Judaica* claims that her *Dictionary* is "significant for the sympathetic tone of the article on the Jews;" and there is much truth in this assessment. For example, she seemed genuinely disturbed by their history of persecution. She also received information on Judaism from sympathetic correspondents like Henri Baptiste Grégoire (1750-1831), the famous French bishop who pleaded for tolerance toward Jews. And, in fact, the account of Judaism in Adams's survey is free of derisive comments or demeaning labels. In general, she provided a fair portrait.[18]

Yet, in her treatment of Judaism, she also added a substantial description of "The London Society for Promoting Christianity amongst the Jews." This might seem odd, even condescending or annoying, to some contemporary readers; but this "benevolent" cause was dear to Adams's heart. Like the members of this British organization, Adams was "devoutly waiting for the redemption of Israel." This hope, together with her admiration for Jewish persistence and her sorrow at Jewish suffering, helped animate her long labors on her two-volume study of the history of that religion. *The History of the Jews from the Destruction of Jerusalem to the Present Time*, published in the United States in 1812 and later in British and German editions, was well received. In particular, the members of the London group praised her work. Adams corresponded with its members and leaders, and she even established an American branch. On 5 June 1816, the year before the last edition of her *Dictionary* appeared, Adams founded "The Female Society of Boston and the Vicinity for Promoting

[17] Adams, *Dictionary*, 371-72. Adams also included a number of entries on various Western philosophers and philosophical schools that have challenged traditional Christian teachings. See "Sceptics" and "Spinosists."

[18] *Encyclopedia Judaica*, s.v. "Adams, Hannah." Adams and Grégoire, the French Catholic, had a substantial correspondence. See the seventeen letters from Grégoire to Adams, written between 1805 and 1823, in the Hannah Adams Papers, New England Historic Genealogical Society.

Christianity amongst the Jews." She acted as its corresponding secretary. Her commitment to this cause did not disable her as a scholar. As I have indicated, and others have noted, Adams's depiction of Judaism in her *Dictionary* certainly was not hostile. Yet, to the attentive reader, her passionate concern to bring the Jews to Christianity was not entirely hidden either.[19]

For Adams, Islam did not fit into the divine plan in quite the way that the Jews did. Her coverage reflected that belief. Yet Adams did include seven entries on Islam. She acknowledged the two main branches of Islam in one-line descriptions under "Schaites" (Shi'ites) and "Somnites" (Sunni). Two important Islamic movements are mentioned as well. Adams offered a fifty-five line account of Sufism ("Sufis"), the Islamic mystical tradition. Incorporating more recent developments, Adams also recounted the history and beliefs of the Wahhabi movement ("Wahabees"). Wahhabism, which rejected Sufism, was an Islamic reform movement founded by Ibn 'Abd al-Wahhab (1703-92). As Adams noted, Wahhab emphasized, among other things, the unity of God and condemned the creeping polytheism found in the popular veneration of Muslim saints. But the most important and comprehensive depiction of Islam was found in the four-and-one-half page entry under the term "Mahometans." In general, Adams represented the tradition fairly. She recounted the familiar details of Muhammad's life, even offering some praise: "He was endowed with a subtle genius, and possessed of great enterprise and ambition." She also provided a relatively sound overview of common Muslim beliefs. As promised, she let adherents speak for themselves by quoting from one original source.

Her portrait of Islam was less hostile than that of many other Westerners of her day, but her commitments and concerns found their way into the account in small ways too. For instance, she spoke of Muhammad's "pretensions" to a divine mission. She also anticipated a concern of her Christian readers: Islam had spread widely and rapidly, and some Muslims had cited this as evidence of its veracity—as Adams and others had pointed to Christianity's success to support its own claims to divine origin. In her main entry on Islam, Adams offered a response:

---

19 Hannah Adams, *A Concise Account of the London Society for Promoting Christianity Amongst the Jews* (Boston: John Eliot, 1816), 3. Hannah Adams, *The History of the Jews from the Destruction of the Temple to the Nineteenth Century*, 2 vols. (Boston: John Eliot, 1812). On the founding of the American branch of the London Society see "Religious Intelligence: Societies for Promoting Christianity among the Jews," *Christian Disciple* 4 (Nov. 1816): 249-255 and "Letter from Mr. Hawtrey to Miss Hannah Adams," *Christian Disciple* 5 (Feb. 1817): 62.

Muhammad's success was tainted. He "contrived by permission of polygamy and concubinage to make his creed patatable [*sic*] to the most depraved of mankind." Perpetuating another Western stereotype, she claimed that the founder also propagated his message by the sword. In other words, Christians need not be disturbed by the success of Islam since it attracted the most undesirable persons by the most violent means.

Zoroastrianism, the other major Western religion that Adams described, had not spread widely enough to worry Adams and her Christian contemporaries. There was, then, less coverage and no apologetics. She did offer her readers a sketch of this ancient Persian tradition, however, in four entries. As I noted above, the basic overview is found under "Gaurs." There she provided some basic information about the founder, Zarathustra (or "Zoroaster"), his teachings, and Zoroastrianism's most sacred text, the Avesta (or "Zend"). She portrayed the Magi, most famous for having visited Jesus' manger in Bethlehem, as "an ancient Persian sect who believed in two co-eternal principles." She even had some praise for this priestly tribe or caste who hailed from west of Persia and came to embrace Zoroastrianism: their priests attained to "extraordinary skill in philosophy." Adams acknowledged the Zoroastrians who settled on the West coast of India from the eighth century onward in a one sentence account ("Persees"). In the final, and perhaps most surprising, entry on this tradition, Adams briefly discussed the founder's worldview under the broad label, "Oriental Philosophy." Few modern readers would expect an overview of "Oriental Philosophy" to include only the teachings of Zarathustra. We are reminded of the historical gap that lies between us and this text in other ways too: Adams would not have classified Zoroastrianism with the other major Western religions, as most scholars today would. For her, that religion was yet another region of that extremely vast and mostly uncharted territory that she and her contemporaries called "heathenism."

"Heathenism"

The more than thirty-five entries on "heathen" or "pagan" traditions refer to the religions of Asian countries and ancient peoples, literate and non-literate, that remained beyond the reach of Judaism, Christianity, and Islam. Among the several "ancient nations" of the Middle East and Europe that Adams depicted were the Egyptians. For Adams and many of her contemporaries, Egypt was one of the most "renowned" and "refined" of the ancient nations. In separate entries she also noted the religions of other peoples such as the Babylonians, Greeks, Canaanites, and Celts (see

"Babylonians," "Grecians," "Sammans," and "Celtes"). The Celts, for instance, were "one of the primitive nations by which most parts of Europe were peopled." She referred to the Druids, the priestly class that presided over the ritual sacrifices of the Celts, in this main article and in a separate entry (see "Druids").

Several entries also dealt with the religions of non-literate peoples in Africa, the Americas, and the Pacific. Mostly because of recent interest shown by Christian missionaries, Adams's account of the "South Sea Islanders" was relatively substantial. A passing reference to the significance of thunder for natives in Brazil is found elsewhere in the volume ("Brazilians"), but the primary account of the natives of the Americas is found in the entry on "Indians." That five-page entry surveys the traditions of North, Central, and South America. As expected, Adams distorted the beliefs and practices of this great variety of peoples in some ways, but her account was remarkably free of open hostility. This might be even more surprising since she would have been educated in the local lore of her home town, and that lore included the story of an Indian raid that wiped out most of Medfield. We cannot know to what extent Adams saw native peoples as violent barbarians; but, with few exceptions, she managed to avoid dismissive labels and derogatory asides. (She did mention, however, "the *savage* tribes of Guiana.") Even where her account might seem to lead toward negative judgments, Adams sometimes invited the reader to pause just short of unqualified condemnation. For example, she anticipated and softened the implied criticism of the Amazonian tribes' use of religion to sanction war by comparing them to nominal Christians in the "civilized" West. "Upon their going out to war they hoist at the prow of their canoes that idol, under whose auspices they look for victory; but *like too many Christians*, they never pray to their gods, except in cases of difficulty, when they feel their need of divine assistance or support."[20]

Adams devoted three pages to the devotions of other native peoples—those of Africa (see "Negroes"). She failed to cite Charles de Brosses's book, *Du culte des dieux fétiches* (1760), but Adams relied heavily on a term that de Brosses had introduced ("fetishism") to interpret the beliefs and practices of these tribes. She hinted that native Africans approximate the beliefs of Westerners in their common affirmation of "a supreme Being" and "a future state." The implication, which few of her readers would have missed, was that there is some hope for these non-Christians since a

[20] Italics mine.

residue of an original monotheism and the distorted outlines of right belief could be found among them. Yet Adams allowed the condescending and Christian-centered perspective of her sources to seep into her account. In its most benign form, this perspective yielded a portrait of exotic tribes who worship the divine through the forms of nature—mountains, trees, and birds. In its most hostile form, some Africans (the inhabitants of "Benin") were portrayed as devil-worshippers. These pagans, Adams and her sources reported incredulously, even add to their offense by portraying this demonic figure as—the word was italicized for emphasis—*white*.

Some residue of incredulity, condescension, even hostility, can be found in Adams's accounts of Asian peoples and religions too. Yet, in general, Adams fairly transmitted the received knowledge about Asia. In fact, in her descriptions of Asian traditions, as throughout the volume, she always was more generous and judicious than the authors she consulted. For Adams, and the authors she read, Asian religions included Hinduism, Buddhism, Confucianism, Daoism, and Shinto. Actually, the Western intellectuals who read about Asian religions—and the traders, missionaries, and diplomats who encountered them directly—often had difficulty distinguishing among them. Until the middle of the nineteenth century or so, "The Orient" remained a single mass of "otherness"—even for many of the most sophisticated writers. The commonalties, most Western interpreters agreed, seemed much more important than the differences among them. The Asian religions were not-Christian. Asians themselves were, well, not-us. For those interested in making more precise distinctions, the sources were limited and contradictory. Confusions persisted. As late as 1845, for example, Ralph Waldo Emerson, one of the most sympathetic and influential American students of Asian religions, mistakenly identified the *Bhagavad Gita* as that "much renowned book of Buddhism."[21]

Academic Sinology and Indology began in Europe only several years before the final edition of Adams's *Dictionary* appeared; but among late-eighteenth and early-nineteenth century Americans who could draw distinctions, Confucianism and Hinduism were most widely known and most popularly appreciated. Systematic trade with China opened in 1784, and so Americans, especially on the major sea ports of the east coast, began their rather unsystematic introduction to its culture. Americans

---

21 Ralph L. Rusk, ed., *The Letters of Ralph Waldo Emerson* (New York: Columbia University Press, 1939), 3: 179. For an overview of American views of Asian religions in this period see Carl T. Jackson, *The Oriental Religions and American Thought: Nineteenth Century Explorations* (Westport, Conn.: Greenwood, 1981).

influenced by the Enlightenment were less enamored of Confucianism than many of their most prominent European counterparts, but still they followed the British and Continental pattern by celebrating the discovery of a tolerant and rational "natural religion" in Confucianism. The year 1784 also was important for the Western awareness of Hinduism. It was then that Sir William Jones and a small group of British gentlemen founded the Asiatik Society of Bengal. That society's journal would help to introduce Americans to Asian religions in general and Hinduism in particular. (In fact, at Ezra Stiles' suggestion, Adams consulted that journal as she wrote the last two editions of her book.) Buddhism, on the other hand, was only beginning to be understood. The first Pali grammar in a European language did not appear until 1826, and Eugene Burnouf would not publish his pathfinding survey of Indian Buddhism until more than a decade after Adams died. Buddhism's origins remained obscured; and, as the passage from Emerson's letter indicates, it was often confused with Hinduism. Daoism and Shinto, the other Asian religions known to Adams, were noted in passing in comprehensive surveys of the time; but those traditions remained relatively unexplored territory until the end of the nineteenth century.[22]

In the first edition of Adams's survey, Asian religions were conflated and confined in a long appendix; but by the fourth edition the treatment had been expanded and, in some cases, refined. Perhaps more important, Adams followed the lead of a British editor of her book and inserted separate entries for Asian religions among the existing accounts of Western and non-literate traditions. The arrangement had become alphabetical, not theological. In an important sense, the religions of Asia, while still remote, finally had found a place on the religious map. That is why we have reprinted the fourth edition here: it was Adams's most comprehensive and textured account of the religious world. In that edition, Adams covered Asia in thirteen entries. As we read those entries we are reminded again that her world is not ours. Her Asia is not ours.

---

[22] Among the many influential articles published in the journal of the Asiatik Society was William Jones, "On the Gods of Greece, Italy, and India," *Asiatik Researches* 1 (1788): 221-275. On the history of the organization and its publications see Royal Asiatic Society of Bengal, *One Hundreth Jubilee of the Royal Asiatic Society of Bengal (1784-1934) and the Bicentenary of Sir William Jones (1746-1946)* (Calcutta: Printed by G. E. Bingham, Baptist Mission Press, n.d.). Ezra Stiles to Hannah Adams, 12 June 1794, The Hannah Adams Papers, New England Historic Genealogical Society. Eugéne Burnouf and Christian Lassen, *Essai sur le pali* (Paris: Dondey-Dupré, 1826). Eugéne Burnouf, *L'Introduction à l'histoire du buddhisme indien* (Paris: Imprimerie royale, 1844).

Adams ignored completely some traditions that originated in Asia. For instance, in the main entry on India ("Hindoos") she overlooked two traditions that originated there, Jainism and Sikhism. Adams included a separate entry for Shinto ("Sintoos") but not Daoism or Confucianism (see "Chinese").

"Hindoos," however, did receive substantial attention in a five-page entry (see also "Yogeys"). Relying on the reports of Baptist missionaries and the investigations published in *Asiatik Researches,* and especially the pioneering work of Sir William Jones, Adams put together an account that included most of the beliefs and practices that had fascinated—and repulsed—early Western observers. She explicitly noted, or implied, Western parallels: in their belief in Brahma, the creator, Vishnu, the sustainer, and Shiva, the destroyer, Hindus affirm a "three-fold divinity." Using Western language to record Hindu beliefs, she noted that adherents acknowledged a number of Vishnu's "*incarnations*." Hindu ritual sacrifices seemed to resemble those of the Jews. Distorting the Indian tradition, Adams also followed one source in reporting that "the necessity of some *atonement* for *sin* is one of the prevailing ideas among the Hindoos." As with the continuities she found in non-literate religions, these parallels between Hinduism and the Judeo-Christian tradition would have reassured her readers that there were bits of religious truth buried beneath the layers of superstition. But some beliefs and practices seemed so discontinuous, and so barbaric, that interpreters could not hide their horror. For instance, Adams, and other Westerners, focused on the practice of *satī* : "There subsists to this day among the Hindoos a voluntary sacrifice of too singular and shocking a nature to pass unnoticed; which is that of wives burning themselves with the bodies of their deceased husbands."[23]

Adams's Western, even explicitly Christian, outlook shaped her description of Hinduism in other ways too. She included a description of Protestant missionary activity in India, for instance. Even one of Hinduism's acknowledged virtues, tolerance, was turned against the tradition. Adams recorded Sir William Jones's observation—and there is much truth in it—that the lack of missionary success in India could be traced to Hindus' tendency to embrace Jesus as one more incarnation of Vishnu. That might be one possible strategy for incorporating Christian and Hindu beliefs, but Adams and most of her contemporaries were not

---

[23] Italics mine.

interested in synthesis. They preferred conversions. Even Hindu inclusivism, then, came to be seen as an annoying trait.

Adams's assessment of Buddhism was scattered in five entries. It was scattered because Adams failed to see fully the connections among the various forms of Asian Buddhism. There was no single overview article. Instead descriptions appeared, often using different key terms, in portraits of religion in Burma ("Birmins"), Japan ("Budso" and "Japanese"), China ("Chinese"), and Tibet ("Thibetians"). There was no discussion of Buddhism in India because, like other Western interpreters before the mid-nineteenth century, Adams did not realize that the origins of that same tradition that had spread throughout Asia were to be found in India. She saw that Chinese and Burmese Buddhism had been transplanted from India. In the entry on Burmese Buddhism she noted that that it "originated from the same source as the Hindoo but differs in some of its tenets." Viewing Burmese Buddhism from the perspective of Indian Hinduism, she reported that adherents worship "Boodh," the ninth incarnation of Vishnu. Adams also noted the Indian roots of "the sect of Foe" (Buddhism) in China (see "Chinese"). But Westerners in general, and Adams in particular, did not yet have the textual sources or linguistic skills to fully understand Buddhism's Indian beginnings or to find the link between the teachings of China's "Foe" and Burma's "Boodh."

Yet her evaluation of Buddhism was more nuanced than that of Hinduism. It was less consistently and explicitly negative. Tibetan Buddhism, for instance, seemed only slightly worse off than Roman Catholicism. Like Western interpreters for centuries, Adams stressed the parallels. Tibetans, of course, did not know of divine revelation in Jesus; but they did have monks, beads, incense, icons, and even a "pope" (the Dali Lama). Drawing on an interpretive tradition established by the narratives of Jean Baptise DuHalde (1674-1743) and Per Osbeck (1723-1805), Adams distinguished between popular ("external doctrine") and elite ("internal doctrine") forms of Chinese Buddhism. Adams, and the writers she consulted, liked the popular form much better. The "priests" of that popular Buddhism—presumably she meant Pure Land Buddhism—extorted money from the followers; yet, in general, that sect seemed benign, even positive. They seemed to believe in reward and punishment in a future life. Their ethics also seemed praiseworthy: "They enjoin all works of mercy and charity; and forbid cheating, impurity, wine, lying, and murder; and even the taking of life from any creature." On the other hand, Adams closely followed her direct source, Osbeck, in describing the elite tradition of Chinese Buddhism as a negation of all that the West held dear.

"The internal doctrine of this sect, which is kept secret from the common people," Adams reported, "teaches a philosophical atheism, which admits neither rewards nor punishments after death; and believes not in a providence, or the immortality of the soul; acknowledges no other god than the *void*, or *nothing* ; and makes the supreme happiness of mankind to consist in a *total inaction*, an *entire sensibility*, and a *perfect quietude*."[24]

Hannah Adams's Place in the History of the Study of Religion

In the above passage, and a few others, Adams seemed to violate her methodological principles by recording, almost word for word, negative descriptions. She sometimes seemed blind to the ways in which a borrowed term or phrase violated her commitment to impartiality. Yet, to her credit, she never treated a sect or religion more hostilely than her sources had. Even if she failed to comply fully with her announced guidelines, her *Dictionary* advanced the study of religion. It did so because she so consistently approximated the impartiality she had sought and, even more, simply because she had articulated such goals in the first place. Her commitment to impartiality, together with her careful scrutiny and critical treatment of available sources, placed her at the forefront of modern Western efforts to understand the religious world. She should be counted as one of the American pioneers or precursors of the modern academic study of religion.

To say that Adams was a pioneer is not to say that she stood alone. Her *Dictionary* was linked with two related European literary genres—philosophical dictionaries and religious compendia. If Adams's perspective was more conventionally Christian than that of either Voltaire (1694-1778) or Pierre Bayle (1647-1706), the format of her book owed much to these and other seventeenth- and eighteenth-century philosophical dictionaries. The other, more important, tradition that Adams's book continued was that of

---

24 Adams's interpretation of China went back to the writings of DuHalde because two of her sources, Stiles and Osbeck, had followed that Jesuit interpreter closely. Osbeck, for instance, followed DuHalde's interpretations of Chinese religions and even quoted from them at length. See P. [Jean Baptiste] Du Halde, *The General History of China...*, 4 vols., trans. R. Brookes (London: John Watts, 1736). Stiles, *United States Elevated to Glory and Honour*. *Peter Osbeck, A Voyage to China and the East Indies...*, 2 vols., trans. John Reinhold Forster (London: Benjamin White, 1771): 1: 278-87. On the American confrontation with the allegedly "negative" elements of Buddhism see Thomas A. Tweed, "'The Seeming Anomaly of Buddhist Negation': American Encounters with Buddhist Distinctiveness, 1858-1877," *Harvard Theological Review* 83 (Jan. 1990): 65-92.

compendia of religions. These began appearing at least as early as the seventeenth century. One of the first was Alexander Ross's *Pansebia; Or, A View of All Religions in the World* (1653). But like most of the overviews that followed, Ross's book was hardly as comprehensive as its title suggested, and its prominent Christian author, who served as the King's chaplain in his later years, showed little inclination to treat non-Christian traditions with any sympathy. Other notable British and Continental works in this tradition included not only Broughton's *Historical Dictionary of All Religions* but also Bernard Picart's *Cérémonies et coutumes religieuses de tous les peuples du monde* (1723-43), Charles François Dupuis' *Origine de tous les cultes* (1795), Christoph Meiners's *Allgemeine kritische Geschichte der Religionen* (1806-07), and Benjamin Constant's *De la religion, considérée dans sa source, ses formes, et ses développments* (1824-31). Adams was not as theoretically sophisticated as most of these authors, but her *Dictionary* should be listed among these other pioneering works because of its approach and comprehensiveness.[25]

Adams also is important because she was among the earliest *American* students of world religions. Others in America, from Cotton Mather to John Adams, had shown limited interest in Asian religions and cultures. After 1784, some American traders, travelers, and diplomats had direct contact with Asian religions. Amasa Delano (1763-1823), for example, published a *Narrative of Voyages and Travels*, which described, for instance, the religions and cultures of China and India. During the first decades of the nineteenth century, American Protestant missionaries such as Adoniram Judson (1788-1850), who were filled with compassion for the lost souls in Asia, sent back reports. William Bentley (1759-1819), the Unitarian minister of the East Church in Salem, learned Arabic and Persian and investigated Asian traditions from his second-floor study. Bentley, an acquaintance of Adams's, also helped to spread and maintain interest in Asian, especially Chinese, traditions through his work for the

---

[25] Pierre Bayle, *Dictionnaire historique et critique* (1697; Paris: Desoer, 1820). Bayle took as his model the *Grand Dictionnaire historique*, first published by Moréri in Paris in 1674. Bayle's work, in turn, provided one of the models for Voltaire's *Dictionnaire philosophique* (1764). Alexander Ross, *Pansebia; Or, A View of All Religions in the World* (London: 1653). Bernard Picart, *Cérémonies et coutumes religieuses de tous les peuples du monde* (Amsterdam: J. F. Bernard, 1723-43). Charles François Dupuis, *Origine de tous les cultes, or religion universelle*, 7 vols. (Paris: H. Agasse, 1795). Christoph Meiners, *Allgemeine kritische Geschichte der Religionen*, 2 vols. (Hannover: Helwing, 1806-07). Benjamin Constant, *De la religion, considérée dans sa source, ses formes, et ses développments*, 5 vols. (Paris: Bosange, 1824-31).

East India Marine Society in Salem. But he failed to publish the results of his wide-ranging study in any systematic form. As far as I can tell, then, Adams's only serious rival among her contemporaries for the title of American pioneer was Joseph Priestley (1733-1804), the Unitarian scientist and author who emigrated to the United States in 1794. In 1799, fifteen years after the first edition of Adams's volume appeared, Priestley published *A Comparison of the Institutions of Moses with Those of the Hindoos and other Ancient Nations.* This book, however, was less comprehensive than Adams's: it focused on Hinduism and Judaism. It was much more explicitly polemical too. Focusing instead on Adams's successors, some might wish to elevate to the status of "pioneer" a few Americans who wrote and lectured on world religions later in the nineteenth century. James Freeman Clarke (1810-88), for example, authored a popular survey of world religions and became the nation's first academic lecturer in "comparative religion" at Harvard Divinity School in 1867. William Farfield Warren (1833-1929) became the first occupant of the first professional chair in "comparative theology" in America when he took that position at Boston University in 1873. These and other writers were important, but Adams had led the way.[26]

If Adams's survey was as important as I suggest, then it is not surprising to find that its author was well known in the Boston area, and beyond, during her lifetime. A reviewer of the fourth edition assumed that his readers knew the author and her works. The minister who wrote the review, Samuel Willard (1775-1859) of Deerfield, Massachusetts, opened his very positive evaluation by reporting that he would not offer much background since "the author of this work is in such full possession of publick regard, from the benefit conferred by her writings, and the merits of her several productions are so generally known." Her fame was less widespread elsewhere, but she had readers and admirers scattered throughout the United States and Great Britain. The anonymous reviewer of her posthumously published *Memoirs* claimed that "her reputation had extended through her own land, and was well known abroad." Adams's surviving correspondence offers some support for this claim. For example,

[26] Amasa Delano, *Narrative of Voyages and Travels in the Northern and Southern Hemispheres: Comprising Three Voyages Round the World; Together with A Voyage of Survey and Discovery, in the Pacific Ocean and Oriental Islands* (Boston: E.G. House, 1817). Joseph Priestley, "A Comparison of the Institutions of Moses with Those of the Hindoos and Other Ancient Nations," in *The Theological and Miscellaneious Works of Joseph Priestley*, 25 vols. (London: Printed by G. Smallfield, 1817-32), 17: 130-319.

she received fan mail from South Carolina. Martha Ramsay, a woman from Charleston, wrote a letter praising the second edition of her *Dictionary*. "I think your work far exceeds anything of the kind yet attempted, and one which no person or inquiring mind, having once perused would willingly be without." Some readers in the following generation remembered her and admired her work. For example, her *Dictionary* influenced some later attempts to survey the religious landscape. It provided the model for Vincent L. Milner's *Religious Denominations of the World*, published in 1872, fourty-one years after her death. Milner's volume reprinted material from Adams's book, and it was remarkably similar in structure and approach.[27]

But most later American survey writers underemphasized or ignored Adams's early contributions. In one sense, this is not surprising: her sources quickly became outdated due to the proliferation of new translations and authoritative accounts during the nineteenth century. It also makes sense that the conservative Protestant authors of the many compendia that appeared in the nineteenth century ignored her work: they did not share her commitment to impartiality. It is more difficult to explain, however, her loss of stature among New England liberals. Unitarian and Transcendentalist writers in the Boston area—including Lydia Maria Child, James Freeman Clarke, and Samuel Johnson—authored important works on the world religions starting in the 1850s. These works were the successors to the compendia of Adams's generation, and they anticipated the even more sophisticated surveys that began to appear in the last decades of the nineteenth century and the first of the twentieth. Yet Clarke, Johnson, and Child seem to have failed to acknowledge publicly Adams's important contributions. In one of the most surprising and inexplicable developments, Child, who knew Adams and her work, claimed originality for her impartial approach to the study of religions. In the preface to the first volume of her three-volume *The Progress of Religious Ideas* (1855), Child complained about the "one-sidedness" of previous overviews. Her book, she promised her readers, would be novel: "The facts it contains are very old; the novelty it claims is

---

[27] [Samuel Willard], *North American Review* 7 (May 1818): 86. Review of *A Memoir of Miss Hannah Adams*, by Hannah Adams, *Christian Examiner* 13 (Sept. 1832): 133. Martha Ramsay to Hannah Adams, 28 Mar. 1804, Hannah Adams Papers, New England Historic Genealogical Society. Vincent L. Milner, *Religious Denominations of the World: Comprising a General View of the Origin, History, and Condition of the Various Sects of Christians, the Jews, and Mahometans, As Well as the Pagan Forms of Religion Existing in the Different Countries of the Earth* (Philadelphia: Bradley, Garretson, and company, 1872).

the point of view from which those facts are seen and presented." Her approach would be new, Child explained, because she had written "with complete impartiality." No one else had done that: "I am not aware of any one who truly reverenced the spirit of Christianity, has ever before tried the experiment of placing it precisely on a level with other religions, so far as the manner of representation is concerned." It is difficult to know what Child meant by this. Did she mean that Adams had not succeeded in her attempts at impartiality? Did she think that Adams had not even attempted impartiality? Or did she—this seems difficult to imagine—simply forget Adams's book? In any case, Adams received less notice and praise from the independent and academic scholars who followed her than we might have expected.[28]

And many of those who have remembered Adams, have dismissed her contributions as insignificant. Perhaps taking the lead from Adams's own self-deprecating comments, the author of one entry in a biographical dictionary concluded that "her works contain nothing original." In a collection of essays on New England religious history published in 1917, Dean William Wallace Fenn of Harvard Divinity School seemed to go out of his way to dismiss her: he called her "a literary lady of very local and temporary renown." A more recent evaluation, which appeared in a highly respected reference work, suggested that although she was admired by her contemporaries, "her writings are of no lasting consequence."[29]

But she has not been wholly forgotten or universally dismissed. A vast number of students of women's history have remembered her as the first woman to earn her living by writing in America. She often has been grouped with Catharine Sedgwick, Harriet Beecher Stowe, and Elizabeth Stuart Phelps, and other early women writers. Students of New England religious history, especially Unitarian history, remember her disputes with Jedidiah Morse and her acquaintances with major Unitarian ministers. The author of one of the earliest and most comprehensive histories of the field of "comparative religion," Louis Henry Jordon, listed five Americans who wrote during the second half of the nineteenth century among its "founders and masters." Adams, however, was the only American

---

[28] Lydia Maria Child, *The Progress of Religious Ideas Through Successive Ages*, 3 vols. (New York: Francis; London: S. Low, 1855), 1: viii, ix, x. James Freeman Clarke, *Ten Great Religions* (Boston: James R. Osgood, 1871). Samuel Johnson, *Oriental Religions and Their Relation to Universal Religion*, 3 vols. (Boston: Houghton Mifflin, 1872, 1877, 1885).

[29] *Dictionary of American Biography*, s.v. "Adams, Hannah." John Winthrop Planter, et. al, *The Religious History of New England* (Cambridge: Harvard UP, 1917): 104. *Notable American Women*, s.v. "Adams, Hannah."

included—with Europeans such as Constant, Meiners, Müller and others—among the field's "prophets and pioneers." In this 1905 volume Jordon acknowledged that Adams had failed to implement fully her plan for impartiality, but he argued that her work was a "really notable undertaking" considering her period and limitations. It pointed toward the new field of comparative religion that would get under way in the 1870s.[30]

Adams might not have been the *only* American "prophet and pioneer" of the study of religion, as Jordon proclaimed: others played important early roles. At the same time, most of the negative judgments of Adams's significance seem unfair. While the view from her window might have

---

[30] A wide range of entries in biographical dictionaries recognize Adams as the first woman to earn her living in America. For example, see *The National Cyclopedia of American Biography*, s.v. "Adams, Hannah." The only two articles devoted exclusively to Adams, both emphasize her importance as a female author. See Elizabeth Porter Gould, "Hannah Adams: The Pioneer Woman in American Literature," *New England Magazine* 10 (May 1894): 363-69 and Gene Gleason, "A Mere Woman," *American Heritage* 24 (Dec. 1972): 80-84. Adams also is mentioned in many, even most, overviews of American women's history. Usually she has been mentioned at or near the start of a chapter on women authors or professionals. See Phebe A. Hanaford, *Women of the Century* (Boston: B. B. Russell, 1877), 175-76; Mrs. John A. Logan, *The Part Taken by Women in American History* (Wilmington: The Perry-Nalle Publishing Company, 1912), 793-94; Inez Haynes Irwin, *Angels and Amazons: A Hundred Years of American Women* (Garden City, New York: Doubleday, Doran, and Company, 1934), 21-22. More recent work on women's history also has noted her importance as the first American woman to earn her living by writing. See Nancy F. Cott, *The Bonds of Womanhood: 'Women's Sphere' in New England, 1780-1835* (New Haven: Yale University Press, 1977), 7. One recent article has mentioned, more specifically, her role as an early female history-writer. See Nina Baym, "Women and the Republic: Emma Willard's Rhetoric of History," *American Quarterly* 43 (Mar. 1991): 1. Several historians writing about the American, and especially Unitarian, encounter with Asian religions have noted Adams's significance. Sydney E. Ahlstrom, *The American Protestant Encounter with World Religions*, The Brewer Lectures on Comparative Religion (Beloit, Wisconsin: Beloit College, 1962), 21; George Hunston Williams, "The Attitude of Liberals in New England Toward Non-Christian Religions, 1784-1885," *Crane Review* 9 (Winter 1967): 61-66; Jackson, *Oriental Religions and American Thought*, 16-19. Most histories of the field of "comparative religion" overlook Adams. See Morris Jastrow, Jr., *The Study of Religion*, Classics in Religious Studies Series (1901; reprint, Chico, California: Scholars Press, 1981); Jan deVries, *Perspectives in the History of Religions*, trans. Kees W. Bolle (1961; Berkeley: University of California Press, 1967); and Eric J. Sharpe, *Comparative Religion: A History* (New York: Charles Scribner's Sons, 1975). One notable exception is Jordon's book: Louis Henry Jordon, *Comparative Religion: Its Genesis and Growth* (1905; reprint, Atlanta: Scholars Press, 1986), 146-49. According to Jordon, the five American "founders and masters" of the field included James Freeman Clarke, Samuel Johnson, William Fairfield Warren, Crawford Howell Toy, and Frank Field Ellinwood. See Jordon, *Comparative Religion*, 197-202.

been distorted in some ways, Adams managed to provide a remarkably comprehensive and surprisingly impartial perspective on the religious landscape. For what she attempted, as much as what she accomplished, Adams should be counted among the American pioneers of the study of religion.

DICTIONARY OF ALL RELIGIONS: **SOME KEY ENTRIES**

* = main entry

CHRISTIANITY
- Arminians
- Baptists
- Calvinists
- *Christians
- Congregationalists
- Deists
- Dorellites (A perfectionist community founded by William Dorrell)
- Dunkers (Church of the Brethren)
- English Church (The Church of England)
- Friends (Quakers)
- Infidels
- Lutherans
- Mennonites
- Methodists
- Millennarians (Millennialism)
- New Jerusalem Church (Swedenborgians)
- Presbyterians
- Puritans
- Roman Catholics
- Separates ("New Light" Congregationalists and Baptists in America)
- Shakers
- Unitarians
- Unitas Fratrum (Moravians)
- Universalists
- Jemima Wilkinson (Founder of Universal Friends)

JUDAISM
Cabbalists (Followers of the Kabbalah, or "received tradition.")
Essenes
Hebrews
*Jews
Karaites (Sect that recognizes only Hebrew scriptures as authoritative)
Rabbinists (Followers of the Kabbalah)
Sadducees
Talmudists
Therapeutae (Jewish ascetic and contemplative group in Alexandria)
Zabathai Zevi (Shabbetai Tsevi [1626-76] of Turkey.)
Zealots

ISLAM
*Mahometans
Musselmans (Muslims)
Schaites (Shi'a Muslims)
Somnites (Sunni Muslims)
Sufis
Wahabees (Muslim sect founded in the eighteenth century)

HEATHENISM
Heathen
*Pagans

ZOROASTRIANISM
*Gaurs (Zoroastrians)
Magi
Oriental Philosophy (The philosophy of Zoroaster)
Persees (The Parsis, Zoroastrianism of India)

NON-LITERATE RELIGIONS
*Indians (Native religions of the Americas)
Brazilians
*Negroes (Native African religions)
Pelew Islands
South Sea Islanders

ANCIENT RELIGIONS AND NATIONS
Celtes
Druids
Egyptians
Grecians
Sabeans (ancient inhabitants of Arabia)
Sammans (ancient Chaldeans, Syrians, and Canaanites)
Zabeans (Chaldeans, Persians, and other "ancient idolaters")

ASIAN RELIGIONS
Birmins (Buddhism in Burma)
Budso (Buddhism in Japan)
*Chinese (Confucianism, Daoism, and Buddhism in China)
Gymnosophists ("Naked sages." Greek term to describe Indian monks.)
*Hindoos (Religion in India--Hinduism)
*Japanese (Religion in Japan--Shinto and Japanese Buddhism)
Seeks (Sikhs)
Sintoos (Followers of Shinto in Japan)
Thibetians (Tibetan Buddhists)
Yogeys (Indian Yoga)

A NOTE ON THE TEXT

This text is a reproduction of the fourth edition of Hannah Adams's survey of religions. The first edition was published as *An Alphabetical Compendium of the Various Sects Which Have Appeared from the Beginning of the Christian Era to the Present Day* (Boston: B. Edes and Sons, 1784). The second and third editions, from different publishers, appeared in 1791 and 1801: Hannah Adams, *A View of Religions, in two parts* (Boston: J. W. Folsom, 1791) and Hannah Adams, *A View of Religions, in two parts* (Boston: Manning & Loring, 1801). The fourth edition, which was most comprehensive, was published as *A Dictionary of All Religions and Religious Denominations, Jewish, Heathen, Mahometan, and Christian, Ancient and Modern* (Boston: Cummings and Hilliard, 1817).

We gratefully acknowledge the assistance of the staff at Andover-Harvard Library at Harvard Divinity School. This Scholar's Press edition is a reproduction of a volume that was shelved in that library. The original was in less than ideal condition, and so this reprint is flawed as well. We hope that readers will overlook these minor defects as they consult this pioneering survey of the religious landscape.

A DICTIONARY OF ALL RELIGIONS AND RELIGIOUS DENOMINATIONS,

JEWISH, HEATHEN, MAHOMETAN, AND CHRISTIAN,

ANCIENT AND MODERN.

WITH AN

APPENDIX,

CONTAINING

A SKETCH OF THE PRESENT STATE OF THE WORLD, AS TO POPULATION, RELIGION, TOLERATION, MISSIONS, ETC. AND THE ARTICLES IN WHICH ALL CHRISTIAN DENOMINATIONS AGREE.

BY HANNAH ADAMS.

PROVE ALL THINGS; HOLD FAST THAT WHICH IS GOOD.—*Apostle Paul.*

Fourth edition, with corrections and large additions.

PUBLISHED

BY JAMES EASTBURN AND COMPANY,

AT THE LITERARY ROOMS, CORNER OF BROADWAY AND PINE STREET, N. YORK;

AND

BY CUMMINGS AND HILLIARD,

NO. 1, CORNHILL, BOSTON.

1817.

PRINTED BY HILLIARD AND METCALF,
At the University Press in Cambridge, Mass.

ADVERTISEMENT.

The reader will be pleased to observe, that the following rules have been carefully adhered to through the whole of this performance.

1. To avoid giving the least preference of one denomination above another: omitting those passages in the authors cited, where they pass their judgment on the sentiments, of which they give an account: consequently the making use of any such appellations, as Heretics, Schismatics, Enthusiasts, Fanatics, &c. is carefully avoided.

2. To give a few of the arguments of the principal sects, from their own authors, where they could be obtained.

3. To endeavour to give the sentiments of every sect in the general collective sense of that denomination.

4. To give the whole, as much as possible, in the words of the authors from which the compilation is made, and where that could not be done without too great prolixity, to take the utmost care not to misrepresent the ideas.

TO THE

HON. JOHN ADAMS, LL. D.

FORMERLY PRESIDENT OF THE UNITED STATES.

SIR,

SENSIBLE of the honour I received by your permitting me to prefix your name to the second and third editions of this work, I am desirous that the present should appear under the same respectable and distinguished patronage.

The talents and virtues which you have exhibited, both in public and private life, will, I trust, be duly appreciated by the rising generation; and it is my ardent wish, that your ability and integrity may be perpetuated in your descendants.

I am most respectfully,

Sir, your most obliged

and very humble servant,

HANNAH ADAMS.

Boston, November, 1817.

PREFACE.

The candid reception which the public have given to the three preceding editions of the View of Religions encourages me to publish a fourth edition, with an account of a number of denominations, which have been recently formed. A London edition of this work, by the late Rev. Dr. Andrew Fuller, has been found useful in this compilation. This excellent man observes in his Preface, that "The design of such a work is not to convey an idea of all religious principles being equally true, or safe to those who imbibe them; but to exhibit the multiplied speculations of the human mind in as just and impartial a manner as possible. Such things exist or have existed in the world, whether we know them or not; and the reading of them in a proper spirit may induce us to cleave more closely to the law and to the testimony; forming our religious principles by their simple and obvious meaning; and avoiding, as a mariner would avoid rocks and quicksands, every perversion of them in support of a preconceived system."

I respectfully acknowledge having derived much assistance from Mr. Thomas Williams' "Dictionary of all Religions, including the substance of Miss H. Adams' View of Religions reduced to one alphabet." I have adopted his title, and inserted a number of his alterations and additions in this edition. The articles I have selected and published verbatim from Mr. Williams' work are distinguished by an asterisk(*) placed at the beginning of each, according to his method. But having, in the first edition of my View of Religions prescribed rules to myself, from which I have not knowingly deviated in the subsequent editions, I have avoided inserting any thing from Dr. Fuller or Mr. Williams, which appeared to me an infringement of these rules.

I have therefore omitted quoting the remarks which Mr. Williams makes upon the different denominations; for whether correct or not, the inserting of them would be an infringement of the first rule in the Advertisement of my work.

With regard to many of the ancient sects, it is well known that little has been preserved, and therefore little can be expected. The accounts of these, as Mr. Williams justly observes, "have necessarily been taken from early ecclesiastical history, which was by no means written with the candour and impartiality of modern times." As for modern sects, it has been the practice in this candid age to let them speak for themselves. This liberal principle has been adopted in all the editions of my work, where I had an opportunity to peruse their own authors. But as the account of the Jesuits is chiefly taken from Protestant ecclesiastical historians, it may be proper to add, that many individuals of this order undoubtedly deserve the following character given of them by a Roman Catholic author. "The severity of their manners, their temperance, their personal decency and disinterestedness did them honour as religious men and as citizens."* The great and good Bourdaloue, one of the most celebrated preachers in the reign of Lewis XIV, was a Jesuit.

The first part of the Appendix, "Containing a sketch of the present state of the world as to population, religious toleration, missions, &c." is the work of Mr. T. Williams, excepting a few additions relative to recent events, which have taken place since the publication of his Dictionary. This intelligence is chiefly contained in the notes to his statements.

The last part of the Appendix, which mentions the central points in which the various denominations of Christians are united, was published in the second and third editions of this work; and is inserted with a few additions. After perusing accounts of such a variety of opinions on religion, it is pleasant to find even a few articles in which the great body of Christians are agreed.

In giving this work to the public, I have only to request a continuance of the same candid indulgence I have so long experienced. I shall be highly gratified, if seeing such a diversity of sentiment amongst Christians might induce those, who peruse this work, to search the scriptures as the only foundation for their faith and practice. And in all their researches after truth may they imitate the candour of the late pious and ingenious Dr. Watts. This excellent man observes, that "From my own experiment, I can easily guess what confounding intricacies of thought others pass through in their honest searches after truth. These conflicts did exceedingly enlarge my soul, and stretched my charity to a vast extent. I see, I feel, and am assured, that several men may be very sincere, and yet entertain notions of divinity, all widely different. I confess, now and then some opinions, or some unhappy occurrences are ready to narrow and confine my affections again, if I am not watchful over myself; but I pray God to preserve upon my heart a strong and lasting remembrance of those days, and those studies, whereby he laid within me the foundation of so broad a charity."†

* Butler's Life of Fenelon.

† Watts' Orthodoxy and Charity united.

INTRODUCTION,

CONTAINING A BRIEF ACCOUNT OF THE WORLD AT THE TIME OF CHRIST'S APPEARANCE UPON EARTH.

SECTION I.

WHEN Jesus Christ made his appearance on earth, a great part of the world was subject to the Roman empire. This empire was much the largest temporal monarchy that had ever existed: so that it was called, "all the world." (Luke ii. 1.) The time when the Romans first subjugated the land of Judea, was between sixty and seventy years before Christ was born; and soon after this, the Roman empire rose to its greatest extent and splendour. To this government the world continued subject till Christ came, and many hundred years afterwards. The remoter nations, who had submitted to the yoke of this mighty empire, were ruled either by Roman governours, invested with temporary commissions, or by their own princes and laws, in subordination to the republic whose sovereignty was acknowledged, and to which the conquered kings, who were continued in their own dominions, owed their borrowed majesty. At the same time the Roman people and their venerable senate, though they had not lost all shadow of liberty, were yet in reality reduced to a state of servile submission to Augustus Cæsar; who by artifice, perfidy, and bloodshed, attained an enormous degree of power, and united in his own person the pompous titles of *Emperour, Pontiff, Censor, Tribune of the people:* in a word, all the great offices of the state.*

* Mosheim's Ecclesiastical History, vol. i. p. 16.

At this period the Romans, according to Daniel's prophetic description, had trodden down the kingdoms, and by their exceeding strength, devoured the whole earth. However, by enslaving the world, they civilized it; and whilst they oppressed mankind, they united them together. The same laws were every where established, and the same languages understood. Men approached nearer to one another in sentiments and manners; and the intercourse between the most distant regions of the earth was rendered secure and agreeable. Hence the benign influence of letters and philosophy was spread abroad in countries which had been before enveloped in the darkest ignorance.*

Just before Christ was born, the Roman empire not only rose to its greatest height, but was also settled in peace. Augustus Cæsar had been for many years establishing the state of the Roman empire, and subduing his enemies, till the very year that Christ was born: then all his enemies being reduced to subjection, his dominion over the world appeared to be settled in its greatest glory. This remarkable peace, after so many ages of tumult and war, was a fit prelude to the ushering of the glorious Prince of Peace into the world. The tranquillity, which then reigned, was necessary to enable the ministers of Christ to execute with success their sublime commission to the human race. In the situation into which the providence of God had brought the world, the gospel in a few years reached those remote corners of the earth, into which it could not otherwise have penetrated for many ages.

All the heathen nations, at the time of Christ's appearance on earth, worshipped a multiplicity of gods and demons, whose favour they courted by obscene and ridiculous ceremonies, and whose anger they endeavoured to appease by the most abominable cruelties.†

* Robertson's Sermon on the Situation of the world at the time of Christ's appearance.

† See Mosheim and Robertson.

Every nation had its respective gods, over which one more excellent than the rest presided; yet in such a manner that the supreme Deity was himself controlled by the rigid decrees of fate, or by what the philosophers called *eternal necessity*. The gods of the east were different from those of the Gauls, the Germans, and other northern nations. The Grecian divinities differed from those of the Egyptians, who deified plants, and a great variety of the productions both of nature and art. Each people had also their peculiar manner of worshipping and appeasing their respective deities. In process of time, however, the Greeks and Romans grew as ambitious in their religious pretensions as in their political claims. They maintained that their gods, though under different appellations, were the objects of religious worship in all nations; and therefore they gave the names of their deities to those of other countries.*

The deities of almost all nations were either ancient heroes, renowned for noble exploits and worthy deeds, or kings and generals who had founded empires, or women who had become illustrious by remarkable actions or useful inventions. The merit of those eminent persons, contemplated by their posterity with enthusiastic gratitude, was the cause of their exaltation to celestial honours. The natural world furnished another kind of deities; and as the sun, moon, and stars shine with a lustre superiour to that of all other material beings, they received religious homage from almost all the nations of the world.†

* Mosheim, vol. i. p. 18.

† The learned Mr. Bryant, in his analysis of ancient mythology, supposes that the worship of the powers of nature, principally the sun, was the original idolatry, which prevailed in all nations; that the characters of the pagan deities of different countries melt into each other; and that the whole crowd of gods and goddesses mean only the powers of *nature*, (especially the *sun*) branched out and diversified by a number of different names and attributes. Sir William Jones, in his history of the antiquities of Asia, appears to have embraced the same opinion. See Bryant, vol. i. p. 2,308. See also Sir William Jones' Dissertation of the gods of Greece, Italy, and India.

From those beings of a nobler kind, idolatry descended into an enormous multiplication of inferiour powers; so that in many countries, mountains, trees, and rivers, the earth, and sea, and wind, nay, even virtues and vices, and diseases, had their shrines attended by devout and zealous worshippers.*

These deities were honoured with rites and sacrifices of various kinds, according to their respective nature and offices. Most nations offered animals; and human sacrifices were universal in ancient times. They were in use among the Egyptians till the reign of Amasis: they were never so common among the Greeks and Romans: yet they were practised by them on extraordinary occasions. Porphyry says that the Greeks were wont to sacrifice men when they went to war. He relates also that human sacrifices were offered at Rome till the reign of Adrian, who ordered them to be abolished in most places.†

Pontiffs, priests, and ministers, distributed into several classes, presided over the pagan worship, and were appointed to prevent disorder in the performance of religious rites. The sacerdotal order, which was supposed to be distinguished by an immediate intercourse and friendship with the gods, abused its authority in the basest manner, to deceive an ignorant and wretched people.‡

The religious worship of the pagans was confined to certain times and places. The statues, and other representations of the gods, were placed in the temples, and supposed to be animated in an incomprehensible manner; for they carefully avoided the imputation of worshipping inanimate beings: and therefore pretended that the divinity represented by the statue was really present in it, if the dedication were truly and properly made.§

* Mosheim, vol. i. p. 20.

† Dr. Priestley's Discourses relating to the Evidences of Revealed Religion.

‡ Notwithstanding the ignorance which prevailed respecting religion, the Augustan was the most learned and polite age the world ever saw. The love of literature was the universal passion.

§ Mosheim, vol. i. p. 22.

Besides the public worship of the gods, to which all, without exception, were admitted, there were certain religious rites celebrated in secret by the Greeks, and several eastern countries, to which a small number was allowed access. These were called mysteries;* and persons who desired an initiation were obliged previously to exhibit satisfactory proofs of their fidelity and patience, by passing through various trials and ceremonies of the most disagreeable kind. The secret of these mysteries was kept in the strictest manner, as the initiated could not reveal any thing that passed in them, without exposing their lives to the most imminent danger.

These secret doctrines were taught in the mysteries of Eleusis, and in those of Bacchus, and other divinities; but the reigning religion was totally external. It held out no body of doctrines, no public instruction to participate on stated days in the established worship. The only faith required was, to believe that the gods exist, and reward virtue either in this life or in that to come;—the only practice, to perform at intervals some religious acts, such as appearing in the solemn festivals, and sacrificing at the public altars.†

The spirit and genius of the pagan religion was not calculated to promote moral virtue. Stately temples, expensive sacrifices, pompous ceremonies, and magnificent festivals, were the objects presented to its votaries. But just notions of God, obedience to his moral laws, purity

* The vulgar were carefully excluded from these secrets, which were reserved for the nobility and sacerdotal tribe. The priests, who had devised these allegories, understood their original import, and bequeathed them, as an inestimable legacy, to their children. In order to celebrate these mysteries with the greater secrecy, the temples were so constructed as to favour the artifice of the priests. The fanes, in which they used to execute their sacred functions, and perform the ceremonies of their religion, were subterraneous mansions, constructed with such wonderful dexterity, that every thing which appeared in them breathed an air of solemn secrecy. See Encyclopedia Brittannica, vol. xii. p. 501.

† Travels of Anacharsis the Younger in Greece, by the Abbe Barthelemi, vol. ii. p. 311.

2

of heart, and sanctity of life, were not once mentioned as ingredients in religious service. No repentance of past crimes, and no future amendment of conduct, were ever prescribed by the pagans, as proper means of appeasing their offended deities. Sacrifice a chosen victim, bow down before a hallowed image, be initiated in the sacred mysteries, and the wrath of the gods shall be averted—the thunder shall drop from their hands.*

The gods and goddesses, to whom public worship was paid, exhibited to their adorers examples of egregious crimes, rather than of useful and illustrious virtues. It was permitted to consider Jupiter, the father of the gods, as an usurper, who expelled his father from the throne of the universe, and who was in his turn to be one day driven from it by his son.† The priests were little solicitous to animate the people to virtuous conduct, either by precept or example: they plainly enough declared, that all which was essential to the true worship of the gods was contained in the rites and institutions which the people had received by tradition from their ancestors. Hence the wiser part of mankind, about the time of Christ's birth, looked upon the whole system of religion as a just object of ridicule and contempt.

The consequence of this state of theology was an universal corruption of manners, which discovered itself in the impunity of the most flagitious crimes.‡ The colours are not too strong which the apostle employs in drawing the character of the heathens. Rom. i. 21, 22. Eph. iv. 17, 18, 19.

At the time of Christ's appearance on earth, the religion of the Romans, as well as their arms, had extended itself throughout a great part of the world. Those nations, who before their subjection had their own gods, and their own particular religious institutions, were persuaded by de-

* Robertson. † Travels of Anacharsis. ‡ Mosheim, vol. i. p. 23.

grees to admit into their worship a great variety of the sacred rites and customs of the conquerors.*

When from the sacred rites of the ancient Romans we pass to review the other religions which prevailed in the world, it will appear obvious that the most remarkable may be properly divided into two classes; one of which will comprehend the religious systems which owe their existence to political views, and the other of those which seem to have been formed for military purposes. The religions of most of the eastern nations may be ranked in the former class, especially that of the Persians, Egyptians and Indians, which appear to have been solely calculated for the preservation of the state, the support of the royal authority and grandeur, the maintenance of public peace, and the advancement of civil virtues. The religious system of the northern nations may be comprehended under the military class, since all the traditions among the Germans, the Britons, the Celts, and the Goths, concerning their divinities, have a manifest tendency to excite and nourish fortitude, ferocity, an insensibility of danger and contempt of life.†

At this time Christianity broke forth from the east like a rising sun, and dispelled the universal religious darkness which obscured every part of the globe. "The noblest people (says Dr. Robertson) that ever entered upon the stage of the world, appear to have been only instruments in the divine hand for the execution of wise purposes concealed from themselves. The Roman ambition and bravery paved the way, and prepared the world for the reception of the Christian doctrine. They fought and conquered, that it might triumph with the greater ease. (See Isai. x. 7.) By means of their victories, the overruling providence of God established an empire, which really possesses that perpetuity and eternal duration which they vainly arrogated to their own. He erected a throne which shall contin-

* Mosheim, vol. i. p. 24.

† Ibid. vol. i. p. 25.

ue forever; and of the *increase of that government there shall be no end.*"*

It has been mentioned, to the honour of Christianity, that it rose and flourished in a learned, inquiring, and discerning age: and made the most rapid and amazing progress through the immense empire of Rome to its remotest limits, when the world was in its most civilized state, and in an age that was universally distinguished for science and erudition.†

SECTION II.

The state of the Jews was not much better than that of other nations, at the time of Christ's appearance on earth. They were governed by Herod, who was himself tributary to the Roman people. His government was of the most vexatious and oppressive kind. By a cruel, suspicious, and overbearing temper, he drew upon himself the aversion of all, not excepting those who lived upon his bounty.

Under his administration, and through his influence, the luxury of the Romans was introduced into Palestine, accompanied with the vices of that licentious people. In a word, Judea, governed by Herod, groaned under all the corruption which might be expected from the authority and example of a prince, who, though a Jew in outward profession, was, in point of morals and practice, a contemner of all laws, human and divine.‡

After the death of this tyrant, the Romans divided the government of Judea between his sons. In this division one half of the kingdom was given to Archelaus, under the title of Exarch. Archelaus was so corrupt and wicked a prince, that at last both Jews and Samaritans joined in a

* Isaiah, ix. 7.

† Addison's Evidences and Harwood's Introduction, vol. i. p. 32.

‡ Mosheim, vol. i. p. 32.

petition against him to Augustus, who banished him from his dominions about ten years after the death of Herod the Great. Judea was by this sentence reduced to a Roman province, and ordered to be taxed.*

The governours whom the Romans appointed over Judea were frequently changed, but seldom for the better. About the sixteenth year of Christ, Pontius Pilate was appointed a governour, the whole of whose administration, according to Josephus, was one continual scene of venality, rapine, and of every kind of savage cruelty. Such a governour was ill calculated to appease the ferments occasioned by the late tax. Indeed Pilate was so far from attempting to appease, that he greatly inflamed them, by taking every occasion of introducing his standards, with images, pictures, and consecrated shields, into their city; and at last by attempting to drain the treasury of the temple, under pretence of bringing an aqueduct into Jerusalem. The most remarkable transaction of his government, however, was his condemnation of Jesus Christ; seven years after which he was removed from Judea.†

However severe the authority which the Romans exercised over the Jews, yet it did not extend to the entire suppression of their civil and religious privileges. The Jews were in some measure governed by their own laws, and permitted the enjoyment of their religion. The administration of religious ceremonies was committed as before to the high priest, and to the sanhedrim; to the former of whom, the order of priests and levites was in the usual subordination; and the form of outward worship, except in a very few points, suffered no visible change. But, on the other hand, it is impossible to express the disquietude and disgust, the calamities and vexations, which this unhappy nation suffered from the presence of the Romans, whom their religion obliged them to regard as a polluted and idolatrous people; particularly from the avarice and cruelty

* Mosheim, vol. i. p. 31. † Encyc. Brit. vol. ix. p. 136.

of the pretors, and the frauds and extortions of the publicans: so that, all things considered, their condition, who lived under the government of the other sons of Herod, was much more supportable than the state of those who were immediately subject to the Roman jurisdiction.*

It was not, however, from the Romans only that the calamities of this miserable people proceeded. Their own rulers multiplied their vexations, and debarred them from enjoying any little comforts which were left them by the Roman magistrates. The leaders of the people, and the chief priests, were, according to the account of Josephus, profligate wretches, who had purchased their places by bribes, or by other acts of iniquity, and who mantained their ill-acquired authority by the most abominable crimes. The inferiour priests, and those who possessed any shadow of authority, were become dissolute and abandoned to the highest degree. The multitude, excited by these corrupt examples, ran headlong into every kind of iniquity; and by their endless seditions, robberies, and extortions, armed against themselves both the justice of God and the vengeance of man.†

About the time of Christ's appearance, the Jews of that age concluded the period pre-determined by God to be then completed, and that the promised Messiah would suddenly appear. Devout persons waited day and night for the consolation of Israel; and the whole nation, groaning under the Roman yoke, and stimulated by the desire of liberty or of vengeance, expected their deliverer with the most anxious impatience.

Nor were these expectations peculiar to the Jews. By their dispersion among so many nations, by their conversation with the learned men among the heathens, and by the translations of their inspired writings into a language almost universal, the principles of their religion were spread all over the east. It became the common belief that a

* Mosheim.

† Mosheim, vol. i. p. 38.

Prince would arise at that time in Judea, who would change the face of the world, and extend his empire from one end of the earth to the other.*

The whole body of the people looked for a powerful and warlike deliverer, who they supposed would free them from the Roman authority. All considered the whole of religion as consisting in the rites appointed by Moses, and in the performance of some external acts of duty. All were unanimous in excluding the other nations of the world from the hopes of eternal life.

The learned among the Hebrew nation were divided into a great variety of sects; and defended their tenets with the greatest zeal and pertinacity. The Samaritans were, in particular, violently opposed to the Jews. A particular account of their opinions, as well as those of the Pharisees, Sadducees, Essenes, &c. will be explained under each denomination in the Dictionary.

Whilst the learned and sensible part of the Jewish nation was divided into a variety of sects, the multitude was sunk into the most deplorable ignorance of religion; and had no conception of any other method of rendering themselves acceptable to God, than by sacrifices, washings, and other external rites and ceremonies of the Mosaic law. Hence proceeded that dissoluteness of manners, which prevailed among the Jews during Christ's ministry on earth. Hence also the divine Saviour compares the people to sheep without a shepherd, and their doctors to men who, though deprived of sight, yet pretended to show the way to others.†

In taking a view of the corruptions, both in doctrine and practice, which prevailed among the Jews at the time

* Robertson.—About this period the pagans expected some great king, or glorious person, to be born. Hence Virgil, the Roman poet, who lived at this time, in his fourth eclogue, describes the blessings of the government of some great person, who was, or should be born about this time, in language agreeable to the Jewish prophet's description of the Messiah and his kingdom.

† Mosheim, vol. i. p. 38.

of Christ's appearance, we find that the external worship of God was disfigured by human inventions. Many learned men have observed that a great variety of rites were introduced into the service of the temple, of which no traces are to be found in the sacred writings. This was owing to those revolutions which rendered the Jews more conversant than they had formerly been with the neighbouring nations. They were pleased with several of the ceremonies which the Greeks and Romans used in the worship of the pagan deities, and did not hesitate to adopt them in the service of the true God, and add them as an ornament to the rites which they had received by divine appointment.

The Jews multiplied so prodigiously, that the narrow bounds of Palestine were no longer sufficient to contain them. They poured, therefore, their increasing numbers into the neighbouring countries with such rapidity, that at the time of Christ's birth there was scarcely a province in the empire, where they were not found carrying on commerce, and exercising other lucrative arts. They were defended in foreign countries against injurious treatment by the special edicts of the magistrates. This was absolutely necessary, since in most places the remarkable difference of their religion and manners from those of other nations, exposed them to the hatred and indignation of the ignorant and bigoted multitude. "All this (says Dr. Mosheim) appears to have been most singularly and wisely directed by the adorable hand of an interposing providence, to the end that this people, which was the sole depository of the true religion, and of the knowledge of one supreme God, being spread abroad through the whole earth, might be every where, by their example, a reproach to superstition, contribute in some measure to check it; and thus prepare the way for that yet fuller discovery of divine truth, which was to shine upon the world from the ministry and gospel of the Son of God."*

* Mosheim, vol i. p. 42.

SECTION III.

At the important era of Christ's appearance in the world, two kinds of philosophy prevailed among the civilized nations. One was the philosophy of the Greeks, adopted also by the Romans; and the other that of the Orientals, which had a great number of votaries in Persia, Syria, Chaldea, Egypt, and even among the Jews. The former was distinguished by the simple title of *philosophy;* the latter was honoured by the more pompous appellation of *science* or *knowledge,* since those who adhered to the latter sect pretended to be the restorers of the knowledge of God which was lost in the world. The followers of both these systems, in consequence of vehement disputes and dissensions about several points, subdivided themselves into a variety of sects. It is however to be observed, that all the sects of the oriental philosophy deduced their various tenets from one fundamental principle, which they held in common; but the Greeks were much divided about the first principles of science.

Amongst the Grecian sects there were some who declaimed openly against religion, and denied the immortality of the soul; and others who acknowledged a Deity, and a state of future rewards and punishments. Of the former kind were the Epicureans and Academics, of the latter the Platonists and Stoics. See an account of those respective denominations in the dictionary.

The oriental philosophy was popular in several nations at the time of Christ's appearance. Before the commencement of the Christian era it was taught in the east, whence it gradually spread through the Alexandrian, Jewish, and Christian schools.

Those who professed to believe the oriental philosophy, were divided into three leading sects, which were subdivided into others. Some imagined two eternal principles, from whence all things proceeded; the one presiding over light, the other over matter, and by their perpetual conflict explaining the mixture of good and evil that appears in the universe. Others maintained that the being, which presided over matter, was not an eternal principle, but a subordinate intelligence; one of those which the supreme God produced from himself. They supposed that this being was moved by a sudden impulse to reduce to order the rude mass of matter which lay excluded from the mansions of the Deity, and also to create the human race. A third sect entertained the idea of a triumvirate of beings, in which the *supreme Deity* was distinguished both from the *material* evil principle, and from the Creator of this sublunary world.—That these divisions did really subsist, is evident from the history of the Christian sects which embraced this philosophy.*

From blending the doctrines of the oriental philosophy with Christianity, the Gnostic sects, which were so numerous in the first centuries, derive their origin. Other denominations arose, which aimed to unite Judaism with Christianity. Many of the pagan philosophers, who were converted to the Christian religion, exerted all their art and ingenuity to accommodate the doctrines of the gospel to their own schemes of philosophy. In each age of the church new systems were introduced, till, in process of time, we find the Christian world divided into that prodigious variety of sentiment, which is exhibited in the following pages.

* Mosheim, vol. i. pp. 70, 71.

A

DICTIONARY

OF ALL

RELIGIONS.

ABRAHAMITES, different denominations in the middle ages, called after their respective leaders; one of which was condemned by Theophilus for worshipping images, and another united with the *Paulicians.**

ABYSSINIAN CHURCH, that established in the empire of Abyssinia. They maintain that the *two* natures are united in Christ, without either confusion or mixture; so that though the nature of our Saviour be really *one*, yet it is at the same time two-fold and compound.

The Abyssinian church embraced these tenets in the seventh century. They disown the pope's supremacy, and transubstantiation, though they believe the real presence of Christ in the sacrament, and administer the communion in both kinds. Like the Roman catholics, they offer their devotions and prayers to the saints, and believe in a state of purgatory. They use *confession*, and receive *penance* and *absolution* from the priests.† Their divine service consists in reading the Scriptures, administering the Eucharist, and reading some Homilies of the Fathers. They use different forms of baptism; and keep both Saturday and Sunday as sabbaths. They are circumcised, and abstain from swine's flesh; not out of regard to the Mosaic law, but purely as an ancient custom of their country. They read the whole four evangelists regularly every year in their churches; and when they speak of an event, they say, "It happened in the days of Matthew," *i. e.* while Matthew was reading in

* Dictionary of Arts and Sciences, vol. i. p. 10.

† Mosheim, vol. ii. p. 172. vol. iii. p. 492. Mod. Univ. Hist. vol. xv. p. 174—177. Ludolph's Hist. of Ethiopia.

their churches. They are a branch of the *Cophts*.

*ACACIANS, two ancient sects, the one followers of Acacius, an Arian Bishop of Cæsaria: the other named after Acacius Patriarch of Constantinople, who favoured the Eutychians.†

*ACADEMICS, an ancient Philosophical sect, which taught in a grove near Athens, sacred to Academus, who was one of their heroes. They were originally the disciples of Socrates and Plato; but in after times neglected the plain and useful truths which they had taught, and devoted themselves to the most abstruse and incomprehensible studies: they have been confounded, by Mr. Hume and others, with the Sceptics.‡

ACEPHALI, [headless,] a branch of the Eutychians, who had been deserted by their chief.

ADAMITES, a denomination in the second century, who asserted, that since their redemption by the death of Christ they were as innocent as Adam before the fall, and are accused of praying naked in their assemblies. It was renewed in the fifteenth century by one Picard, a native of Flanders.§

ADESSENARIANS, [from *Adesse*, to be present,] a branch of the Sacramentarians, believed the literal presence of Christ's body *in* the elements of the eucharist, though in a different manner from the Romanists.

ADIAPHORISTS, those moderate Lutherans who followed Melancthon, and subscribed the *interim*. See *Lutherans*.

ADOPTIANI, a sect, who in the eighth century taught that Jesus Christ was not the natural, but *adopted* Son of God.‖

AERIANS, a denomination which arose about the year 342. They were so called from one Aerius, a monk, and Semi-Arian. He opposed episcopacy, prayers for the dead, stated fasts and feasts, &c.¶

AETIANS, a branch of Arians in the fourth century, who are said to have maintained that *faith* without *works* was sufficient to salvation; and that no sin, however grievous, would be imputed to the faithful; and they pretended to immediate revelations.**

AFGHANS, a people in India, inhabiting a province of Cabul, or Cabulistan, who boast of being descended from Saul, the first king of Israel. They say that their great ancestor was raised from the rank of a shepherd, not for any

* Dictionary of Arts and Sciences, vol. i. p. 10. † Ency. Brit.
‡ Ency. Perthens.
§ Mosheim, vol. i. p. 418. Broughton's Hist. Library, vol. i. p. 49.
‖ Dict. of Arts and Scien. vol. i. p. 49. ¶ Mosheim, vol. i. p. 314.
** Broughton, vol i. p. 24.

princely qualities which he possessed, but because his stature was exactly equal to the length of a rod given by the angel Gabriel to the prophet Samuel, as the measure of royal stature.

This story is supposed to be one of the fictions which Mahomet borrowed from the latter rabbins. Sir William Jones, however, though he gave no credit to this fable, seems to have had no doubt but that the Afghans are descendants of Israel carried off in the captivity of the ten tribes.

This great man strongly recommended an inquiry into the language, literature, and history of the Afghans. "We learn," said he, "from Esdras, that the ten tribes, after a wandering journey, came to a country, called Arsareth, where we may suppose they settled. Now the best Persian historians affirm, that the Afghans are descended from the Jews; and they have among themselves traditions of the same import. It is even asserted that their families are distinguished by the names of Jewish tribes, though since their conversion to Islamism they have studiously concealed their origin. The language they use has a manifest resemblance to the Chaldaic, and a considerable district under their dominions is called Hazareth, which might easily have been changed from Arsareth."*

AGNOETÆ, [unknowing,] a denomination of the fourth century, followers of Theophronius, the Cappadocian, who called in question the omniscience of God; alleging that he knew things past only by memory, and future only by an uncertain prescience. Another sect of the same name arose about the year 535, who followed the sentiments of Themistius, deacon of Alexandria, who, from Mark xiii. 32, denied that Christ, in any sense, knew the day of judgment.†

†**AGONISTICI,** a name given to certain followers of Donatus, who used to attend the public markets, fairs, &c. to *contend* in favour of his principles. They were properly itinerant *Polemics;* and are sometimes called Circuitores, Circelliones,‡ &c.

AGYNIANS, a small sect about the end of the seventh century. They condemned the use of certain meats, and *marriage,* whence their name.

ALBANENSES, and **ALBANOIS** were petty sects of the eighth century, the probable remains of the *Gnostics* and *Mancheans,* which see.

ALBIGENSES, so called from their first residence in Albi and Albigeois. A denomination remarkable for their oppo-

* Asiatic Researches, vol. ii. p. 76, and Works of Sir William Jones, vol. i. p. 336. † Broughton, p. 26. ‡ Ency. Brit.

sition to the discipline and ceremonies of the church of Rome. Their opinions were similar to the *Waldenses*, which see.

ALLENITES, the disciples of Henry Allen, of Nova Scotia, who began to propagate his doctrines in that country about the year 1778, and died in 1783, during which time he made many proselytes, and at his death left a considerable party behind him, though now much declined. He published several treatises and sermons, in which he declares, that the souls of all the human race are emanations, or rather parts of the one great Spirit; that they were all present in Eden, and were actually in the first transgression. He supposes that our first parents in innocency were pure spirits, and that the material world was not then made; but that in consequence of the fall, that mankind might not sink into utter destruction, the world was produced, and men clothed with material bodies; and that all the human race will, in their turn, be invested with such bodies, and in them enjoy a state of probation for immortal happiness.*

ALMARICIANS, the followers of Almaric, professor of logic and theology at Paris, in the fifteenth century. He opposed the worship of saints and images; and his enemies charged him with maintaining that in his time the reign of the Holy Spirit commenced, in which the sacraments and all external worship were to be abolished.†

ALOGIANS, a denomination in Asia Minor in the second century; so called because they denied the divine λόγος, or word, and the writings of St. John, attributing them to Cerinthus. But Dr. Lardner denies the existence of such a sect, as not being mentioned by any contemporary writer.‡

§AMERICAN SECT, New, a congregation lately arisen in Pennsylvania, among the Welsh emigrants to that country under the auspices of the late Rev. M. J. Rees, who died at Somerset, in that state, in 1804. Their tenets are comprised in the following articles of their religious constitution. The convention shall be called the *Christian Church*, and never by any other name. Jesus Christ is the *only* head: believers in him, the *only* members: and the New Testament, the *only* rule of the fraternity. In mental matters, each member shall enjoy his own sentiments, and freely discuss every subject: but in discipline, a strict conformity with the precepts of Christ is required. Every distant society shall have the same power of admitting members, electing officers, &c. Delegates from the different congre-

* Manuscript from a clergyman in Nova Scotia, 1783. † Mosheim, vol. iii. 120, &c. ‡ Broughton, vol. i. p. 33. § Lardner's Heretics, p. 446.

gations shall meet from time to time, to consult the general interest. At every meeting for religious worship, collections shall be made for the poor, and the promulgation of the gospel *among the Heathen.**

AMMONIANS, so called from Ammonius Saccas, who taught with the highest applause in the Alexandrian school, about the conclusion of the second century. This learned man attempted a general reconciliation of all sects, whether philosophical or religious; his creed was therefore a mixture of Christianity and oriental Philosophy, in which he was deeply skilled.

With regard to moral discipline, Ammonius permitted the people to live according to the law of their country, and the dictates of nature: but a more sublime rule was laid down for the wise. They were to raise above all terrestrial things, by the towering efforts of holy contemplation, those souls, whose origin was celestial and divine. They were ordered to extenuate, by hunger, thirst, and other mortifications, the sluggish body, which restrains the liberty of the immortal spirit, that in this life they might enjoy communion with the supreme Being, and ascend after death, active and unincumbered to the universal Parent, to live in his presence forever.†

AMSDORFIANS, the followers of Amsdorf, a kind of Antinomians in the sixteenth century, who are said to have maintained that good works were not only unprofitable, but even opposite and pernicious to salvation.‡

†ANABAPTISTS, (re-baptizers,) a sect which arose in the time of Luther's Reformation in Germany, and excited various insurrections, under pretence of erecting the kingdom of Christ on earth.§ See *Fifth Monarchy Men.* It is but justice to remark, that this sect agreed scarcely in any thing with the modern *Baptists*, except in the circumstances of rejecting infant baptism, and practising immersion. See *Baptists.*

†ANCHORITES, (*or Anchorets,*) Hermits: certain primative monks who chose the solitude of caves and deserts to avoid the temptations of the world.

ANGELITES, a denomination which sprung up about the year 494; so called from Angelium, in Alexandria, where they held their first meetings. They were called likewise from different leaders, Serverites, Damianists and Theodosians. They denied that either of the persons of the Trinity were self-existent; but taught there is a common Deity existing in them all; and that each is God

* Evans' Sketch of all Religions.

† Mosheim, vol i. p. 137—144.

‡ Dict. Art. Scien. vol. i. p. 131.

§ Scotch Theolog. Dict.

by a participation of this Deity.*

ANOMŒANS, a name by which the pure Arians were distinguished in the fourth century, from the Semi-Arians. The word is taken from Ἀνόμοιος, different, dissimilar. †See *Arians.*

ANTHROPOMORPHITES, a sect in the tenth century; so denominated from Ανθρωπος man, and Μορφη shape: because they maintained that the Deity was clothed with a human form, and seated like an earthly monarch upon a throne of state; and that his angelic ministers were beings arrayed in white garments, and furnished with natural wings. They take every thing spoken of God in scripture in a literal sense, particularly when it is said that *God made man after his own image.*‡

***ANTIBURGHERS**, dissenters from the Church of Scotland, chiefly in matters of church government; and from the Burgher Seceders, in refusing the Burgess oath. See *Burghers* and *Seceders.*§

ANTINOMIANS. They derive their name from αντι against, and νόμος law, as being against the moral law; not merely as a covenant of life, but also as a rule of conduct to believers.

In the sixteenth century, while Luther was eagerly employed in censuring and refuting the popish doctors, who mixed the law and gospel together, and represented eternal happiness as the fruit of legal obedience, a new teacher arose, whose name was John Agricola, a native of Isleben, and an eminent doctor in the Lutheran church. His fame began to spread in the year 1538, when from the doctrine of Luther now mentioned, he took occasion to advance sentiments which drew upon him the animadversion of that reformer.

The doctrine of Agricola is said to be in itself obscure, and is thought to have been misrepresented by Luther, who wrote against him with acrimony, and first styled him and his followers Antinomians. Agricola defended himself, and complained that opinions were imputed to him, which he did not hold.

The writings of Dr. Crisp, in the seventeenth century, have been generally considered as favourable to Antinomianism, though he acknowledges, that "in respect to the rule of righteousness, or the matter of obedience, we are under the law still; or else (as he adds) we are lawless, to live every man as seems good in his own eyes, which no true Christian dares so much as to think." The following sentiments, however,

* Broughton, vol. i. p. 49. † Ibid. p. 51.
‡ Broughton, vol. i. p. 55. Mosheim, vol. ii. p. 227.
§ Scotch Theolog. Dict. ‖ Mosheim, vol. iv. p. 321.

among others appear to be taught in his sermons. "The law is cruel and tyrannical, requiring what is naturally impossible. The sins of the elect were so imputed to Christ, as that though he did not commit them, yet they became actually his transgressions, and ceased to be theirs. Christ's righteousness is so imputed to the elect, that they, ceasing to be sinners, are as righteous as he was."*

"An elect person is not in a condemned state while an unbeliever, and should he happen to die before God call him to believe, he would not be lost. All signs and marks of grace are doubtful evidences of heaven; it is the voice of the Spirit of God to a man's own spirit, speaking particularly in the heart of a person, *Son, be of good cheer, thy sins are forgiven thee,* that is the great and only evidence which can determine the question. The whole essence of faith is nothing else but the echo of the heart, answering the foregoing voice of the Spirit, and word of grace; the former declaring, *Thy sins are forgiven thee;* the latter answering, My sins are forgiven me. God sees no sin in believers, nor does he afflict them on this account. Repentance and confession of sin are not necessary to forgiveness. A believer may certainly conclude before confession, yea, as soon as he hath committed sin, the interest he hath in Christ, and the love of Christ embracing him."

Some of the principal passages of scripture, from whence these sentiments were defended, are the following: *He was made sin for us, who knew no sin.—Who shall lay any thing to the charge of God's elect?—Their sins and their iniquities will I remember no more.—All things work together for good to them that love God.* 2 Cor. v. 21. Rom. viii. 33. Heb. viii. 12. Rom. viii. 28.†

Many of those, who in the present day adopt these principles, reject the moral law as a rule of conduct to believers, disown personal and progressive sanctification, and hold it inconsistent for a believer to pray for the forgiveness of his sins. These are properly Antinomians.

There are others who reject these notions, and many of those advanced by Dr. Crisp, who yet have been denominated, by their opponents, Antinomians.

* Most of those who are styled Antinomians, believe that the justification of sinners is an eternal act of God, not only preceding all acts of sin, but the existence of the sinner himself; though some suppose with Dr. Crisp, that the elect were justified at the time of Christ's death. For a particular account of the shades of difference among this denomination, the reader is referred to the authors mentioned in the following page.

† Crisp's Sermons, vol. iv. p. 94, 116, 119, 269, 270, 276, 298, 363, 466, 493, &c.

Some of the chief of those, whose writings have been considerd as favouring Antinomianism, are, Crisp, Eaton, Richardson, Saltmarsh, Town, Hussey, &c. These have been answered by Gataker, Sedgwick, Bull, Williams, Beart, &c. to which may be added, Fletcher's Four Checks to Antinomianism; and Bellamy's Essay on the nature and glory of the Gospel.

Mr.Evans asserts, that "there are many Antinomians, indeed, of a singular cast in Germany, and other parts of the continent; they condemn the moral law as a rule of life, and yet profess a strict regard to the interests of practical religion."

*ANTIPÆDOBAPTISTS, those who reject infant baptism. See *Baptists*.

ANTISABBATARIANS, those who reject the observation of the Sabbath, under the idea that it was obligatory on the Jews only; and maintain that no one day is now more holy than another.

ANTITACTÆ, a branch of the Gnostics, who held that God, the Creator of the universe, was good and just; but that one of his creatures had created evil, and engaged mankind to follow it in opposition to God; and that it is the duty of mankind to oppose the author of evil, in order to avenge God of his enemy. See *Gnostics*.

ANTITRINITARIANS, a general name given to all those who deny the doctrine of the Trinity, and particularly to the Arians and Socinians.

APELLÆANS, followers of Apelles in the second century, who believed in a supreme God, and in an inferiour one formed by him. He denied the resurrection.‡

APHTHARTODOCITES, a sect in the sixth century, who held that the body of Jesus Christ was *incorruptible*, and not subject to death. They were a branch of the Eutychians.§

APOCARITÆS, a sect in the third century sprung from the Manicheans, who held that the soul of man was of the essence of God.‖

APOLLINARIANS, a denomination in the fourth century, who asserted that Christ's person was composed of a union of the true divinity and a human body, endowed with a sensitive soul; but without the reasonable one, the divinity supplying its place; the human body united to the divine spirit making one nature only.¶

APOSTOLICS, a denomination in the twelfth century, who professed to exhibit in their lives and manners the piety and virtues of the holy apostles. They held it unlawful to take

* Scotch Theol. Dict.

‡ Lardner's Heretics, 315, &c.

§ Broughton, vol. i. p. 58.

‖ Ib. p. 60.

¶ Formey's Eccles. Hist. vol. i. p. 79.

an oath, renounced the things of this world, and preferred celibacy to wedlock.*

AQUARIANS, a denomination in the second century, who, under pretence of abstinence, made use of water instead of wine in the eucharist. See *Encratites.*

ARABACI. They sprung up in the year 207, denied the immortality of the soul, and believed that it perishes with the body; but maintained, at the same time, that it was to be again recalled to life with the body, by the power of God.†

ARCHONTICS, a denomination which appeared about the year 175; who held that archangels created the world, denied the resurrection of the body, and maintained that the God of sabaoth exercised a cruel tyranny in heaven. They defended their doctrines by books of their own composing, styled "The Revelation of the Prophets," and the Harmony.

ARIANS, a denomination, which arose about the year 315, and owed its origin to Arius, presbyter of Alexandria, a man of a subtle turn, and remarkable for his eloquence. He maintained that the Son was totally and essentially distinct from the Father; that he was the first and noblest of all those beings whom God the Father had created out of nothing, the instrument by whose subordinate operation the Almighty Father formed the universe, and therefore inferiour to the Father both in nature and dignity. He added, that the holy Spirit was of a different nature from that of the Father and of the Son, and that he had been created by the Son. However, during the life of Arius, the disputes turned principally on the divinity of Christ.

The original Arians were divided among themselves, and torn into factions, regarding each other with the bitterest aversion, of whom the ancient writers make mention under the names of Semi-Arians, Eusebians, Aetians, Eunomians, Acacians, Psatyrians, and others, most of which are described in this work under their respective heads.

The modern Arians, to prove the subordination and inferiority of Christ to God the Father, argue thus: There are various passages of scripture where the Father is styled the one, or only God. *Why callest thou me good? There is none good but one, that is God.* (Matt. xix. 17.) The Father is styled God with peculiarly high titles and attributes. (See Matt. xxiii. 9.—Mark v. 7. &c.) It is said in Ephesians iv. 6. *There is one God and Father of all, who is above all.* Our Lord Jesus Christ expressly speaks of another God distinct from himself. See Matt.

* Mosheim, vol. ii. p. 457.

† Mosheim, vol. i. p. 294.

‡ Echard's Eccles. Hist. vol. ii. p. 542.

xxvii. 46.—John xx. 17.) He not only owns another than himself to be God, but also that he is above and over himself. He declares that *his Father is greater than he,* John xiv. 28. Our Lord also says, *He came not in his own but in his Father's name and authority;* that he sought not his own, but God's glory; nor made his own, but God's will his rule. See John vi. 38; xii. 49; xiv. 10.

In the solemn prayer, uttered by our Lord just before his crucifixion, he declares, *This is life eternal, that they might know thee, the only true God, and Jesus Christ, whom thou hast sent.* John xvii. 3. Our Lord addresses one person, calling that person *The only true God.* That this person addressed was the Father, is evident from the commencement of the prayer, *Father, the hour is come,* (verse 1.) and from the repetition of the title Father in several of the subsequent verses (verse 5, 11, 21, 24, 25.) It follows therefore, that the Father *is the only true God.*

Other passages of Scripture, which prove the same doctrine, are those in which Christ asserts, that the Father alone knew the day of general judgment, Matt. xxiv. 36. Mark xiii. 32. *But of that day and that hour knoweth no man, no, not the Angels which are in heaven, neither the Son, but the Father only.* If any one being besides the Father were God, he would have known the day of judgment; since therefore the Father alone knew this day, it is evident that he alone is the omniscient God.

The Apostles also declare, that our Lord Jesus Christ was not God, but a being distinct from him; that he was subordinate and inferiour to the Father, and derived all his wisdom and power from him. 1 Cor. viii. 6. *But to us there is but one God, the Father.* Ephes. iv. 6. *One God and Father of all. Ye are Christ's, and Christ is God's.* 1 Cor. iii. 23. that is, as Christians are subject to the dominion of Christ, so Christ is subject to the dominion of God. *The head of Christ is God.* 1 Cor. xi. 3. The one infinite mind is repeatedly called not only the Father of Jesus, but likewise his God. Ephes. i. 3. *Blessed be the God and Father of our Lord Jesus Christ.* See also Rom. xv. 6. 2 Cor. i. 3. Colossians i. 3. 1 Peter i. 3. It is said in 1 Cor. xv. 24, that *Christ will deliver up the kingdom to God, even the Father.* Therefore he will be subjected to him, and is consequently inferiour.

There are numerous texts of Scripture, in which it is declared that religious worship is referred to the Father only. See Matt. iv. 10. John iv. 23. Acts iv. 24. 1 Cor. 1—4. In all these, and various other passages, prayers were addressed to *the God and Father of our Lord Jesus Christ.*

Modern Arians are distinguished by the titles *High* and *Low;* the former, like the Semi-Arians, raising the character of Christ as nearly as possible to the divinity; and the latter sinking it very nearly to mere humanity. The term Arian is now indiscriminately applied to those who consider Jesus simply subordinate to the Father. Some of them believe Christ to have been the Creator of the world; but they all maintain that he existed previously to his incarnation, though in his pre-existent state they assign him different degrees of dignity. (See *Unitarians of Dr. Price's description.)* See also *Pre-existents.*

The opinion of the Arians concerning Christ, differs from the Gnostics chiefly in two respects,—(1.) The Gnostics supposed the pre-existent spirit which was in Jesus to have been an emanation from the supreme Being, according to the principles of the philosophy of that age, which made creation out of nothing, to be an impossibility. But the Arians supposed the pre-existent spirit to have been properly created, and to have animated the body of Christ instead of the human soul.—(2.) The Gnostics supposed that the pre-existent spirit was not the maker of the world; but was sent to rectify the evils which had been introduced by the Being who made it. But the Arians supposed that their Logos was the Being, whom God had employed in making the universe, as well as in all his communications with mankind.*

For the difference between Arians and Socinians. See *Socinians.*

ARISTOTELIANS, the disciples of Aristotle, a famous Grecian philosopher, who flourished about 485 years before Christ. He taught that the universe existed from eternity, but admitted the existence of a Deity, whom he styled the first Mover; and whose nature he represented as somewhat similar to a principle of power, giving motion to a machine. In producing motion, he taught, that the Deity acts not voluntarily, but necessarily;—not for the sake of other beings, but for his own pleasure; and that happy in the contemplation of himself, he is entirely regardless of human affairs. Nothing occurs in his writings, which decisively determines whether he supposed the soul of man mortal or immortal.

Respecting ethics, he taught, that happiness consists in the virtuous exercise of the mind;

* Mosheim's Eccles. Hist. vol. i. p. 335, 442, 443. Formey's Eccles. Hist. vol. i. p. 76. Priestley's Hist. of Early Opinions, vol. iv. p. 168 Clarke's Scripture Doctrine of the Trinity, p. 1, 2, 3, 46. Emlyn's Extracts, p. 9, 10, 11, 21. Yates' Vindication of Unitarianism, p. 69, 70, 79. Theological Repository, vol. iv. p. 276. Doddridge's Lectures, p. 401. Evans' Sketch, p. 59. See also Ben Mordecai's Apology, written by Mr. Henry Taylor.

and that virtue consists in preserving that mean in all things, which reason and prudence prescribe. It is the middle path between two extremes, one of which is vicious through excess, the other through defect.*

ARMENIANS, a division of Eastern Christians, so called from Armenia in Asia, a country they originally inhabited. Their sentiments are similar to those of the Greek Church. See that article.

In the rites and ceremonies of the Armenian church, there is so great a resemblance to those of the Greeks, that a particular detail might be superfluous. Their liturgies also are either essentially the same, or at least ascribed to the same author. See *Syrian Christians.*

The Armenian was considered as a branch of the Greek Church, professing the same faith, and acknowledging the same subjection to the See of Constantinople, till near the middle of the sixth century. At that time the doctrine of the Monophysites spread far and wide through the regions of Africa and Asia, comprehending the Armenians also among its votaries. When they receded from holding communion with the Greeks, they made no change in their ancient Episcopal form of church government; but only claimed the privilege of choosing their own spiritual rulers.

The Armenians are scattered all over Asia, and have formed settlements, wherever they have found an opening for trade. They have churches at Calcutta, Madras, Bombay, and in all the principal trading countries in that part of the globe, and extend to Jerusalem, Constantinople, and Russia.†

ARMINIANS. They derive their name from James Arminius, who was born in Holland 1560. He was the first pastor of Amsterdam, afterwards professor of divinity at Leyden; and attracted the esteem and applause of his very enimies by his acknowledged candour, penetration and piety. He had been a pupil of Theodore Beza, who adhered to the Calvinistic doctrines in the strictest manner, but Arminius thinking the tenets of Calvin, with regard to *free-will, predestination* and *grace,* contrary to the mild and amiable perfections of the Deity, began to express his doubts concerning them in the year 1591; and upon further inquiry, adopted sentiments more nearly resembling those of the Lutherans, than of the Calvinists.

The principal tenets of the Arminians are comprehended in five articles, to which are added a few of the arguments

* Enfield's Philosophy, vol. i.

† Broughton's Hist. Lib. vol. ii. p. 229. Dallaway's Hist. of Constantinople, p. 383.

they make use of in defence of their sentiments.

I. That God has not fixed the future state of mankind by an absolute, unconditional decree; but determined from all eternity to bestrow salvation on those, who he foresaw would persevere unto the end in their faith in Jesus Christ; and to inflict everlasting punishments on those, who should continue in their unbelief, and resist unto the end his divine succours.

For, as the Deity is just, holy and merciful; wise in all his counsels, and true in all his declarations to the sons of men, it is inconsistent with his attributes, by an antecedent decree, to fix our commission of so many sins in such a manner, that there is no possibility for us to avoid them. And he represents God dishonourably, who believes, that by his revealed will he hath declared he would have all men to be saved, and yet by an antecedent secret will, he would have the greater part of them to perish. That he has imposed a law upon them, which he requires them to obey on penalty of his eternal displeasure, though he knows they cannot do it without his irresistible grace; and yet is absolutely determined to withhold this grace from them, and then punish them eternally for what they could not do without his divine assistance.

II. That Jesus Christ, by his death and sufferings, made an atonement for the sins of all mankind in general, and of every individual in particular; that, however, none but those who believe in him can be partakers of their divine benefit.

That is, the death of Christ put all men in a capacity of being justified and pardoned, upon condition of their faith, repentance, and sincere obedience to the laws of the new covenant.

For the scriptures declare, in a variety of places, that Christ died for the whole world. John iii. 16, 17. *God so loved the world, that he gave his only begotten Son, that whosoever believed on him, might not perish, but have everlasting life*, &c. 1 John ii. 2. *He is the propitiation, not only for our sins, but for the sins of the whole world.* And the apostle expresses the same idea in Heb. ii. 9, when he says, *Christ tasted death for every man.* Here is no limitation of that comprehensive phrase.

If Christ died for those who perish, and for those who do not perish, he died for all. That he died for those who do not perish, is confessed by all; and if he died for any who may or shall perish, there is the same reason to affirm that he died for all who perish. Now that he died for such, the scripture says expressly in 1 Cor. viii. 11. *And through thy knowledge shall the weak brother perish, for whom Christ died.* Hence it is evident, Christ died for those who perish, and for those who do not perish: therefore he died for all men.

III. That mankind are not totally depraved; and that the sin of our first parents is not imputed to us, nor shall we be hereafter punished for any but our own personal transgressions.

For, if all men are utterly unable to do good, and continually inclined to all manner of wickedness, it follows they are not moral agents. For how are we capable of performing our duty, or of regulating our actions by a law, commanding good and forbidding evil, if our minds are bent to nothing but what is evil? Then sin must be natural to us; and if natural, then necessary with regard to us; and if necessary, then no sin. For what is natural to us, as hunger, thirst, &c. we can by no means hinder; and what we can by no means hinder, is not our sin. Therefore mankind are not totally depraved.

That the sin of our first parents is not imputed to us is evident, because as the evil action they committed was personal, so must their real guilt be personal, and belong only to themselves, and we cannot in the eye of justice and equity be punishable for their transgressions. See Jer. xxxi. 29, 30.

IV. That there is a measure of grace given to every man to profit withal, which is neither irresistible nor irrevocable; but is the foundation of all exhortations to repentance, faith, &c. For if conversion be wrought only by the overpowering operation of God, and man is purely passive in it, vain are all the commands and exhortations to wicked men to *turn from their evil ways; to cease to do evil, and learn to do well; to put off the old man, and put on the new.* See Isai. i. 16. Deut. x. 16. Eph. iv. 22, and various other passages of scripture to the same purpose. Were an irresistible power necessary to the conversion of sinners, no man could be converted sooner than he is; because before this irresistible action came upon him, he could not be converted, and when it came upon him he could not resist its operation. And therefore no man could reasonably be blamed for having lived so long in an unconverted state, and it could not be praiseworthy in any person who was converted, since no man can resist an overpowering operation.

V. That true believers may fall from their faith, and forfeit finally their state of grace.

For, the doctrine of a possibility of the final departure of true believers from the faith is expressed in Heb. vi. 4, 5, 6. *It is impossible for those who were once enlightened, &c. if they shall fall away, to renew them again to repentance.* See also 1 Cor. ix. 27. 2 Pet. ii. 18—20. And many other passages of scripture to the same purpose.

All commands to persevere and stand fast in the faith, show that there is a possibility that believers may not stand fast and persevere unto the end. All cautions to Christians not to fall from grace, are evidences and suppositions that they may fall. For what we have just reason to caution any person against, must be something which may come to pass, and be hurtful to him. Now such caution Christ gives his disciples, Luke xxi. 34. To those who had like precious faith with the apostles, St. Peter saith, *Beware, lest, being led away by the errour of the wicked, you fall from your own steadfastness.* 2 Pet. iii. 17. Therefore he did not look upon this as a thing impossible; and the doctrine of perseverance renders those exhortations and motives insignificant, which are so often to be found in scripture.

In these points, which are considered as fundamental articles in the Arminian system, the doctrine of free-will, as implying a self-determining power in the mind, is included. See *Freewillers* and *Pelagians*.*

ARNOLDISTS, the followers of Arnold of Brescia, in the twelfth century, who maintained publicly, that the treasures and revenues of popes, bishops, and monasteries, ought to be solemnly transferred to the rulers of each state; and that nothing was to be left to the ministers of the gospel but a spiritual authority, and a subsistence drawn from tithes, and from the voluntary oblations of the people.†

ARTEMONITES, a denomination in the second century, so called from Artemon, who taught that at the birth of the man Christ, a certain divine energy, or portion of the divine nature, united itself to him.

ARTOTYRITES, a sect in the second century, charged with celebrating the eucharist with bread and cheese: saying that the first oblations of men were of the fruits of the earth and of sheep. They admitted women to the priesthood.‡

ASCLEPIDOTÆANS, a sect in the third century; so called from Asclepidotus, who taught, like the modern Socinians, that Jesus Christ was a mere man.

ASCODOGRITES, a denomination which arose in the year 181. It is said they brought into their churches, bags, skins, or bottles, filled with new wine, to represent the new wine mentioned by

* Mosheim's Eccles. Hist. vol. v. p. 3, 7, 8. Whitby on the Five Pints, p. 106, 107, &c. Taylor on Original Sin, p. 13—125. Stackhouse's Body of Divinity. Correspondence between Clarke and Leibnitz, and between Priestley and Price.

† Mosheim, vol. ii. p. 450. ‡ Broughton, vol. i. p. 85.

Christ; then danced round these bottles, and intoxicated themselves with the wine. They are likewise called Ascitæ, and both words are derived from the Greek ασκὸς, a *bottle.**

ASCODRUTES, a branch of Gnostics in the second century, who asserted that divine mysteries, being the images of invisible things, ought not to be represented by visible things, nor incorporeal things by corporeal and sensible. Therefore they rejected baptism and the eucharist.†

*ASSIDEANS, a party of Jews, which joined Mattathias in fighting for the freedom of their country. See 1 Macc. ii. 42; vii. 13.

ASSURITANS, a branch of the Donatists, who held that the Son was inferiour to the Father, and the Holy Ghost to the Son. See *Donatists.*

ATHANASIANS, the followers of Athanasius, bishop of Alexandria, who flourished in the fourth century. He was bishop forty six years; and his long administration was spent in a perpetual combat against the Arians, and in defence of the doctrine of the Trinity.—The scheme of Athanasius is thus expressed in the creed which bears his name.‡ "The Catholic faith is this, that we worship one God in Trinity and Trinity in unity. For there is one person of the Father, another of the Son, and and another of the Holy Ghost. But the Godhead of the Father, of the Son, and of the Holy Ghost, is all one; the glory equal, the majesty coeternal." See *Trinitarians.*

This system also includes in it, the belief of two natures in Jesus Christ, viz. the divine and human, forming one person.

To prove the divinity of Christ, and his coequality with the Father, this denomination argue thus:

In John i. 1. it is expressly declared, that *In the beginning was the Word, and the Word was with God, and the Word was God.*

That "the Word," in whatever way we choose to translate the original term, which is so rendered, whether we retain this rendering, or give the preference to *wisdom* or *reason,* is here to be understood as a designation of Jesus Christ, appears evident from the whole of the subsequent context. It is said in the fourteenth verse, *and the Word was made flesh, and dwelt among us, (and we beheld his glory, the glory as of the only begotten of the Father,) full of grace and truth.* Sup-

* Broughton, vol. i. p. 191.

† Ibid. p. 83.

‡ It has been supposed that this creed, which bears the name of Athanasius, was not drawn up by Athanasius, bishop of Alexandria; it is commonly attributed to Vigilius, the African, who lived about the end of the fifth century. See Evans' Sketch, and Adams' Religious World Displayed.

posing it then to be admitted, that "the Word" here does not mean an attribute, or an abstract quality personified, but a person; and that this person is Jesus Christ:—it is clear, that the verse contains a plain and express declaration of his true and proper Divinity, *The Word was God.*

Christ's divinity and coequality with the Father, are plainly taught in Philip. ii. 5, 6, 7, &c. *Let this mind be in you, which was also in Christ Jesus, who, being in the form of God, thought it not robbery to be equal with God, but made himself of no reputation, and took upon him the form of a servant, &c.*

Our divine Saviour says of himself, *I and my Father are one,* John x. 30. *He that has seen me, has seen the Father.* John xiv. 9. *All things that the Father hath, are mine.* John xvi. 15. Those high and strong expressions teach, that he is the Supreme God.

The prophets describe the true God as the only Saviour of sinners. Hosea xiii. 4. *Thou shalt know no God but me; for there is no Saviour besides me.* Jesus Christ not only professes to save sinners, but he calls himself the Saviour by way of eminence. Hence it is evident, that he assumes a character, in the most emphatical way, which the God of Israel had challenged and appropriated to himself.

The titles given to Christ in the New Testament are the same with those given to God in the Jewish scriptures. Jehovah is the incommunicable name of the Supreme God, signifying his eternal, independent and immutable existence. This name, which is appropriated to God, (Psalms lxxxiii. 18.) is given to Christ. Romans xiv. 11. Heb. i. 10. Jesus is the person spoken of by St. John, whose glory Esaias is declared to have seen, when he affirms, he saw the Lord of Hosts. Therefore Jesus is the Lord of Hosts.

The attributes, which are sometimes appropriated to God, are applied to Christ.

Omniscience is ascribed to Christ. John xvi. 30. *Now we are sure, that thou knowest all things.* To be the searcher of the heart, is the peculiar and distinguishing characteristic of the one true God, as appears from Jer. xvii. 10. Yet our blessed Lord claims this perfection to himself. *I am he,* saith he, *that searcheth the reins, and the heart.* Rev. ii. 23.

Omnipresence, another divine attribute, is ascribed to Christ. Matt. xviii. 20. *Where two or three are gathered together in my name, there am I in the midst of them.*

Immutability is ascribed to Christ. Heb. i. 10, 11, 12. *Thou art the same, and thy years shall not fail.* This is the very description, which the psalmist gives of the immutability of the only true God. See also Heb. xiii. 8.

Eternity is ascribed to Christ, Rev. i. 8. The Son's being Jehovah, is another proof of his eternity, that name expressing necessary existence.

Christ is also said to have almighty power. Heb. i. 3. See also Philip. iii. 21, &c.

The truth and faithfulness of God are ascribed to Christ. *I am*, says he, *the truth*, &c.

Divine works are also ascribed to Christ, viz. creation, preservation, and forgiveness of sins.

There are numerous texts of scripture, which assert that Christ is the creator of all things. See Heb. i. 10. *Thou, Lord, in the beginning hast laid the foundation of the earth, and the heavens are the works of thy hands*. See also Rev. iii. 14. 1 Cor. viii. 6. and various other passages.

The work of creation is every where in scripture represented, as the mark and characteristic, of the true God. See 2 Kings xix. 15. Psalm xix. 1. Hence it is evident, that Christ, the creator, is the true God.

Preservation is ascribed to Christ. Heb. i. 3. *Upholding all things by the word of his power*.

Christ himself says, in Matt. ix. 6. *The Son of Man hath power on earth to forgive sins*.

Christ's being appointed the Supreme Judge of the world, is an evidence that he is the true God. The God of Israel is emphatically styled, the Judge of all.*

Religious worship, though appropriated to God, was, by divine approbation and command, given to Christ. In Heb. i. 6. the apostle, speaking of Christ, says, *Let all the angels of God worship him*. See also Luke xxiv. 52. John v. 23. Rev. i. 5, 6; v. 13. &c.

The scripture every where asserts, that God alone is to be worshipped. The same scripture asserts, that our blessed Saviour is to be worshipped. Thus St. Stephen adores him with direct worship: *Lord Jesus, receive my spirit*. The obvious consequence of which is, our blessed Saviour is God.

This denomination allege, that divine titles, attributes, works, and worship, are also ascribed to the Holy Ghost.

Many plead, that the Holy Spirit is called Jehovah in the Old Testament, by comparing Acts xxviii. 26. with Isa. vi. 9. And He also appears to be called God, Acts v. 4.

Eternity is clearly the property of the Holy Ghost, who is styled, by the author of the epistle to the Hebrews, *the Eternal Spirit*. Heb. ix. 14.

Omnipresence is a necessary proof of divinity. This attribute belongs to the Holy Spirit: for thus saith the inspired poet, *Whither shall I go from thy Spirit?* Psa. cxxxix. 7.

* See Mr. Alexander's Essay on the real Deity of Jesus Christ.

Omniscience is ascribed to the Spirit. 1 Cor. ii. 10. *For the Spirit searcheth all things, even the deep things of God.*

St. Paul declares, that his ability to work all manner of astonishing miracles, for the confirmation of his ministry, was imparted to him by the Spirit. Rom. xv. 19.

The principal passages of Scripture which are alleged to prove that divine worship is given to the Spirit, are Matt. xxviii. 19. Is. vi. 3—9. Acts xxviii. 25.

The Trinity of persons in the Godhead appears from the form of baptizing *in the name of the Father, of the Son, and of the Holy Ghost.* And also from the Apostolic benediction. *The grace of the Lord Jesus Christ, the love of God, and the communion of the Holy Ghost be with you all, Amen.* The Trinity in unity is one Supreme Being, distinguished from all others by the name Jehovah. Deut. vi. 4. *The Lord our God is one Jehovah.* Yet Christ is Jehovah. Jer. xxiii. 6.—so is the Spirit. Ezek. viii. 3. Therefore Father, Son, and Holy Ghost are one Jehovah. They are three persons, but have one name and one nature.*

ATHEISTS, those who do not believe in the existence of a God, but attribute surrounding nature and all its astonishing phenomena to chance, or to a fortuitous concourse of atoms: This is called *speculative Atheism.* Professing to believe in God, and yet acting contrary to this belief, is styled *practical Atheism.* The name of Atheist is composed of two Greek terms, α and Θεὸς, signifying without God, and in this sense the appellation occurs in the New Testament. Ephes. ii. 12. *Without God,* (or Atheists) *in the world.* Plato distinguishes three kinds of Atheists. 1. Those, who deny the existence of the gods absolutely. 2. Those, who deny their interference in human affairs. 3. Those, who admit both, but conceive them indifferent to human crimes. The first of these, however, are the only Atheists in the strict and proper sense of the word. The latter are rather practical Atheists; and the evidences of a Deity are so numerous and strong, that many have doubted the existence of a real Atheist. Some, however, in most countries, have avowed the principles. In the seventeenth century, Benedict Spinosa, a Jew of Amsterdam, was its noted defender; and Lucillo Vanini, an Italian of eccentric character, was condemned and executed 1616 at Toulouse, for his Atheistical tenets, which he and eleven others had underta-

* Waterland's Sermons, p. 34, 69, 97, 164. Abbadie on the Divinity of Christ, p. 58, 65, 242. Jones' Doctrine of the Trinity, p. 2, 34, 62. Watts' Christian Doctrine of the Trinity. Doddridge's Lectures, p. 392. Robinson's Plea. Vindication of Christ's Divinity, p. 263, 269. Wardlaw's Discourses. Reply to Yates.

ken to disseminate all over Europe. In the early days of the French revolution, the leading members of the convention endeavoured to suppress all religion, except the worship of their tutelary goddess Liberty; and for this purpose they shut up the churches, abolished the Sabbath, and inscribed upon the burying grounds, "Death is an eternal sleep."

Lord Bacon says, that "a smattering in philosophy may lead a man into Atheism, because he looks no farther than second causes; but by diving deeper into it, he will behold the chain of them linked together, which will certainly bring him back to God and providence."*

AUDÆANS, a sect in the fourth century; so called from Audæus, who is said to have attributed to the Deity a human form.† See *Antropomorphites.*

AUGUSTINES, an order of Monks, who followed the rule of St. Augustin, by contraction St. Austin, having all things in common, &c. A convent of these gave name to Austin Friars. See *Monks.*

AZYMITAE, a name given by the Greeks in the eleventh century to the Latin church, because they used unleavened bread in the eucharist.‡

B

BABYLONIANS, or ancient Assyrians. The religion of this great nation has been considered to be involved in much obscurity. It appears, however, that they were great students in the heavens, and blended their religion with astronomy. They worshipped the sun, moon, and stars, particularly Venus. At length their astronomy sunk into astrology, and their learned men became diviners and fortune-tellers, while the multitude, from worshipping the heavenly bodies themselves, became devotees to the idols they had made to represent them. This appears to have been the state of the religion of the Babylonians at the time of Nebuchadnezzar, when the unbounded ambition of that monarch introduced an addition to the established worship of the land by the deification of himself.§

BAPTISTS, or Antipædobaptists. This denomination claim an immediate descent from the Apostles, and assert, that the constitution of their churches is from the authority of Jesus Christ himself, and his immediate successors. Many others indeed deduce their origin as a sect, from much later times, and affirm, that they first sprang up in Germa-

* Ency. Brit. Buck's Theol. Dict. † Mosheim, vol. i. p. 350.
‡ Hist. Dict. vol. i. § Bellamy's History of Religion, p. 38, 40.

ny in the sixteenth century. This denomination of Christians is distinguished from others by their opinions respecting the mode and subject of baptism. Instead of administering the ordinance by sprinkling or pouring water, they maintain that it ought to be administered only by immersion; such they insist is the meaning of the Greek word βαπτίζω, to wash or dip, so that a command to baptize is a command to immerse. They also defend their practice from the phrase, *buried with him in baptism*, from the first administrators repairing to rivers, and the practice of the primitive church after the Apostles.

With regard to the *subjects* of Baptism, this denomination allege, that it ought not to be administered to children or infants at all, nor to adults in general; but to those only, who profess repentance for sin and faith in Christ. Our Saviour's commission to his apostles, by which Christian baptism was instituted, is to *go and teach all nations, baptizing them;* &c. that is, not to baptize all they meet with, but first to examine and instruct them, and whoever will receive instruction to baptize in the *name of the Father, and of the Son, and of the Holy Ghost.* This construction of the passage is confirmed by another passage; *Go ye into all the world, and preach the Gospel to every creature; he that believeth and is baptized, shall be saved.* To such persons, and to such only this denomination says, baptism was administered by the apostles and the immediate disciples of Christ; for those who were baptized in primitive times are described as repenting of their sins, and believing in Christ. See Acts ii. 38; viii. 37. and other passages of scripture.

They farther insist, that all positive institutions depend entirely upon the will and declaration of the institutor; and that therefore reasoning by analogy from previous abrogated rites, is to be rejected, and the express commands of Christ respecting the mode and subjects of baptism ought to be our only rule.

The Baptists in England form one of the three denominations of Protestant Dissenters. The constitution of their churches, and their modes of worship are Congregational or Independent. They bore a considerable share of the persecutions of the seventeenth and preceding centuries, for there were some among the Lollards and Wickliffites who disapproved of infant baptism. There were many of this persuasion among the Protestants abroad. In Holland, Germany, and the North, they went by the names of Anabaptists and Mennonites; and in Piedmont and the South, they were found among the Albigenses and Waldenses.

The Baptists subsist under two denominations; the particular or Calvinistical, and the general or Arminian. The former is by far the most numerous. Some of both denominations allow of mixed communion* with Pædobaptists; others disallow it, and allege, that it would be inconsistent in them to admit unbaptized persons, (as others are in their view,) to unite with them in this ordinance.

A few of this denomination observe the seventh day of the week as the Sabbath, apprehending the law which enjoined it not to have been repealed by Christ, or his apostles. See *Sabbatarians.*

A considerable number of the general Baptists have embraced Arianism, or Socinianism, on account of which several of their ministers and churches, who disapprove of these principles, have, within the last forty years, formed themselves into a distinct connexion, called The New Association. The churches in this union keep up a friendly acquaintance, in some outward things, with those from whom they are separated; but in things they deem more essential, disclaim any connexion with them; particularly as to changing ministers and the admission of members.

The Baptists in America, and in the East and West Indies, are chiefly Calvinists. But from nearly the first rise of this denomination in America, there have been some who have opposed a number of the principal articles in the Calvinistic creed. This party have increased, and are denominated Free Will Baptists. See *Free Willers.*

The Baptists in Scotland, having imbibed a considerable part of the principles of Glass and Sandeman, have no connexion with the others. When the English Baptists, however, engaged in a mission to the East, they very liberally contributed towards the translation of the scriptures into the Eastern languages.† See *Haldamites.*

* The Rev. Robert Hall, who holds an eminent rank among the dissenters in England, has lately published a work, "On the Terms of Communion, with a particular view to the Case of the Baptists and Pædobaptists." He asserts in his preface to this work, that "There is no position in the whole compass of theology, of the truth of which he feels a stronger persuasion, than that no man, or set of men, are entitled to prescribe as an indispensable condition of communion, what the New Testament has not enjoined as a condition of salvation." To establish this position is the principal object of his work. Those who wish to see the arguments he makes use of, are referred to his ingenious publication.

† Gale's Reflections on Wall's History. Stennet's Answer to Addington. Booth's Pædobaptism Examined, second edition. McLean on the Commission. Baptist Confession of Faith. Rippon's Baptist Register, vol. i. p. 172, vol. ii. p. 361.

The different denominations of Baptists all unite in pleading for universal liberty of conscience. See *Mennonites, Dunkers,* &c.

BARDESANISTES, a denomination in the second century, the followers of Bardesanes, a native of Edessa, and a man of a very acute and penetrating genius.

The sum of his doctrine was as follows:

I. That there is a Supreme God, pure and benevolent, absolutely free from all evil and imperfection; and that there is also a prince of darkness, the fountain of all evil, disorder, and misery.

II. That the Supreme God created the world without any mixture of evil in its composition: he gave existence also to its inhabitants, who came out of his forming hand, pure and incorrupt, endued with subtle ethereal bodies, and spirits of a celestial nature.

III. That, when the prince of darkness had enticed men to sin, then the Supreme God permitted them to fall into sluggish and gross bodies, formed of corrupt matter by the evil principle. He permitted also the depravation and disorder, which this malignant being introduced, both into the natural and moral world; designing, by this permission, to punish the degeneracy and rebellion of an apostate race. And hence proceeds the perpetual conflict between reason and passion, in the mind of man.

IV. That, on this account, Jesus descended from the upper regions, clothed not with a real, but with a celestial and aërial body, and taught mankind to subdue that body of corruption, which they carry about with them in this mortal life; and by abstinence, fasting, and contemplation, to disengage themselves from the servitude and dominion of that malignant matter, which chained down the soul to low and ignoble pursuits.

V. That those, who submit themselves to the discipline of this Divine Teacher, shall, after the dissolution of this terrestrial body, mount up to the mansions of felicity, clothed with ethereal vehicles, or celestial bodies.

This denomination was a branch of the Gnostics.* See *Gnostics.*

BARLAAMITES, a denomination in the sixteenth century, followers of Barlaam, a Neapolitan monk, who was called a heretic for asserting that the light, which surrounded Christ on Mount Tabor, was not an emanation of the divine essence.†

BASILIDIANS, a branch of the Egyptian Gnostics in the second century. They acknow-

* Mosheim's Eccles. Hist. vol. i. p. 179, 180.

† Mosheim, vol. iii. p. 374, new edition.

ledged the existence of one supreme God, perfect in goodness and wisdom, who produced from his own substance seven beings, or *aions*, of a most excellent nature. Two of these *aions*, called Dunamis and Sophia, (i. e. *power* and *wisdom*,) engendered the angels of the highest order. These angels formed a heaven for their habitation, and brought forth others of a nature somewhat inferiour to their own, to the amount of three hundred and sixty five, under their mighty chief Abraxas.

It may be worthy of remark, that by this sect the word *aion*, from expressing only the duration of beings, was by a metonymy employed to signify the beings themselves. Thus the supreme Being was called *aion;* and the angels were distinguished by the title of *aions*. All this will lead us to the true meaning of that word among the Gnostics. They had formed to themselves the notion of an invisible world, composed of entities, or virtues, proceeding from the Supreme Being, and succeeding each other at certain intervals of time, so as to form an eternal chain, of which our world was the terminating link. To the beings which formed this eternal chain, the Gnostics assigned a certain term of duration, and a certain sphere of action. Their terms of duration were at first called *aions;* and themselves were afterwards metonymically distinguished by that title.

These beings, advanced to the government of the world which they had created, fell by degrees from their original purity, and soon manifested the fatal marks of depravity and corruption.* See *Gnostics*.

BAXTERIANS, so called from the learned and pious Mr. Richard Baxter, who was born in the year 1615. His design was to reconcile Calvin and Arminius. For this purpose he formed a middle scheme between their systems. He taught that God had elected some, whom he is determined to save, without any foresight of their good works; and that others to whom the gospel is preached have common grace, which if they improve, they shall obtain saving grace, according to the doctrine of Arminius. This denomination own, with Calvin, that the merits of Christ's death are to be applied to believers only; but they also assert that all men are in a state capable of salvation; to support which opinion, this learned author alleges, that it was the nature of *all* mankind which Christ assumed at his incarnation, and the sins of *all* mankind were the occasion of his suffering; that therefore it is not to the elect only, but to *all* mankind, that Christ has commanded his

* Mosheim, vol i. p. 181—183. Lardner's Heretics, p. 76, &c.

ministers to proclaim his gospel, and offer the benefits which he hath procured.*

*BEGHARDS, [i. e. hard-beggars,] feminine BEGUINES, so called from their importunity in prayer, and sometimes taken more literally; this was a term applied (like *Methodists*) to not less than thirty petty sects of very different characters in the twelfth and thirteenth centuries.†

BEHMENISTS, a name given to those mystics who adopted the explication of the mysteries of nature and grace as given by Jacob Behmen.—This writer was born in the year 1575, at Old Siedenburg near Gorlitz, in Upper Lusatia. He was a shoemaker by trade; and is described as having been thoughtful and religious from his youth up, taking peculiar pleasure in frequenting public worship. At length seriously considering that speech of our Saviour, *My Father which is in heaven will give the Holy spirit to him that asketh him*, he was thereby awakened to desire that promised Comforter; and, continuing in that earnestness, he was at last, to use his own expression, "surrounded with a divine light for seven days, and stood in the highest contemplation and kingdom of joys!" After this, about the year 1600, he was again surrounded by the divine light, and replenished with the heavenly knowledge; insomuch that by his inward light he saw into the essences, uses, and properties of things, which were discovered to him by their lineaments, figures, and signatures. In the year 1610, he had a third special illumination, wherein still farther mysteries were revealed to him; but it was not till the year 1612, that Behmen committed these revelations to writing. His first treatise is entitled, *Aurora*, which was seized by the senate of Gorlitz before completed. His next production is called *The Three Principles*, by which he means the dark world, or hell; the light world, or heaven; and the external or visible world, which we inhabit. In this work he more fully illustrates the subjects treated of in the former, and supplies what is wanting in that work, showing, (1.) How all things came from a working-will of the holy, triune, incomprehensible God, through an outward, perceptible, working, triune power of fire, light, and spirit, in the kingdom of heaven.—(2.) How and what angels and men were in their creation; that they are in and from God, his real offspring; that their life begun in and from this divine fire, which is the Father of light, generating a birth of light in their souls; from both which proceeds the

* Baxter's Cath. Theol. p. 51, 53. Baxter's End of Controv. p. 154.
† Mosheim, vol. iii. p. 232, 288, &c. new edit.

holy Spirit, or breath of divine love in the triune creature, as in the triune Creator.—(3.) How some angels, and all men, are from God, and what they are in their fallen state.—(4.) How the earth, stars, and elements were created, in consequence of the fall of angels.—(5.) Whence there is good and evil in all this temporal world; and what is meant by the curse that dwells in it.—(6.) Of the kingdom of Christ, how it is set in opposition to the kingdom of hell.—(7.) How man, through faith in Christ, is able to overcome the kingdom of hell, and thereby obtain eternal salvation.—(8.) How and why sin and misery shall only reign for a time, until God shall, in a supernatural way, make fallen man rise to the glory of angels.

The next year Behmen produced his *Three-fold Life of Man, according to the three principles.* In this work he treats more largely of the state of man in this world:—That he has—1. That immortal spark of life which is common to angels and devils:—2. That divine life which forms the difference between both; and 3. The life of this external and visible world. The first and last are common to all men; but the second only to a true Christian.

Behmen wrote several other treatises, but these are the basis of all his other writings. His conceptions are often clothed under allegorical symbols; and in his latter writings he has frequently adopted chemical phrases which he borrowed from conversation with learned men. But as to the matter contained in them, he disclaims having borrowed it either from men or books. He died in the year 1624, and his last words were, "Now I go hence into paradise!"*

Behmen's principles were adopted by the late ingenious and pious Mr. Law, who has clothed them in a more modern dress, and in a less obscure style; for whose sentiments, see article *Mystics*.

BENEDICTINES, Monks of the order of St. Benedict, who were obliged to perform their devotions seven times a day, and subjected to many privations. They claim the honour of converting the English nation and of founding the Metropolitan church of Canterbury.

BEREANS, a sect of Protestant Dissenters from the church of Scotland, who take their title from, and profess to follow the example of the ancient Bereans, (Acts xvii. 11.) in building their system of faith and practice upon the scriptures alone, without regard to any human authority whatever.

Mr. Barclay, a Scotch clergyman, was the founder of this denomination. They first as-

* Behmen's Works, vol. i. p. 6—20; vol. ii. p. 1. Okely's Memoirs of Behmen, p. 1—8.

sembled as a separate society of Christians in the city of Edinburgh, 1773.

The Bereans agree with the established churches of England and Scotland respecting the trinity, predestination and election, though they allege that these doctrines are not consistently taught in either, but they differ from them in various points. Particularly, they reject all natural religion; and assert, that our knowledge of God is from revelation alone.

They hold faith to be a simple credence in God's word. They consider personal assurance* as of the essence of faith. They argue, that God has expressly declared, *He that believeth shall be saved;* and therefore it is not only absurd but impious, and in a manner calling God a liar, for a man to say, "I believe the Gospel, but have doubts nevertheless of my own salvation." They maintain that unbelief is the unpardonable sin.

They consider a great part of the Old Testament-history, and the whole book of Psalms, as typical or prophetic of Christ, and do not apply them to the experience of private Christians. See *Hutchinsonians.*

In admitting to communion, this denomination do not require that account of personal experience which many other churches do. When they exclude unworthy members for immoral conduct, they do not think themselves authorized to deliver them over to Satan, as the apostles did; that power they consider as restricted to the apostles, and to the inspired testimony alone; and not to be extended to any church on earth, or any number of churches, or of Christians, whether decided by a majority of votes, or by unanimous voices.†

The doctrines of the Bereans have found converts in England, Scotland, and America.

BERENGARIANS, a denomination in the eleventh century, followers of Berengarius, who asserted that the bread and wine in the Lord's supper are not really and essentially, but *figuratively*, changed into the body and blood of Christ. But his followers were divided in opinion: all agreed that the elements are not essentially changed, though some allowed them to be changed in effect.‡

BERYLLIANS, so called from one Beryllus, an Arabian bishop in the third century.

* Mr Barclay says, "By whatever evidence I hold the resurrection of Jesus, by the same precise evidence I must hold it for a truth that I am justified—for God hath equally asserted both."—On this M'Lean remarks—"The resurrection is a truth independent of my believing, and the subject of direct testimony; but my justification is not declared to be a truth until I believe the former; nor is directly asserted, but promised on that provision. *If thou shalt believe*, &c. Rom. x. 9." See M'Lean's Commission of the Apostles.

† See Barclay's Works. Nicols' Essays, &c.

‡ Dict. of Arts and Sciences, vol. i. p. 289.

He taught that Christ did not exist before Mary; but that a portion of the divine nature was united to him at his birth.*

*BETHLEHEMITES, a sect, or rather a religious order, distinguished by a red star on their breast, which they called the Star of Bethlehem. They settled at Cambridge in the thirteenth century.†

*BEZPOPOFTSCHINS, a class of Russian Dissenters, including all those who either have no regular priests, or who refuse to acknowledge those of the established church: they are the *Duhobortsi, Pomoryans, Theodosians,* and ten others, which will be found under their places in the alphabet.‡

BIDDELIANS, the followers of John Biddle, a Socinian, who in the year 1644 erected an independent congregation in London. He taught that Jesus Christ hath no other than a human nature; and yet, like Socinus, made no scruple of calling him God, on account of the divine sovereignty with which he was invested.§ See *Socinians.*

BIRMANS, inhabitants of the Birman country in India. Their Religion originated from the same source as the Hindoo, but differs in some of its tenets. They are worshippers of Boodh, in which form they believe Vishnu appeared in his ninth incarnation, and forbade the depriving any being of life. They therefore eat no animal food; and believe that, after having undergone a number of transmigrations, they shall at last be either received to their Olympus, or sent to a place of punishment.

The Birmans do not torture their bodies like the Hindoos; but think it meritorious to mortify them by a voluntary abstemiousness and self-denial.‖

BOGOMILES, a sect in the twelfth century, which sprung from the Massalians. They derived their name from the divine mercy, which its members are said to have incessantly implored; for the word *bogomiles,* in the Mysian tongue, signifies *calling for mercy from above.*

Basilius, a monk at Constantinople, was their founder, and the doctrines he taught, it is said, were similar to those of the Manicheans.¶

*BOHEMIAN BRETHREN, a Society of Christian Reformers, which sprang up in Bohemia about 1467; in 1535 they united with the Lutherans and afterwards with the Zuinglians.

BONOSIANS, a branch of the Photinians, who followed the opinions of Bonosus, bishop of Sardica. See *Photinians.*

BORRELISTS, so named

* Mosheim, vol. i. p. 248. † Buck's Theol. Dict.
‡ Pinkerton's Greek Church, p. 305.
§ Lindsey's View of the Unitarian Doctrine and Worship, p. 289.
‖ Symes' Embassy to Ava. ¶ Mosheim, vol. ii. p. 444.

from their leader, Adam Borrel, of Zealand, a learned man, about the time of the Reformation, who is charged with undervaluing the Church, [i. e. of Rome,] its priests, and services. He asserted that all Christian churches had degenerated from the pure apostolic doctrines. His followers lead a very austere life, and employ a great part of their goods in alms and works of piety.*

BOURIGNONISTS, a denomination in the seventeenth century, which sprang from the famous Antoinette Bourignon de la Ponte, a native of Flanders, who pretended to be divinely inspired, and set apart to revive the true spirit of Christianity that had been extinguished by theological animosities and debates. The leading principles which run through her productions are as follow:—That man is perfectly free to resist or receive divine grace. That God is ever unchangeable love towards all his creatures, and does not inflict any arbitrary punishment; but that the evils they suffer are the natural consequences of sin. That true religion consists not in any outward forms of worship, nor systems of faith; but in an entire resignation of the will to God.†

This lady was educated in the Roman Catholic religion; but she declaimed equally against the corruptions of the church of Rome and those of the reformed churches: hence she was opposed and persecuted by both catholics and protestants. She maintained that there ought to be a toleration of all religions.

Those who are desirous of seeing a particular account of the life and writings of this lady, may consult an abridgment of the "Light of the World," published in 1786, by the New Jerusalem church.

***BRAMINS,** (formerly called Brachmans,) the Priests of Brachma, the supreme God of the *Hindoos*, which see.

***BRAZILIANS.** The natives of Brazil were so much terrified by thunder, that it was not only the object of religious reverence, but the most expressive name in their language; for the Deity was called *Toupan*, the thunderer.

BRETHREN & SISTERS OF THE FREE SPIRIT. They, about the thirteenth century, gained ground imperceptibly in Italy, France, and Germany. They took their denomination from the words of Paul, (Rom. viii. 2—14.) and maintained that the true children of God were invested with the privilege of a full and perfect freedom from the jurisdiction of the law. They were called by the Germans and Flemish, *Beghards* and *Beguttes*, names giv-

* Broughton, vol. i. p. 170.

† Dufresnoy's Chronological Tables, vol. ii. p. 253. Mosheim, vol. v. p. 64. Light of the World, p. 27—430. Mad. Bourignon's Letters.

en to those who made an extraordinary profession of piety and devotion.

The sentiments taught by this denomination were as follow:—That all things flowed by emanation from God, and were finally to return to their divine source:—That every man, by the power of contemplation, might be united to the Deity in an ineffable manner; and that they who, by long and assiduous meditation had plunged themselves, as it were, into the abyss of the divinity, acquired thereby a most glorious and sublime liberty; and were not only delivered from the violence of sinful lusts, but even from the common instincts of nature.

They treated with contempt every external act of religious worship; looking upon prayer, and the sacraments as the elements of piety, adapted to the capacity of children, and as unnecessary to the perfect man, whom long meditation had raised into the bosom and essence of the Deity.*

***BRETHREN & CLERKS OF THE COMMON LIFE**, a fraternity of the order of St. Augustine, who are commended for promoting the cause of religion and learning, about the time of the reformation.†

BROWNISTS, the name given for some time to those who were afterwards known in England and Holland under the denomination of *Independents*. It arose from a Mr. Robert Brown, who about 1590 was a teacher amongst them in England, and at Middleburg, in Zealand. He was a man of education, zeal, and abilities. The separation, however, does not appear to have originated in him: for by several publications of those times, it is clear that these sentiments had, before his day, been embraced, and professed in England, and churches gathered on the plan of them. Nor did the sect call themselves Brownists; but considered it rather as a nick-name given them by their adversaries.‡

This denomination did not differ in point of doctrine from the church of England, or from the other puritans; but they apprehended that, according to scripture, every church ought to be confined within the limits of a single congregation, and have the complete power of jurisdiction over its members, to be exercised by the elders within itself, without being subject to the authority of bishops, synods, presbyteries, or any ecclesiastical assembly, composed of the deputies from different churches. See *Independents*.

***BUCHANITES**, a Sect in Scotland which arose about

* Mosheim, vol. iii. p. 122—124. † Ibid.

‡ Examination of Barrow. Canne's Necessity of Separation, p. 153. Gifford's Plain Declaration, p. 1, 2. Also Neal's Puritans, p. 428.

1783. They believed in a Mrs. Buchan of Glasgow, who gave herself out to be the Woman spoken of in the Apocalypse, and promised to conduct her followers to heaven without dying: but she died soon after, and with her the sect ended.*

BUDNEIANS, a branch of the Socinians, which appeared in the year 1589, and maintained that Christ was not begotten by any extraordinary act of divine power; but that he was born like other men in a natural way, and not a proper object of divine worship.† See *Socinians.*

BUDSO, a form of Pagan worship, introduced into Japan, from China and Siam. Its author is supposed to have been Budha, whom the Indian bramins conceive to be their god Vishnu, who, they say, made his ninth appearance in the world, under the form of a man, so named. See *Hindoos.*

***BURGHERS**, a numerous and respectable class of seceders, from the church of Scotland, originally connected with the Associate Presbytery; but some difference arising about the lawfulness of the Burgess oath, a separation took place in 1739, and those who refused the oath, were called Antiburgers.* See *Seceders.*

C

CABBALISTS, certain doctors among the Jews, who pretend to derive from tradition an acromatic or secret science, called the Cabbala. This science is divided into three sorts. By the first kind, the Jews extract recondite meanings from the words of scripture. The second is a kind of magic, in employing the words and letters of scripture in certain combinations, which they suppose have power over the good and evil spirits of the invisible world familiar with them. The third, which is properly the Cabbala, is an art, by which they profess to raise mysterious expositions of the scriptures upon the letters of the sentences, to which they apply them.

The cabbalists suppose every letter, point, or accent of the law to contain some hidden mystery, which was revealed to Moses on Mount Sinai, but not written, (whence it is called the oral law,) but handed down by tradition among these mystic doctors.‡

* Scotch Theolog. Dict.

† Mosheim, vol. iv. p. 199.

‡ Butler's Horæ Biblicæ.

It is said, that the cabbalistic mysteries are at present despised by the more intelligent part of the Jewish nation.

CAINIANS, a denomination which sprang up about the year 130, so called on account of their great respect for Cain. They pretend that the virtue which had produced Abel was of an order inferiour to that which had produced Cain; and that this was the reason why Cain had the victory over Abel and killed him.

The morals of this denomination were said to be very defective.*

CALIXTINS, a branch of the Hussites, in Bohemia and Moravia, in the fifteenth century. The principal point in which they differed from the church of Rome, was the use of the chalice, (calix,) or communicating in both kinds. *Calixtins* was also a name given to those among the Lutherans, who followed the opinions of George Calixtus, a celebrated divine in the seventeenth century, who endeavoured to unite the Romish, Lutheran, and Calvinistic churches in the bonds of charity and mutual benevolence, taking the apostle's creed as his foundation of union.†

CALVINISTS. They derive their name from John Calvin, who was born at Nogen, in Picardy, in 1509. He first studied the civil law, and was afterwards made professor of divinity at Geneva, in the year 1536. His genius, learning, eloquence, and piety rendered him respectable even in the eyes of his enemies.

The name of Calvinists was first given to those who embraced not merely the doctrine, but the church-establishment and discipline established at Geneva, and to distinguish them from the Lutherans. But since the meeting of the Synod of Dort, the name has been chiefly applied to those who embrace Calvin's leading views of the gospel, to distinguish them from the Arminians.

The leading principles by which Calvinists are distinguished from Arminians, are reduced to five articles, and which from their being the principal points discussed at the Synod of Dort, have since been denominated the *five points.*

These are *predestination, particular redemption, total depravity, effectual calling,* and the certain *perseverance of the saints.*

The following statement comprises the principal tenets of the Calvinists, to which are added a few of the arguments they allege in defence of their sentiments.

I. That God has chosen a certain number of the fallen race of Adam in Christ, before the foundation of the world, unto eternal glory, according to his immutable purpose, and of his free grace and love, with-

* Ency. Brit. † Broughton, vol. i. p. 192. Mosheim, vol. iv. p. 450, 451.

out the foresight of faith, good works, or any conditions performed by the creature, as the cause of his election; and that the rest of mankind he was pleased to pass by, and ordain them to dishonour and wrath for their sins, to the praise of his glorious justice.*

For, as the Deity is infinitely perfect and independent in all his acts, the manifestation of his essential perfections must be the supreme end of the divine counsels and designs. Prov. xvi. 4. *The Lord has made all things for himself,* &c. Since God is omniscient, it is evident that he foresaw from eternity whatever should come to pass; but there can be no prescience of future contingents; for what is certainly foreseen, must infallibly come to pass; consequently the prescience of the Deity must be antecedent to his decrees.

The sacred scriptures assert the divine sovereignty in the clearest terms. Rom. ix. 21. *Hath not the potter power over the clay of the same lump, to make one vessel unto honour, and another to dishonour?* See from verse eleventh to the end of the chapter, and also Rom. viii. 30; xi. 5, 7. Eph. i. 4. Acts xiii. 48, &c.

II. That Jesus Christ, by his death and sufferings, made an atonement for the sins of the elect only.

The advocates for particular redemption admit that the death of Christ is sufficient to expiate the sins of the whole world; yet, say they, it was the will of God, that Christ by the blood of the cross, should efficaciously redeem those only who were from eternity elected to salvation, and given to him by the Father.†

For, there are express texts of scripture which testify that Christ did not die for all men. See John vi. 37. *All that the Father giveth me shall come to me,* &c. And in John x. 11, our Lord styles himself *the good Shepherd, who lays down his life for his sheep.* See also John xvii. 9.

III. That mankind are totally depraved, in consequence of the fall of the first man, who being their public head, his sin involved the corruption of all his posterity; and this corruption extends over the whole soul, and renders it unable of itself to turn to God, or to do any thing truly good; and exposes it to his just displeasure, both in this world and that which is to come.

For the inspired pages assert the original depravity of mankind, in the most emphatical terms. Gen. viii. 21. *The imagination of man's heart is evil from his youth.* Psalm xiv. 2, 3. *The Lord looked down from heaven upon the children of men, to see if there were any that did understand and seek after God.*

* The most prominent feature of this system is, the election of some, and reprobation of others, from all eternity.

† Acta Synodi, Sess. 136, p. 250.

They are all gone aside, they are altogether become filthy; there is none that doeth good, no not one. To the same purport see Rom. iii. 10, 11, 12, &c. And it is evident, that Adam's sin was imputed to his posterity, from Rom. v. 19. *By one man's disobedience many were made sinners,* &c. The scriptures also teach, that all sin exposes us to everlasting destruction. See Gal. iii. 10. 2 Cor. iii. 6, 7. and Rom. v. 14.

The total depravity of human nature is also evident from the universal reign of death over persons of all ages and in all times;—from the propensity to evil, which appears in mankind, and impels them to transgress God's law;—from the necessity of regeneration;—the nature of redemption;—and the remains of corruption in the saints.

IV. That all whom God hath predestinated unto life, he is pleased in his appointed time effectually to call by his word and Spirit, out of that state of sin and death in which they are by nature, to grace and salvation by Jesus Christ.

In proof of this doctrine, the Calvinists allege, among others, the following scripture passages. *Whom he did predestinate, them he also called, &c. That ye may know what is the exceeding greatness of his power to us-ward who believe, according to the working of his mighty power, &c. For we are his workmanship, created in Christ Jesus unto good works.* See Rom. viii. 30. Ephes. i. 19, 20; ii. 9, 10. 2 Cor. iv. 6.

If there were any thing in us which renders the grace of God effectual, we should have cause for boasting; but the apostle emphatically says, *Where is boasting? It is excluded.* Rom. iii. 27.

V. That those whom God has effectually called and sanctified by his spirit, shall never finally fall from a state of grace.

For, say they, this doctrine is evident from the promises of persevering grace in the sacred scriptures. *I will put my fear in their hearts, and they shall not depart from me. This is the Father's will, that of all he hath given me, I should lose nothing.* And the apostle exclaims with triumphant rapture, *I am persuaded that neither life, nor death, &c. shall be able to separate us from the love of God, which is in Christ Jesus our Lord.*

Such were the doctrines of the first Calvinists, and such, in substance, are those of the present time. In this however, as in every other denomination, there are considerable shades of difference.

Some think Calvin, though right in the main, yet carried things too far; these are commonly known by the name of Moderate Calvinists. Others think he did not go far enough; and these are known by the name of High Calvinists; by many called Antinomians.

It is proper to add, that the Calvinistic system includes in it the doctrine of a Trinity.*

Atonement,† and justification by faith alone, or by the imputed righteousness of Christ.‡ For a more copious elucidation of these sentiments, see the articles *Hopkinsians, Predestinarians,* and *Necessarians.*

CAMERONIANS, a party in Scotland, who took their denomination from Richard Cameron, a famous field preacher, who refused to accept the indulgence to tender consciences granted by Charles II. as such an acceptance seemed an acknowledgment of the king's supremacy, and that he had before a right to silence them. Cameron made a separation from his Presbyterian brethren, in 1666, and afterwards headed a rebellion, in which he was killed. His party were never entirely reduced till the revolution, when they voluntarily submitted to King William.§

CAMERONIANS, (or *Cameronites,*) is also the donomination of a party of moderate Calvinists in France, who asserted that God does not move the will physically, but only morally, in virtue of its dependance on the judgment of the mind. They derived this name from John Cameron, a famous professor, first at Glasgow, where he was born in 1580, and afterwards at Bordeaux and Saumur; at which last place he promulgated his doctrine of grace and free will, which was followed by Amyraut, Cappel, Bochart, Daille, and other learned reformed ministers, who judged Calvin's doctrines on these points too harsh.||

CAMISARS. See *French Prophets.*

CAPUTIATI, a sect in the twelfth century; so called from wearing a singular kind of *cap* with a leaden image of the Virgin Mary. They declared publicly, that their purpose was

* Both the Calvinists and Arminians, who formed the Synod of Dort, were however on the article of the Trinity generally agreed.

† This is observed by Mr. Evans, in his Sketch of Denominations, &c. who states the Calvinistic doctrine of atonement to be, that "Christ, by his death, made satisfaction to divine justice for the elect, appeasing the anger of the Divine Being, and effecting, on his part, a reconciliation." This doctrine, however, he says, is reprobated by some of their divines; and he instances in the writing of Dr. Magee on the Atonement and Mr. Fuller, the latter of whom observes, "If we say, a way was opened by the death of Christ, for the free and consistent exercise of mercy in all the methods which sovereign wisdom saw fit to adopt, perhaps we shall include every material idea, which the scripture gives us of that important event." See Fuller on Deism. See also Fuller's Calvinistic and Socinian Systems Compared.

‡ Mosheim's Eccles. Hist. vol. iii. p. 352; vol. iv. p. 70. Calvin's Institutes, p. 127. Assembly's Confession of Faith, p. 35, 36, &c. Charnock's Works, vol. ii. p. 1352. Twisse's Works, p. 225. Dr. Edwards' Veritas Reduc. p. 56, 89, &c. Edwards on Original Sin, p. 18—40, &c. Toplady's Works.

§ Scotch Theol. Dict. || Encyclopædia, vol. iv. p. 61.

to level all distinctions among mankind, and to restore their natural equality.*

CAROLOSTADIANS, followers of Carolostadt, a colleague of Luther. He denied the real presence in the eucharist, and declaimed against human learning.†

CARPOCRATIANS, a denomination which arose towards the middle of the second century; so called from Carpocrates, whose philosophical tenets agreed in general with those of the Egyptian Gnostics; but he is charged with licentious principles and conduct.‡ See *Gnostics.*

CATAPHRYGIANS. See *Montanists.*

*CATECHUMENS, the lowest order of Christians in the primitive church, being such as were under Catechetical Instruction previous to Baptism.‡

CATHARISTS, a branch of the Paulicians in the twelfth century, of very austere manners. See *Paulicians.*

*CATHOLICS. See *Roman Catholics.*

*CELTES, (or CELTÆ,) one of the primitive nations, by which most parts of Europe were peopled. The Druids were their priests and judges. Their Religion was pure Paganism without images, but they worshipped in consecrated groves.§ See *Druids* and *Pagans.*

CERDONIANS, followers of Cerdo, a branch of the Gnostics in the second century, which were also called *Marcionites.*

CERINTHIANS, a denomination which arose in the first century; so called from Cerinthus, who taught that the creator of the world, whom he considered also as the sovereign of the Jews, was a being endowed with the greatest virtues, and derived his birth from the supreme God—that this being fell by degrees from his primitive dignity—that the supreme God, in consequence, determined to destroy his empire, and sent for this purpose one of the glorious *aions,* whose name was Christ—that Christ chose for his habitation the person of Jesus, the son of Joseph and Mary; and descending in the form of a dove, entered into him while he was receiving the baptism of John—that Jesus, after his union with Christ, opposed himself to the god of the Jews, and was by his instigation seized and crucified—that when Jesus was taken captive, Christ ascended up on high, so that the man Jesus alone was subjected to the pains of an ignominious death.

Cerinthus required of his followers, that they should worship the supreme God, in conjunction with the Son; that they should abandon the God of the Jews, whom he looked upon as the creator of the world; that they should retain a part of the law given by Moses, but employ their principal attention

* Mosheim, vol. ii. p. 456, 457. † Ibid. vol. iv. p. 28, 30.
‡ Ibid. vol. i. p. 184, 185. § Ency. Perth.

and care to regulate their lives by the precepts of Christ. To encourage them to this, he promised them the resurrection of this mortal body, after which was to commence a scene of the most exquisite delights during Christ's earthly reign of a thousand years, which was to be succeeded by a happy and never-ending life in the celestial world.* See *Gnostics*.

CHAZINZARIANS, that is, worshippers of the cross, a sect which arose in the seventh century in Armenia.†

CHILIASTS. See *Millenarians*.

CHINESE. The religion of this great and ancient nation was certainly patriarchal, and supposed to be derived from Joktan, the brother of Peleg. (Gen. x. 29, 30.) This has degenerated to Paganism, which among their *literati* may be refined to a sort of philosophical atheism; but among the vulgar is as gross idolatry as that of other heathen nations. The grand *Lama*, or Pope of the Chinese and Tartars, who resides at Thibet in Tartary, is their visible deity, and treated with more distinction than the Pope himself, in the zenith of his power and glory, and attended by 20,000 priests or *lamas*. In addition to this general system of religion, which is founded on their sacred books, said to have descended from the skies, there are three grand sects, of which we shall give a brief account; and those three are again subdivided into as many as the Christian world itself.

1. The sect of *Tao-se*, or the followers of *Laokium*, who lived, as they pretend, 500 years before Christ, and taught that God was corporeal. They pay divine honours to this philosopher, and give the same worship, not only to many emperours who have been ranked with the gods, but also to certain spirits, under the name of *zamte*, who preside over all the elements. Their morality consists in calming the passions, and disengaging themselves from every thing which tends to disquiet the soul, to live free from care, to forget the past, and not be apprehensive for the future. There are also magicians,—some of whom pretend that they derive from their founder the secret of making an elixir, which confers immortality.

2. The most predominant sect is that of *Foe*, who (according to their chronology) flourished 1000 years before our Saviour, and who became a god at the age of 30 years. This religion was transmitted from India to China 65 years after the birth of Christ. A large number of temples, or pagodas, are reared to this deity, some of which are highly magnificent, and a number of bonzes, or priests, consecrated to his service. He is represented shining in light, with his hands hid under his robes, to

* Mosheim, vol. i. p. 117, 118.

† History of Religion, vol. iv.

show that he does all things invisibly. The doctors of this sect teach a double doctrine, the one *external*, the other *internal.* According to the former they say, all the good are recompensed, and the wicked punished, in places destined for each. They enjoin all works of mercy and charity; and forbid cheating, impurity, wine, lying, and murder; and even the taking of life from any creature whatever. For they believe that the souls of their ancestors transmigrate into irrational creatures; either into such as they liked best, or resembled most, in their behaviour; for which reason they never kill any such animals.*

They build temples for Foe, and monasteries for his priests, providing for their maintenance, as the most effectual means to partake of their prayers. These priests pretend to know into what bodies the dead are transmigrated; and seldom fail of representing their case to the surviving friends as miserable or uncomfortable, that they may extort money from them to procure the deceased a passage into a better state, or pray them out of purgatory, which forms a part of their system.†

The *internal* doctrine of this sect, which is kept secret from the common people, teaches a philosophical atheism, which admits neither rewards nor punishments after death; and believes not in a providence, or the immortality of the soul; acknowledges no other god than the *void,* or *nothing;* and makes the supreme happiness of mankind to consist in a *total inaction,* an *entire insensibility,* and a *perfect quietude.*‡

3. A sect which acknowledges for its master the philosopher *Confucius,* (or *Kung-fut-si,*) who lived about 500 years before our Saviour. This religion, which is professed by the literati, and persons of rank in China and Tonquin, consists in a deep inward veneration for the God, or King of Heaven, and in the practice of every moral virtue. They have neither temples nor priests, nor any settled form of external worship: every one adores the Supreme Being in the way he likes best.§

Confucius, like Socrates, did not dive into abstruse notions, but confined himself to speak with the deepest regard of the great Author of all beings, whom he represents as the most pure and perfect essence and fountain of all things; to inspire men with greater fear, veneration, gratitude, and love of him; to assert his divine providence over all his creatures; and to represent him as a being of such infinite knowledge, that even our most secret thoughts are not hidden from him; and of such

* Osbeck's Voyage to China, vol. i. p. 280.

† Modern Universal History, vol. viii. p. 112—114.

‡ History of Don Ignatius, vol. ii. p. 102.

§ Kaimes, vol. iv. p. 230.

boundless goodness and justice, that he can let no virtue go unrewarded, or vice unpunished.

Mr. Maurice, the author of Indian Antiquities, asserts, that Confucius strictly forbade all images of the Deity, and the deification of dead men; and that in his dying moments he encouraged his disciples, by predicting that *in the west the Holy One would appear !*

The Chinese honour their dead ancestors, burn perfumes before their images, bow before their pictures, and invoke them as capable of bestowing all temporal blessings.*

It is remarked, that "None of the different systems of religion," above mentioned, "can be said to be the prevailing creed in China; or what is more remarkable, can be found existing pure and distinct from the rest. The greater part of the Chinese have no decided opinion whatever on the subject, and are either complete atheists, or, if they acknowledge a Supreme Being, utterly ignorant in what view he ought to be regarded; while they all combine with their peculiar sentiments the multifarious superstitions of the more popular sects. Of all these tolerated and established religious persuasions the emperour is the supreme head; without whose permission not one of them can enjoy a single privilege or point of pre-eminence; and who can diminish or increase, at his pleasure, the number of their respective temples or priests."†

CHRISTIANS. The disciples and followers of Jesus Christ were first called Christians at Antioch,‡ A. D. 42. They were eminently distinguished by the sublime virtues which adorned their lives, and the miraculous gifts and graces bestowed by God upon them.

The history of our Saviour, as recorded in the New Testament, forms the basis of the Christian system, and as this book is happily in the hands of all our readers, it is unnecessary to enter into particulars.

The evidences of the Christian religion are comprised under historical testimony,§ prophecies, miracles, the internal

* Maurice's Ind. Antiq. vol. v. p. 468.

† American edition of the Edinburgh Encyclopædia, vol. vi. part I. p 91.

‡ Acts xi. 26. Antioch seems to have been a kind of head quarters to the Christians, and from hence they sent missionaries in various directions. See Calmet's Dictionary, vol v.

§ See an excellent defence of the truth of the Christian revelation in the article *Christianity*, in the Edinburgh Encyclopædia. It is chiefly confined to the exposition of the historical argument for the truth of Christianity; and the aim of the author is to prove the external testimony to be so sufficient, as to leave infidelity without excuse, even though the remaining important branches of the Christian defence had been less strong and satisfactory than they are. This able workwas written by the Rev. Thomas Chalmers, D. D. of Glasgow, Scotland. It has been published in a duodecimo volume at Philadelphia and at Hartford. The compiler of this work is much gratified to hear that its success has been proportionate to its merits.

evidence of its doctrines and precepts, and the rapidity of its first propagation among the Jews and Gentiles. Though thinking Christians have in every age differed widely respecting some of the doctrines of this religion, yet they are fully agreed in the divinity of its origin, and the benevolence of its tendency.*

CHRISTIANS OF ST. JOHN, so called because they pretend to have received their faith and traditions from John the Baptist. They always inhabit near a river, in which they baptize; for they never baptize but in rivers, and only on Lord's days. Before they go to the river, they carry the infant to church, where there is a bishop, who reads certain prayers over the head of the child; thence they carry the child to the river, with a train of men and women, who, together with the bishop, go up to the knees in water. Then the bishop reads again certain prayers out of a book; which done, he sprinkles the infant three times, saying, *In the name of the Lord, first and last of the world and paradise, the high Creator of all things.* After this the bishop reads again in his book, while the godfather plunges the child all over in the water; after which they all go to the parent's house to feast. They have no knowledge of the doctrine of the trinity; only they say that Christ is the Spirit and Word of the eternal Father. They confess that he became man to free us from the punishment of sin: but when the Jews came to take him, he eluded their cruelty with a shadow.

They have no canonical books, but a number full of charms and traditions. Their chief festivals are three: one in memory of the creation; another on the feast of St. John; and the third, which lasts five days, in June, during which time they are all rebaptized.†

CHRISTIANS OF ST. THOMAS, a denomination in the peninsula of India, so called because they have a peculiar veneration for that apostle, who preached the gospel and suffered martyrdom, as is said, in that peninsula. See *Syrian Churches*.

CHRISTO SACRUM, a society founded in 1801, at Delft, by Onder de Wingaard, an old Burgomaster of that city, an intelligent man, privately instigated, it is said, by the Mennonites, enemies of the reformed. Though there are found among them disciples of Calvin and Luther, the Mennonites are, however, the most numerous. The members of this assembly repeat incessantly that they are not a sect, but a society, whose object is to unite all religions. They admit whoever believes in the divinity of Jesus Christ, and in the redemption of man-

* Evans' Sketch of Religious Denominations, p. 30

† Tavinier's Travels, p. 90, 93.

kind by the merits of the passion of the Saviour. The society began with four members, and immediately increased to two or three thousand; as yet they have no public worship except at Delft. Their temple is ornamented with some elegance; three seats and as many pulpits, which rise gradually, are designed for those who read, who chant, and who preach.

The worship is divided into two parts;—adoration and instruction. The first takes place every Sunday towards five or six o'clock in the evening; they set forth especially the greatness of God as manifested in the wonders of creation. The instruction takes place once a fortnight, also in the evening; when the principles of revealed religion are developed. The Lord's supper is celebrated six times in a year; the assembly are prostrated during the prayer and blessing.

The society has published some small pieces, of which the first presents in the frontispiece the emblem which it has adopted; it is a cross placed on the gospel and decalogue, and applied to a crown of palm, in which is inscribed in Dutch these words of Jesus Christ; *I am the way, the truth and the life; no one can come to the Father but by me.**

***CHURCH OF ENGLAND.** See *English Church.*

CIRCUMCELLIANS, (in Latin *Circumcelliones,*) a branch of the Donatists. They abounded chiefly in Africa. They had no fixed abode; but rambled about begging, or rather exacting a maintenance from the country people.†

COCCEIANS, a denomination of the seventeenth century; so called from John Cocceius, professor of divinity in the university of Leyden. He represented the whole history of the Old Testament as a mirror, which held forth an accurate view of the transactions and events that were to happen in the church under the dispensation of the New Testament, and unto the end of the world. He maintained that by far the greatest part of the ancient prophecies foretold Christ's ministry and mediation, and the rise, progress, and revolutions of the church; not only under the figure of persons and transactions, but in a literal and direct manner: and that Christ was the substance of the Old Testament as well as of the New.

Cocceius also taught, that the covenant made between God and the Jews was of the same nature as the new covenant by Jesus Christ: that the law was promulgated by Moses, not merely as a rule of obedience, but also as a representation of the covenant of grace: that when the Jews had provoked the Deity by their various transgressions, (particularly by the worship of the golden calf,) the severe yoke of the ceremonial

* Gregorie's History of Religious Sects, vol. i.

† Broughton, vol i. p. 249.

law was added as a punishment: that this yoke, which was painful in itself, became doubly so on account of its typical signification; since it admonished the Israelites from day to day of the imperfection of their state, filled them with anxiety, and was a perpetual proof that they had merited the righteous judgment of God, and could not expect, before the coming of the Messiah, the entire remission of their iniquities: that indeed good men, under the Mosaic dispensation, were after death made partakers of glory; but that, nevertheless, during the whole course of their lives they were far removed from that assurance of salvation, which rejoices the believer under the dispensation of the gospel; and that their anxiety flowed from this consideration, that their sins, though they remain unpunished, were not yet pardoned, because Christ had not as yet offered himself up to make an atonement for them.* See *Hutchinsonians*.

COLARBARSIANS. See *Marcosians*.

COLLEGIATES, a name given to a society of Mennonites in Holland, because they called their religious assemblies *colleges*. They are also called Rhinstergers.† See *Mennonites*.

COLLUTHIANS, followers of Colluthus, a priest of Alexandria who is said to have taught that God was not the author of the evils and afflictions of this life.‡

COLLYLYRIDIANS, an Arabian sect in the fourth century; who idolized the Virgin Mary as a goddess, offering to her little cakes.§

CONGREGATIONALISTS, a denomination of protestants, who maintain that each particular church has authority from Christ for exercising government, and enjoying all the ordinances of worship within itself.

The platform of church discipline which was drawn up in 1648, and agreed upon by the elders and messengers of the churches, assembled in the synod at Cambridge, in New England, defines a congregational church to be, by the institution of Christ, a part of the militant visible church, consisting of a company of saints by calling, united in one body by a holy covenant, for the public worship of God, and the mutual edification of one another in the fellowship of the Lord Jesus.

According to this platform, such as are admitted members of churches ought to be first examined: for the eunuch of Ethiopia, before his admission, was examined by Philip, whether he did believe in Jesus Christ with all his heart.

The qualifications necessary to be found in all church members, are repentance from sin, and faith in Jesus Christ. This

* Mosheim, vol. iv. p. 545—548.
† Ibid. vol. v. p. 59. Collier's Historical Dictionary.
‡ Broughton, vol. i. p. 264. § History of Religion, vol. iv.

denomination differed originally from the *Independents* in this respect, that they invited councils, which are to advise only; but the Independents formerly decided all difficulties within themselves. They are now, however, considered as one denomination.* See *Independents*.

CONONITES, the followers of Conon, Bishop of Tarsus, in the sixth century; who taught that the body never lost its essential form; that its matter alone was subject to corruption and decay, and was to be restored when this mortal shall put on immortality.†

*CONSUBSTANTIALISTS, who believed the doctrine of consubstantiation, namely, that the *real* body of Christ is present with the bread and wine, instead of their being converted into it by transubstantiation. The term consubstantial (Ὁμοούσιος) was also used in the Arian controversy to distinguish the Athanasians. See *Lutherans*, and *Arians*.

COPHTS, a numerous denomination of Christians in Egypt, Syria, Nubia, and the adjacent countries. They are subject to the patriarch of Alexandria, who is said to have no less than 140 bishoprics in those parts subject to him, besides the bishop of the Abyssinians, who is nominated and consecrated by him. The patriarch makes a short discourse to the priests once a year; and the latter read legends from the pulpit on great festivals, but never preach. Their church service is performed in Arabic, and modern Coptic. They followed the doctrine of the Jacobites with regard to the nature of Christ and baptism by fire; and the ceremonies which they observe are much the same with those of the Greek Church.‡ See *Jacobites* and *Greek Church*.

CORNARISTS, the disciples of Theodore Cornhert, who maintained that every religious communion needed reformation; but that no person had a right to engage in accomplishing it, without a mission supported by miracles.§

CORRUPTICOLÆ, a sect of the sixth century, who maintained that the body of Christ was corruptible, like that of other men.‖

CRISPITES, the followers of Dr. Crisp, whose name has been already mentioned under the article Antinomians, where it appears, that the doctor did not refuse obedience to the divine law, either in theory or practice. The Calvinists in general, however, suppose that he was not accurate in his ideas of the substitution of Christ in the place of the redeemed, but carried the doctrine of commu-

* Platform of Church Discipline, 1648. Neal's New England, vol. ii. p. 314.
† Mosheim, vol. i. p. 473.
‡ Father Simons' Religion of the Eastern Nations, p. 110.
§ Ency. vol. v. p. 433. ‖ Dictionary of Arts and Sciences, vol. i. p. 492.

tation to an extreme that represented the Saviour as himself a sinner through his union with the elect.*

Dr. Gill in 1746 reprinted Crisp's Works with notes, in which he justified some of his peculiar expressions and apologized for others. His sermons produced a seven years' theological warfare, Dr. Daniel Williams being his principal antagonist. See *Neonomians.*

*CRUSADERS, a multitude gathered from all the countries of Christendom, who undertook a *Crusade (Croisade)* or holy war under the banners of the cross, to recover Palestine from the Turks. To this wild scheme they were first excited by Peter the hermit, who, under the auspices of Pope Martin II. gathered nearly a million of persons, mercenaries and enthusiasts, who in 1096 first invaded the holy land with a partial success. This encouraged them to seven other successive crusades, of which the last was in 1270, and left the object unaccomplished. It has been calculated that two millions of persons perished in these several expeditions, and left a warning to posterity against engaging in such wild projects under the influence of religious frenzy.†

*CYNICS, a sect of snarling philosophers who were proud of showing their contempt, not only for riches and state, but for the arts and sciences, and all the comforts of civilized life. This sect was founded by Antisthenes of Athens, but carried to its highest glory by Diogenes, who wandered like a beggar in a ragged cloak, and carried with him a tub which served him for his lodging.‡

D

*DALEITES, the followers of David Dale, a very industrious manufacturer, a most benevolent Christian, and the humble pastor of an independent congregation at Glasgow. At first he formed a connexion with the *Glassites,* in many of whose opinions he concurred: he separated from them, chiefly on the ground of preferring practical to speculative religion, and christian charity to severity of church discipline. As he grew rich by industry, he devoted all his property to doing good, and ranks high among the philanthropists of his age.§

DAMIANISTS, disciples of Damian, bishop of Alexandria in the sixth century. Their opinions were similar to those of the *Angelites.*

DANCERS, a sect which

* Buck's Theol. Dict. Hist. of Dissenters, vol. i. p. 399. † Ency. Brit.
‡ Stanley's Hist. of Philosophy. § Scotch Theolog. Dict.

arose at Aix-la-Chapelle in 1373, whence they spread through Liege, Hainault, and other parts of Flanders. It was customary for persons of both sexes, publicly, as well as in private, to begin dancing of a sudden; and, holding each others' hands, to continue their motions with extraordinary violence, till they dropt breathless together. They affirmed, that during these intervals of agitation, they were favoured with wonderful visions. Like the Flagellants, they wandered about from place to place; had recourse to begging for their sustenance; and treated with the utmost contempt both the priesthood and the church.*

The clergy supposed them to be possessed, and applied exorcism, as they say, with complete success. M. Bonnet, however, gives the honour of these holy dances to the Catholic church, and F. Menestrier says the *choir* originally received its name from being the part of the church where the priests used to dance together; and the custom of religious dancing was continued by the *Brandons* in France as low down as the beginning of the eighteenth century.†

DAVIDISTS, or *David-Georgians*, the followers of David George, of Delft, in the sixteenth century, who acquired great reputation by his prudent conversation. He deplored the decline of vital and practical religion, and endeavoured to restore it among his followers; but rejected, as mean and useless, the external services of the church. Many extravagancies are charged on him, which perhaps were founded on the unguarded expressions of his illiterate zeal. He was condemned for a heretic after his death, and his body burned; but he left disciples, which appear to be men of good report.‡

DEISTS, a class of men whose distinguishing character is, not to profess any particular form or system of religion; but who merely acknowledge the existence of a God, and profess to follow the law and light of nature, rejecting all divine revelation, and consequently Christianity. The denomination was first assumed early in the sixteenth century, by some persons who wished to clear themselves from the charge of atheism. P. Viret, in 1563, speaks of deists as a new name, applied to those who professed to believe in God, but rejected Jesus Christ.

Lord Ed. Herbert, baron of Cherbury, who flourished in the seventeenth century, has been regarded as the most eminent of the deistical writers, and appears to be one of the first who formed deism into a system; and asserted the sufficiency, universality, and absolute perfection of natural religion, with a view to discard all extraordina-

* Mosheim, vol. iii. p. 206. † Burney's Hist. of Music, vol. ii. p. 27.
‡ Mosheim, vol. iv. p. 164. Crosby, Eng. Bap. vol. i. p. 64.

ry revelation as useless and needless. He reduced this universal religion to five articles, which he frequently mentions in his works. 1. That there is one supreme God. 2. That he is to be worshipped. 3. That piety and virtue are the principal parts of his worship. 4. That if we repent of our sins, God will pardon us. 5. That there are rewards for good men, and punishments for bad men, in a future state.*

The Deists are classed by some of their own writers into two sorts, *mortal* and *immortal* deists. The latter acknowledge a future state, the former deny it, or at least represent it as a very uncertain thing.

Dr. S. Clarke, taking the denomination in the most extensive signification, distinguishes deists into four sorts. 1. Such as believe the existence of an infinite, eternal Being, who made the world, though they suppose he does not concern himself in its government. 2. Those who believe not only the being, but also the providence of God, with respect to the natural world; but who, not allowing any difference between moral good and evil, deny that God takes any notice of the moral conduct of mankind. 3. Such as believe in the natural attributes of God and his all-governing providence, and have some notion of his moral perfections, yet deny the immortality of the soul; believing that men perish entirely at death, without any future renovation. 4. Such as admit the existence of God, together with his providence, as also all the obligations of natural religion; but so far only as these things are discoverable by the light of nature alone, without any divine revelation.

Some of the deists have attempted to overthrow the Christian dispensation, by representing the absolute perfection of natural religion. Others, as Blount, Collins, and Morgan, have endeavoured to gain the same purpose, by attacking particular parts of the Christian scheme, by explaining away the literal sense and meaning of certain passages, or by placing one portion of the sacred canon in opposition to the other. A third class, wherein we meet with the names of Shaftsbury and Bolingbroke, advancing farther in their progress, expunge from their creed the doctrine of future existence, and deny or controvert all the moral perfections of the Deity.

The deists of the present day are distinguished by their zealous efforts to diffuse the principles of infidelity among the common people. Hume, Bolingbroke, and Gibbon addressed themselves solely to the more polished classes of the community; and would have thought their refined speculations debased by an attempt to enlist disciples among the populace. But

* Leland's View of Deistical Writers, vol. i. p. 2, 3.

of late the writings of Paine, and others, have diffused infidelity among the lower orders of society: and deism has even led to atheism, or a disbelief of all superiour powers.*

DESTRUCTIONISTS, a denomination of Christians who teach that the final punishment threatened in the gospel to the wicked and impenitent, consists not in eternal misery, but in a total extinction of being; and that the sentence of annihilation shall be executed with more or less torment, in proportion to the greater or less guilt of the criminal.

The name assumed by this denomination, takes for granted that the scripture word *destruction* means annihilation. In strict propriety of speech they should therefore be called *Annihilationists*. This doctrine is largely maintained in the sermons of Mr. S. Bourn, of Birmingham; by Mr. J. N. Scott, Mr. J. Taylor, of Norwich, and many others.

In defence of the system, Mr. Bourn argues as follows: There are many passages of scripture, in which the ultimate punishment to which wicked men shall be adjudged, is defined in the most precise terms, to be an everlasting *destruction* from the power of God, which is equally able to destroy as to preserve. So when our Saviour is fortifying the minds of his disciples against the wrath of men, he expresses himself thus: *Fear not them that kill the body*, but *him who is able to destroy both soul and body in hell.* And when he says, *These shall go away into everlasting punishment, but the righteous into life eternal*, Mr. B. understands, by that *eternal punishment*, which is opposed to *eternal life*, not a state of perpetual misery, but total and *everlasting destruction from the presence of the Lord*, which is 'the second death,' from which there is no resurrection.† Mr. Bourn alleges, that the figures, by which the eternal punishment of wicked men is described, agree to establish the doctrine of the annihilation of the finally impenitent. One figure or comparison often used, is that of combustible materials thrown into a fire, which will consequently be entirely consumed, if the fire be not quenched. So the cities of Sodom and Gomorrah are said to have suffered the vengeance of an eternal fire; that is, they were so effectually consumed or destroyed, that they could never be rebuilt; the expression of *eternal fire* signifying the irrevocable destruction of those cities, not the degree or duration of the misery of the inhabitants, who perished. The images of the *worm that dieth not, and the fire that is*

* Leland's View of Deistical Writers, vol. i. p. 2, 3. Broughton's Hist. Lib vol. i. p. 316. Voltaire's Universal Hist. vol. ii. p. 259. Ogilve's Inquiry, p. 57. Hall's Sermon on Modern Infidelity. Dwight's Century Sermon preached Jan. 7, 1801.

† Bourn's Serm. vol. i. p. 379—395.

not quenched, used in Mark ix. 44. are set in opposition to entering into life, and intended to denote a period of life and existence.

To this scheme Dr. *Jon. Edwards* opposes many objections, as—1. That the punishment of annihilation admits of no degrees.—2. That this destruction is not described as the end, but the beginning of misery.—3. That annihilation is not an exertion, but a suspension only of divine power.—4. That the punishment of the wicked is to be the same as that of the fallen angels, Matt. xxv. 41.—5. That the state of final punishment is attended with weeping and gnashing of teeth, Matt. xxiv. 51.—6. As the happiness of the just does not consist in eternal *being*, but *well*-being, so the punishment of the wicked requires the idea of eternal suffering to support the contrast.*

*DIACONOFTSCHINS, the followers of Alexander, a *Deacon* (whence their name) of the church of Vetka, from which he separated in 1706, from some dispute relative to the chrism and the sign of the cross; and this sect has since separated into three or four minor ones, all equally zealous dissenters. See *Raskolniks*.†

DIGGERS, a name given to those in the fifteenth century, who, being persecuted, were obliged to hold their assemblies in caverns and caves dug in the earth. They are said to have despised the church of Rome and its ministers.‡

DIMOERITES, See *Apolinarians*.

*DISSENTERS, all who dissent from the doctrines of the church of England, of which the principal denominations are—Presbyterians, Independents, and Baptists; to which may be added Quakers, Methodists, and many others. See *Nonconformists*.

*DISSIDENTS, a term applied to the reformed churches in Poland. By the *pacta conventa* they claim a free toleration of their religion, but this has been often interrupted.§

DOCETÆ, a sect in the first and second centuries, who held that Jesus Christ was born, lived in the world, died, and rose again, not in reality, but in *appearance* only.‖ See *Gnostics*.

DOMINICANS, a religious order, in some places called Jacobins, and in others Predicants, or preaching friars. The Dominicans take their name from their founder, Dominic de Guzman, a Spaniard, born in 1170, at Calaroga, in Old Castile. He was first canon and archdeacon of Orsuna; and afterwards preached with great zeal and vehemence against the Albigenses in Languedoc, where he laid the first foundation of his order, which was confirmed in 1216, by a bull of Honorius

* Edwards' 'Salvation of all men examined,' chap. v.
† Pinkerton's Greek Church, p. 302. ‡ Broughton, vol. i. p. 328.
§ Buck's Theol. Dict. ‖ Broughton, vol. i. p. 339.

III. under the title of St. Augustin, to which Dominic added several severe precepts and observances. He obliged the brethren to take a vow of absolute poverty, and to abandon entirely all their revenues and possessions, and assume the title of Preaching Friars, because public instruction was the main end of their institution. This order long retained a high degree of authority. But their influence began to decline towards the beginning of the sixteenth century, in consequence of their pretended apparitions and miracles, to terminate their dispute with the Franciscans.* See *Franciscans*.

DONATISTS, a denomination which arose by a schism in the fourth century. They derived their name from Donatus, a learned bishop of Numidia. They maintained that their community was alone to be considered as the true church, and avoided all communication with others, as degenerated and impure. They re-baptized those came over to their party from other churches, and, if ministers, re-ordained them. They were much persecuted by the orthodox, though they agreed with them in point of faith, and are not charged with immorality. They remained till the sixth century.†

DORRELLITES, the followers of Dorrel, a sectary, who appeared at Leyden in Massachusetts in 1797, and pretended to be a prophet, sent to supersede the dispensation of Jesus Christ, and claimed divine worship in his stead. It appears, from an account of his tenets, which was taken down from his own mouth, by the Rev. John Taylor of Deerfield, that he denied the foreknowledge of God, and his almighty power. "Jesus Christ," said he, "is to substance a spirit, and is God. He took a body, died, and never rose from the dead. None of the human race will ever rise from their graves. The resurrection spoken of in scripture, is only one from sin to spiritual life, which consists in perfect obedience to God. Written revelation is a type of the substance of the true revelation, which God makes to those whom he raises from spiritual death. The substance is God revealed in the soul; those who have it are perfect, are incapable of sinning, and have nothing to do with the Bible." Dorrel denied future judgment; and asserted, that neither prayer nor any other worship is necessary.‡

*DOSITHEANS. The founder of this sect was a magician of Samaria, who pretended to be the Messiah. He had thirty disciples answering to the days of the month, and among them a woman, whom he called the *moon*. They practised circumcision, and rigid fastings, and in whatever attitude the Sabbath found them, they remained during its continuance. At last to make it

* Mosheim, vol. iv. p. 19. † Mosheim, vol. i. p. 333. ‡ See Mass. Spy, 1798.

believed he was taken to heaven, he retired into a secret cavern, and starved himself to death: some remains of this sect were found in Egypt in the sixth century.*

*DRUIDS, the priests or ministers of religion among the Gauls. They were chosen out of the best families, and divided into different classes—bards, who were both poets and musicians—priests and divines—and moral philosophers, who were instructors of youth and sometimes judges. They wore long white robes and chaplets, carried wands, with a mystic symbol round their necks, called the druid's *egg*. They admitted no images in their religious worship, which was performed in groves of oak; but they paid peculiar honours to the misletoe.

Mr. *Bryant* maintains that the sun was the grand object of their worship, and that Stonehenge exhibits the remains of one of their vast temples, consisting of massy stones in a circular form in the open air, sometimes poised on each other in the manner of rocking stones.†

DUHOBORTSI, a sect of Russian dissenters, who sprang up among the common peasants about the middle of the last century. Their name is supposed to have been given them in 1788 by an archbishop, who by this designation intended to point out the errors contained in their doctrines, for Dahoborets literally signifies. *a wrestle with the spirit.* They call themselves Christians, and all others they denominate men of the world.

The chief and distinguishing dogma of this denomination is, the worshipping God in spirit and in truth; and hence they not only throw aside all the ceremonies of the Greek Church, but also reject baptism and the Lord's Supper,—regeneration and spiritual baptism in their opinion are the same.

They hold no particular creed, but only say in regard to themselves, that they are of the law of God, and of the faith of Jesus. The symbol of faith of the Greek Church, or the Nicene creed, they not only respect, but confess all that it contains to be truth; they merely, however, assign it a place among their common psalms.

They do not consider it to be essential to salvation, that a man should be a member of their society; they say, that it is necessary only to understand the ways of the Lord, and to walk in them, and to fulfil his will, for this is the way of salvation.

"Excepting their principles of faith," says Mr. Pinkerton, "the Duhobortsi, in their domestic and social life, may serve as an example to all other sects." They lead most exemplary lives; they are sober, industrious, diligent in their occupation, and

* Mosh. vol. i. p. 139, 140. Basnage's Hist. of the Jews, book ii chap. 13.
† Ency. Brit.

of good and gentle dispositions. Laziness and drunkenness are vices not suffered among them.

They have no stated place appointed for worship, as they account all places equally holy. Neither do they appoint any particular days for this purpose, as they suppose all days alike. They hold their meetings in private houses. In the course of their meetings, they pray one after another, sing psalms, and explain the word of God. They have no appointed priest, but confess Jesus Christ to be the only just, pure, and undefiled priest, and to be their only teacher. Every one speaks according to the grace given him, for the admonishing and comforting of his brethren. Even women are not excluded; for say they, "have not women enlightened understanding as well as men?"

The virtue which shines with the greatest lustre among this denomination, is *brotherly love.* They have no private property, but all things common. They are hospitable to strangers, compassionate to such as are in distress, and merciful to their beasts.

They have no kind of punishments among them, except expulsion from their society; and this only for such transgressions, as prove the person to have lost the spirit of Christianity. Those, who are excluded, may be restored, on giving evidence of their repentance.

They have no magistrates in their society, and no written laws or regulations; but the society at large governs itself, and each individual in it. They are seldom troubled with divisions and animosities, although two or three young families live together in one house. Their children are in the strictest subjection to their parents, and in general, young people among them pay the most profound respect to the aged.

The manner, in which this denomination educate their children, is simple and peculiar to themselves. As soon as a child begins to speak, the parents teach him to get by heart short prayers and psalms, and relate to him such passages of the sacred history as are calculated to engage his attention. In this manner, they continue to instruct their children in the doctrines of the gospel, till they are of age. When the children have thus committed to memory several prayers and psalms, they go to the meetings, repeat their prayers and sing psalms, with the rest. In this way the sentiments of the parents are, by little and little, instilled into their children, and seated in their young minds by the exemplary conduct of their parents. Hence it has often been observed, that the children of the Duhobortsi are distinguished among all other children, like stalks of wheat among oats.

This denomination suffered

continued persecution from all quarters, until the reign of Alexander. In 1801 two senators were sent to review the affairs of the government in the Ukraine. They were the first who represented this people to the emperour in a true light. They were prior to this, scattered in different provinces. The emperour gave them permission to settle at a place called Molishnia Vodi. Here they formed two settlements in 1804.*

DULCINISTS, the followers of Dulcinus of Lombardy, in the fourteenth century; who, after predicting the downfal of the Pope, took arms to fulfil his own prophecy, and perished miserably in the attempt. He joined the Apostolics and became a leader in their sect before he founded one of his own.†

DUNKERS, a denomination which took its rise in the year 1724. It was founded by Conrad Peysel, a German, who, weary of the world, retired to an agreeable solitude within fifty miles of Philadelphia, for the more free exercise of religious contemplation. Curiosity attracted followers, and his simple and engaging manners made them proselytes. They soon settled a little colony, called Euphrata, in allusion to the Hebrews, who used to sing psalms on the border of the river Euphrates. They are said to derive their name from baptizing by immersion, which they perform thrice. And as they presented themselves to the ordinance in a peculiar manner, bowing forward, (perhaps kneeling in the water, as an act of worship,) they were in ridicule called *Tumblers.* This is the more probable, as it appears their baptism was accompanied with the *laying on of hands* and prayer while in the water.

Their habit seems peculiar to themselves, consisting of a long tunic, or coat, reaching down to their feet, with a sash, or girdle, round the waist, and a cap, or hood, hanging from the shoulders, like the dress of the Dominican friars. The men do not shave the head or beard. The men and women have separate habitations and distinct governments. For these purposes, they have erected two large wooden buildings, one of which is occupied by the brethren, the other by the sisters of the society; and in each of them there is a banqueting-room, and an apartment for public worship: for the brethren and sisters do not meet together even at their devotions. They live chiefly upon roots and other vegetables; the rules of their society not allowing them flesh, except on particular occasions,

* For farther particulars respecting the Duhobortsi, see Pinkerton's Present state of the Greek church in Russia, p. 250, 251, 252, &c. See also Christian Disciple for Feb. 1817.

† Mosheim, vol. iii. p. 91.

when they hold what they call a love-feast; at which time the brethren and sisters dine together in a large apartment, and eat mutton, but no other meat. In each of their little cells they have a bench fixed, to serve the purpose of a bed, and a small block of wood for a pillow. The Dunkers allow of no intercourse between the brethren and sisters, not even by marriage.

The principal tenet of the Dunkers appears to be this: That future happiness is only to be attained by penance and outward mortifications in this life; and that as Jesus Christ by his meritorious sufferings became the redeemer of mankind in general, so,—each individual of the human race, by a life of abstinence and restraint, should work out his own salvation. They are charged with holding the doctrine of supererogation: they deny the eternity of future punishments, and believe that the souls of the just are employed to preach the gospel to those who have had no revelation in this life. They suppose the Jewish sabbath, sabbatical year, and year of jubilee, are typical of certain periods after the general judgment, in which the souls of those who are so far humbled as to acknowledge God and Christ, are received to felicity; while those who continue obstinate are reserved in torments until the grand period typified by the jubilee arrives, in which all shall be made eventually happy. They also deny the imputation of Adam's sin to his posterity. So that they are general baptists and universalists. But they disclaim violence even in cases of self-defence, and suffer themselves to be defrauded or wronged rather than go to law; on which accounts they have been called the *harmless* Dunkers.

Their church government and discipline are the same with those of the English Baptists, except that every brother is allowed to speak in the congregation; and their best speaker is usually ordained to be their minister. They have deacons and deaconesses from among their ancient widows and exhorters, who are all licensed to use their gifts statedly.*

*DURSIANS or *Duruzians*, a fierce people inhabiting the wilds of mount Libanus, and in the eleventh century engaged in the holy war. There is evidence, that they embraced the general profession of Christianity; but their peculiar tenets were kept so secret, that they cannot now be ascertained with certainty: it is probable however that they were Manicheans.†

* Caspipina's Lett. p. 70—72. Review of North America, vol. i. p. 225. Adams' 'Religious world displayed,' and Winchester's Dialogues.

† Mosheim, vol. iv. p. 270.

E

EBIONITES, a denomination in the first and second centuries; so called from their leader Ebion, or from their *poverty*, which *Ebion* signifies in Hebrew. They believed the divine mission of Christ, and, it is said, his participation of a divine nature; yet they regarded him as a man, born of Joseph and Mary, according to the ordinary course of nature. They asserted, that the ceremonial law, instituted by Moses, was not only obligatory upon the Jews, but also upon all others, and that the observance of it was essential to salvation. They observed both the Jewish sabbath and the Lord's day; and in celebrating the eucharist made use of unleavened bread. They abstained from the flesh of animals, and even from milk. They rejected the old testament, and in the new testament received only the gospel of St. Matthew, and a book which they styled, "The gospel according to the Hebrews."

Some ancient writers distinguish two kinds of Ebionites;—the one, usually called Nazarenes, and only Judaizing Christians, who mingled the institutions of Moses with those of Christ: (See *Nazarenes*) and the other, Unitarians, who denied the divinity of Jesus, and rejected a part of the scriptures.*

ECLECTICS, a name given to certain ancient philosophers, who endeavoured to form a system of opinions by selecting from every sect those doctrines, which seemed to approach nearest to the truth. Hence their denomination, derived from εκλέγω, "I choose," may be considered as referring either to "one who chooses," or one which may be chosen.

The eclectic philosophy was in a flourishing state at Alexandria, when our Saviour was upon earth. Its founders wished to be considered as chiefly followers of Plato, whose philosophy they made the foundation of their system. But they did not scruple to join with his doctrines, whatever they thought conformable to reason in the tenets of other philosophers. Potamon, a Platonist, appears to have been the projector of this plan. The eclectic system was brought to perfection by Ammonius Saccas, who blended Christianity with his philosophy, and founded the sect of the *Ammonians*, or *New Platonists*, in the second century. See *Ammonians*.

The moral doctrine of the Alexandrian school was as follows:—The mind of man, originally a portion of the divine

* Mosheim, vol. i. p. 173, 174. Hearne's Ductor Historicus, vol. ii. pp. 74. Priestley's Enquiry, &c.

Being, having fallen into a state of darkness and defilement by its union with the body, is to be gradually emancipated from the chains of matter, and rise by contemplation to the knowledge and vision of God. The end of philosophy, therefore, is the liberation of the soul from its corporeal imprisonment. For this purpose the Eclectic philosophy recommends abstinence, with other voluntary mortifications, and religious exercises.

In the infancy of the Alexandrian school, not a few of the professors of Christianity were led, by the pretensions of the Eclectic sect, to imagine that a coalition might, with great advantage, be formed between its system and that of Christianity. This union appeared the more desirable, when several philosophers of this sect became converts to the christian faith. The consequence was, that pagan ideas and opinions were by degrees mixed with the pure and simple doctrines of the gospel.*

EFFRONTES, sectaries, so called from shaving their foreheads till they bled, (which they called the baptism of blood,) and then anointing them with oil; using no other baptism, and denying the person and deity of the Holy Ghost.†

EGYPTIANS, ancient, one of the most renowned of the early nations, who, like the Babylonians, originally worshipped the sun, and afterwards inferiour deities, which they esteemed emanations from it. "They were refined in their superstitions above all nations in the world; and conferred the names and titles of their deities upon vegetables and animals of every species; and not only upon these, but also upon the parts of the human body, and the very passions of the mind. Whatever they deemed salutary, or of great value, they distinguished by the title of sacred, and dedicated it to some god. They had many emblematical personages, set off with the heads of various animals, to represent particular virtues and affections, as well as to denote the various attributes of their gods."‡ Thus they "worshipped the creature more than the Creator;" and were given up to idolatry beyond other countries, becoming the source of superstition to all the eastern nations. They paid particular honours to the serpent and crocodile, and to the Ibis, as a most useful animal. Apis was worshipped in the form of an ox or cow, and Osiris as a goat; and the souls of their superiour deities were supposed to reside in the stars or planets. Some have taken great pains to prove that their idols had originally a reference to the scripture history, and particularly to the patriarch Joseph.§

* Enfield's Philos. Edinburgh Ency. Mosheim, vol. i. p. 37, 171.
† Ross' View of all Religions, p. 233. ‡ Bryant's Analysis, vol. i. p. 333.
§ Bellamy's Hist. of all Religions, p. 21, &c.

EICETÆ, a sect in the year 680, who affirmed that, in order to make prayer acceptable to God, it should be performed with agitations both of mind and body.* See *Dancers*.

ELCESAITES, the followers of Elxai (or Elcesia,) a sectary of the second century, whether Jew or Christian is uncertain; but he held the doctrine of two principles, and other points of Manicheanism. He was succeeded by Saturninus.†

ENCRATITES, or *Continents*, a sect in the second or third century, who condemned marriage; forbade the eating of flesh, or the drinking of wine; rejected all the comforts and conveniences of life, and practised great mortification of the body. They appear to have been a branch of the Manicheans.‡

ENERGICI, sectaries in the sixteenth century, charged with holding that the eucharist was the *energy* and *virtue* of Jesus Christ; not his body, nor a mere representation thereof.§

ENGLISH CHURCH. The church of England is Episcopal, and boasts a regular succession of bishops, from the times of the apostles, conveyed to them by the church of Rome. See *Episcopalians*.

The reformation was introduced into England during the reign of Henry VIII, who upon his altercation with the Pope, took the management of ecclesiastical affairs into his own hands, and styled himself *the supreme head of the church*, which title has since been given to the English monarchs. Under the king, the church of England is governed by two archbishops and twenty four bishops. The various grades among the clergy are styled, deans, archdeacons, rectors, vicars, &c.

The liturgy was introduced in the reign of Edward VI, and re-established in that of Elizabeth, with some few alterations. During the reign of this queen, the thirty nine articles were also established. It has been generally held by most, if not all Calvinists, both in and out of the establishment, that the doctrinal articles of the English church are Calvinistic. This opinion, however, has been warmly controverted by others, who interpret them in favour of Arminianism. The former opinion has been defended by Dr. Scott, Mr. Toplady, Dr. Haweis, Sir R. Hill, and more recently by Mr. Overton. The latter has been as strenuously maintained by Dr. Kipling, Mr. Daubeny, and the present bishop of Lincoln; and the dispute has never run higher upon the subject, than it has done of late years. "Each party," says Mr. Adam, "seem to understand the articles exclusive-

* Dufresnoy's Chronological Tables, vol. i. p. 213.
† Mosheim, vol. i. p. 216, new ed.
‡ Mosheim, vol. i. 180.
§ History of Religion, vol. iv.

ly in their own sense. But as some of our reformers were inclined to Calvinism, and others to Arminianism, it is, perhaps, more natural to believe with some of our ablest divines, that the thirty-nine articles were framed with comprehensive latitude, and that neither Calvinism, nor Arminianism was meant to be exclusively established.

The law requires all persons, who are admitted into holy orders, to subscribe to the thirty-nine articles. In the course of the last century, disputes arose among the English clergy respecting the propriety of subscribing to any human formulary of religious sentiments. An application for its removal was made in parliament in 1772, by the petitioning clergy, and received the most public discussion in the house of Commons, but was rejected in the house of Lords.

The churches of England and Ireland were united by the union of 1801, and form a grand national establishment; but with a free toleration of dissenters in their principles and worship, without admitting them to any of its emoluments, and excluding them from many offices in the state.*

The episcopal church in the United States of America, which is wholly independent of that of England, has organized her government, owing to dissimularity of circumstances, in a very different manner. In this organization, indeed, the principle is by both churches recognized, that all orders of the church, affected by the laws, should have a vote in making them. And therefore the general convention, which is the highest legislative authority of the protestant episcopal church, is composed of two houses, the house of bishops, and the house of clerical and lay deputies, consisting of deputies from the different state or diocesan conventions of the church; and the concurrence of both houses is necessary to every act of the convention; and in the house of clerical and lay deputies, the two orders, clerical and lay, have a negative upon each other. The general convention meets triennially. In every state or diocess, there is a convention, consisting of the bishop, the clergy and laity, who are represented by delegates from the congregations, and which usually meet once a year. Visitations are made by the bishops to their respective diocesses, for the purpose of examining the state of the church, inspecting the behaviour of the clergy, and administering the rite of confirmation.

The thirty-nine articles have been adopted by the church in the United States, and are con-

* Adam's Religious World displayed, vol. ii. p. 337. Evans' Sketch 12 ed. p. 119. Toplady's Historical Proof of the Calvinism of the Church of England. Overton's True Churchman. Kipling on the articles. Daubeny's Vindiciæ Eccles. Angl. Bp. of Lincoln's Charge, and Mr. Scott's Answer.

tained in all late editions of the book of common prayer, but subscription to them is not required in candidates for holy orders, as in England.

EONITES, the followers of Eon d' Etoile, a lunatic gentleman of Bretagne, in the twelfth century, who imagined that he was appointed to judge both the quick and dead. He ended his days in a miserable prison; but persecution and death in the most dreadful forms, could not persuade his infatuated disciples to abandon his cause.*

EOQUINIANS, so called from Eoquinus in the sixteenth century, who is said to have taught that Christ did not die for the wicked, but for the faithful only.†

***EPEFANOFTSCHINS**, a small Russian sect, followers of a monk of Kieff, who got himself ordained a bishop through forged letters of recommendation. Being imprisoned on a discovery of the cheat, he died in confinement, but is by his sect esteemed a martyr. Their sentiments are nearly the same as the *Starobredsi*, or old ceremonialists.‡

EPICUREANS. They derive their name from Epicurus, the philosopher, who was born in the 109th olympiad, or about 240 years before Christ. He accounted for the formation of the world by supposing that a finite number of that infinite multitude of atoms, which fills the immense space of the universe, falling fortuitously into the region of our world, were in consequence of their innate motion collected into one rude and indigested mass. All the various parts of nature were formed by those atoms, which were best fitted to produce them. The fiery particles formed themselves into air, and from those which subsided, the earth was produced. The mind, or intellect, was formed of particles most subtle in their nature, and capable of the most rapid motion. The world is preserved by the same mechanical causes by which it was framed, and from the same causes it will at last be dissolved.

Epicurus admitted that there were in the universe divine natures: but asserted that these happy beings did not incumber themselves with the government of the world; yet that on account of their excellent nature they are proper objects of reverence.

The science of physics was, in the judgment of Epicurus, subordinate to that of ethics; and his whole doctrine concerning nature was professedly adapted to rescue men from the dominion of troublesome passions, and lay the foundation of a tranquil and happy life. He taught that man is to do every thing for his own sake; that he

* Mosheim, vol. ii. p. 457, 458. Broughton's Hist. Lib. vol. i. p. 361.
† Ross' View of Religions, p. 234. ‡ Pinkerton's Russian Church, p. 304.

is to make his own happiness his chief end, and do all in his power to secure and preserve it. He considered pleasure as the ultimate good of mankind: but asserts, that he does not mean the pleasures of the luxurious; but principally the freedom of the body from pain, and of the mind from anguish and perturbation. His followers however applied the principle to sensual indulgence, and this made his philosophy so popular that people of high rank and luxurious character generally embraced it. The virtue he prescribes is resolved ultimately into our private advantage, without regard to the excellence of its own nature, or to its being commanded by the Supreme Being.*

EPISCOPALIANS, an appellation given to those who assert, that episcopacy is of divine right, and was the constitution of the primitive church. They maintain that bishops, [ʼεπίσκοπους] presbyters, (or priests) and deacons, are three distinct orders in the church; and that the bishops have a superiority over both the others directly from God; in proof of this they allege, that during our Saviour's stay upon earth, he had under him two distinct orders of ministers—the twelve, and the seventy; and after his ascension, we read of apostles, presbyters, and deacons in the church. That the apostolic, or highest order, is designed to be permanent, they think, is evident from bishops being instituted by the apostles themselves, to succeed them in great cities, as Timothy at Ephesus, Titus at Crete, &c. It appears that Timothy and Titus were superiour to modern presbyters, from the offices assigned them. Timothy was by Paul empowered to preside over the presbyters of Ephesus, to receive accusations against them, (1 Tim. v. 19.) to exhort, to charge, and even to rebuke them; and Titus was, by the same apostle, left in Crete for the express purpose of setting things in order, and ordaining presbyters in every city.

They contend that bishops, in the sense in which they use the term, certainly existed in the churches as early as A. D. 160. They lay great stress on the writings of the Christian Fathers on this point, and in particular on Clement, on the Epistles of St. Ignatius.† The Roman and English are the principal episcopal churches in the west of Europe.

ERASTIANS, the followers of Erastus, a German divine of the sixteenth century. The pastoral office, according to him, was only persuasive, like a professor of sciences over his students without any power annexed; the Lord's supper, and

* Leland's Discourses on the Christian Revelation.

† Dr. Edwards' Remains, p. 229. Ency. vol. vi. p. 689—692. Adam's Religious World displayed, vol. ii. p. 275, &c.

other ordinances of the gospel, were to be free and open to all; the minister might dissuade the vicious and unqualified from the communion—but might not refuse it, or inflict any kind of censure; the punishment of all offences being referred to the civil magistrate.*

ESSENES, a Jewish sect, which maintained that rewards and punishments extended to the soul only, and considered the body as a mass of malignant matter, and the prison of the immortal spirit. The greatest part of them considered the laws of Moses as an allegorical system of spiritual and mysterious truth, and renounced all regard to the outward letter in its explanation. The leading traits in the character of this sect were, that they were sober, abstemious, peaceable, lovers of retirement, and had a perfect community of goods. They paid the highest regard to the moral precepts of the law; but neglected the ceremonial, excepting what regarded personal cleanliness, the observation of the sabbath, and making an annual present to the temple at Jerusalem. They commonly lived in a state of celibacy, and adopted the children of others, to educate them in their own principles and customs. Though they were in general averse to oaths, they bound all whom they initiated by the most sacred vows to observe the duties of piety, justice, fidelity, and modesty; to conceal the secrets of the fraternity; to preserve the books of their instructors, and with great care to commemorate the names of the angels.

Philo mentions two classes of Essenes, one of which followed a practical, the other a theoretical institution. The latter, who were called *Therapeutæ*, placed their whole felicity in the contemplation of the divine nature. Detaching themselves entirely from secular affairs, they transferred their property to their relations and friends, and retired to solitary places, where they devoted themselves to a holy life. The principal society of this kind was formed near Alexandria, where they lived not far from each other in separate cottages, each of which had its own sacred apartments, to which the inhabitants retired for the purposes of devotion.†

Philo says, lib. v. cap. 17. the Essenes were in number about four thousand in Judea; and Pliny seems to fix their principal abode above Engedi, where they fed on the fruit of palm trees. He adds, that they lived at a distance from the seashore, for fear of being corrupted by the conversation of strangers.

We do not see that Jesus

* Neal's History of the Puritans, vol. iii. p. 140.

† Enfield's Hist. of Philos. vol. ii. p. 186. See also Josephus' Antiq. and Prideaux's Connect. Calmet's Dictionary.

Christ hath spoken of them, or that he preached among them. It is not improbable, that John Baptist lived among them, till he began to baptize and preach. The wilderness, where Pliny places the Essenes, was not very far from Hebron, which is thought by some to be the place of John's birth.*

ETHNOPHRONES, i. e. Paganizers, a sect in the eighth century, who, professing christianity, joined thereto all the ceremonies of paganism; such as judicial astrology, divinations of all kinds, &c.; and who observed the feasts, times, and seasons, of the Gentiles.†

EUCHITES. See *Massalians.*

EUDOXIANS, a branch of the Arians in the fourth century; so called from Eudoxus, who, after the death of Arius, became head of the party.‡ See *Arians.*

EUNOMIANS. See *Arians.*

EUSEBIANS, the followers of Eusebius, the very learned bishop of Cæsarea, in the fourth century. He maintained a subordination of persons in the godhead, which has subjected him to the charge of Arianism, though, as many think, unjustly. See *Arians.*§

EUSTATHIANS, a rigid denomination in the fourth century, so called from Eustathius, a monk. He prohibited marriage, the use of wine and flesh, and obliged his followers to quit all they had, as incompatible with the hopes of heaven.‖

EUTUCHITES, a kind of religious stoics in the third century, who held that our souls are placed in our bodies to honour the angels, who created them; and that we ought to rejoice equally in all events, because to grieve, would be to dishonour our creators.¶

EUTYCHIANS, a denomination in the fifth century, so called from Eutyches, abbot of a certain convent of monks at Constantinople, and the very opposite to the Nestorians. He maintained, that there was only one nature in Jesus Christ. The divine nature, according to them, had so entirely swallowed up the human, that the latter could not be distinguished: so that it was inferred our Lord had nothing of humanity but the appearance. See *Jacobites.*

Eutychus began to propagate his opinions about the year 448, when he was rather advanced in years, and they were immediately condemned by a synod held by Flavian at Constantinople; the next year they were justified by the council of Ephesus, and again condemned two years after by the council of Caledon; such is the fallibility of human nature!**

* Calmet's Dictionary, vol. i. † Broughton. ‡ History of Religion, vol. iv.
§ Mosheim, vol. i. p. 291. ‖ Mosheim, vol. i. p. 313.
¶ Broughton, vol. ii. p. 532. ** Mosheim, vol. i. p. 413.

F

FAMILISTS, or family of Love, a denomination which appeared in Holland about the year 1555, and derive their origin from one Henry Nicholas, of Westphalia. He pretended that there was no knowledge of Christ, nor of the scriptures, but in his family. He quoted 1 Cor. xiii. 9, 10. *For we know but in part, and we prophecy in part; but when that which is perfect is come, then that which is in part shall be done away;* and hence inferred that the doctrine of the apostles was imperfect, and to be superseded by the more perfect revelation made to *The Family of Love.*

This denomination taught, (1.) That the essence of religion consisted in the feelings of divine love; and that it was a matter of indifference what opinions Christians entertained concerning points of faith, provided their hearts burned with the sacred flame of piety and love. (2.) That the union of the soul with Christ transforms it into the essence of the Deity. (3.) That the letter of the scripture is useless; and those sacred books ought to be interpreted in a spiritual or allegorical manner. (4.) That it was lawful on some occasions to prevaricate in evidence.*

This sect appeared in England about the year 1580; where, when their founder was discovered, their books were ordered to be publicly burnt, and the society was dispersed.

FARVONIANS, a branch of the Socinians; so called from Farvonius, who flourished in the sixteenth century. He asserted, that Christ had been produced out of nothing by the Supreme Being, before the creation of the world; and warned his disciples against paying religious worship either to the Son or Spirit.† See *Socinians.*

FIFTH MONARCHY-MEN, a denomination which arose in the seventeenth century. They derived their name from maintaining that there will be a *fifth universal monarchy* under the personal reign of Jesus Christ upon earth. Their leader was Thomas Venner, a cooper, who, in his conventicle in Coleman Street, having warmed the passions of his audience, sallied forth toward St. Paul's Church-Yard, on Sunday Jan. 6, 1660, determined to set up the new monarchy, and vainly expecting Jesus Christ from heaven to their support. The military were called out against them, but it was three days before they were subdued, many being killed, and of the rest, Venner

* Mosheim, vol. iv. p. 165. Broughton, vol ii. p. 30. More's Mystery of Godliness, p. 356. Fulfilling of the Scriptures, vol. i. p. 166.

† Mosheim, vol. iv. p. 291, 202.

and ten others were hanged in different parts of the city.*

FLACIANS, the disciples of M. Flacius Illyricus in the sixteenth century; who was a learned and zealous disciple of Luther, and one of the authors of the famous German Ecclesiastical History, called *Centuriæ Magdeburgensis*. He maintained that original sin is 'the very *substance* of human nature.'† See *Calvinists*.

FLAGELLANTS, a denomination which sprang up in Italy in the year 1260, and was thence propagated through almost all the countries of Europe. They derive their name from the latin, *flagello*, to *whip*. The society that embraced this new discipline, ran in multitudes, composed of persons of both sexes, and of all ranks and ages, through the public streets, with whips in their hands, lashing their naked backs with astonishing severity, thinking to obtain the divine mercy for themselves and others, by their voluntary mortification and penance.—This sect re-appeared in the fourteenth and fifteenth centuries, maintaining that their penance was of equal virtue with the sacraments; that the forgiveness of all sins was to be obtained thereby; that the law of Christ was soon to be abolished; and that a new law, enjoining the baptism of blood, to be administered by whipping, was to be substituted in its place.‡

FLANDRIANS. See *Mennonites*.

FLORINIANS, so called from Florinus, a branch of the Valentinians in the second century. See *Valentinians*.

FRANCISCANS, an order of friars founded in 1209, by St. Francis of Assini, who had led a dissolute life, but a fit of sickness produced an entire change in his method of living; and at the age of twenty one he solemnly determined to practise the most rigorous self-denial; and had the courage to support that resolution, without the least deviation, during a life of forty six years. Absolute poverty was his fundamental rule, which he rigorously enjoined on all his followers. Some years afterwards, this rule was relaxed by the indulgence of several popes; but this occasioned a schism in the order, and divided them into two parties. Those who adhered strictly to the austere rules of their founder were called Fraticelli, or Little Brothers, which name Francis himself had assumed out of humility, and prescribed it to his followers. They were also called Spiritual, while the others were styled Brethren of the Community. This religious order acquired great reputation and influence; and it is said that previous to

* Mosheim, vol. iv. p. 533.

† Ibid. p. 43.

‡ Mosheim, vol. iii. p. 94, 206, 277.

the death of St. Francis it amounted to more than fifty thousand persons. The Franciscans maintained that the Virgin Mary was born without original sin, which the Dominicans denying, occasioned a contention, which ended much to the disgrace of the latter.* See *Dominicans.*

FRATICELLI, i. e. *Little Brothers*, a sect which appeared in Italy about 1298, and spread all over Europe. They pretended that ecclesiastics ought to have no possessions of their own. This term had been honourably applied, as we have seen, to the *spiritual* or stricter kind of Franciscans; but, when used in reference to the Catharists and Waldenses, was considered as a term of reproach and ridicule.†

FRATRES ALBATI, or White Brethren. They derived their name and origin from a certain priest, who, in the fifteenth century, descended from the Alps, arrayed in a white garment, and accompanied by a prodigious number of both sexes, who after the example of their chief were clothed in white linen. They went in a kind of procession through several provinces, following a cross, which their leader had erected like a standard. The new chief exhorted his followers to appease the anger of an offended deity; emaciated his body by voluntary acts of mortification and penance; and attempted to excite Europe to renew the crusades.‡

FREETHINKERS, an appellation assumed by certain persons, who disbelieved Christianity, and boasted their freedom from religious prejudices. See *Deists.*

*FREETHINKING Christians, a name lately adopted by a society which arose in the year 1799, and has ever since regularly assembled in London, calling itself a *church of God*, founded on the principles of free inquiry. Their first members separated from a congregation of trinitarian dissenters in Parliament Court Chapel, Bishopsgate Street; they rejected the doctrine of the trinity, the atonement, and other points of Calvinism; then the sacraments and the immateriality of the soul; and lastly, the inspiration of the scriptures and public worship; for they have neither singing nor prayer in their assemblies, and regard the bible only as an authentic history.

These freethinking Christians readily admit that, since their first assembling as a body, their sentiments have undergone considerable alteration on points of primary importance; but they contend that this is the natural consequence of free inquiry; that men who had heretofore been the slaves of errour, could

* Mosheim, Eccles. Hist. vol. iii. p. 192. Eustace's Classical Tour through Italy, vol. ii. p. 197.

† Broughton, vol. i. p. 427.

‡ Mosheim, vol. iii. p. 122.

not but advance in the attainment of truth, after adopting a system which left thought unrestrained, and conscience free; and they are still ready to renounce any opinion, whenever it shall appear to them untenable. In consequence, their public meetings, which are mostly on Sunday forenoons, resemble rather a debating society, than a christian church. The elder opens the meeting by stating the subject for consideration, and, at his call, several speakers successively address the meeting. It is not unusual to hear among them a difference of opinion; and they are all prompt to controvert the current doctrines of the christian world, to show their dissent from all sects and parties, and their aversion to the clergy, and to christian ministers of all denominations.

This society was little known till the year 1808, when they advertised their intention of publicly inquiring into the "existence of a being, called *the devil.*" So singular a notice could not fail of drawing a considerable number of persons to their assembly, especially on a Sunday morning. The landlord of the house at which they met, in the Old 'Change, alarmed for his personal security, obliged them to remove, and they engaged the large room at the Paul's Head, Cateaton street. Here the magistracy interfered; but as they had taken the precaution to license themselves under the toleration act, nothing could be done legally to restrain them. Since then they have set up a periodical publication under the title of the "Freethinking Christian's Magazine," in which they profess to disseminate christian, moral, and philosophical truth; and they have erected a handsome meeting-house in the crescent behind Jewin Street, Cripplegate, where this weekly assembly, consisting of members and strangers, is said to amount to between four and five hundred persons.

The following appears to be the latest summary of their opinions. "The christian religion," they say, "consists in the worship of one God, eternal, just, and good; and in an obedience to the commands of Jesus, his messenger on earth, who taught the wicked to repent of the errour of their ways, and that God was ever ready to receive them. Forms and ordinances, parade and show, are no parts of his system; but virtue and purity of heart can alone prepare man for a blissful existence beyond the grave; the wisdom and hope of which were furnished by the resurrection of the teacher of their faith, *a member of earth, and an heir of immortality.*"*

FREE-WILLERS, Arminians, characterized by their ad-

* Freethinking Christian's Mag. The True Design of the Church of God, &c. Evans' Sketch, 13th ed. p. 311, &c.

herence to the doctrine of Free-will, as implying a self-determining power in the mind. Dr. Clarke defines liberty to be 'a power of self-motion, or self-determination,' which definition implies that in our volitions we are not acted upon. Activity, and being acted upon, are incompatible with one another. In whatever instances, therefore, it is truly said of us that we act, in those instances we cannot be acted upon. A being, in receiving a change of its state from the exertion of an adequate force, is not an agent. Man, therefore, could not be an agent, were all his volitions derived from any force, or the effects of any mechanical causes. In this case, it would be no more true that he ever acts, than it is true of a ball, that it acts when struck by another ball. To prove that a self-determining power belongs to the will, it is urged that we ourselves are conscious of possessing such liberty. We blame and condemn ourselves for our actions; have an inward sense of guilt, shame, and remorse of conscience; which feelings are inconsistent with the scheme of necessity. We universally agree that sôme actions deserve praise, and others blame; for which there would be no foundation, if we were invincibly determined in every volition. Approbation and blame are consequent upon free actions only. It is an article in the christian faith, that God will render rewards and punishments to men for their actions in this life. We cannot maintain his justice in this particular, if men's actions be necessary, either in their own nature, or by divine decrees and influence. Activity and self-determining power are also alleged to be the foundation of all morality, and the greatest possible happiness.* See *Necessarians.*

FRENCH PROPHETS. They first appeared in Dauphiny and Vivarais. In the year 1688, five or six hundred protestants, of both sexes, gave themselves out to be prophets, and inspired of the Holy Ghost, and they soon amounted to many thousands. They had strange fits, which came upon them with tremblings and faintings, as in a swoon, which made them reel and stagger till they dropped. They beat themselves, fell on their backs, shut their eyes, and heaved their breasts, as in fits: and when they came out of these trances said, they saw the heavens open, the angels, paradise, and hell; and then began to prophesy.

The burden of their discourses was, *Repent, amend your lives: the end of all things draweth nigh!* The walls of their assemblies, and, when in the open air, the hills rebounded with their loud cries for mercy: and with im-

* See Locke on Free Will. Letters between Clarke and Leibnitz. The Correspondence between Drs. Priestley and Price.

precations against the priests, the church, and the pope, with predictions of the approaching fall of popery.

In the year 1706, three or four of these prophets came over into England, and brought their prophetic spirit with them, which discovered itself by extacies, agitations, and inspirations under them, as it had done in France.: and they propagated the like spirit to others, so that before the year was out, there were two or three hundred of these prophets in and about London, of both sexes, of all ages; men, women, and children; and they had delivered four or five hundred prophetic warnings.

The great thing they pretended by their spirit was, to give warning of the near approach of the kingdom of God, the happy times of the church, the millenium-state. Their message was, that the grand jubilee, the acceptable year of the Lord, the accomplishment of those numerous passages in scripture concerning the *new heavens*, and the *new earth*, &c. was *now* even at the door—that this great work was to be wrought on the part of man by spiritual arms only, proceeding from the mouths of those who should, by inspiration of the Spirit, be sent forth in great numbers, to labour in the vineyard—that this mission of his servants should be witnessed to by signs and wonders from heaven, by a deluge of judgments on the wicked throughout the world; as famine, pestilence, earthquakes, &c.—that the exterminating angels should root out the tares, and leave upon earth only good corn; and that the works of men being thrown down, there should be but one Lord, one faith, one heart, and one voice, among mankind. They declared, that all these great things would be manifest over the whole earth within the term of three years.

These prophets also pretended to the gift of languages, of discerning the secrets of the heart; the power of conferring the same spirit on others, and the gift of healing by the laying on of hands. To prove that they were really inspired by the Holy Ghost, they alleged the complete joy and satisfaction they experienced, the spirit of prayer which was poured forth upon them, and the answer of their prayers by the Most High.*

FRIENDS, or Quakers, a religious society which began to be distinguished about the middle of the seventeenth century. Their doctrines were first promulgated in England, by George Fox, about the year 1647, for which he was imprisoned at Nottingham, in the year 1649, and the year following at Derby. The appellation of *Quakers* was given them by way of contempt: some say on account of their

* Chauncey's Works, vol. iii. p. 2—39. Prophetical Warnings of the Eternal Spirit. A Brand snatched from the burning, &c.

tremblings under the impression of divine things; but *they* say, it was first given them by oné of the magistrates who committed G. Fox to prison, on account of his bidding him and those about him, to *tremble* at the word of the Lord.

From their first appearance, they suffered much persecution. In New England they were treated with peculiar severity, though the settlers themselves had but lately fled from persecution.

During these sufferings they applied to King Charles II. for relief, who in 1661 granted a mandamus, to put a stop to them. Neither were the good offices of this prince in their favour confined to the colonies; for in 1672 he released under the great seal four hundred of these suffering people, who were imprisoned in Great Britain.

In 1681 Charles II. granted to William Penn the province of Pennsylvania. Penn's treaty with the Indians, and the liberty of conscience which he granted to all denominations, even those which had persecuted his own, do honour to his memory.

In the reign of James II. the *Friends*, in common with other English dissenters, were relieved by the suspension of the penal laws. But it was not till the reign of William and Mary, that they obtained any thing like a proper legal protection.

An act was made in the year 1696, which, with a few exceptions, allowed to their affirmation the legal force of an oath, and provided a less oppressive mode for recovering tithes under a certain amount; which provisions under the reign of George I. were made perpetual. For refusing to pay tithes, &c. however, they are still liable to suffer in the exchequer and ecclesiastical court, both in Great Britain and Ireland.

The doctrines of the society of Friends have been variously represented, and it is too much to suppose so large a denomination can be perfectly unanimous. The following account, however, has been drawn up by one of themselves, and nearly in the words of their own most approved writers.

1. They believe that *God is one:* and that this one God is Father, Son, and Holy Ghost, as in Matt. xxviii. 19.* To the assertion that they deny the Trinity, *Wm. Penn* answers, "Nothing less: they do believe in the holy Three, or the trinity of Father, Word, and Spirit, according to the scriptures; but they are very tender of quitting scripture terms and phrases for schoolmen's; such as distinct and separate persons and subsistences, &c. and they judge that a curious inquiry into those high and divine relations, though never so great truths in themselves, tends little to godliness, and less to peace."

2. They believe that *Christ* is

* Claridge.

both God and man in wonderful union; that he suffered for our salvation, was raised again for our justification, and ever liveth to make intercession for us. And in reply to the charge, that the Quakers deny Christ to be *God, Wm. Penn* says, "A most untrue and uncharitable censure: for their great and characteristic principle is, that Christ, as the divine Word, lighteth the souls of all men who come into the world, with a spiritual and saving light, (according to John i. 9—12.) which none but the Creator of souls can do."

3. They believe the *scriptures* to be of divine authority, given by the inspiration of God through holy men: that they are a declaration of those things most surely believed by the primitive Christians; and that they contain the mind and will of God, and are his commands to us: in that respect they are his *declaratory* word, and therefore are obligatory on us, and are profitable for doctrine, reproof, &c. They love and prefer them before all books in the world, rejecting all principles and doctrines that are repugnant thereunto. "Nevertheless," says *Barclay*, "because they are only a declaration of the fountain, and not the fountain itself, they are not to be esteemed the *principal* ground of all truth and knowledge, nor the *primary* rule of faith and manners; but a *secondary* rule, subordinate to the spirit, from whom they have all their excellence and certainty."

They object to calling the scriptures the *word* of God, as being a name applied to Christ by the sacred writers themselves, though too often misunderstood by those who extol scripture above the immediate teaching of Christ's spirit in the heart; whereas without the last, the first cannot be profitably understood.

4. On the *original and present state* of man, *Wm. Penn* says, "The world began with innocency; all was then good that God had made; but this happy state lasted not long; for man, lost the divine image, the wisdom, power, and purity he was made in; by which, being no longer fit for paradise, he was expelled that garden as a poor vagabond, to wander in the earth." Respecting the state of man under the fall, *Barclay* observes, "Not to dive into the curious notions which many have concerning the condition of Adam before the fall, all agree in this, that he thereby came to a very great loss, not only in the things which related to the outward man, but in regard of that true fellowship and communion he had with God. So that though we do not ascribe any whit of Adam's guilt to men, until they make it theirs by the like acts of disobedience; yet we cannot suppose that men who are come of Adam naturally, can have any good thing in their nature, which he, from

whom they derive their nature, had not himself to communicate to them. And whatever real good any man doth, it proceedeth not from his nature, as the son of Adam; But from the seed of God in him, as a new visitation of life, in order to bring him out of his natural condition."

5. On *man's redemption* through Christ. They believe that God who made man had pity on him; and in his infinite goodness and wisdom provided a mean for the restoration of fallen man, by a nobler and more excellent Adam, promised to be born of a woman; and which, by the dispensation of the Son of God in the flesh, was personally and fully accomplished in him, as man's Saviour and Redeemer.

Respecting the doctrines of *satisfaction* and *justification*, they say, We believe that Jesus Christ was our holy sacrifice, atonement, and propitiation—that God is just in forgiving true penitents upon the credit of that holy offering—that what he did and suffered, satisfied and pleased God, and was for the sake of fallen man who had displeased him. *Penn.*

6. *On immediate revelation.* They believe that the saving, certain, and necessary knowledge of God, can only be acquired by the inward, immediate revelation of God's spirit. They prove this from 1 Cor. ii. 11, 12; xii. 3. Heb. viii. 10. Where the law of God is put into the mind, and written in the heart, there the object of faith and revelation of God is inward, immediate, and objective: "but these divine revelations," says *Barclay*, "as they do not, so neither can they at any time contradict the scripture testimony, or right and sound reason."

7. *On universal and saving light.* They affirm, that "God hath given to every man a measure of the light of his own Son, (John i. 9.) and that God by this light invites, calls, and strives with every man, in order to save him; which as it is received, works the salvation of all, even of those who are ignorant of the death of Christ, and of Adam's fall: but that this light may be resisted, in which case God is said to be resisted and rejected, and Christ to be again crucified; and to those who thus resist and refuse him he becomes their condemnation."

8. *On perfection and perseverance.* They assert that as many as do not resist this light, become holy and spiritual; bringing forth all those blessed fruits which are acceptable to God: and by this holy birth, (to wit, Jesus Christ formed within us, and working in us,) the body of death and sin is crucified, and we are freed from actually transgressing the law of God. And they entertain worthier notions of God, than to limit the operations of his grace to a partial cleansing of the soul

from sin, even in this life. (Matt. v. 48. 1 John ii. 14; iii. 3.) Yet this perfection still admits of a growth; and there remains always a possibility of sinning, where the mind does not most diligently and watchfully attend to the Lord.

9. Concerning *worship*. They consider as obstructions to pure worship, all forms which divert the attention of the mind from the secret influences of the Holy Spirit. Yet, although true worship is not confined to time and place, they think it incumbent on christians to meet often together, in testimony of their dependence on their heavenly Father, and for a renewal of their spiritual strength. When thus met, they believe it to be their duty patiently to wait for the arising of that life which, by subduing those thoughts, produces an inward silence, and therein affords a true sense of their condition; believing even a single sigh, arising from such a sense of our infirmities and of the need we have of divine help, to be more acceptable to God, than any performance, however specious, originating in the will of man.

10. *On the ministry*. As by the light, or gift of God, all true knowledge in things spiritual is received, so by the same, as it is manifested in the heart, every true minister of the gospel is ordained and prepared for the work. Moreover, they who have this authority, may and ought to preach the gospel, though without human commission or literature.* (1 Pet. iv. 10, 11.) *Barclay*.

11. *On baptism and the supper*. They believe that as there is *one Lord* and *one faith*, so there is *one baptism;* which is *not the putting away the filth of the flesh, but the answer of a good conscience before God*. And this baptism is a pure and spiritual thing, by which we are buried with him, that being washed and purged from our sins, we may walk in newness of life; of which the baptism of John was a figure, which was commanded for a *time*, and not to continue *forever*. (Matt. iii. 11.) Hence it follows that the baptism which Christ commanded, (Matt. xxviii. 19.) must relate to his own baptism, and not to that of John: to say it must be understood of water is but to beg the question, the text being wholly silent thereon.—With respect to the other rite, termed *the Lord's supper*, they believe that the communion of the body and blood of Christ is spiritual, which is the participation of his flesh and blood, by which the inward man is daily nourished in the hearts of those in whom Christ dwells; and that this is most agreeable to the doctrine of Christ concerning this matter. (John vi. 53, 54.) *Barclay*.

12. *On the resurrection*. They believe the resurrection, ac-

* They allow females to preach, who are called thereto and moved by the spirit.

cording to the scripture, not only from sin, but also from death and the grave. They believe that as our Lord Jesus was raised from the dead by the power of the Father, and was the first fruits of the resurrection, so every man in his own order shall arise; they that have done well *to the resurrection of eternal life, but they that have done evil to everlasting condemnation.* And as the celestial bodies do far exceed the terrestrial, so they expect our spiritual bodies in the resurrection shall far excel what our bodies now are. (*Penn* and *Sewell.*)

Having treated of the principles of religion as professed by the *Friends*, we now proceed to notice some tenets which more immediately relate to their conduct among men.

1. On *oaths* and *war.*—With respect to the former of these they abide *literally* by these words of our Saviour: *But I say unto you, swear not at all; neither by heaven, &c. but let your communication be yea, yea; nay, nay; for whatsoever is more than these cometh of evil.* (Matt. v. 34—37.)

To prove that *war* is not lawful to christians, they likewise argue thus:—(1.) Christ commands, that we should love our enemies. (2.) The apostle James testifies that wars and strifes come from the lusts which war in the members of carnal men. (3.) The apostle Paul admonisheth christians that they defend not themselves, neither avenge, by rendering evil for evil; but give place unto wrath, because vengeance is the Lord's. (4.) The prophets Isaiah and Micah have expressly foretold that *in the mountain of the house of the Lord, Christ shall judge the nations;* and then *they shall beat their swords into ploughshares, &c.* and *there shall be none to hurt nor kill in the holy mountain of the Lord.* (Barclay.)

2. On *deportment*—(1.) They affirm that it is not lawful for christians either to give or receive such flattering titles of honour, as your Holiness, your Majesty, your Excellency, &c.; because these titles are no part of that obedience which is due to magistrates or superiours; neither doth the giving them add to, or the not giving them diminish from, that subjection we owe them. But they do not object to employ those titles which are descriptive of their station or office; such as *king, prince, duke, earl, bishop,* &c. Neither do they think it right to use what are commonly called compliments; such as *your most obedient servant,* &c. Such customs have led christians to lie; so that to use falsehood is now accounted civility. They disuse those names of the months and days, which, having been given in honour of the heroes and false gods of the heathen, originated in their flattery or superstition: they likewise condemn the custom of speaking to a single person in the plural

number, as having also arisen from motives of adulation.—(2.) They affirm that it is not lawful for christians to kneel, or prostrate themselves to any man, or to bow the body, or to uncover the head to them; because these are the outward signs of our adoration towards God. (3.) They affirm that it is not lawful for christians to use superfluities in apparel, which are of no use, save for ornament and vanity. (4.) That it is not lawful to use games, sports, or plays among christians, under the notion of recreation, which do not agree with christian gravity and sobriety. They allege that the chief end of religion is to redeem men from the spirit and vain conversation of the world, and to lead them into inward communion with God; therefore every thing ought to be rejected that wastes our precious time, and diverts the heart from that evangelical spirit which is the ornament of a christian.

With regard to *religious liberty*, they hold that the rights of conscience are sacred and unalienable, subject only to the control of the Deity, who has not given authority to any man, or body of men, to compel another to his religion. *(Barclay.)*

3. On their *church government*, or *discipline*. To effect the salutary purposes of discipline, they have established monthly, quarterly, and yearly meetings. A monthly meeting is usually composed of several particular congregations, situated within a convenient distance from each other. Its business is to provide for the subsistence of the poor, (for they maintain their *own* poor,) and for the education of their offspring; to examine persons desiring to be admitted into membership; to deal with disorderly members, and if irreclaimable, to disown them. (Matt. xviii. 15—17.)

All marriages are proposed to these meetings for their concurrence, which is granted, if upon inquiry, the parties appear clear of other engagements, and if they also have the consent of their parents or guardians; without which no marriages are allowed: for this society has always scrupled to acknowledge the exclusive authority of the priests to marry. Their marriages are solemnized in a public meeting for worship; and the monthly meeting keeps a record of them; as also of the births and burials of its members. This society does not allow its members to sue each other at law; it therefore enjoins all to end their differences by speedy and impartial arbitration: and if any refuse to act according to these rules, they are disowned. Several monthly meetings compose a quarterly meeting, to which they send representatives, and to which appeals lie from the monthly meetings. The yearly meeting has a general superintendence of the society in the country in which it is established; and as particular exigencies arise, makes such regulations as appear to be requisite; and appeals from the quarterly meetings are here finally determined. There are also meetings of the female Friends, held at the same times and places (in separate apartments) to regulate matters relative to their own sex. There are likewise meetings for sufferings, composed of members chosen at the quarterly meetings. They were so called in times of persecution, and are now continued to superintend the general concerns of the society.*

G

GAIANITÆ, a denomination which sprang from the Eutychians. They derive their name from Gaian, a bishop of Alexandria, in the sixth century, who is said to have denied that Jesus Christ, after the hypostatical union, was subject to any of the infirmities of human nature.

GALILEANS, or GAULANITES,† a political sect, or rather party among the Jews, the followers of Judas, a native of Gaulan in Galilee, who in the tenth year of Jesus Christ excited his countrymen, the Galileans, and many other Jews, to take arms, and venture upon all extremities, rather than pay tribute to the Romans. The principles he instilled into his party were, not only that they were a free nation, and ought not to be in subjection to any other; but that they were the elect of God, that he alone was their governour, and that therefore they ought not to submit to any ordinance of man. Though Judas was unsuccessful, and his party in their very first attempt was entirely routed and dispersed; yet so deeply had he infused his own enthusiasm into their minds, that they never rested, until in their own destruction they involved the city and temple.

GALLICAN CHURCH. Notwithstanding the established religion of France is Roman Catholic, and the king of France is called *eldest son of the church*, the Gallican clergy have ever been more exempt from the temporal dominion of the pope than those of any other country, and that in two respects: (1.) The pope has not authority to command any thing in which the civil laws of the

* Sewell's history of the people called Quakers, 8vo ed. vol. i. p. 45—432; vol. ii. p. 552. R Claridge's life and posthumous Works, p. 414—442. Penn's Works, folio edit. vol. i. p. 859, 860; vol. ii. p. 783—878. Barclay's Works, folio edit. p. 84—876. A Summary of the History, Doctrine, &c. of the Friends, p. 4—21. Bevan's Refutation of the more modern misrepresentations of Friends, p. 21—95. Clarkson's Portraiture of Quakerism, &c.

† Acts v. 37. See Calmet's Dict. in *Judas*, vol. i. new ed.

kingdom are concerned.—(2.) Though the pope's supremacy is owned in spiritual matters, yet his power is limited and regulated by the decrees and canons of ancient councils received in the realm.

In the established church, Jansenists were very numerous. The bishoprics and prebendaries were all in the gift of the king; and no other catholic state, except Italy, had so numerous a clergy as France, among whom were eighteen archbishops, and a hundred and eleven bishops.

Since the repeal of the edict of Nantz, in the seventeenth century, the protestants have suffered much from persecution: but a law, which did great honour to Lewis XVI. late king of France, gave to his non-Roman Catholic subjects, as they were called, all the civil advantages of their catholic brethren.

The French clergy amounted to one hundred and thirty thousand, the higher orders of which enjoyed immense revenues; but the cures, or great body of acting clergy, seldom possessed more than about 30*l.* a year. The clergy, as a body, independent of their tithes, possessed a revenue, arising from property in land, amounting to five millions sterling annually: at the same time they were exempt from taxation. Before the levelling system had taken place, the clergy signified to the commons the instructions of their constituents, to contribute to the exigencies of the state in equal proportion with the other citizens. Not contented with this offer, the tithes and revenues of the clergy were taken away; in lieu of which, it was agreed to grant a certain stipend to the different ministers of religion: but the possessions of the church were considered as national property by a decree of the constituent assembly.* The religious orders; viz. the communities of monks and nuns, possessed immense landed estates; and after having abolished the orders, the assembly seized the estates for the use of the nation: the gates of the cloisters were now thrown open. The next step of the assembly was to establish what is called *the civil constitution of the clergy*. This decree, though opposed with energetic eloquence, was passed, and was soon after followed by another, obliging the clergy to swear to maintain their civil constitution. Every artifice and every menace was used to induce them to take the oath: great numbers, however, refused, (among whom were a hundred and thirty eight bishops,) and were driven from their sees and parishes; three hundred of the priests being massacred in one day in one city. All the other pastors who adhered to their religion were either sacrificed or compelled to seek a refuge among foreign nations.†

Notwithstanding this, May

* Encyclopædia, vol. xvi. p. 130.

† Barruel's Hist. of the Clergy.

28, 1795, a decree was obtained for the freedom of religious worship, and in the following June, the churches in Paris were opened with great ceremony. The theophilanthropists, headed by Paine, attempted to convert the people from atheism to a popular kind of deism, though with small and temporary success; and they soon vanished from the country. See *Theophilanthropists.*

Buonaparte was an avowed friend to religious toleration, and showed in many cases a partiality to the protestants, and a great antipathy to the catholic priests, whom he justly suspected inimical to his authority. The protestant religion, however, did not spread, the people being so deeply tinctured with infidelity as to show a total indifference to religion, while at the same time they were satiated with infidelity, so that they seem to have banished the subject from their thoughts.*

Upon the late restoration of the Bourbons, the Roman Catholic religion has been re-established with all its pomp and splendour. At the same time, we learn, that the protestant religion is far from having been annihilated. Hundreds of protestant ministers, and thousands of believers in protestantism being found in that community in the south of France: though it is said by some, that they are much declined in zeal and purity, both of doctrine and manners.†

GAULANITES. See *Galileans.*

GAURS, or **Guebres,** a sect in Persia, who pretended to be the successors of the ancient magi, the followers of Zoroaster. Though said to be numerous, they are tolerated in but few places. A combustible ground, about ten miles distant from Baku, a city in the north of Persia, is the scene of their devotions, where are several small temples: in one of which the Guebres pretend to preserve the sacred flame of the universal fire, which rises from the end of a large hollow cane, stuck into the ground, resembling a lamp burning with pure spirits; or rather similar to the gas lights now exhibited in many parts of our country.

This religion was founded by Zoroaster, who lived about the year of the world 2860, and taught his followers to worship God only under the form of fire; considering the brightness, purity, and incorruptibility of that element, as bearing the most perfect resemblance to the nature of the good Deity; while he considered darkness to be emblematic of the evil principle.‡

Zoroaster compiled a book for

* Monthly Mag. vol vii. p 129. † Evangelical Magazine, 1814, p. 399.

‡ Of the two opposing principles, the good one was called Oromasdes, and the evil, Ahriman. Some have asserted, that the ancient Persians held a co-eternity of these two principles. Other writers say, that the evil principle was

the use of the priests, who were to explain it to the public at large. This book was called the *zend*; i. e. *a kindler of fire*, because it was for the use of those who worshipped the fire; but the allegorical meaning was to kindle the fire of religion in their hearts. In this book there are so many passages taken out of the old testament, that some learned men have supposed the author was a Jew. He gives almost the same account of the creation of the world, and of the ancient patriarchs, as we find recorded in scripture. He enjoins, relating to clean and unclean beasts, the same as was done by Moses, and in the same manner orders the people to pay tithes to the priests. The rest of the book contains the life of the author, his pretended visions, the methods he used in order to establish his religion, and concludes with exhortations to obedience. Yet, notwithstanding the striking similarities between the *zend* and the laws of Moses, it will not follow from hence that Zoroaster was a Jew. The Chaldeans and Persians were inquisitive people; they even sent students to India and Egypt; and, when the Jews were in a state of captivity among them, they would naturally inquire into the mysteries of their religion.

GAZARES, a denomination which appeared about the year 1197, at Gazare, a town of Dalmatia. They held almost the same opinions with the Albigenses; but their distinguishing tenet was, that no human power had a right to sentence men to death for any crime whatever.

*GENTILES, a term which the Jews applied to all foreigners; so the Greeks called all other nations barbarians.

GENTOOS. See *Hindoos.*

GEORGIANS. See *Iberians.*

*GLASSITES, the followers of Mr. John Glass of Perth. He was a minister of the established church at Tealing, near Dundee, but expelled for preaching against the Scotch league and covenant, and maintaining the pure spirituality of Christ's kingdom, with some other points afterwards taught by Sandeman. (See *Sandemanians.)* His principal work is entitled, 'The Testimony of the King of Martyrs.'

GNOSIMACHI, the professed enemies to the *Gnosis*, i. e. the speculative knowledge of Christianity. They rested

created out of darkness, and that Oromasdes first subsisted alone; that by him the light and darkness were created; and that in the composition of this world good and evil are mixed together, and so shall continue till the end of all things, when each shall be separated and reduced to its own sphere. Others have endeavoured to account for the origin of the prince of darkness thus: "Oromasdes," say they, "said once within his mind, 'How shall my power appear, if there be nothing to oppose me?' This reflection called Ahriman into being, who thenceforward opposed all the designs of God; and thereby, in spite of himself, contributes to his glory." See Heckford on Religions, p. 109.

wholly on good works, calling it a useless labour to seek for science in the scriptures. In short, they contended for the practice of morality in all simplicity, and blamed those, who aimed at a deeper insight into the mysteries of religion. They were the reverse of the Gnostics.—See the following article.

GNOSTICS. This denomination sprang up in the first century, as is supposed among the disciples of Simon Magus, who united the principles of his philosophy, with those of Christianity ; and were distinguished by the appellation of *Gnostics*, from their boasting of being able to restore mankind to the knowledge (γνωσις) of the Supreme Being, which had been lost in the world. This party was not conspicuous for its numbers or reputation before the time of Adrian. It derives its origin from the oriental philosophy.* The hypothesis of a soul distinct from the body, which had pre-existed in an angelic state, and was (for some offence committed in that state) degraded and confined to the body as a punishment, had been the great doctrine of the eastern sages from time immemorial. Not being able to conceive how evil in so great an extent could be subservient to good, they supposed that good and evil had different origins. They looked upon matter as the source of all evil, and argued in this manner: There are many evils in this world, and men seem impelled by a natural instinct to the practice of those things which reason condemns; but that eternal mind, from which all spirits derive their existence, must be inaccessible to all kinds of evil, being of a most perfect and beneficent nature. Therefore the origin of those evils with which the universe abounds, must be sought somewhere else than in the Deity. Now there is nothing without or foreign to the Deity but *matter :* therefore matter is the centre and source of all evil. Having assumed these principles, they proceeded further, and affirmed that matter was eternal, and derived its present form, not from the will of the supreme God, but from the creating power of some inferiour intelligence, to whom the world and its inhabitants owed their existence.

In their system it was generally supposed, that all intelligences had only one source, viz. the Divine Mind. And to help out the doctrine concerning the origin of evil, it was imagined, that though the Divine Being himself was essentially and perfectly good, those intelligences, or spirits, who were derived from him, and especially those who were derived from *them*, were capable of depravation.

The great boast of the Gnostics, was their doctrine con-

* See *Gaurs*, above.

cerning the derivation of various intelligences (called *aions*) from the Supreme Mind, which they thought to be done by emanation or efflux: and as those were equally capable of producing other intelligences in the same manner, and some of them were male, and others female, there was room for endless combinations of them. For a farther elucidation of the term *aions*, see the article *Basilidians*.

The oriental sages expected the arrival of an extraordinary messenger of the Most High, invested with a divine authority, endowed with the most eminent sanctity and wisdom; and peculiarly appointed to enlighten with the knowledge of the Supreme Being, the darkened minds of miserable mortals. When these philosophers afterwards discovered, that Christ and his followers wrought miracles of the most amazing kind, and of the most salutary nature, they were easily induced to connect their fundamental doctrines with those of Christianity, by supposing him the great messenger expected from above, to deliver men from the power of the malignant genii, to whom, according to their doctrine, the world was subjected; and to free their souls from the dominion of corrupt matter. But though they considered him as the son of the Supreme God, sent from the *pleroma*, or habitation of the everlasting Father, they denied his deity, looking upon him as inferiour to the Father. They also rejected his humanity, upon the supposition that every thing concrete and corporeal is in itself essentially and intrinsically evil. Hence the greater part of the Gnostics denied that Christ was clothed with a real body, or that he really suffered the pains and sorrows of the cross. They maintained, that he came to mortals with no other view than to deprive the *aions*, or spiritual tyrants of this world, of their influence upon virtuous and heaven-born souls; and, destroying the empire of these wicked spirits, to teach mankind how they might separate the divine mind from the impure body, and render the former worthy of being united to the Father of spirits. It has been supposed that the apostle Paul, when he censures "endless genealogies and old wives' fables," (1 Tim. i. 4.) has reference to the philosophy of the Gnostics.

Their persuasion, that evil resided in matter, rendered them unfavourable to wedlock, and led them to hold the doctrine of the resurrection of the body in great contempt. They considered it as a mere clog to the immortal soul, and supposed that nothing was meant by it, but either a moral change in the minds of men, which took place before they died; or that it signified the ascent of the soul to its proper abode in the superiour regions, when it was disengaged from its earthly incumbrance.

As the Gnostics were philosophic and speculative people, and affected refinement, they did not make much account of public worship, or of positive institutions of any kind: they are said not to have had any order in their churches.

As many of this denomination thought that Christ had not any real body, and therefore had not any proper flesh and blood, it seems, on this ground, when they used to celebrate the eucharist, they did not make any use of wine, which represents the blood of Christ, but of water only.

We have little account of what they thought with respect to baptism; but it seems that some of them at least disused it: and it is said that others abstained from the eucharist and from prayer.

The greatest part of this denomination adopted rules of life, which were full of austerity, recommending a strict and rigorous abstinence; and prescribing the most severe bodily mortifications, from a notion that they had a happy influence in purifying and enlarging the mind, and in disposing it for the contemplation of celestial things.

The *Egyptian* Gnostics are distinguished from the Asiatic by rejecting the evil principle of the Persians—by making Jesus and Christ two persons, and by less severity of life and manners.*

These branches of the Gnostics were subdivided into various denominations. See *Antitactæ, Ascodrutes, Bardesanistes, Basilidians, Carpocratians, Cerdonians,* Cerinthians, Marcosians, Ophites, Saturnians, Simonians,* and *Valentinians.*

GORTONIANS, a sect that made great disturbance in New England in 1643. S. Gorton was their leader, and was charged with antinomian sentiments.†

***GOSPELLERS**, a sect which arose at the time of the reformation in England, and which, speaking slightly of the law and all its obligations, and talking highly of grace, are charged with introducing antinomianism into that country.‡

***GRECIANS.** The ancient Greeks derived their theology and mythology from Egypt or Syria, or perhaps both. Mr. *Bryant* says, those, who derived their religion from Egypt and the East, misconstrued every thing they borrowed, and added many opinions of their own.§ Others suppose the Greek mythology a corruption of the scripture history, and much learned ingenuity has been employed to show that the

* Mosheim, vol. i. p. 69—109. Priestley's Eccles. History, vol. i. p. 51—186. History of early opinions, vol. i. p. 120. Percival's Dissertations.

† Hutchinson's Hist. vol. i. p. 117.

‡ Grant's History of the Eng. Church, vol. i. p. 408.

§ Bryant's Analysis, vol. i. p. 396.

gods of Greece borrowed their history from the Jewish patriarchs. Saturn is supposed to have been Noah; Neptune—Japheth; Apollo—Joshua; Bacchus—Moses; and so of the rest, except Jupiter or Jove, the Supreme God, whose name is derived from *Jah*, or the incommunicable name, *Jehovah*.* The probability seems to be that in the first instance most pagan nations worshipped the sun and other heavenly bodies, and afterwards those heroes, or secondary gods, whose history they borrowed from tradition, and improved by poetic fables, till they formed the elegant system of the Greek mythology.

GREEK CHURCH. In the eighth century, there arose a difference between the eastern and western churches, which caused much contention during the ninth century; and in the eleventh a total separation took place. At that time the patriarch Michael Cerularius, who was desirous to be freed from the papal authority, published an invective against the Latin church, and accused its members of maintaining various errours. Pope Leo IX retorted the charge, and sent legates from Rome to Constantinople. The Greek patriarch refused to see them; upon which they excommunicated him and his adherents publicly in the church of St. Sophia, A. D. 1054. The Greek patriarch excommunicated those legates with all their adherents and followers, in a public council; and procured an order of the emperour for burning the act of excommunication, which they had pronounced against the Greeks. This rupture has never been healed: and at this day a very considerable part of the world profess the religion of the Greek, or eastern church. The Nicene and Athanasian creeds are the symbols of their faith.

The principal points, which distinguish the Greek church from the Latin, are as follow:—(1.) They maintain, that the Holy Ghost proceeds from the Father *only*, and not from the Father and the Son.—(2.) They disown the authority of the pope, and deny that the church of Rome is the true catholic church.—(3.) They do not affect the character of infallibility.—(4.) They utterly disallow works of supererogation, indulgences, and dispensations.—(5.) They admit of prayers and services for the dead, as an ancient and pious custom; and even pray for the remission of their sins: but they will not allow the doctrine of purgatory, nor determine any thing dogmatically concerning the state of departed souls.—(6.) Some, as the Georgians, defer the baptism of their children till they are three or four or more years of age.—(7.) The chrism, or baptismal unction, immediately follows baptism. The priest

* Stillingfleet's Orig. Sacræ. B. iii. ch. v. Bell. Hist. of Relig. p. 93, &c.

anoints the person baptized in the principal parts of his body, with an ointment consecrated with many curious ceremonies for that purpose by a bishop; this chrism is called the unction with ointment, and is a mystery peculiar to the Greek communion, holding the place of confirmation in that of the Roman: it is styled *the seal of the gift of the Holy Ghost.*—(8.) They insist, that the sacrament of the Lord's supper ought to be administered in both kinds: and they give the sacrament to children after baptism.—(9.) They exclude confirmation and extreme unction out of the seven sacraments; but they use the holy oil, or *euchalaion,* which is not confined to persons in the close of life, like the extreme unction of the Roman church: but is administered, if required, to devout persons upon the slightest malady. Seven priests are required to administer this sacrament regularly, and it cannot be administered at all by less than three. After the oil is solemnly consecrated, each priest, in his turn, anoints the sick person, and prays for his recovery.—(10.) They deny auricular confession to be a divine precept, and say it is only a positive institution of the church. Confession and absolution constitute this mystery in the Greek church, in which penance does not make a necessary part.—(11.) They do not pay any religious homage to the eucharist.—(12.) They administer the communion to the laity, both in sickness and health.—(13.) They do not admit of images or figures in bass-relief, or embossed work; but use painting and sculpture in silver.—(14.) They permit their *secular** clergy to marry once; but never twice, unless they renounce their function, and become laymen.—(15.) They condemn all fourth marriages.

The invocation of saints and transubstantiation, are alike received by the Greek and Latin churches. They observe a number of holydays, and keep four fasts in the year more solemn than the rest; of which the fast in lent, before easter, is the chief.

The service of the Greek church is too long and complicated to be particularly described in this work: the greatest part consists in psalms and hymns.—Five orders of priesthood belong to the Greek church; viz. bishops, priests, deacons, sub-deacons, and readers; which last includes singers, &c. The episcopal order is distinguished by the titles of metropolitan, arch-bishops, and bishops. The head of the Greek church, the patriarch of Constantinople, is elected by twelve bishops, who reside nearest that famous capital; but the right of confirming this election belongs at present to the Turkish emperour. The power

* Their regular or monastic clergy are never allowed to marry.

of this prelate is very extensive. He calls councils by his own authority to govern the church, and with permission of the emperour, administers justice in civil cases among the members of his communion. The other patriarchs are those of Jerusalem, Antioch, and Alexandria, all nominated by the patriarch of Constantinople, who enjoys a most extensive jurisdiction. For the administration of ecclesiastical affairs, a synod is convened monthly, composed of the heads of the church resident in Constantinople. In this assembly the patriarch of Constantinople presides, with those of Antioch and Jerusalem, and twelve archbishops.

In regard to discipline and worship, the Greek church has the same division of the clergy into regular and secular, the same spiritual jurisdiction of bishops and their officials, the same distinction of ranks and offices with the church of Rome.

The Greek church comprehends in its bosom a considerable part of Greece, the Grecian isles, Wallachia, Moldavia, Egypt, Abyssinia, Nubia, Lydia, Arabia, Mesopotamia, Syria, Silicia, and Palestine; Alexandria, Antioch, and Jerusalem; the whole of the Russian empire in Europe; great part of Siberia in Asia; Astracan, Casan, and Georgia.

The riches of some of the Greek churches and monasteries, in jewels, (particularly pearls,) in plate, and in the habits of the clergy, are very great, and reckoned not much inferiour to those in Roman Catholic countries.* See *Russian Church*.

*GYMNOSOPHISTS, a sect of Indian philosophers, famous in antiquity for their strict adherence to the principles of the religion they professed, their devotedness to the study of wisdom, and their aversion to indolence and idleness. They believed in the immortality and transmigration of the soul, and placed the chief happiness of man in a contempt of the delusive pleasures and attractions of this mortal life. They dwelt in woods, where they lived upon the wild products and fruits of the earth, and never drank wine, nor married. In some cases they did not form themselves into societies, but each had his private recess, where he studied and performed his devotions by himself. These were a kind of hermits, of which some are said to have dwelt on a mountain in Ethiopia.

They were called *Gymnosophists*, i. e. naked philosophers, not because they went absolutely naked, but perhaps in ridicule, because they wore only

* Ricaut's State of the Greek Church. King's History of the Greek Church, p. 11—134. Father Simon's Religion of the Eastern Nations, p. 5—8. Thevenot's Travels, p. 412. Broughton's Hist. Lib. vol i. p. 145. History of Religion, vol. vi. p. 251—253. Pinkerton's Greek Church in Russia.

what was required for decency and convenience. Some of them attained to eminence in the sciences, and practised medicine. They are supposed to have had their origin from the Bramins.*

H

HALCYONS, a denomination which arose in 1802, and took the title of the Halcyon Church in Columbia. This church admits men of different sentiments into its fellowship; they profess to adhere strictly to the scriptures, and renounce all manner of creeds and confessions of faith.

They deny the doctrine of the trinity; and say, "there is no other God, nor person in the godhead, but the Father—and the Messiah is the personality of the Father," and "the Father cannot be known as a person, only as he was pleased to assume personality in his anointed." They also deny the doctrine of the eternal punishment of the wicked. They assert that both the fallen angels and wicked men will cease to exist at the close of the mediatorial kingdom of our Saviour.

They practise baptism in this manner: those who profess their faith in Christ, walk down to the water in procession, with a large congregation, accompanied with vocal and instrumental music, and are baptized by pouring water on the head, in the name of our Lord Jesus Christ, and using these words: "By the authority of the great head of Zion, I baptize thee in the name of our Lord Jesus Christ, by whom is exhibited, in one glorious person, Father, Son, and Holy Ghost. Amen."

The members of the Halcyon church devote their children to the Lord, not by baptism, but by dedicating them to the Lord, and placing them under the guardianship of the church, the members of which receive them in their arms; and petition the Lord for a blessing on them, and watch over them, that they may receive a religious education.†

HALDANITES, so called from Messrs. Robert and James Haldane, brothers of very respectable characters, who possess an ample fortune. These gentlemen seceded from the church of Scotland, and are what is called open communion Baptists. They admit to the fellowship of their churches, all whom they consider christians, though differing from them about baptism, and other subjects. Saintship they consider

* Ency. Perth.

† Halcyon Epistle, addressed to christians of all denominations, published 1803.

as the basis of christian union, and believe that the bible teaches christians mutual forbearance, *&c.

The first object the Messrs. Haldanes had in view, was to devote themselves to the propagation of the gospel in India; but being prevented by the East India Company, they turned their attention to its dissemination at home. Accordingly in 1797, they formed a society, whose professed object was to send forth men to preach the gospel in those parts of Scotland where they conceived this blessing was not enjoyed in its purity, and where it was not regularly dispensed. The members of this society travelled at different times, through the greater part of Scotland, preaching the gospel to their countrymen, and it was their invariable rule, not to receive any compensation for their labours. They spent large sums in the erection of convenient places of worship in Edinburgh and in Glasgow, and in other means of promoting religion.

This society reject all creeds and confessions of faith, and profess to take the scriptures as the sole rule of doctrine, discipline, and worship. They are independents in the strictest sense of the word; and no denomination disclaim more than they, either following men, or being followed by others in matters of religion.

The Messrs. Haldanes are pastors over a considerably large church in Edinburgh. When they became baptists, a very considerable number of the church separated. Some of these united together as a church, chose pastors, and to this day continue independents. Another part of them are under the pastoral care of Mr. Innes, who became a baptist, after examining the subject. His change of sentiment did not occasion a separation, as from his first settlement differences in opinion were made a subject of forbearance, which was not the case at first with the Messrs. Haldanes. Messrs. Erving and Wardlaw were in union with these gentlemen previous to their becoming baptists. At that time, and for some time after, various religious subjects were under discussion at Glasgow, and in several other places, where there were churches. These discussions led to inquiry in the various churches connected with them; under some of them a separation took place. The Messrs. Haldanes, and also Erving and Wardlaw, are said to favour some of the doctrines of Sandeman.

A few years since, a number of ministers came from Scotland to America, in the character of missionaries of the independent persuasion, and some of them were patronized by the liberal Robert Haldane of Edin-

* See a tract written by Mr. James Haldane on that subject; and also his Remarks on Mr. Jones' Review of his observations on forbearance.

burgh. These missionaries, after travelling a short time in different parts of the United States, were led to embrace the baptist sentiments. Some churches have been founded by the converts;—among others, Mr. Walter Balfour has gathered a small church in Boston and Charlestown, to which he still ministers.

These churches disapprove of all connexion with the world, in the support of the gospel and with other churches in choosing and ordaining elders. They deny, that present ministers are successors of the apostles in the sense frequently conveyed on baptismal and other occasions; and that their office, as teachers and rulers in the church, should be known by any distinction in dress or titles. They maintain weekly communion—reject creeds and confessions of faith; and use no platform of church government but the scriptures.

They have been supposed by some to have imbibed Sandeman's notions of faith, divine influence, religious experience, &c. This charge they deny; but admit that they favour some of the doctrines of Sandeman, because they conceive they are taught in the scriptures.*

HATTEMISTS derive their name from P. Van Hattem, a minister in the province of Zealand, in the seventeenth century. He interpreted the Calvinistic doctrine concerning absolute decrees, so as to deduce from it the system of a fatal and uncontroulable necessity. He denied the difference between moral good and evil, and the corruption of human nature. Hence he concluded, that mankind were under no sort of obligation to endeavour after a regular obedience to the divine laws; but that the whole of religion consisted, not in acting, but in suffering; and that all the precepts of Christ are reducible to this one—that we bear with patience the events that happen, and make it our study to maintain tranquillity of mind. He also affirmed, that Christ had not satisfied the divine justice by his death and sufferings: but had only signified to us thereby that the Deity was propitious towards mankind. He maintained farther, that this was Christ's manner of justifying sinners: and also that God does not so properly punish men *for* their sins, as *by* them.† See *Necessarians.*

*HEATHEN, a term which, like Gentiles, was applied formerly to all nations but the Jews, and is still applicable to all pagan nations.

*HEBREWS, the posterity of *Eber*, the ancestor of Abraham (Gen. xi. 16—26) and the

* Benedict's History of the Baptists, vol. ii. p. 407, 408, 409.
The compiler of this work has been favoured by Mr. Balfour, mentioned above, as the pastor of a church of weekly communion baptists, with much of the information contained in this article.

† Mosheim, vol. iv. p. 553—554.

Jews. So Paul, being by both parents a Jew, calls himself an Hebrew of the Hebrews, Phil. iii. 5. Some think, however, that the term was used in allusion to its original import, a *pilgrim* or stranger; so they read, Gen. x. 21. Shem was the father of all the children not of Eber, but of *passage* or pilgrimage, i. e. of all pilgrims.* See Heb. xi. 12—16.

HELCESAITES, or **Helsaites**: See *Elcesaites;* and to what is there said, it may be added, that they appear to be a party of Ebionites, called also Ossens, Sampseans, and Ampsenians, who subsisted under one or other of these names through most part of the second and third centuries. Their opinions are involved in much obscurity: thus far seems to be ascertained, that they rejected certain parts of both the old and new testaments; and in some cases excused apostasy, or at least admitted of equivocation, when called upon to renounce christianity.†

***HELLENISTS**, Jews who speak the Greek language. Acts vi. 1.‡ To such we are indebted for the Greek version of the old testament, commonly called the Septuagint, or the version of the *seventy*. Others think they were Grecian proselytes to the Jewish religion, Grecian Jews.§

***HEMERO-BAPTISTS**, a Jewish sect which practised *daily* baptism, or frequent religious washings; which is said to have been the case also with the *Christians* of *St. John*, at least on some occasions.‖

HENRICIANS, the followers of one Henry, a pious and zealous monk of the twelfth century. He rejected the baptism of infants, censured with severity the licentious manners of the clergy, whom he in vain attempted to reform, and treated the festivals and ceremonies of the church with great contempt. He died in prison.¶

HERACLEONITES, the followers of Heracleon, from whom they were named.** See *Valentinians*.

HERMOGENIANS, a denomination which arose towards the close of the second century; so denominated from Hermogenes, a painter by profession. He regarded matter as the turbid fountain of all evil, and could not persuade himself that God had created it, because he was willing to attribute to him nothing but good; he believed however, that from this eternal mass of evil and corruption, the Deity formed this beautiful world, and its inhabitants, both celestial and terrestrial.††

HERNHUTTERS, Mora-

* Parkhurst's Greek Lex. in Ἑβραῖος.

† Lardner's Heretics, p. 424, &c. ‡ Doddridge in loc.

§ Wolfius in loc. Parkhurst's Greek Lex. in Ἑλληνιστής.

‖ Scotch Theol. Dict. ¶ Mosh. vol. ii. p. 448. ** Brough. vol i. p. 484.

†† Mosheim, vol. i. p. 190. Lardner's Heretics, p. 374, &c.

vians, or united brethren, so called from their settlement at Hernhuth. See *United Brethren.*

HERODIANS, those Jews who adhered to Herod and the Roman government, and in many instances symbolized with the heathen, in opposition to the patriotic party, which adhered closely to the Mosaic law, and groaned under this foreign yoke. They were chiefly Sadducees, and persons of licentious manners.* See *Mark* viii. 15.

HETEROUSIANS, a name given to one of the Arian divisions, which taught that the nature of the Son was not even similar to that of the Father. See *Homoiousians.*

HIERACITES, a denomination in the third century; so called from their leader Hierax, a philosopher and magician of Egypt, who maintained that the principal object of Christ's ministry, was the promulgation of a new law, more severe and perfect than that of Moses. Hence he concluded that the use of flesh, wine, wedlock, and of other things agreeable to the outward senses, which had been permitted under the Mosaic dispensation, was absolutely prohibited by Christ. He is said to have excluded from the kingdom of heaven children who died before they had arrived to the use of reason; and that upon the supposition that God was bound to administer rewards to those *only* who had fairly finished their victorious conflict with the body and its lusts: he maintained also that Melchisedec was the Holy Ghost. His disciples taught, that the Word, or Son of God, is contained in the Father, as a little vessel in a great one; whence they had the name of *Metangismonites,* from the Greek word *μεταγγισμονος.* He also denied the doctrine of the resurrection.†

HINDOOS, or HINDUS, otherwise called *Gentoos,* the original inhabitants of Hindoostan or Indostan and the bramins are their priests. They pretend that their legislator, Brama, bequeathed to them a book, called the *vedas,* containing his doctrines and instructions. The shanscrit‡ language, in which the vedas§ are written, was, for many centuries, concealed in the hands of the bramins; but has at length been brought to light, by the indefatigable industry of the

* Stackhouse's Hist. of the Bible, vol. v. p. 128. † Mosheim, vol. i. p. 246.

‡ The shanscrit language was till lately little known even in Asia. It is deemed sacred by the bramins, and confined solely to the offices of religion. The import of its name is, according to the eastern style, *the language of perfection.* Encyclopædia, vol. xiv. p. 520.

§ The antiquity of the vedas has been much questioned by European scholars. There is a very able treatise on the subject, by R. T. Coleridge, Esq. in the eighth vol of the Asiatic Researches. He thinks interpolations will be found in their sacred writings or vedas, and says that such have been found by Sir Wm. Jones and Mr. Blaquiere; but adds, that the greatest part of the books, received by the learned Hindus, will assuredly be found genuine.

late learned and ingenious Sir Wm. Jones and others.

The Rev. Mr. Maurice, a learned writer of the present day, has, in an elaborate work, entitled, "A history of the antiquities of India," traced the origin of the Hindoo nation, and developed their religious system. The following imperfect sketch of the religion of Hindostan, is taken from that author.

He supposes that the first migration of mankind took place before the confusion of tongues at Babel, from the region of Ararat, where the ark rested. By the time the earth was sufficiently dry for so long a journey, either Noah himself, or some descendant of Shem, gradually led on the first journey to the western frontiers of India; that this increasing colony flourished for a long succession of ages in primitive happiness and innocence; practised the purest rites of the patriarchal religion, without images and temples, till at length the descendants of Ham invaded and conquered India, and corrupted their ancient religion.

According to the Hindoo theology, Brahme,* the great being, is the supreme, eternal, uncreated God. Brama, the first created being, by whom he made and governs the world, is the prince of the beneficent spirits. He is assisted by Vishnu, the great preserver of men, who, nine several times, appeared upon earth, and under a human form, for the most beneficent purposes. Vishnu is often styled Crishna, the Indian Apollo, and in his character greatly resembles the Mithra of Persia. This prince of the benevolent Deutas has for a coadjutor Mahadeo, or Siva, the destroying power of God. And this three-fold divinity, armed with the terrours of almighty power, pursue through the whole extent of creation the rebellious Deutas, headed by Mahasoor, the great

* According to Sir W. Jones, the supreme God Brahme, in his triple form, is the only self-existent divinity acknowledged by the philosophical Hindoo. When they consider the divine power, as exerted in creating or giving existence to that which existed not before, they call the Deity Brahme. When they view him in the light of destroyer, or rather changer of forms, he is called Mahadeo, Siva, and various other names. When they consider him as the preserver of created things, they give him the name of Vishnu; for since the power of preserving creation by a superintending providence belongs eminently to the godhead, they hold that power to exist transcendently in the preserving member of the triad, whom they suppose to be every where always; not in substance, but in spirit and energy. See Asiatic Researches.

Following the leading ideas of Sir W. Jones, Mr. Maurice asserts, that there is a perpetual recurrence of the sacred triad in the Asiatic mythology; that the doctrine of a trinity was promulgated in India, in the geeta, 1500 years before the birth of Plato; for of that remote date are the Elephanta cavern, and the Indian history of Mahabharat, in which a triad of Deity are alluded to, and designated. Hence he supposes that the doctrine of a trinity was delivered from the ancient patriarchs, and diffused over the east during the migration and dispersion of their Hebrew posterity.

malignant spirit who seduced them, and dart upon their flying bands the fiery shafts of divine vengeance.

The nine incarnations of Vishnu, represent the Deity descending in a human shape to accomplish certain awful and important events, as in the instance of the three first; to confound blaspheming vice, to subvert gigantic tyranny, and to avenge oppressed innocence, as in the five following; or finally, as the ninth to abolish human sacrifices.

The Hindoo system teaches the existence of good and evil genii, or, in the language of Hindostan, debtas, dewtas, or devitas. These are represented as eternally conflicting together; and the incessant conflict which subsisted between them filled creation with uproar, and all its subordinate classes with dismay.

The doctrine of the metempsychosis, or transmigration of souls, is universally believed in India, from which country it is supposed to have originated many centuries before the birth of Plato, and was first promulgated in the geeta of Uyasa, the Plato of India. This doctrine teaches that degenerate spirits, fallen from their original rectitude, migrate through various bobuns, in the bodies of different animals.

The Hindoos suppose that there are fourteen bobuns, or spheres; seven below, and seven above the earth. The spheres above the earth are gradually ascending. The highest is the residence of Brahma and his particular favourites. After the soul transmigrates through various animal mansions, it ascends up the great sideral ladder of seven gates, and through the revolving spheres, which are called in India, the bobuns of purification.

It is the invariable belief of the bramins that man is a fallen creature. Their doctrine of the transmigration of the soul is built upon this foundation. The professed design of the metempsychosis was to restore the fallen soul to its pristine state of perfection and blessedness. The Hindoos represent the Deity as punishing only to reform his creatures. Nature itself exhibits one vast field of purgatory for the classes of existence. Their sacred writings represent the whole universe as an ample and august theatre for the probationary exertion of millions of beings, who are supposed to be so many spirits degraded from the high honours of angelical distinction, and condemned to ascend, through various gradations of toil and suffering,* to that exalted sphere of perfection and happiness which

* It is supposed that Pythagoras derived his doctrine of transmigration from the Indian bramins; for in that ancient book, the institutes of Menu, said to be compiled many centuries before Pythagoras was born, there is a long chapter on transmigration and final beatitude. It is there asserted, that so far as vital souls, addicted to sensuality, indulge themselves in forbidden pleasures, even

they enjoyed before their defection.

This doctrine, so universally prevalent in Asia, that man is a fallen creature, gave birth to the persuasion, that by severe sufferings, and a long series of probationary discipline, the soul might be restored to its primitive purity. Hence oblations the most costly, and sacrifices the most sanguinary, in the hope of propitiating the angry powers, forever loaded the altars of the pagan deities. They had even sacrifices denominated those of *regeneration*, and those sacrifices were always profusely stained with blood.

The Hindoos suppose that the vicious are consigned to perpetual punishment in the animation of successive animal forms, till, at the stated period, another renovation of the four jugs, or grand astronomical periods, shall commence upon the dissolution of the present. Then they are called to begin anew the probationary journey of souls, and all will be finally happy.

The destruction of the existing world by fire is another tenet of the bramins.

The temples, or pagodas, for divine worship in India, are magnificent; and their religious rites are pompous and splendid. Since the Hindoos admit that the Deity occasionally assumes an elementary form, without defiling his holiness, they make various idols to assist their imaginations, when they offer up their prayers to the invisible Deity.

Besides the daily offerings of rice, fruits, and ghee, at the pagodas, the Hindoos have a grand annual sacrifice, not very unlike that of the scape-goat among the Hebrews.* They inculcate various and frequent ablutions, which are intended as means of purifying their souls from sin.

to the same degree shall the acuteness of their senses be raised in their future bodies, that they may suffer analogous pain.

* The necessity of some atonement for sin, is one of the prevailing ideas among the Hindoos. Hence they sacrifice certain animals at stated seasons, and particularly a horse, which is the victim above referred to; and hence the voluntary tortures which they inflict upon themselves. Mr. Swartz, one of the Malabarian missionaries, who was instrumental in converting two thousand persons to the christian religion, relates that a certain man on the Malabar coast had inquired of various devotees and priests how he might make atonement; and at last he was directed to drive iron spikes, sufficiently blunted, through his sandals; and on these spikes he was to place his naked feet, and walk about four hundred and eighty miles. If, through loss of blood, or weakness of body, he was necessitated to halt, he was obliged to wait for healing and strength. He undertook his journey; and while he halted under a large shady tree, where the gospel was sometimes preached, one of the missionaries came and preached in his hearing from these words: "The blood of Jesus Christ cleanseth from all sin." While he was preaching, the man rose up, threw off his torturing sandals, and cried out aloud, *This is what I want;* and he became a living witness of the truth of that passage of scripture, which had such a happy effect upon his mind. See Baptist Annual Register for 1794.

The Hindoo religionists are divided into a great variety of sects, but ultimately branch forth into two principal ones; those of Vishnu and Siva, the worshippers of the Deity in his preserving and destroying capacities.

There subsists to this day among the Hindoos a voluntary sacrifice of too singular and shocking a nature to pass unnoticed; which is that of the wives burning themselves with the bodies of their deceased husbands. These women are trained from their infancy in the full conviction of their celestial rank; and the belief that this voluntary sacrifice is the most glorious period of their lives; and that thereby the celestial spirit is released from its transmigrations, and the evils of a miserable existence, and flies to join the spirit of their deceased husbands in a state of purification.

In a particular district of Bengal, religious veneration is paid to the *cow;* in former times it was universal through Hindostan. This animal is venerated in a religious sense, as holding in the rotation of the metempsychosis the rank immediately preceding the human form; and in a political sense as being the most useful and necessary of the whole animal creation, to a people forbidden to feed on any thing which has breathed the breath of life.

From the earliest period, the people of India, like the Chinese, seem to have maintained the same religion, laws, and customs. The religion of the Hindoos, though involved in superstition and idolatry, seems to have been originally pure; inculcating the belief of an eternal and omnipotent Being; their subordinate deities, Brama, Vishnu, and Siva, being only representatives of the wisdom, goodness, and power of the supreme Brahme, whom they call "*The Principal of Truth, the Spirit of Wisdom, and the Supreme Being;*" though others think them emblematic of the mysterious doctrine of the trinity, as believed by the ancient Hebrews.

It is a singular circumstance that there is a striking similarity between the sacred rites of the Hindoos and those of the ancient Jews; for instance, between the character of the bramins or priests, and the Jewish levites; between the ceremony of the scape-goat, and a Hindoo ceremony, in which a horse is used for the goat. Many obsolete customs, alluded to in the old testament, might also receive illustration from the religious ceremonies of the Hindoos. They are perfectly indifferent about making proselytes or converts to their religion, alleging, that all religions are equally acceptable to the supreme Being; and that his wisdom and power would not have permitted such a variety, if he had not found pleasure in beholding them.

Mr. Halhed, in his code of Gentoo laws, has translated

an extract from a preliminary discourse to their code, which represents the Gentoo as the most tolerant of all religions. According to this extract, "the diversities of belief among mankind, are a manifest demonstration of the power of the supreme Being. For it is evident that a painter, by sketching a multiplicity of figures, and by arranging a variety of colours, procures reputation among men; and a gardener gains credit by producing a number of different flowers. It is, therefore, absurdity and ignorance, to view in an inferiour light, him, who created both the painter and gardener." Our author goes on to infer, from the varieties in created things, that the supreme Being has appointed and views different forms of religious worship with complacency. It has, however, been said, that even the tolerance of which the Gentoo religion boasts, is confined to the diversities among themselves. But Sir Wm. Jones thinks, that the reason christianity is not more readily received among them—is, that they confound their own religion with it, and consider the advent of Christ, as nothing more than one of the incarnations of Vishnu.

The baptist society, which was founded in 1792, for evangelizing the heathen, first sent two of their ministers; viz. Mr. *J. Thomas*, and Mr. *W. Carey*, to this country: and all their communications, as well as the testimonies of many others who have made particular inquiry into these things, fully confirm the above remarks.

For seven years Mr. Carey and his colleague, with another who joined them, seem to have laboured without any real success. But in the latter end of the year 1800, after the arrival of four more missionaries, and when they had formed a settlement at Serampore, in the vicinity of Calcutta, success began to attend their labours. The new testament, which had been translated into Bengalee, was now printed; and several of the natives, who, it had been said, would never relinquish *caste*, cheerfully made this sacrifice, and were baptized in the name of the Lord Jesus. From that time to this they have been gradually increasing; and the scriptures have been translated into several of the eastern languages; missionaries have also been sent from other societies.

HOFFMANISTS, those who espoused the sentiments of Daniel Hoffman, professor in the university of Helmstadt, who in the year 1598 taught that the light of reason, even as it appears in the writings of Plato and Aristotle, is adverse to religion; and that the more the human understanding is cultivated by philosophical study, the more perfectly is the enemy supplied with weapons of defence.*

* Enfield's History of Philosophy, vol. ii. p. 5.

HOMOIOUSIANS, a name given to a branch of the Arians, who maintained that the nature of the Son was *similar* to that of the Father. See *Arians.*

HOPKINSIANS, or **Hopkintonians**, so called from the Rev. Samuel Hopkins, D. D. pastor of the first congregational church at Newport: who in his sermons and tracts has made several additions to the sentiments first advanced by the celebrated Jonathan Edwards, late president of New Jersey college.

The following is a summary of their distinguishing tenets, with a few of the reasons by which they are supported.

I. That all true virtue, or real holiness, consists in *disinterested benevolence.* The object of benevolence is universal being, including God and all intelligent creatures. It wishes and seeks the good of every individual, so far as is consistent with the greatest good of the whole, which is comprised in the glory of God, and the perfection and happiness of his kingdom. The law of God is the standard of all moral rectitude, or *holiness.* This is reduced into love to God, and to our neighbour: and universal good-will comprehends all the love to God, our neighbour, and ourselves, required in the divine law; and therefore must be the whole of holy obedience. Let any person reflect on what are the particular branches of true piety; and he will find that disinterested affection is the distinguishing characteristic of each. For instance: all which distinguishes pious fear from the fear of the wicked, consists in love. Holy gratitude is nothing but good will to God and man, ourselves included, excited by a view of the good will and kindness of God. Justice, truth, and faithfulness, are comprised in universal benevolence; so are temperance and chastity: for an undue indulgence of our appetites and passions is contrary to benevolence, as tending to hurt ourselves or others; and so opposite to the general good and the divine command. In short, all virtue is nothing but love to God and our neighbour, made perfect in all its genuine exercises and expressions.

II. That all sin consists in *selfishness.* By this is meant an interested affection, by which a person sets himself up as the supreme, or only object of regard; and nothing is lovely in his view, unless suited to promote his private interest. This self-love is, every degree of it, enmity against God: it is not subject to the law of God, and is the only affection that can oppose it. It is the foundation of all spiritual blindness, and the source of all idolatry and false religion. It is the foundation of all covetousness and sensuality; of all falsehood, injustice, and oppression; as it excites mankind, by undue methods, to invade the property of others. Self-love produces all the violent passions; envy, wrath, clamour, and evil speaking: and every thing contrary to the divine law, is briefly comprehended in this fruitful source of iniquity, *self-love.*

III. That there are no promises of regenerating grace made to the actions of the unregenerate. For as far as men act from self-love, they act for a bad end: for those, who have no true love to God, really fulfil no duty when they attend on the externals of religion.*

IV. That the impotency of sinners, with respect to believing in Christ, is not natural, but *moral:* for it is a plain dictate of common sense, that natural impossibility excludes all blame. But an unwilling mind is universally considered as a crime, and not as an excuse; and is the very thing wherein our wickedness consists.

V. That, in order to faith in Christ, a sinner must approve in his heart of the divine conduct, *even though God should cast him off forever;* which however neither implies love to misery, nor hatred of happiness.† For if the law is good, death is due to those who have broken it; and the judge of all the earth cannot but do right. Gen. xviii. 25. It would bring everlasting reproach upon his government to spare us, considered merely as in ourselves. When this is felt in our hearts, and not till then, we shall be prepared to look to the free grace of God, through Christ's redemption.

VI. That the infinitely wise and holy God has exerted his omnipotent power, in such a manner as he purposed should be followed with the existence and entrance of *moral evil* in the system. For it must be ad-

* The author of the moral Disquisitions, while comparing Hopkinsian-Calvinists with real Calvinists, has this inference: "It is evident that Hopkinsian sentiments are only the genuine, flourishing, and fruitful branches of the calvinistic tree: for the Hopkinsians plead that there is no duty in the actions of sinners, because they are totally depraved. The broad foundation, which supports our ample superstructure, was long since deeply and firmly laid in the first principles of calvinism. To support our theory we need no first principles, except those which Calvinists have adopted and improved against Pelagians and Arminians." See Spring's moral Disquisitions, p. 40.

† "As a particle of water is small, in comparison of a generous stream, so the man of humility feels small before the great family of his fellow-creatures. He values his soul; but when he compares it to the great soul of mankind, he almost forgets and loses sight of it: for the governing principle of his heart is to estimate things according to their worth. When, therefore, he indulges a humble comparison with his Maker, he feels lost in the infinite fulness and brightness of divine love, as a ray of light is lost in the sun, and a particle of water in the ocean. It inspires him with the most grateful feelings of heart, that he has opportunity to be in the hand of God, as clay in the hand of the potter; and as he considers himself in this humble light, he submits the nature and size of his future vessel entirely to God. As his pride is lost in the dust, he looks up with pleasure towards the throne of God, and rejoices with all his heart in the rectitude of the divine administration."

mitted on all hands, that God has a perfect knowledge, foresight, and view of all possible existences and events. If that system and scene of operation, in which moral evil should never have existence, was actually preferred in the divine mind, certainly the Deity is infinitely disappointed in the issue of his own operations.

VII. That the introduction of *sin* is, upon the whole, for the general *good*. For the wisdom and power of the Deity are displayed in carrying on designs of the greatest good: and the existence of moral evil has, undoubtedly, occasioned a more full, perfect, and glorious discovery of the infinite perfections of the divine nature, than could otherwise have been made to the view of creatures.

VIII. That repentance is *before* faith in Christ. By this is not intended, that repentance is before a speculative belief of the being and perfections of God and of the person and character of Christ; but only, that true repentance is previous to a saving faith in Christ, in which the believer is united to Christ, and entitled to the benefits of his mediation and atonement. So Christ commanded, *Repent ye, and believe the gospel;* and Paul preached *repentance towards God, and faith towards our Lord Jesus Christ.* Mark i. 15. Acts xx. 21.

IX. That, though men became sinners by Adam, according to a divine constitution, yet they were, and are accountable for no sins but personal; for (1.) Adam's act, in eating the forbidden fruit, was not the *act* of his posterity; therefore they did not sin at the same time he did. (2.) The sinfulness of that act could not be *transferred* to them afterwards: because the sinfulness of an act can no more be tranferred from one person to another, than an act itself. (3.) Therefore Adam's act, in eating the forbidden fruit, was not the *cause,* but only the *occasion* of his posterity's being sinners. Adam sinned, and now God brings his posterity into the world sinners.

X. That though believers are justified *through* Christ's righteousness, yet his righteousness is not *transferred* to them. For personal righteousness cannot be transferred from one person to another, nor personal sin, otherwise the sinner would become innocent and Christ the sinner. (See *Crispians.*) The scripture, therefore, represents believers as receiving only the *benefits* of Christ's righteousness in justification, or their being pardoned and accepted for Christ's righteousness' sake: and this is the proper scripture notion of imputation. Jonathan's righteousness was imputed to Mephibosheth, when David showed kindness to him for his father Jonathan's sake. 2 Sam. ix. 7.

The Hopkinsians warmly advocate the doctrine of the divine decrees, that of particular election, total depravity, the special influences of the spirit of God in regeneration, justification by faith alone, the final perseverance of the saints, and the consistency between entire freedom and absolute dependence; and therefore claim it as their just due, since the world will make distictions, to be called *Hopkinsian Calvinists.**

In this place it may be proper to notice the difference between Calvinists and Hopkinsians, which consists in the following particulars: Firstly, on the origin of sin. Secondly, on the consequences of Adam's sin. Thirdly, on the nature and character of virtue or holiness. Fourthly, on the nature of sin. Fifthly, on the nature and extent of the atonement. Sixthly, on the effects of divine influences. Seventhly, on justification. Eighthly, on the christian graces.

Firstly, *on the origin of sin.* Calvinists, though they maintain, that "God hath decreed whatsoever comes to pass;" yet deny that he is the efficient author of sin;—but the Hopkinsians assert, that God is the efficacious cause of all volitions in the human heart, whether good or evil.†

Secondly, *on the consequences of Adam's sin.* The Calvinists maintain, that "All mankind sinned in and fell with Adam, in his first transgression:" the Hopkinsians assert, that Adam alone was guilty of original sin; that guilt is a personal thing, and can no more be transferred than action. Calvinists‡ maintain, that mankind, since the fall, labour under a natural or physical incapacity to obey God;—but the Hopkinsians suppose, that total depravity consists in the opposition of the heart or will, to do what they are really able to perform; which they call *moral inability.*

Thirdly, *on the nature and character of virtue or holiness.* Calvinists maintain, that holiness in a moral agent consists in the conformity of the whole being to the will of God. The Hopkinsians assert, that holiness in a moral agent consists exclusively in disinterested benevolence, and that those who love God for what he is, abstractedly considered, will be willing§ to sacrifice their temporal and eter-

* Hopkins on Holiness, p. 7—202. Edwards on the Will, p. 234—289. Bellamy's True Religion Delineated, p. 16. Edwards on the Nature of True Virtue. Bellamy's Dialogues, p. 185. West's Essays on Moral Agency, p. 170—181. Spring's Nature of Duty, p. 23. Moral Disquisitions, p. 40. Manuscript by Dr. Emmons.

† Dr. Hopkins says, that "God is as much the author of sinful, as of holy volitions, and that the professed Calvinist, who denies this, is not so consistent with himself as the Arminian." See Hopkins' System, vol. i. p. 197.

‡ Some who call themselves Calvinists maintain with the Hopkinsians, that the inability of sinners is of a moral nature.

§ The willingness Hopkinsians contend for, is restricted to those moments, while as yet the regenerate man has no certain evidence that he is a christian, or that God will save him.

nal interest for the glory of God, and the greater good of the whole. Calvinists maintain, that love to God originates from a sense of his goodness to us in particular, as well as from a consideration of the perfections of his nature; and deny that love to God implies in any circumstances a willingness to be eternally condemned.

Fourthly, *on the nature of sin.* Calvinists define sin to be, " any want of conformity unto, or transgression of the law of God." The Hopkinsians assert, that sin consists exclusively in selfish moral exercises.

Fifthly, *on the extent and nature of the atonement.* Many of the Calvinists maintain that Jesus Christ, by his death and sufferings, made an atonement for the sins of the elect only. The Hopkinsians assert, that the atonement was coextensive with the effects of the fall; and that Christ died not for a select number only, but for all mankind; they suppose, however, that though by the atonement* a way was opened for all, yet none but those who were elected to eternal life will be saved.

The Calvinists maintain that Christ was substituted for the elect, to obey and suffer in their stead, and was by imputation legally guilty, and that God cannot consistently with his justice, refuse to pardon those, whom Christ has ransomed by undergoing the penalty due to their sins. On the other hand, the Hopkinsians assert, that the atonement differs essentially from all notions of debt and credit, and is simply an exhibition of God's hatred to sin, and regard to his holy law. By the atonement, a way is opened for the great governour of the world, consistently to bestow or withhold mercy as should most effectually answer the purposes of divine goodness.

Sixthly, *on the effects of divine influences.* The Calvinists maintain that " effectual calling is the work of God's spirit, whereby convincing us of our sin and misery, enlightening our minds in the knowledge of Christ, and renewing our wills, he doth persuade and enable us to embrace Jesus Christ, freely offered to us in the gospel. The Hopkinsians assert, that " effectual calling consists in God's creating in the hearts of sinners, by his own immediate energy, a willingness to be saved." They teach, that all God performs by his holy spirit is to make them willing to do, what they are really able to do before.

The Calvinists maintain, that the best actions of good men are blended with imperfection; but some of the most eminent of the Hopkinsian divines teach that every moral exercise of a

* The Hopkinsians say, that " atonement and redemption are widely different in their nature and effects; the former sets open the door of mercy, the latter applies the benefits of Christ." See the Triangle, p. 62

renewed person, is either perfectly good or perfectly evil.*

Seventhly, *on justification.* The Calvinists maintain, that "justification is an act of God's free grace, wherein he pardoneth all our sins, and accepteth us as righteous in his sight, only for the righteousness of Christ, imputed to us and received by faith alone." The Hopkinsians teach that, though the righteousness of Christ is the only ground of a sinner's justification, his righteousness is not transferred to them. According to their system, neither sin nor holiness can be transferred, either from Adam to his posterity, or from Christ to his people.

Eighthly, *on the christian graces.* The Calvinists maintain, that true faith in Christ is the beginning of spiritual life, and the foundation of all the other christian graces. The Hopkinsians assert, that repentance is previous to faith; and that love comprehends in its essence all the christian graces.

The reader may compare the standard works of the Calvinists and Hopkinsians, from which the general collective sentiments of each denomination may be known. There are so many shades of difference between Calvinists and Hopkinsians; and Hopkinsians differ so much among themselves, that it is next to impossible to draw the line between them, so as to do perfect justice to all.

Those who wish to see a more detailed account of the real and verbal differences between Calvinists and Hopkinsians, may consult Ely's Contrast, Wilson's Letters to Ely, the Triangle, a Series of Numbers upon Three Theological Points, &c. published at New York, 1816—1817, and Wilson on the atonement, published at Philadelphia, 1817.

HUGONOTS, or HUGUENOTS, a name given by way of contempt to the reformed, or protestant Calvinists in France, about 1560. The name is variously derived; some take it from a gate in Tours, called *Hugon*, where they first assembled; others from a faulty French pronunciation of the German word *eidgnossen*, or confederates; and others from the first words of their original protest, or confession of faith, "*Huc nos venimus*," &c. The persecution which these people underwent has scarcely its parallel in history; in 1572, upwards of 70,000 of them were butchered in various parts of France, on the memorable eve of St. Bartholomew; nor were their sufferings much mitigated till Henry IV. in 1598, published the edict of Nantz, which secured them the free exercise of their religion. But in

* This doctrine is not held universally among the Hopkinsians; but it is advocated by Dr. Emmons and Dr. Strong.

1685 this edict was cruelly and suddenly revoked by Louis XIV. when the persecution again began; their churches were demolished, their estates confiscated, their persons insulted by the bigoted soldiery; and after the loss of innumerable lives, 500,000 of them were driven into exile in foreign countries.*

*HUMANITARIANS, a term applied to those modern Socinians who maintain with Dr. Priestley the *simple humanity* of Christ; or that Jesus was "a mere man, the son of Joseph and Mary, and naturally as fallible and peccable as Moses, or any other prophet."† See *Socinians* and *Unitarians*.

*HUSSEYITES, a name appropriated to the admirers of Mr. Joseph Hussey, formerly of Cambridge, a learned but eccentric divine. His principal peculiarities of opinion were—the pre-existence of Christ's human soul, or rather of a spiritual or glorious body, in which he appeared to the patriarchs, &c. his high supra-lapsarian notions of the divine decrees, and his objection to all offers or invitations to unconverted sinners.‡ See *Supra-lapsarians* and *Crispites*.

HUSSITES, the followers of John Huss, an eminent divine of Bohemia. He adopted the opinions of Wickliff, and defended them before the council of Constance, who condemned him as an heretic; and he heroically suffered martyrdom in the cause of the reformation, A. D. 1415. His death however excited an open rebellion, and his followers, under the heroic Fiska, became very formidable both to the emperour and the pope, until they at length divided and were overcome.§

HUTCHINSONIANS, the followers of John Hutchinson, Esq. a very learned, ingenious, and laborious layman of Yorkshire, in the last century. After receiving a liberal education, he was appointed successively steward to Mr. Bathurst, the Earl of Scarborough, and the Duke of Somerset. In these situations he paid particular attention to mineralogy and fossils, and formed that fine collection, afterwards bequeathed by Dr. Woodward to the university of Cambridge. He soon, however, confined his attention to scripture philosophy, and from the sacred writings alone formed that system which is usually called by his name. His writings make twelve volumes in octavo, published successively between the years 1724 and 1748.

Mr. Hutchinson begins with discarding what is usually called natural religion, and de-

* Mosheim, vol. iii. p. 404—448. new ed.

† Priestley's Defence of Unitarianism for 1806, p. 101, 102.

‡ Hussey's Glory of Christ unveiled—Operations of grace, but no offers, &c.

§ Mosheim, vol. iv. p. 384—vol. v. p. 117.

rives all his science from the Hebrew scriptures, which he considers as the fountain of true knowledge, both in philosophy and religion.

The *Hebrew* he considers as the primitive language of mankind, and revealed immediately from heaven; but the points and accents he totally discards, considering the Jews as bad guides in the study of the old testament. To every Hebrew root he affixes one radical idea, which he supposes to pervade all its forms; and for this radical idea he trusts more to his own ingenuity and industry in examining the sacred books, than to either lexicographers or translators, as will be seen in the following instances.

The Hebrew name of God, which he calls *Aleim,* he considers as strictly plural, and referring to the persons of the trinity; and the construction of the noun plural with the verb singular, (which is an hebraism,) he views as referring to the unity of the divine essence.

A considerable point of philosophy is founded on the Hebrew *Shemim,* or *names* of the celestial fluid, in the three conditions of fire, light, and spirit; these he explains as the primary emblems of the trinity; observing that the Father is called in scripture "a consuming fire," (Deut. iv. 24.) the Son "the true light," (John i. 9.) and the name of third person is the Holy Spirit—the same word in the sacred languages (as in some others) signifying both spirit and *wind,* or the air in motion.

It should have been remarked that *Alue,* the participle of *Aleim,* is by Mr. Hutchinson appropriated to the second person of the trinity; and as he thinks the noun plural means the *swearers,* or the sacred persons bound by *oath* in covenant for man's redemption; so by *Alue* he understands *that* person on whom the curse of the oath fell, (for he supposes every oath to imply a curse or penalty,) namely, the Son of God incarnate to bear "the curse" for our salvation.

The word *berith,* usually translated *covenant,* he supposes to mean strictly *the purifier;* and, instead of "making a covenant," he would read "cutting off a purifier," alluding to the Lord Jesus, who is compared to "a refiner's fire," and to "fuller's soap," (Mal. iii. 2.) as being the great purifier of his people.

Another term of mysterious import in this system is that of *Cherubim,* which he does not refer to the angelic orders; but considers the cherubic form, namely, the ox, the lion, and the eagle, as typical, firstly of the trinity of nature, (as Mr. Hutchinson speaks,) namely, fire, light, and air; and secondly, as referring to the sacred trinity of persons in the godhead; and the junction of the lion and man, in this emblematic figure, he understands as pointing out the union of the human nature to the Son of God, who is called "the lion of the tribe of Judah."

Thus, from these and some few other radical words, Mr. Hutchinson founds, not only a peculiar theology, but a system of philosophy materially different from that of Sir Isaac Newton. Sir Isaac supposes a vacuum in nature, but Mr. Hutchinson a plenum; conceiving the whole system of nature a vast sphere, in the centre of which is placed the sun: this he considers as an orb of fire, emitting light to the extremities of the system, where it is condensed into air, (or material spirit,) and reverting back to the sun, as it approaches its source is melted (or rather *ground*) into light and fire. In the immense distance of the circumference of this system he places the fixed stars; but admits no other solar system than one, beyond the limits of which he conceives there can be nothing beside outer and utter darkness.

It is an axiom with Mr. Hutchinson, that all our ideas are borrowed from external objects; hence his science is a kind of allegorical philosophy; and he has a peculiar way of spiritualizing the scriptures in reference to scientific objects—as for instance, the cherubim in the tabernacle and temple, as above explained.

It is impossible here to produce (much less examine) the various scriptures on which Mr. Hutchinson and his followers rest their hypothesis; the inquisitive reader will refer to the authorities below. It may be proper to add, that they adopt the copernican (which they esteem the spiritual) system of the heavens, and confirm their notion of the indentity of fire, light, and air, by the modern experiments in electricity.

In expounding the old testament, particularly the psalms, the Hutchinsonians follow the *Cocceians,* (which see) and consider Jesus Christ and his redemption as the sum and substance of the scriptures.*

HYPSISTARII, worshippers of the *most high,* [υψιστος,] a denomination in the fourth century, whose doctrine is reported to have been an assemblage of paganism, judaism, and christianity. They adored the most high God with the christians; but they also revered fire and light with the pagans, and observed the sabbath and the distinction of meats with the jews. They are supposed by some to be a branch of the *Massalians.*†

* Hutchinson's Works, vol. iii. p. 10, &c. Spearman's Inquiry, p. 260—273. Hodge's Elihu, p. 35. Lee's Sophron, vol. i. p. 31; vol. iii. p. 663. Jones' Lectures, p. 9, 10. Skinner's Ecclesiastical History of Scotland, vol. ii. p. 673—676. Forbes' Works. Pike's Philosophia Sacra.

† Encyclopedia, vol. ix. p. 48

I & J

JACOBITES, a denomination of eastern christians in the sixth and seventh centuries, so denominated from Jacob Bardeus, or Ranzalus, a disciple of Eutyches and Dyoscorus. His doctrines spread in Asia and Africa to that degree, that the denomination of the Eutychians was swallowed up by that of the Jacobites, which also comprehended all the Monophysites of the East; i. e. such as acknowledged but one nature, and that human, in Jesus Christ; including the Armenians and Abyssinians. They denied the doctrine of the trinity, and made the sign of the cross with one finger, to intimate the oneness of the godhead.

The Jacobites are of two sects; some following the rites of the Latin church, and others continuing separated from the church of Rome.*

The name Jacobites was used in England in the seventeenth century as a political distinction, to mark the adherents of king James II. who were also called *Nonjurors*. A term very near this, viz. *Jacobins*, was used also to designate the violent party in the French revolution, on account of their holding their meetings in a convent of Jacobins in Paris.

JANSENISTS, a denomination of Roman Catholics in France, which was formed in the year 1640. They follow the opinions of Jansenius, bishop of Ypres, from whose writings the following propositions are said to have been extracted:—1. That there are divine precepts, which good men, notwithstanding their desire to observe them, are nevertheless absolutely unable to obey; nor has God given them that measure of grace which is essentially necessary to render them capable of such obedience.—2. That no person, in this corrupt state of nature, can resist the influence of divine grace, when it operates upon the mind.—3. That, in order to render human actions meritorious, it is not requisite that they be exempt from necessity; but that they be free from constraint.—4. That the semi-pelagians err greatly, in maintaining that the human will is endowed with the power of either receiving or resisting the aids and influences of preventing grace.—5. That whoever affirms that Jesus Christ made expiation, by his sufferings and death, for the sins of all mankind, is a Semi-Pelagian. Of these propositions Pope Innocent X. condemned the first four as heretical, and the last as rash and impious. But he did this without asserting that these were the doctrines of Jansenius, or

* Encyclopedia, vol. ix.

even naming him, which did not satisfy his adversaries, nor silence him. The next pope however, Alexander VII. issued a bull, in which he denounced the said propositions as erroneous doctrines of Jansenius, which excited no small troubles in the Gallican church.

This denomination was also distinguished from many of the Roman Catholics by their maintaining that the holy scriptures and public liturgies should be given to the people in their mother tongue: and they consider it as a matter of importance to inculcate upon all christians, that true piety does not consist in the performance of external devotions, but in inward holiness and divine love.

It is said that Jansenius read through the whole of St. Augustine's works, ten, and some parts thirty times; from these he made a number of *excerpta*, which he collected in his book called *Augustinus*. This he had not the courage to publish; but it was printed after his death, and from it his enemies, the Jesuits, extracted the propositions above named.*

Many of the Jansenists were distinguished for their strict piety, and severe moral discipline. They complained of the corruptions of the church of Rome, censured the licentiousness of the monastic orders, and insisted upon the necessity of reforming their discipline, according to the rules of sanctity, abstinence, and self-denial, that were originally prescribed by their respective founders. The celebrated Pascal, and Quesnel, men eminently distinguished for talents and piety, are ranked among the followers of Jansenius.

JAPANESE. The religion of these islanders is paganism, but under some peculiar forms which deserve attention—particularly, the *Sinto*, the ancient idol worship of the Japanese: the *Budso*, or foreign idol worship, introduced from China: and the religion of their philosophers and moralists.

I. The *Sintos* have some obscure and imperfect notions of the immortality of the soul, and a future state of bliss and misery; they acknowledge a supreme Being, who, they believe, dwells in the highest heaven: and admit of some inferiour gods, whom they place among the stars; but they worship and invoke those gods alone whom they believe to have the sovereign control over this world, its elements, productions, and animals: these, they suppose, will not only render them happy here, but, by interceding for them at the hour of death, may procure them a happy condition hereafter. Hence their *dairis*, or ecclesiastical chiefs, being thought lineally descended from the eldest and most favoured sons of these deities, are supposed to be the true and living images of their gods.

* Mosheim, vol. ii. p. 262. Toplady, Hist. vol. i. p. 92.

The Sintos believe that the soul, after quitting the body, is removed to the high sub-celestial fields, seated just beneath the dwelling places of their gods; that those, who have led a good life, find immediate admission, while the souls of the wicked are denied entrance, and condemned to wander till they have expiated their crimes.

Their religion enjoins abstaining from blood, from eating flesh, or being near a dead body; by which a person is for a time rendered unfit to visit their temples, or to appear in the presence of their gods. It also commands a diligent observance of the solemn festivals, in honour of their gods; pilgrimages to the holy places at Isje; that is, to the temple of Tensio-Dai-Sin, the greatest of all the gods of the Japanese; and the chastisement and mortification of their bodies. But few of them pay much regard to this precept.

II. The most essential points of the *Budso* religion are: That the souls of men and animals are immortal, and both of the same substance, differing only according to the bodies in which they are placed: and that after the souls of mankind have left their bodies, they shall be rewarded or punished according to their behaviour in this life. Their god Armida is the sovereign commander of heaven; and is considered as the patron and protector of human souls; and to obtain his approbation it is requisite to lead a virtuous life, and do nothing contrary to the five commandments, viz. not to kill any thing that has life; not to steal; not to commit fornication; to avoid lies, and all falsehood; not to drink strong liquors. On the other hand, all the vicious, priests or laymen, are, after death, sent to a place of misery, to be tormented for a certain time, according to the nature and number of their crimes, the number of years they lived upon earth, and their opportunities for becoming good and virtuous. Yet they suppose the miseries of these unhappy souls may be greatly alleviated by the virtuous lives of their relations and friends, and still more by the prayers and offerings of the priests to their great god, Armida. When vicious souls have expiated their crimes, they are sent back to animate such vile animals as resembled them in their former state of existence. From the vilest of these transmigrating into other and nobler, they, at last, are suffered again to enter human bodies; and thus have it in their power, by their virtue and piety, to obtain an uninterrupted state of felicity.

III. The philosophers and moralists pay no regard to any of the forms of worship practised in the country. Their supreme good consists in the pleasure and delight which arise from the steady practice of virtue. They do not admit of the transmigration of souls; but believe that there is an universal soul diffused throughout nature, animating all things, and reassuming departed souls as the sea does the rivers. This universal spirit they confound with the supreme Being.

These philosophers consider self-murder as an heroic and commendable action, when it is the only means of avoiding a shameful death, or of escaping from the hands of a victorious enemy. They conform to the general custom of their country, in commemorating their deceased parents and relations, by placing all sorts of provisions on a table provided for the purpose; but they celebrate no other festivals, nor pay any respect to the gods of the country.*

*JASIDEANS, or JESDÆANS, a wandering, ferocious tribe, who frequent the Gordian mountains and the deserts of Curdistan, in Persia. Their priests and rulers are clothed in black, and the rest in white garments. Their religion seems composed of some fragments of christianity, mingled with their ancient pagan superstitions. They pay especial marks of respect, if not worship, to the evil genius, whom they call Carubin or Cherubin, and consider him as one of the chief ministers of the great and good supreme Being, the chief object of their worship, and whose name in the Persian language is Jazid or Jesdan, from which their denomination is probably derived.†

IBERIANS, certain eastern christians of Iberia, now called Georgia, whose tenets are said to be the same with those of the *Greek* church.

*ICONOCLASTES, image breakers; (from εικων, *an image*, and κλαειν, *to break;)* was a name given to those who rejected the use of images in churches, and on certain occasions vented their zeal in destroying them. The great opposition to images began under Bardanes, a Greek emperour in the beginning of the eighth century; and was revived again, a few years after, under Leo the Isaurian, who issued an edict against image worship, which occasioned a civil war in the islands of the Archipelago, and afterwards in Italy; the Roman pontiffs, and the Greek councils, alternately supporting it. At length images were rejected by the Greek church, which, however, retains pictures in churches, though her members do not worship them; but the Latin church not only retained images, but made them the medium, if not the object of their worship, and are therefore called *Iconoduli*, or *Iconolatræ*, i. e. image-worshippers.‡ See *Ikonobortsi.*

*JERUSALEM. See *New-Jerusalem Church*.

* Payne's Epitome of Hist. vol. ii. p. 36—53.
† Mosheim, vol. iv. p. 270.
‡ Mosheim, vol. ii. p. 262, and 887.

JESUITS, a celebrated religious order in the Roman Catholic church, founded by Ignatius Loyola, a Spanish knight, who was born of a respectable family at Loyola, in the province Guipuscoa, in Spain, in 1491. The early part of his life was spent in the military service, in which he acquired great reputation. But when his leg was broken by a cannon ball, at the seige of Pampeluna, in 1521, he employed himself during his confinement, in reading "the Lives of the Saints," which made such a strong impression on his mind, that he determined to renounce the world, to make a pilgrimage to Jerusalem, and to devote himself to the service of God. From this time he led a most austere life, and was indefatigable in his exertions to make converts. His efforts were at length crowned with success. In the year 1537, he gained a number of followers, who bound themselves by five rules, which inculcated the duties of self-mortification and charity, enforced the precepts and practice of virtue, and professed to labour assiduously, without the hope of reward, for the glory of God. They called themselves, "The Society of Jesus." Their zeal was increased by the sanction of the Roman pontiff, Paul III. who by his bull, dated March 1545, permits them to alter, annul or revive, at pleasure, as times, places, and circumstances may require, their constitutions made, or to be made. In another bull dated November, 1549, he gives the general complete jurisdiction over the members, and power over the funds of the society, together with the privilege of sending any individual of the order wherever he may please. The Pope appointed Loyola the first general of this society. He died in 1556, and was canonized 1609. At that time all the miracles of the apostolic ages were said to have been wrought by the influence of his superiour sanctity.

As the object of the order was to obtain influence in all quarters of the globe, and among all classes of men, they naturally became missionaries, school-masters, and confessors. And in a short time they were almost the exclusive, and certainly the most distinguished instructors of youth in every catholic country. They cultivated learning, because they perceived its use in governing mankind, and were not only theologians, but grammarians, critics, mathematicians, philosophers, and poets. They were the confessors of almost every catholic monarch, and person of distinguished rank.

Their wealth, notwithstanding "a vow of poverty," which they found little difficulty in evading, was immense. They obtained a license to trade with the nations whom they undertook to convert. They made themselves masters of a very large province in South America. And thus, although when Loyola, in 1540, petitioned the Pope to authorize the institution of the order, he had only ten disciples, in the year 1608 the number of Jesuits amounted to 10,581. In 1710, the order possessed 24 professed houses, 59 houses of probation, 341 residences, 612 colleges, 200 missions, 150 seminaries, and the society consisted of 19,998 members.

They were expelled from England by proclamation, 2 James I, in 1604—from Venice, in1606—Portugal, 1759—France, 1764—Spain and Sicily, 1767; and finally the celebrated Pope Clement XIV. in July 1773, signed a brief, which suppressed this famous order.

The doctrinal points, which are ascribed to the Jesuits, in distinction from many others of the Roman communion, are as follow.*

I. This order maintained, that the Pope is infallible; that he is the only visible source of that universal and unlimited power, which Christ has granted to the church: that all bishops and subordinate rulers derive from him alone, the authority and jurisdiction, with which they are invested; and that he alone is the supreme lawgiver of that sacred community; a law-giver, whose edicts and commands it is, in the highest degree, criminal to oppose, or dispute, or disobey.

II. They comprehend within the limits of the church, not only many, who live separate from the communion of Rome, but even extend the inheritance of eternal salvation to nations, that have not the least knowledge of the christian religion, or of its divine author; and consider as true members of the church, open transgressors who profess its doctrines.

III. The Jesuits maintain, that human nature is far from being deprived of all power of doing good: that the succours of grace are administered to all mankind, in a measure sufficient to lead them to eternal life and salvation: that the operations of grace offer no violence to the faculties and powers of nature, and therefore may be resisted: and that God, from all eternity, has appointed everlasting rewards and punishments, as the portion of men in a future world, not by an absolute, arbitrary, and unconditional decree, but in consequence of that divine and unlimited prescience, by which he foresaw the actions, merits, and characters, of every individual.

IV. They represent it, as a matter of perfect indifference, from what motives men obey the laws of God, provided these laws are really obeyed; and maintain, that the service of those, who obey from the fear

* This is the representation, which is given by the adversaries of this order. The compiler of this work had not an opportunity to see any of the Jesuits' writings in their own defence.

of punishment, is as agreeable to the Deity, as those actions, which proceed from a principle of love to him and his laws.

V. They maintain, that the sacraments have in themselves an instrumental and efficient power; by virtue of which they work in the soul, independently on its previous preparation or propensities, a disposition to receive the divine grace.

VI. The Jesuits recommend a devout ignorance to such, as submit to their direction, and think a christian ought to yield an unlimited obedience to the orders of the church.

The following maxims are said to be extracted from the moral writings of this order:

I. That persons truly wicked and void of the love of God, may expect to obtain eternal life in heaven, provided, that they be impressed with a fear of the divine anger, and avoid all heinous and enormous crimes, through the dread of future punishment.

II. That those persons may transgress with safety, who have a probable reason for transgressing, i. e. any fair argument or authority in favour of the act they are inclined to perform.

III. That actions intrinsically evil, and directly contrary to the divine law, may be innocently performed by those, who have so much power over their own minds, as to join, even ideally, a good end to this wicked action.

IV. That philosophical sin* is of a very light and trivial nature, and does not deserve the pains of hell.

V. That the transgressions committed by a person, blinded by the seductions of tumultuous passions, and destitute of all sense and impression of religion, however detestable and heinous they may be in themselves, are not imputable to the transgressor before the tribunal of God; and that such transgressions may be often as involuntary, as the actions of a madman.

VI. That the person, who takes an oath, or enters into a contract, may, to elude the force of the one, and obligation of the other, add to the form of the words that express them, certain mental additions and tacit reservations.

This entire society is composed of four sorts of members, viz. novices, scholars, spiritual and temporal coadjutors, and professed members. Beside the three ordinary vows of poverty, chastity, and obedience, which are common to all the monastic tribes, the professed members are obliged to take a fourth, by which they solemnly bind themselves to go, without deliberation or delay, wherever the pope shall think fit to

* By philosophical sin, the Jesuits mean, an action contrary to the dictates of nature and right reason, which is done by a person, who is either absolutely ignorant of God, or does not think of him, during the time this action is committed.

send them. They are governed by a general, who has four assistants. The inferiours of this society are obliged entirely to renounce their own wills, and abide by his directions. Their enterprize has led them into Paraguay, a delightful province of South America ;—here they have founded a government, and instructed and civilized the native Indians.

The general himself is responsible to none but the pope. He nominates all the functionaries of the order, and can remove them at pleasure. Every novice, who offers himself as a candidate for entering into the order, is obliged to confess to his superiour, or to a person appointed by him, not only his sins and defects, but to discover the inclinations, the passions, and the bent of his soul. The society, not satisfied with penetrating in this manner into the inmost recesses of the heart, directs each member to observe the words and actions of novices; they are constituted spies upon their conduct; and are bound to disclose every thing of consequence concerning them to the superiour. In order that this scrutiny into their character may be as complete as possible, a long noviciate must expire, during which they pass through the several gradations of ranks in the society, and they must have attained the full age of thirty three years, before they can be admitted to take the final vows, by which they become members of this society.

The restoration of the order of Jesuits took place in 1814, by a bull of the present pope Pius VII. The apostolic constitutions of pope Paul III. and others are revived in favour of this society; and in short they are placed in the same condition of privilege and power, as they anciently enjoyed. The bull of pope Clement XIV. abolishing the order, is expressly abrogated.*

JEWS, a name derived from the patriarch Judah, and from the predominance of that tribe in after ages, given to all the descendants of his father Jacob, who was also called Israel. Of the ancient Jews, the most authentic accounts may be found in the scriptures. The belief of the modern Jews is expressed by their great Rabbi Maimonides, of the eleventh century, in the following thirteen articles:

I. That God is the creator of all things; that he guides and supports all creatures; that he has done every thing; and that he still acts, and shall act during the whole of eternity.

II. That God is one. There is no unity like his. He alone hath been, is, and shall be, eternally our God.

* Mosheim, vol. iii. p. 465; iv. p. 354, 355. Hist. of Don Ingnatius. Pascal's Letters concerning the Jesuits, 2 vols 8vo. Robertson's Charles V. vol. ii. p. 431. Edinburgh Encyclopedia. Christian Observer, March 1815. February 1817. Buck's Theol. Dict.

III. That God is incorporeal, and cannot have any material properties; and no corporeal essence can be compared with him.

IV. That God is the beginning and end of all things; and shall eternally subsist.

V. That God alone ought to be worshipped; and none besides him adored.

VI. That whatever has been taught by the prophets is true.

VII. That Moses is the father and head of all contemporary doctors, and those, who lived before, or shall live after him.

VIII. That the law was given by Moses.

IX. That the law shall never be altered; and God will give no other.

X. That God knows all the thoughts and actions of men.

XI. That God will regard the works of all those, who have performed what he commands, and punish those, who have transgressed his laws.

XII. That the Messiah is to come, though he tarry a long time.

XIII. That there shall be a resurrection of the dead, when God shall think fit.

The modern Jews adhere still as closely to the Mosaic dispensation, as their dispersed and despised condition will permit them. Their service consists chiefly in reading the law and the prophecies in their synagogues, together with a variety of prayers. They use no sacrifices since the destruction of the temple. They repeat blessings and particular praises to God, not only in their prayers, but on all accidental occasions, and in almost all their actions. They go to prayers three times a day in their synagogues. Their sermons are not made in Hebrew, which few of them now perfectly understand, but in the language of the country where they reside. The passages of scripture and sentences from the doctors are, however, quoted from the Hebrew and explained.

The Jews are strictly prohibited from all vain swearing, and pronouncing any of the names of God without necessity. They abstain from meats prohibited by the levitical law; for which reason, whatever they eat must be dressed by those of their own nation, in a manner peculiar to themselves. In the observance of their religious festivals they perform similar ceremonies to those which were practised by their ancestors. All their rites, precepts, and ceremonies which are not contained in the pentateuch, are founded upon and derive their authority from the Talmud. There is, however, some variation in their customs and ceremonies, and in the liturgies which the nation have made use of at different times, and in various countries. But in the principal points of belief and practice they all agree.

This people acknowledge a twofold law of God,—a written and unwritten one; the former is contained in the five books of Moses; the latter they pretend has been handed down from him by oral tradition. (See *Cabbalists.*) They assert the perpetuity of their law, together with its perfection. They deny the accomplishment of the prophecies in the person of Jesus Christ; alleging that the Messiah is not yet come; and that he will make his appearance with the greatest pomp and grandeur, subduing all nations, and subjecting them to the house of Judah; and making Jerusalem the metropolis of his kingdom.

They say that "during the Messiah's reign, the world will be restored to its former glory, a new heaven and new earth will appear; the former will pass away, mankind will recover their primitive glory, and will be above the angels; satan and his band will be destroyed. The seventh day of the creation was the sabbath, and that day only received a blessing, and was set apart forever to be observed as a holy day; which was a type of the great sabbath; i. e. the world of the Messiah, which also will be called the blessed world."*

When it is urged that the prophets predicted the Messiah's low condition and sufferings, the Jews talk of two Messiahs; one, Ben Ephraim, who they grant to be of a mean and afflicted condition in this world; the other, Ben David, who shall be a victorious and powerful prince.

This people maintain, that the souls of the righteous enjoy the beatific vision of God in paradise, and that the souls of the wicked are tormented in hell with fire and other punishments. They suppose, that the sufferings of the most atrocious criminals are of eternal duration, while others remain only for a limited time in purgatory, which does not differ from hell with respect to the place, but to the duration. They pray for the souls of the dead, and imagine that many are delivered from purgatory on the great day of expiation.

The Rabbinists or modern Pharisees form the bulk of this nation. The two branches of Portuguese and German Jews are of this description, which includes all who admit traditions, &c. They entertain an implacable hatred to the Karaites, or Caraites, who adhere strictly to the text of Moses, and reject the Cabbala.

* This paragraph is extracted from Rabbi Crool's "Restoration of Israel," published 1814. By this work it appears, that the mode of thinking and arguing among the Jews of the present day is similar to that, which was prevalent among their ancestors. The Jews in the time of our Saviour, like those of the present day, expected not a suffering but a triumphant Messiah; and that his appearance and the restoration of Israel are coeval, and closely connected with each other.

There are still, however, a few Sadducees in Africa; and in the East some remains of the ancient sect of the Samaritans—at Gaza, Damascus, and Grand Cairo.

With regard to the ten tribes, Mr. Basnage supposes they still subsist in the East; and Dr. Buchanan observes, that "It has been sufficiently ascertained by the investigation of the learned in India, that the Affghan and Pyran nations consist of the descendants of the ten tribes."

It is impossible to fix the number of people the Jewish nation is at present composed of. But in a pamphlet recently published, entitled, "Of the Jews in the nineteenth century," there is an approximative calculation, though of course in some measure hypothetical, of all the Jews spread over the face of the earth. Our author estimates them at 6,598,000; of which there were 1,000,000 in Poland, before the division of that country in 1772; 200,000 in Russia, comprising Wallachia and Moldavia; 500,000 in the states where the German language is spoken; 80,000 in Holland, and the low countries; 5,000 in Sweden and Denmark; 50,000 in France; 50,000 in England, of whom 12,000 are in London; 200,000 in the states where the Italian language is spoken; 10,000 in Spain and Portugal; 3,000 in the United States of America; 4,000,000 in the Mahometan States of Europe, Asia, and Africa; 500,000 in Persia, and the rest of Asia, comprising China and India.*

The Jews however, since the destruction of Jerusalem, have never been able to regain a permanent settlement in Judea, or indeed in any country on earth; though there is scarcely any part of the globe where they are not to be found. In most countries, they have been terribly massacred. In christendom, they have been despised, calumniated, oppressed, banished, executed, and burned, and in general, have suffered more cruel treatment from christians, than even from Pagans and Mahometans. For a detail of their sufferings the reader is referred to Basnage's History of the Jews. Tovey's Anglia Judaica, &c.

The situation of this people has been greatly meliorated during the last and present century.

France has allowed them the rights of citizens, which induced many of the most wealthy among them to fix their residence in that country. In the city of Paris they have three synagogues and a consistory, composed of three grand rabbis. England, Holland, Poland and Prussia† tolerate and pro-

* See a Pamphlet, styled "The Correspondent," consisting of letters between eminent persons of France and England. London, 1817.

† In Berlin, the Jews have enjoyed singular honours, as men of genius and study. The late Moses Mendelsohn, by the force of his reasoning, has been

tect them. In the United States of America they have never been persecuted, but have been indulged in all the rights of citizens.

In England, energetic attempts are used to effect their conversion. In 1809, the London society was formed "for promoting christianity amongst the Jews." The means adopted by the society are the extensive distribution of bibles and religious tracts among the Jews; establishing weekly and quarterly lectures to be preached to them, the latter of which are styled demonstration sermons, or sermons demonstrative of our Lord Jesus Christ as the true Messiah;—the establishing a charity school for Jewish children, among whom boys of promising talents and piety are prepared for the ministry. And, above all, translating the new testament into pure biblical Hebrew, to be distributed among the dispersed of Israel in every part of the globe.

The management of the society is at present in the hands of the Episcopalians. From intelligence received in 1816, it appears, "that much has been effected in the very few years of the society's operations. A correspondence has been opened with pious and learned christians in various parts of the world; a translation of the new testament into pure biblical Hebrew has been in part accomplished; a large number of Jewish children have been educated, with the full consent of their parents, in the christian faith; an episcopal chapel for the Jews has been erected in that quarter of the city where they most abound; courses of lectures for their benefit have been preached in London, and various other places in England; many works connected with Jewish literature have been published; and above all, some adult Jews, it is hoped, have been truly converted, and admitted by baptism into the christian church. The foreign correspondence of the society seems to indicate that a great change is silently operating throughout the continent; and the society are encouraged to hope and expect a final blessing on their endeavours to promote the salvation of the lost sheep of the house of Israel.*

surnamed the Jewish Socrates; and by the amenity of his diction, the Jewish Plato. Bloch, a Jewish physician, was the first naturalist of the age: Herz is a professor, with four hundred auditors; Mainon, a profound metaphysician. There are Jewish poets, and Jewish artists, of eminence; and, which perhaps exist no where but in Berlin, a Jewish academy of sciences, and a Jewish Literary Journal, composed in Hebrew. See Vaurier, or Sketches of the Times, vol. ii. p. 249.

* Basnage's History of the Jews, p. 110, 115, 227, 746, &c. Encyclopedia, vol. ix. p. 143. Jewish Repository, vol. i. p. 210; vol. ii. p. 289, 320 Levi's Ceremonies of the Jews. Rabbi Crool's Restoration of Israel. Monthly Magazine, 1796. Asiatic Researches, vol ii. p. 76. Works of Sir William Jones, vol. i. p. 336. Christian Observer, 1816.

IKONOBORTSI, a small party of dissenters from the Greek church, who so far retain their zeal against images, that they will not suffer sculptures of any kind, or even *pictures* in their places of worship; and oppose all superstitious reverence to the buildings themselves, saying, the Almighty does 'not dwell in temples made with hands.'* See *Iconoclastes.*

ILLUMINATI, or ILLUMINEES, i. e. the enlightened, a term in the primitive church applied to such as had been instructed and baptized, but has since been adopted by different sects and parties. Such a sect appeared in Spain in 1575. They were charged with maintaining, that mental prayer and contemplation had so intimately united them to God, that they were arrived to such a state of perfection, as to stand in no need of good works, or the sacraments of the church; and that they might commit the grossest crimes without sin.

After the suppression of the Illuminati in Spain, there appeared a denomination in France, which took the same name. It is said they maintained, that one Anthony Bucket, a friar, had a system of belief and practice revealed to him, which exceeded every thing christianity had yet been acquainted with: that, by this method, persons might, in a short time, arrive at the same degrees of perfection and glory, to which the saints and the blessed Virgin have attained; and this improvement might be carried on, till our actions became divine, and our minds wholly given up to the influence of the Almighty. They said further, that none of the doctors of the church knew any thing of religion; that St. Peter and St. Paul were well meaning men, but knew nothing of devotion; that the whole church lay in darkness and unbelief; that every one was at liberty to follow the suggestions of his conscience; that God regarded nothing but himself; and that, within ten years, their doctrine would be received all over the world; that there would be no more occasion for priests, monks, and other religious distinctions.

But the modern Illuminees are said to be a secret society, founded in 1776, by Dr. Adam Weishaupt, professor of canon law in the university of Ingoldstadt; a man of learning and genius, of great activity and insinuating address. He is charged with aiming at the same object that Voltaire, Diderot, and others had attempted some years before, namely, the abolition of christianity, and the establishment of a philosophical infidelity.

The mysteries of this sect are asserted to be comprehended in the following summary.

* Pinkerton's Greek Church, p. 334.

"Liberty and equality are the essential rights that man in his original and primitive perfection received from nature. Property struck the first blow at equality; political societies or governments were the first oppressors of liberty: the supporters of governments and property are the religious and civil laws; therefore to reinstate man in his primitive rites of equality and liberty they begin by destroying these. And it is asserted, that the society have executed, to an alarming degree, its plan for exterminating christianity and destroying government and social order. The means of effecting this was the French revolution, which was in a great measure brought about by the secret influence of this society, and extended over the greater part of Europe. This afforded the French philosophers the opportunity of disseminating their infidel principles among the lower classes of society.

The society of the Illuminati, says the Abbè Barruel, is divided into two grand classes, and each of them is again subdivided into lesser degrees, proportionate to the progress of the adepts.

The first class is that of *preparation*, which contains four degrees; those of *novice*, of *minerval*, of *minor Illuminee*, and *major Illuminee*. Some intermediate degrees belong to this class. The second class is that of the *mysteries*, and this is subdivided into the greater and less mysteries. The latter comprehend the priesthood and administration of the sect, or the degrees of priests, of regents, and of princes.

In the *greater mysteries* are comprised the two degrees of *magi*, or *philosophers*, and of the *man king*. The elect of the latter compose the council and degree of *Areopagites*.

In all these classes, and in every degree, there is a part of the utmost consequence, and which is common to all the brethren. It is that employment known in the society's code of laws, by the appellation of *brother insinuator*, or *recruiter*. The whole strength of the sect depends on this part; for it is this which furnishes members for the different degrees. The insinuators, or recruiters of this society, are sent by their superiours to different towns and provinces, and to distant countries. They are directed carefully to conceal their being Illuminees, and to make the knowledge of human nature their particular study. One of the professors of Illuminism gives the following instruction relating to this kind of science: "The novice must be attentive to trifles, for in frivolous occurrences a man is indolent, and makes no effort to act a part, so that his real character is then acting alone." This assiduous and long continued study of men, enables the possessor of such knowledge to act with men, and by his knowledge of their characters to influence their conduct. For such reasons, this study is continued during the whole progress through the order.

The object of the Illuminees is said to be, to enlist in every country such as have frequently declared themselves discontented with the usual institutions; to acquire the direction of education, of church management, of the professional chair, and of the pulpit; to bring their opinions into fashion by every art, and to spread them among young people, by the help of young writers; to get under their influence reading and debating societies, reviewers, booksellers, and post-masters; journalists, or editors of news-papers, and other periodical works; and to insinuate some of their fraternity into all offices of instruction, honour, profit, and influence, in literary, civil, and religious institutions. It is reported to be one of their established maxims, that "the end sanctifies the means."

Men of high reputation in Great Britain, and on the continent of Europe, have given ample testimony of their belief in the accounts which are given of Illuminism. Bishop Porteus, in his charge to the clergy of his diocess, in the years 1798 and 1799, has the following passage: "It now appears from undoubted evidence, collected from the most authentic sources, and produced about the same time, by two different authors, of different countries and religions, and writing without the least concert or communication with each other, that there have in fact subsisted in the heart of Europe certain sects of men, distinguished by various fanciful names, and various mysterious rites and ceremonies, but all concurring in one common object, namely, the gradual overthrow, not merely of all religion, but of all civil government and social order throughout the world."

The Chevalier Von Hamelberg, in the Prussian service, translated the work of professor Robison into German, and presented it to his sovereign, who expressed the highest approbation of his performance.

On the other hand, the histories of the Abbè Barruel and professor Robison have been called in question by men of learning and extensive information. In particular, the celebrated Gregoire, in his Histoire Des Sectes Religienses, gives a very different account of the Illuminati. He supposes, that the project of Weishaupt and his co-operaters was at first praise-worthy. It, said he, "embraced the plan of diffusing light, union, charity, and tolerance; of abolishing the slavery of the peasantry, the feudal rights, and all those privileges, which in elevating one portion of the community degraded the other; of disseminating instruction among the people, of causing merit to triumph, of establishing individual and political liberty, and gradually and without a shock, of meliorating the social order."

Our author admits, however, that the society was too little rigid with regard to those it admitted. "It is not," says he, "rare in every society to find men who, not being animated with its spirit, counteract its operations; and that of the Illuminees had such men. If they had been only negative members in that way they were injurious. Every thing, which has the air of mystery, awakens suspicion, and favours calumny, and calumny exhausted itself with regard to the invisible society. As soon as the alarm was sounded, it was spread abroad, that this society, numerous, and of high repute, had no other aim than to monopolize all the lucrative and honourable posts; to extinguish the torch of truth, to overturn all government and to destroy all religion."*

*INCORRUPTIBILES, a small party of the Eutychians, who maintained that Christ's body was incorruptible even before its resurrection, so that it did not need the support of food, &c. nor was naturally subject to mortality. They were opposed to the *Corrupticolæ.*

INDEPENDENTS, a denomination of protestants in England and Holland, originally called *Brownists.* They derive their name from maintaining that every particular congregation of christians has an entire and complete power of jurisdiction over its members to be exercised by the elders of each church within itself; independent of the authority of bishops, synods, presbyteries, or any other ecclesiastical assemblies.

This denomination appeared in England in the year 1616. John Robinson, a Norfolk divine, was considered as their founder. He possessed sincere piety, and no inconsiderable share of learning. Perceiving defects in the denomination of the Brownists, to which he belonged, he employed his zeal and diligence in correcting them, and in new-modelling the society. Though the Independents considered their own form of ecclesiastical government as of divine institution, and as originally introduced by the authority of the apostles;–nay, by the apostles themselves; yet, they did not think it necessary to condemn other denominations; but acknowledged that true religion might flourish in those communities which were

* For farther accounts of this society the reader is referred to Barruel's Memoirs of Jacobinism, Prof. Robison's Proofs of a conspiracy against all the religions and governments in Europe, and Gregoire's Histoire Des Sectes Religienses.

under the jurisdiction of bishops, or the government of presbyteries. They approved also of a regular and educated ministry, nor is any person among them permitted to speak in public, before he has submitted to a proper examination of his capacity and talents, and has been approved of by the church to which he belonged.

Their grounds of separation from the established church are different from those of the other puritans. Many of the latter objected chiefly to certain rites, ceremonies, vestments, or forms, or to the government of the church, while yet they were disposed to arm the magistrate in support of the truth; and regretted and complained, that they could not on these accounts conform to it. But Robinson, and his companions, not only rejected the appointments, of the church on these heads, but denied its authority to enact them; contending that every single congregation of christians was a church, and *independent* of all legislation, save that of Christ; standing in need of no such provision or establishment as the state can bestow; and incapable of soliciting or receiving it. Hence they sought not to reform the church, but chose to dissent from it. They admitted there were many godly men in its communion, and that it was reformed from the grossest errours of popery, but thought it still wanted some things essential to a true church of Christ; in particular a power of choosing its own ministers, and a stricter discipline among its members.

In support of the scheme of congregational churches, this denomination observe that the word εκκλησία, which we translate *church*, is always used in the scriptures to signify a *single congregation*, or the place where a single congregation meets. Thus that unlawful assembly at Ephesus, brought together against Paul by the craftsmen, is called a church. (Acts xix. 29—41.) The word, however, is generally applied to a more sacred use: but still it signifies a single congregation. The whole body of the disciples at Corinth is indeed called the *church*, but spoken of as coming together into one place. (1 Cor. xiv. 23.) The whole nation of Israel is also named a church; but it was no more than a single congregation, for it had but one place of public worship, viz. first the tabernacle, and afterwards the temple. The catholic church of Christ, his holy nation and kingdom, is likewise a single congregation, having one place of worship, viz. heaven, wherein all the members hold communion; and will, at last, form one *general assembly and church of the first-born, whose names are written in heaven.*

The independents allege, that the church of Corinth had an entire judicature within itself. For Paul thus addressed them: *Do not ye judge them, which are* *within?* (1 Cor. v. xii.) So they were not dependent upon the apostle, to come to him for a sentence, nor upon the elders of other associated churches.* See *Brownists* and *Congregationalists*.

This denomination is supposed to be of late considerably on the increase; partly by accessions from the Calvinistic Methodists, and partly by their extension into Scotland and Ireland. The creed of the Independents is generally Calvinistic, though with considerable shades of difference; and many in Scotland and Ireland have symbolized with the *Glassites* or *Sandemanians*.

INDIANS, a term alike applicable to the natives of India and America; but as we have considered the former under the name of *Hindoos*, we shall confine this article to the latter; and begin with the natives of North America, noticing some striking peculiarities of their ancient pagan notions and idolatries.

The aborigines of *New England* not only believed in a plurality of gods, who made and govern the several nations of the world, but they made deities of every thing they imagined to be great, powerful, beneficial, or hurtful to mankind; yet they conceived an almighty Being, who dwells in the south-west regions of the heavens, to be superiour to all the rest. This almighty Being they called *Kichtan*, who at first, according to their tradition, made a man and a woman out of a stone; but upon some dislike destroyed them again; and then made another couple out of a tree, from whom descended all the nations of the earth: but how they came to be scattered and dispersed into countries so remote from one another, they cannot tell. They believed their supreme God to be a good being, and paid a sort of acknowledgment to him for plenty, victory, and other benefits: But there is another power, which they call *hobamocko*, (i. e. the devil,) of whom they stood in greater awe, and worshipped merely from a principle of fear. The immortality of the soul was in some sort universally believed among them. When good men die, they said, their spirits go to Kichtan, where they meet their friends, and enjoy all manner of pleasures. When wicked men die, they go to Kichtan also; but are commanded to walk away, and to wander about in restless discontent and darkness forever.†

Mr. Brainerd, who was a pious and successful missionary among the Indians on the Susquehannah and Delaware rivers, in 1744, gives the following account of their religious

* Mosheim, vol. iv. p. 526. Neal's History of the Puritans, vol. iii. p. 142. Goodwin's Works, vol. iv. p. 71. Ency. vol. ix. p. 170.

† Neal's History of New England, vol. i p. 33—35.

sentiments:—"After the coming of the white people, the Indians in *New Jersey*, who once held a plurality of deities, supposed there were only three, because they saw people of three kinds of complexion, viz. whites, negroes, and themselves. It is a notion pretty generally prevailing among them, that it was not the same God that made them who made us; but that they were created after the white people; and it is probable, they suppose, their God gained some special skill by seeing the white people made, and so made them *better*. With regard to a future state of existence, many of them imagine, that the *chichung*, i. e. the shadow, or what survives the body, will at death go southward, to some unknown place, and enjoy some kind of happiness—such as hunting, feasting, dancing, or the like; and never be weary of these pleasures. They believe that most will be happy; and that those who are not so, will be punished only with privation, being excluded from the walls of the good world, where happy spirits reside. These rewards and punishments they suppose to depend entirely on their behaviour towards mankind, and to have no reference to any thing which relates to the worship of the supreme Being."*

The original inhabitants of *Canada*, like other heathen, had an idea of a supreme Being; whom they considered as the creator and governour of the world. It is said that most of the nations which speak the Algonquin language give this being the appellation of the *Great Hare*, but some call him *Michabou*, and others *Atahocan*. They believe that he was born upon the waters, together with his whole court, who were composed of four-footed animals, like himself; that he formed the earth of a grain of sand taken from the bottom of the ocean; and that he created men of the bodies of dead animals. Some mention a god of the waters, who opposed the designs of the Great Hare, who is called the *Great Tiger*. They have a third called *Matcomek*, whom they invoke in the winter season.

The *Agreskoui* of the Hurons, and the *Agreskousé* of the Iroquois, are, in the opinion of these nations, the sovereign being, and god of war. These Indians do not give the same original to mankind with the Algonquins; for they do not ascend so high as the first creation. According to them, there were in the beginning six men in the world; but they cannot tell who placed them there.

The gods of the Indians are supposed to have bodies, and to live much in the same manner as themselves; but without any of the inconveniences to which they are subject. The word

* Brainerd's Journal.

spirit, among them, signifies only a being of a more excellent nature than others.

According to the *Iroquois*, in the third generation there came a deluge, in which not a soul was saved; so that, in order to re-people the earth, it was necessary to change beasts into men. Besides the first Being, or Great Spirit, they hold an infinite number of genii, or inferiour spirits, both good and evil, who have each their peculiar form of worship. They ascribe to these beings a kind of immensity and omnipresence, and constantly invoke them as the guardians of mankind; and they only address themselves to the evil genii, to beg of them to do them no hurt. They believe in the immortality of the soul, and say that the region of their everlasting abode lies so far westward, that the souls are several months in arriving at it, and have vast difficulties to surmount. The happiness that they hope to enjoy is not believed to be the recompense of virtue only, but to have been a good hunter, brave in war, &c. are the chief merits which entitle them to their paradise:* this, they and other American natives describe as a delightful country, blessed with perpetual spring, whose forests abound with game; whose rivers swarm with fish; where famine is never felt, but uninterrupted plenty shall be enjoyed without labour or fatigue.†

Most of the natives of South America have an idea of a supreme Being, whom they call the *Grand Spirit*, by way of excellence; and whose perfections are as much superiour to other beings, as the fire of the sun is to elementary fire. They believe this omnipotent Being is so good, that he could not do evil to any one, even if he were inclined. That, though he created all things by his will, yet he had under him spirits of an inferiour order, who, by his assistance, formed the beauties of the universe; but that man was the work of the Creator's own hands. These spirits are, by the Natches, termed *free servants*, or *agents;* but at the same time they are as submissive as slaves: they are constantly in the presence of God, and prompt to execute his will. The air, according to them, is full of other spirits of more mischievous dispositions, and these have a chief, who was so eminently mischievous, that God Almighty was obliged to confine him; and ever since, those aërial spirits do not commit so much mischief as they did before, especially if they are entreated to be favourable. For this reason the savages always invoke them, when they want either rain or fair weather. They give this account of the

* Charlevoix's Voyage to North America, vol ii. p. 141—155.

† Robertson's History of South America, vol. i. p. 387.

creation of the world, viz. that God first formed a little man of clay, and breathed on his work; and that he walked about, grew up, and became a perfect man: but they are silent as to the creation of women.*

The greatest part of the natives of Louisiana had formerly their temples, as well as the Natches; and in all these temples a perpetual fire was preserved.†

The aborigines of East and West Florida own a supreme benevolent Deity, and a subordinate one, who is malevolent; neglecting the good god, who does no harm, they bend their whole attention to soften the latter, who, they say, torments them day and night.‡

The Apalachians, bordering on Florida, worship the sun, but sacrifice nothing to him which has life: they hold him to be the parent of life, and think he can take no pleasure in the destruction of any living creature. Their devotion is exerted in perfumes and songs.§

The divinities of the ancient inhabitants of *Mexico* were clothed with terrour, and delighted in vengeance. The figures of serpents, of tigers, and of other destructive animals, decorated their temples. Fasts, mortifications, and penances, all rigid, and many of them excruciating to an extreme degree, were the means which they employed to appease the wrath of the gods. But of all offerings, human sacrifices were deemed the most acceptable.‖ At the dedication of the great temple at Mexico, it is reported there were 60 or 70,000 human sacrifices. The usual amount of them was about 20,000.¶

The city of Mexico is said to have contained nearly 2000 small temples, and 360 which were adorned with steeples. The whole empire of Mexico contained above 40,000 temples, endowed with very considerable revenues. For the service in the grand temple of Mexico itself, above 5000 priests were appointed; and the number in the whole empire is said to have amounted to nearly a million. The whole priesthood, excepting that of the conquered nations, was governed by two high-priests, who were also the oracles of the kings. Beside the service in the temple, their clergy were to instruct the youth, to compose the calenders, and to paint the mythological pictures. The Mexicans had also priestesses, but they were not allowed to offer up sacrifices. They likewise had monastic orders, especially one, into which no person was admitted under sixty years of age.**

* Modern Universal History, vol. xl. p. 374.

† Charlevoix's Voyages, vol. ii. p. 273. ‡ Kaimes' Sketches, vol. iv. p. 155.

§ Kaimes' Sketches, vol. iv. p. 216

‖ Robertson's Hist. of South America, vol. ii. p. 384, 385.

¶ Priestley's Lectures on History, p. 440.

** Critical Review, vol. liv. p. 312.

Notwithstanding the vast depopulation of America, a very considerable number of the native race still remains both in Mexico and Peru. Their settlements in some places are so populous, as to merit the name of cities. In the three audiences into which New Spain is divided, there are at least two millions of Indians; a pitiful remnant indeed of its ancient population; but such as still forms a body of people, superiour in number to all the other native inhabitants of this vast country.*

The sun, as the great source of light, of joy, and fertility in the creation, attracted the principal homage of the native *Peruvians*. The moon and stars, as co-operating with him, were entitled to secondary honours. They offered to the sun a part of those productions, which his genial warmth had called forth from the bosom of the earth, and reared to maturity. They sacrificed, as an oblation of gratitude, some of the animals who were indebted to his influence for nourishment. They presented to him choice specimens of those works of ingenuity, which his light had guided the heart of man in forming. But the Incas never stained his altars with human blood; nor could they conceive that their beneficent father, the sun, would be delighted with such horrid victims.†

The savage tribes of *Guiana* believe the existence of one supreme Deity, whose chief attribute is benevolence; and to him they ascribe every good which happens. But as it is against his nature to do ill, they believe in subordinate malevolent beings, like our devil, who occasion thunders, hurricanes, and earthquakes; and who are the authors of death and diseases, and of every misfortune.‡

The natives of *Amazonia* have a vast variety of idols, whom they consider as subordinate to one supreme Being; but of that Being they have very confused notions. They stand in great awe of their priests, and hold them in the utmost veneration. They have a particular house, or rather hut, for the celebration of their ceremonies, and this is to them what others call a church or temple. Here the priests address themselves to their gods, and receive answers from their oracles. When they go to war, they apply to their priests for assistance against their enemies, and the first thing the priests do, is to curse them. Upon their going out to war they hoist at the prow of their canoes that idol, under whose auspices they look for victory; but, like too many called christians, they never pray to their gods, except in cases of difficulty, when they feel their need of divine assistance or support.

* Robertson's History of America, p. 391.

† Robertson's History of America, vol. ii. p. 309, 310.

‡ Kaimes, vol. i. p. 150.

INDWELLING SCHEME. See *Pre-existents*.

***INFIDELS,** or unbelievers in divine revelation, and consequently in christianity, may be divided into two great classes—*Deists* and *Atheists*, which see.

INGHAMITES, the followers of Mr. Ingham, a respectable gentleman of the north of England, who was educated at Queen's College, at the same time with Mr Hervey; and in 1732 joined the society of the first Methodists at Oxford. He accompanied the Mess. Wesleys on their first voyage to Georgia, but returning the next year, attached himself to the United Brethren. Some time after this, itinerating in the north of England he formed several churches on the Independent plan. But in 1760, Mr. Ingham and some of his co-adjutors met with the writings of Messrs. Glass and Sandeman, and adopting some of their notions, both as to doctrine and discipline, began to split into parties, and many went over to their communion. Some thousands, however, adhered to Mr. Ingham, of which there are yet considerable remains. They admitted members by lot, after a public declaration of their experiences, which introduced much confusion and contention. Mr. Ingham pleaded very strongly for the doctrine of imputed righteousness; but objected to the systematic language generally adopted in speaking of distinct persons in the trinity. He practised infant baptism, and approved many things in the writings of Mr. Sandeman. This denomination receive members by the laying on of hands; practise the love feasts, and the kiss of charity. But they did not think with Sandeman that a plurality of elders was necessary to church ordinances.*

INVISIBLES, a name of distinction given to the disciples of Osiander, Flacius, Illyricus, Swenkfeld, &c. because they denied the perpetual visibility of the church.†

JOACHIMITES, a denomination which appeared about the commencement of the thirteenth century; so called from Joachim, abbot of Sora, in Calabria. He foretold the destruction of the church of Rome, and the promulgation of a new and more perfect gospel, in the age of the Holy Ghost, by a number of poor and austere ministers, whom God was to raise up and employ for that purpose. For he divided the world into three ages, relative to the three dispensations of religion which were to succeed each other. The two imperfect ages, viz. the age of the old testament, which was that of the Father, and the age of the new, which was under the administration of the Son, were, according to

* Sketch of the Scotch Independents and the Inghamite churches.
† Collier's Hist. Dict.

his doctrine, now passed; and the third age, even that of the Holy Ghost, was near at hand.*

JOHNSONIANS, the followers of Mr. John Johnson, many years a baptist minister at Liverpool, of whom there are still several congregations in different parts of England.

The following positions are extracted from Mr. Johnson's writings:

I. That true Faith is *not* "a *duty* which God requires of man;" but a grace of "so different a nature, that it is not possible to be made a duty; or [nor] possible to be required of any created being."† Consequently faith is not, in his view, a requirement of the law of God, nor does the law "require any thing properly relating to eternal salvation;"‡ nor is that unbelief which is the reverse of this, (or the want of faith,) a sin, but a "vacuity," or mere "nonentity."§

II. That faith, though "an active principle," is not an act, or "action," or "work" of the soul of man, but "the operation of God;"‖ whence it would seem to follow, that it is not the soul which believes, but this principle of grace within him.

III. That the holiness of the first man, Adam, was inferiour to that of the angels, much more to that of the saints who are raised above the angels; that the first man being "earthy," not only in his body, but his whole person, his holiness could be "only such a resemblance of, and nearness to God, as an *earthy* nature was capable of."¶

IV. That gospel ministers are not to preach the law,** neither "moral duties;" nor "to exhort persons to faith, repentance, love, holiness, &c." which blessings proceed alone from the grace of God:†† nor "to caution and warn them against sinful practices, to teach and instruct them in the regulation of their lives, &c. Our commission (says Mr. J.) is not to preach the law, but the gospel."‡‡

V. That "the blessings of spiritual grace and eternal life, being secured in Christ prior to the fall, were never lost;" and consequently, could not be "restored." Adoption not rising out of salvation, but, on the contrary, salvation from adoption, as being included in it. "So that," says Mr. J. "I cannot conceive any reason, according to the original constitution of things, why grace and glory might not have taken place upon God's elect, according to his everlasting love in adoption, supposing sin or salvation never [had] a being."§§

According to the account

* Mosheim, vol. iii. p. 66. † Faith of God's elect, p. 10. ‡ Ib. p. 28. § Ib. p. 55. ‖ Ib. p. 40. ¶ Ib. p. 44, 69. ** Ib. p. 259. †† Ib. p. 255. ‡‡ Ib. p. 257, 259. §§ Ib. p. 89, 90.

given by the anonymous correspondent of Mr. Evans,* Mr. Johnson's followers reject the doctrine of the trinity; but maintain the indwelling scheme. They deny original sin; yet assert, that no man will savingly believe the gospel, unless brought by the special influence of the spirit to receive it. They deny the natural immortality of the soul; yet maintain the separate existence of the soul between death and the resurrection. Respecting the atonement and perseverance of the saints, they agree with the Calvinists; and with other baptists as to the mode and subjects of baptism. Those who die in infancy, they say, will be raised to life in a pure state, not to inherit the heavenly kingdom, but to inhabit the new earth, which will be formed after the conflagration; on which, they say, Christ and his church will reign a thousand years, and then be removed to some more glorious region. See the account of this denomination in Evans' Sketch, 12 ed. p. 267.†

ISBRANIKI, i. e. the multitude of the elect, a name assumed by certain dissenters from the Russian church, otherwise called *Starovertsi*, i. e. believers in the ancient faith; but generally called by the members of the establishment *Raskolniki*, or schismatics. See those names, and also the *Russian church*.

JUDAIZING Christians. The rise of this denomination is placed under the reign of Adrian. For when this emperour had razed Jerusalem to its foundations, and enacted severe laws against the whole body of the Jews, the greatest part of the christians, who lived in Palestine, to prevent their being confounded with them, abandoned the Mosaic rites, and chose a bishop, named Mark, a foreigner by nation, and an alien from the commonwealth of Israel. Those who were strongly attached to the Mosaic rites separated from their brethren, and founded at Pera, (a country of Palestine,) and in the neighbouring parts, particular assemblies, in which the law of Moses maintained its primitive dignity and authority.

There were, however, in the apostolic age judaizing christians, which set Christ and Moses upon an equal footing of authority; these were afterwards divided into two sects, widely different both in their rites and opinions, and distinguished by the names of *Nazarenes* and *Ebionites*, which see.

JUMPERS, so called from

* The above account was given to Mr. Evans by a preacher among the Johnsonians.

† Dr. Priestley maintained that the ancient Hebrew Christians were Nazarenes; and that the Nazarenes were the same people with the Ebionites, the Socinians of early days. See an account of the Controversy between Dr. Priestly, Dr. Horsley, and others, in General Repository, &c. published at Cambridge, 1812.

their practice of jumping during the time allotted for religious worship and instruction. They originated in Wales, about the year 1760, when the Calvinistic Methodists had made some progress in the principality. Several of the first preachers in that connexion were naturally of very warm tempers, and zealously engaged in promoting their views of religion. Their discourses were calculated to produce a strong sensation among their hearers. Such as were ignorant, and at the same time of a warm temper, under deep impression, gave way to their feelings. They cried out loudly, some uttering one thing and some another in the midst of the congregation: some clapped their hands, others shook hands one with another, and others, rejoicing at the discovery which the gospel makes of a Saviour, began to jump for joy. This was taken notice of, and by some considered as an indication of pious zeal. The custom spread like wild-fire. Very soon jumping began to be considered as a proof that the people enjoyed the presence of God. Many preachers among the independents and baptists imitated the methodists, and discovered their religious zeal by shouting and jumping.

Instances have also been known in Wales, where the clergy were methodistically inclined to this jumping, in the parish churches. This exercise is sometimes continued, with occasional singing or exhortation between, for hours, until the strength of the party is quite exhausted.

Mr. Evans relates, that about the year 1785, he happened to be present accidentally at a meeting which terminated in jumping. It was held in the open air, on a sunday evening, near Newport, Monmouthshire. The preacher was one of lady Huntingdon's students, who concluded his sermon with the recommendation of jumping; and to allow him the praise of consistency, he got down from the chair on which he stood, and jumped along with them. The arguments he adduced for this purpose were, that David danced before the ark; and that the man, whose lameness was removed, leaped and praised God for the mercy which he had received. He expatiated on these topics with uncommon fervency, and then drew the inference, that they ought to show similar expressions of joy for the blessings Jesus Christ had put into their possession. He then gave an impassioned sketch of the sufferings of the Saviour; and hereby roused the passions of a few around him into a state of violent agitation. About nine men and seven women, for some little time, rocked to and fro, groaned aloud, and then jumped with a kind of frantic fury. Some of the audience flew in all directions; others gazed on in silent amazement. They all gradually dispersed except the Jumpers, who continued their exertions from eight in the evening to near eleven at night. They at last kneeled down in a circle, holding each other by the hand, while one of them prayed with great fervour, and then, all rising up from off their knees, departed. But previous to their dispersion, they wildly pointed up towards the sky, and reminded one another that they should soon meet there and be never again separated.

Several of the more zealous itinerant preachers in Wales, recommended the people to cry out Gogoniant,(the Welsh word for glory,) Amen, &c. &c. to put themselves in violent agitation; and finally to jump till they were quite exhausted, so as often to be obliged to fall down on the floor, or on the field where this kind of worship is held.

Some years since, Mr. W. Williams, a blind Welsh poet, wrote a pamphlet in defence of this practice, which was patronized by the abettors of jumping in religious assemblies, but viewed by the serious and grave with disapprobation. It appears from late accounts that the jumpers are comparatively very few, even among the Methodists; and those are persons of very warm tempers, and animated manners.*

K

KARAITES, or CARAITES. This name denotes a scripturist,and is given to a jewish sect which adhered to the literal sense of the old testament, and considered the scriptures as the whole and only rule of their faith and practice. This denomination was given them about thirty years before Christ, when, upon the dissension betwixt Hillel, the president of the Sanhedrim, and Shammai, the vice president, by which their respective pupils were divided into two parties, betwixt whom there were perpetual contests; those that were of the opinion of the Karaites, sided with the school of Shammai, and those who were zealous for traditions, with that of Hillel. According to Dr. Prideaux, they did not absolutely reject traditions, but only refused them the same authority with the written oracles of God. They were distinguished from the Sadducees, by maintaining the doctrines of the immortality of the soul, and future rewards and punishments.† A

* Evans' Tour through Wales, and Bingley's North Wales. Evans' Sketch of Religious Denominations, 12 London Edition.

† Calmet's Dict. in Caraite, chap. xvi, xvii. Prideaux's Conn. vol. ii. p. 388. Jenning's Lectures. Clarke's Travels, vol. ii. p. 348.

considerable number of this sect is still found in Turkey, and other parts of the East.

A colony of Karaite jews reside in a fortress in the Crimea, and enjoy the free exercise of their ancient customs and religious rites. They pretend to have the text of the old testament in its most genuine state, and deem it an act of piety to copy the bible, or pious commentaries upon the text once in their lives. Their character is said to be directly opposite to that which is generally attributed to their brethren, being altogether without reproach. They pay great attention to the education of their children, who are taught publicly in the synagogues. Almost all of them are engaged in trade or manufactures.

KEITHIANS, a party that separated from the quakers, in Pennsylvania, in the year 1691. They were headed by the famous George Keith, from whom they derived their name. Those who persisted in their separation, after their leader deserted them and returned to England, practised baptism, received the Lord's supper, and kept the seventh day sabbath, whence they were called *Quaker-Baptists*, and Sabbatarians: but they retained the language, dress, and manners of the Quakers.*

*KILHAMITES; thus the Methodists of the new connexion are sometimes called, from Mr. Alex. Kilham, who was a distinguished preacher among them, and acted as secretary to the society. See *Methodists*.

*KIRK, The or Church of Scotland, is Calvinistic in doctrine, and presbyterian in discipline; and has been so from the time of the celebrated John Knox, the famous Scotch reformer, who flourished in the sixteenth century. The form of their worship is very simple, without a liturgy and without pomp. Scotland contains about nine hundred parishes, and as many benefices; they are provided for by patrons, and not, in general, elective by the people. See *Presbyterians*.

*KNIGHTS: three orders of knighthood were instituted in the twelfth century for the defence of christianity, and for the annoyance of infidels. 1. The Knights of St. John of Jerusalem were designed to relieve and assist the vast number of pilgrims who visited Jerusalem and the holy land. 2. The *templars* (so called from a palace adjoining Jerusalem) were purely a military order, who were to guard the roads and protect the christians from the Mahometans. 3. The teutonic Knights of St. Mary chiefly devoted their service to the care of the soldiers wounded in the holy wars. The two latter

* Edwards' Hist. of American Baptists, p. 55—60

orders have been long extinct; but the former found an asylum in the Isle of *Malta*.*

KNIPPERDOLINGS, a denomination in the sixteenth century, derived from Bertrand Knipperdoling, who taught a literal millenium; denied justification by faith, original sin, and infant baptism: maintained that every Christian has authority to preach and administer the sacraments; that all things ought to be in common, &c.†

KTISTOLATRÆ, certain of the Monophysites, who maintained that the body of Christ, before his resurrection, was corruptible, like that of other men.‡

L

LABBADISTS, a denomination in the seventeenth century. Their founder, John Labbadie, was a native of France, and remarkable for his natural eloquence and warm enthusiasm. He was educated in the bosom of the church of Rome, but in 1630 he embraced the protestant religion, and became a member of the reformed church, and performed with reputation the ministerial functions in France, Switzerland, and Holland. He at length erected a new community, who, according to the accounts of the Labbadists, did not differ from the reformed church so much in their tenets and doctrines, as in their manners and rules of discipline. Labbadie, however, maintained, that the holy scriptures were not sufficient to lead men to salvation, without certain particular illuminations and revelations from the holy spirit; and that in reading the scriptures, we ought to give less attention to the literal sense of the word, than to the inward suggestions of the spirit, and that the efficacy of the word depended upon him that preached it; that the faithful ought to have all things in common; that there is no subordination or distinction of rank in the true church of Christ; that Christ was to reign a thousand years upon earth; that the contemplative life is a state of grace and union with God, and the very height of perfection; that the christian, whose mind is contented and calm, sees all things in God, enjoys the Deity, and is perfectly indifferent about every thing that passes in the world; and that the christian arrives to that happy state by the exercise of a perfect self-

* Mosheim, vol. iii. p. 18—20. N. Ed.

† Chevrea's Hist. of the World, vol. iii. p. 437.

‡ Mosheim, vol. i. p. 471, 472.

denial, by mortifying the flesh and all sensual affection, and by mental prayer.

Labbadie had the address to ingratiate himself with Elizabeth Princess Palatine, and other ladies of rank and piety. Several persons of distinguished talents became members of this sect; among whom was the celebrated Anne Maria Sehurman of Utrecht, whose extensive erudition rendered her so famous in the republic of letters, during the last century.*

LAMA, worship of the. See *Shamanism.*

LAMPETIANS, the followers of Lampetius, a Syrian monk, who in the seventeenth century taught that, as man is born free, a christian, in order to please God, ought to do nothing by necessity; and that it is therefore unlawful to make vows, even those of obedience. To this system he is said to have added certain tenets of the Carpocratians, &c.†

LATITUDINARIANS, a name which distinguished those in the seventeenth century, who attempted to bring episcopalians, presbyterians, and independents, into one communion, by compromising the difference between them. The chief leaders of this party were the great Chillingworth, and John Hales, to whom may be added More, Cudworth, Gale, Tillotson, and Whitchcot. They were zealously attached to the church of England; but did not look upon episcopacy as indispensable to the constitution of the christian church: hence they maintained, that those who followed other forms of government and worship, were not on that account to be excluded from the communion, or to forfeit the title of brethren. They reduced the fundamental doctrines of christianity to a few points. By this way of proceeding they showed that neither the episcopalians, who, generally speaking, were Arminians, nor the presbyterians and independents, who as generally adopted the doctrines of Calvin, had any reason to oppose each other with such animosity and bitterness, since the subjects of their debates were matters of an indifferent nature, with respect to salvation; and might be variously explained and understood without any prejudice to their eternal interests.‡

LIBERTINES, a sect which arose in Flanders about 1525, probably from the remains of the "*Brethren of the free spirit*," mentioned above. They published no books; but the doctrines they taught, according to Calvin and others, were the following: 1. That the Deity was the sole operating cause in the mind of man, and the immediate author of all human actions. 2. That consequently

* Mosheim, vol. v. p. 492. † Broughton, vol. ii. p. 31.
‡ Mosheim, vol. iv. p. 535. Burnet's History of his own times, p. 186.

the distinctions of good and evil that had been established with respect to those actions, were false and groundless; and that men could not, properly speaking, commit sin. 3. That religion consisted in the union of the spirit, or rational soul, with the supreme Being. 4. That all those who had attained to this happy union by sublime contemplation and elevation of mind, were then allowed to indulge, without exception or restraint, their appetites and passions, as all their actions were then perfectly innocent. 5. That after the death of the body, they were to be united to the Deity.*

LOLLARDS, the followers of Walter Lollard, (or Walter, the Lollard,) who is said to have been an Englishman by birth; but he first propagated his doctrines in Germany, about the year 1315, after which he returned to England, a few years before Wickliff began to oppose the church of Rome. (See *Wickliffites.)* The Lollards rejected the sacrifice of the mass, extreme unction, and penances for sin; insisting that Christ's sufferings were all-sufficient to atone for the sins of those who believed in him. Walter Lollard afterwards returned to the continent, where he sealed his testimony with his blood, being burnt alive at Cologne in 1322.

Many societies of Lollards, of both sexes, were formed in most parts of Germany and Flanders, where they were protected by the magistrates and inhabitants, on account of their usefulness to the sick; but whether they were really the disciples of Walter Lollard, may be questioned; the Alexians or Cellites, had obtained the name of Lollards, from the old German word *lullen, lollen,* or *lallen,* "to sing with a low voice;" to *lull*; because they interred such as died of the plague, which at that period ravaged all Europe, and sung a dirge in a mournful tone, as they conveyed them to the grave. They obtained many papal grants, by which their institute was confirmed, their persons exempted from the cognizance of the inquisitors, and subjected entirely to the jurisdiction of the bishops: and at last, for their farther security, Charles, Duke of Burgundy, in 1472, obtained a bull from Pope Sixtus IV. by which they were ranked among the religious orders, and delivered from the jurisdiction of their bishops; which privileges were yet more extended by Pope Julius II. in 1506.

In England, the followers of Wickliff were called, by way of reproach, *Lollards,* from some affinity in their tenets, which were solemnly condemned by the archbishop of Canterbury and the council of Oxford; and those who adhered to them

* Broughton, vol. ii. p. 543. Mosheim, vol. iv. p. 122, 123.

were for many years subjected to a cruel persecution.*

LUCIANISTS, so called from Lucianus, or Lucius, a disciple of Marcion; who rejected marriage, and denied both the immortality of the soul and the resurrection.† See *Marcionites.*

LUCIFERIANS, a denomination in the fourth century; so called from Lucifer, bishop of Cagliari; a zealous trinitarian, who was on that account banished by Constantius, and afterwards refused to commune with the catholic church, on account of their receiving back on their repentance, those who had gone over to the Arians. They are said to have maintained that the soul was transfused from the parents to the children.‡

LUTHERANS, those who follow the opinions of Martin Luther, an Augustine friar, who was born at Isleben, in Upper Saxony, in the year 1483. He possessed an invincible magnanimity, and an uncommon vigour and acuteness of mind. He first took offence at the indulgences which were granted in 1517, by Pope Leo X. to those who contributed towards finishing St. Peter's church at Rome; Luther being then professor of divinity at Wittemburg. Those indulgences promised remission of all sins, past, present, and *to come,* however enormous their nature, to all who were rich enough to purchase them. At this Luther raised his warning voice; and in ninety five propositions, maintained publicly at Wittemberg, Sept. 30, 1517, exposed the doctrine of indulgences, which led him to attack the authority of the pope. This was the commencement of that memorable revolution in the church, which is styled *the reformation.*

The capital articles which Luther maintained are as follow; to which are added a few of the texts and arguments which he employed in their defence.

I. That the holy scriptures are the only source whence we are to draw our religious sentiments, whether they relate to faith or practice. John v. 39. 2. Tim. iii. 15—17. Reason also confirms the sufficiency of the scriptures: for if the written word be allowed to be a rule in one case, how can it be denied to be a rule in another?

II. That justification is the effect of faith, exclusive of good works; and that faith ought to produce good works purely in obedience to God, and not in order to our justification:§ for St. Paul, in his epistle to the

* Mosheim, vol. iii. p. 355, 357, and 378, New Ed.

† Lardner's Her. p. 287—290.

‡ Mosheim, vol i. p. 314.

§ Luther constantly opposed this doctrine to the Romish tenet, that man by works of his own—prayer, fasting, and corporeal afflictions—might merit and claim pardon; and he used to call the doctrine of justification *by faith alone* "Articulus stantis vel cadentis ecclesiæ."

Galatians, strenuously opposed those, who ascribed our justification (though but in part) to works; *If righteousness come by the law, then Christ is dead in vain.* Gal. ii. 21. Therefore it is evident we are not justified by the law, or by our works; but to him who believeth, sin is pardoned and Christ's righteousness imputed.

III. That no man is able to make satisfaction for his sins: for our Lord teaches us to say, when we have done all things that are commanded, *We are unprofitable servants.* Luke xvii. 10. Christ's sacrifice is alone sufficient to satisfy for sin, and nothing need be added to the infinite value of his atonement.

Luther also rejected tradition, purgatory, penance, auricular confession, masses, invocation of saints, monastic vows, and other doctrines of the church of Rome.

On the points of predestination, original sin, and free-will, Luther coincided with Calvin, but on matters of church discipline they widely differed; likewise on the presence of Christ's body in the sacrament. His followers also deviated from him in some things; but the following may be considered as a fair statement of their principles, and the difference between them and the Calvinists: (1.) The Lutherans have bishops and superintendants for the government of the church. But the ecclesiastical government which Calvin introduced was called presbyterian; and does not admit of the institution of bishops, or of any subordination among the clergy. (2.) They differ in their notions of the sacrament of the Lord's supper. The Lutherans reject *tran*substantiation; but affirm, that the body and blood of Christ are *materially* present in the sacrament, though in an incomprehensible manner; this they called *con*subtantiation. The Calvinists hold, on the contrary, that Jesus Christ is only *spiritually* present in the ordinance, by the external signs of bread and wine. (3.) They differ in their doctrine of the eternal decrees of God respecting man's salvation.* The modern Lutherans maintain that the divine decrees, repecting the salvation and misery of men, are founded upon the divine prescience. The Calvinists, on the contrary, consider these decrees as absolute and unconditional.

The Lutherans are generally divided into the moderate and the rigid. The *moderate* Lutherans are those who sub-

* Though Luther, and many of his German co-adjutors limited the atonement to those who are saved, a great majority of his followers maintained, that Christ actually made a full, a perfect atonement for every individual of the human race. See Wilson on Atonement, p. 22.

mitted to the *interim*, published by the emperour Charles V.* Melanchthon was the head of this party, and they were called *Adiaphorists.* The *rigid* Lutherans are those who would not endure any change in their master's sentiments; of whom M. Flacius was the head.

The Lutherans are partial to the use of instrumental music in their churches, and admit statues and paintings as the church of England does, without allowing them any religious veneration; but the rigid Calvinists reject these, and allow only the simplest forms of psalmody.

The modern Lutherans, about the close of the seventeenth century, enlarged their liberality toward other sects, and gave up the supposed right of persecution. Their public teachers now enjoy an unbounded right of dissenting from the decisions of those symbols of creeds, which were once deemed almost infallible rules of faith and practice. Mosheim attributes this change in their sentiments to the maxim which they generally adopted, that Christians were accountable to God alone for their religious opinions; and that no individual could be justly punished by the magistrate for his erroneous opinions, while he conducted himself like a virtuous and obedient subject, and made no attempts to disturb the peace and order of civil society.

The Lutherans at present admit also into their sacred canon the Epistle of St. James, and the revelation of St. John, which Luther rejected, because he could not explain them.†

The doctrine of consubstantiation, which is maintained by the Lutheran churches, constitutes the principal difference between them and the church of England. See *English church.*

In Sweden and Norway the Lutheran church is episcopal. In Denmark under the name of superintendants, all episcopal authority is retained; whilst through Germany the superiour power is vested in a consistory, over which there is a president, with a distinction of rank and privileges, and a subordination of the inferiour clergy to their superiours, different from the purity of presbyterianism.

The German Lutheran church is a respectable body as to numbers and wealth, in Pennsylvania and Maryland. Their maintaining the doctrine of consubstantiation, and the episcopal form of their ecclesiastical government, keeps them and the German reformed church

* This was a confession of faith enjoined only in the interim, i. e. till a general council should decide the question in dispute.

† Mosheim, vol. iii. p. 331; vol iv. p. 108, 109. Robertson's Charles V. vol. ii. p. 42. Broughton, vol. ii. p. 33—36. Middleton's Biographia Evan. vol. i. p. 158, &c. and Luther on the Galatians, 4to. p. 142—144.

distinct bodies. There is, however, a good understanding between them, and they often officiate in each other's pulpits, and in some instances unite in building a church, in whichthey both worship at different times. This harmony between two denominations, once so much opposed to each other, is owing to the relaxation of the reformed church in some of the peculiar doctrines of Calvinism.*

The Lutherans are also subdivided into a variety of inferiour denominations, as *Amsdorfians*, *Calixtins*, *Flacians*, *Osiandrians*, *Synergists*, *Ubiquitarians*, and *Zuinglians*, of which some account will be found under their respective heads.

M

MACEDONIANS, a denomination of the fourth century, so called after Macedonius, the semi-arian bishop of Constantinople. Socrates, the ecclesiastical historian, says, He considered the Holy Ghost as the "*divine energy* diffused throughout the universe, and not as a person distinct from the Father and the Son;" an opinion that had many partizans, before it was condemned in the council of Constantinople, in the year 381.†

*MAGDALENETTES, a name given to certain communities of nuns, consisting chiefly of penitent courtezans. They were established at Mentz in 1542—at Paris 1492—at Naples 1324—at Rouen and Bordeaux 1618. The propriety of giving this name to such characters has been, however, denied by Mr. Hanway and others, since it is by no means certain that Mary Magdalen was a woman of bad character; and her having been a demoniac by no means implies it.‡ See *Penitents*.

MAGI, (μάγοι, Greek;) interpreters of sacred mysteries. The Magi, or Magians, are an ancient Persian sect, who believed in two co-eternal principles, namely, Oromasdes, the source of all good, and Arimanius, the fountain of all evil. The former they worshipped under the symbol of its purest emblem, a perpetual fire. Their priests attained to such extraordinary skill in philosophy, that some have imagined, they exercised curious and diabolical arts, and hence arose the term Magicians. Others supposed their magic was natural and lawful.

* Evans' Sketch of Religious Denominations. Buck's Theol. Dict. Rush's Account of the German inhabitants of Pennsylvania.

† Mosheim, vol i. p 426.

‡ Scotch Theol. Dict. in Magdalen. Hanway's Letter to the governours of the Magdalen Hospital.

Such were the ancient Magi of the Persians, their descendants in Persia are the Gaurs of the present day.* See *Gaurs*.

MAHOMETANS, or MOHAMMEDANS, derive their name and doctrine from Mahomet, or Mohammed, who was born in Arabia late in the sixth century. He was endowed with a subtle genius, and possessed of great enterprise and ambition. He aimed at the introduction of a new religion, and began his eventful project by accusing both Jews and christians with corrupting the revelations that had been made to them from heaven. He maintained that the prophets, and even Christ himself, had foretold his coming, which he endeavoured to make out from the Arabic version of Deut. xxxii. 2. Psalm l. 2. Isa. xxi. 7, and John xvi. 7; in some of which he pretended that he was literally named, as likewise in other parts of the original gospels; and particularly that he was the *paraclete* promised by our Saviour in the text last referred to.

According to the best Mohammedan authors, his mission was revealed to him in a dream, in the fortieth year of his age. From that moment, say they, Mohammed, under the influence of a holy terrour, devoted himself to a solitary life. He retired to a grotto in the mountain of Hira, which overlooks Mecca. He there passed his days and nights in fasting, prayer, and meditation. In the midst of one of these extacies, the angel Gabriel appeared to him with the first chapter of the koran, and commanded him to read. Mohammed replied, he was unable; upon which the angel repeatedly embraced him, and commanded him to read in the name of his Creator. A few days afterwards, praying upon the same mountain of Hira, Mohammed saw the angel again seated in the midst of the clouds, on a glittering throne, with the second chapter of the koran; and was addressed by him in the following words: "Oh thou who art covered with a celestial mantle, arise and preach!"

Thus Gabriel, say the same writers, communicated by command of the Eternal to his prophet, in the twenty three last years of his life, chapter by chapter, the whole book of the koran.†

These pretensions to a divine mission drew on him a requisition from the inhabitants of Mecca, that he would convince them by working a miracle; but he replied, "God refuses those signs and wonders that would depreciate the merit of faith, and aggravate the guilt of infidelity." He declared that God sent him into the world not only to teach his will, but to compel mankind to embrace it. The magistrates of Mecca were alarmed at the progress of his

* Calmet's Dictionary on the Bible, vol. ii.

† Prideaux's Life of Mahomet. D'Ohosson's Ottoman Empire.

doctrines; and Mohammed, being apprized of their design to destroy him, fled to Medina. From this flight, which happened in the year of Christ 622, his followers compute their era, called in Arabic, *hegira,* or the *flight.*

The book in which the Mohommedan religion is contained is called *alcoran,* or *the koran,* i. e. the *reading;* as we say the *bible,* which means the *book,* by way of eminence. The Mohammedans believe, that this book was taken from the great volume of the *divine decrees,* which has been from everlasting by God's throne, written on a table of vast dimensions, called "the preserved table." Its doctrines made a most rapid progress over Arabia, Syria, Egypt, and Persia; and Mohammed became the most powerful monarch of his time. His successors spread over great part of Asia, Africa, and Europe: and they still give law to a very considerable proportion of mankind.

This rapid and extensive spread of the Moslem faith has not only been urged as an argument in its favour, but been brought into competition with the propagation of Christianity. Two circumstances however must be brought into consideration. Mohammed contrived by the permission of poligamy and concubinage to make his creed palatable to the most depraved of mankind; and at the same time, by allowing its propagation by the sword, to excite the martial spirit of unprincipled adventurers. "The sword, (says he) is the key of heaven and hell:" "and whosoever falls in battle, his sins are forgiven at the day of judgment; and the loss of his limbs shall be supplied by the wings of angels and cherubims."

The great doctrine of the koran is the *unity of God:* to restore which point, Mohammed pretended, was the chief end of his mission; it being laid down by him as a fundamental truth, that there never was, nor can be, more than one true religion. For though particular laws or ceremonies are temporary, and subject to alteration according to divine direction; yet, the substance of religion being truth, continues immutable. And he taught, that whenever this religion became neglected, or essentially corrupted, God informed and admonished mankind thereof by prophets, of whom Moses and Jesus were the most distinguished, till the appearance of Mohammed.

The koran asserts Jesus to be the true Messiah, the word and breath of God, a worker of miracles, a preacher of heavenly doctrines, and an exemplary pattern of a perfect life. Many Mohammedans deny that he was really crucified; but pretend that, to elude the malice of his enemies, he was caught up into paradise, and another person crucified in his stead; though this opinion is by no means universal. They believe that his religion was improved and completed by Mohammed, who was the *seal* of the prophets, and was sent from God to restore the true religion to its primitive simplicity; with the addition however, of some peculiar laws and ceremonies.

The Mohammedans divide their religion into two general parts; faith and practice. Their faith, or theory, is summed up in this confession; *There is but one God, and Mohammed is his prophet.* Under these two propositions are comprehended six distinct branches: Belief in God; in his angels; in his scriptures; in his prophets; in the resurrection and judgment; in God's absolute decrees.

The unity of God is the first principle of their faith. "There is no God but God, and him only we must adore." Of angels it is believed, that they have pure and subtile bodies, created of fire, and that they have various forms and offices; some being employed in writing down the actions of men, others in carrying the throne of God, and other services. They reckon four angels superiour to the rest: Gabriel, who is employed in writing the divine decrees—Michael, the protector of the Jews—Azrael, the angel of death—and Israfil, who will sound the trumpet at the resurrection. They likewise assign to each person two guardian angels. The devil, according to the koran, was once one of the highest angels; but fell through refusing to pay homage to Adam at the command of God.

Besides angels and devils, the Mohammedans are taught to believe an intermediate order of creatures, which they call *jin*, or *genii;* created also of fire, but of a grosser fabric than angels, and subject to mortality. Some of these are supposed to be good, and others bad; and capable of future salvation or damnation, as men are.

As to the scriptures, they are taught by the koran, that God in divers ages of the world gave revelations of his will in writing to his prophets, all of which are lost except the pentateuch, the psalms, the gospel, and the koran, which were successively delivered to Moses, David, Jesus, and Mohammed; which last being the *seal* of the prophets, these revelations are now closed. The number of prophets, who have been from time to time sent into the world they compute at 224 thousand.

Their next article of faith is the general resurrection and a future judgment. But before these, they believe there is an intermediate state, both of the soul and body. When a corpse is laid in the grave, two angels they suppose, come to examine it concerning the unity of God and the mission of Mohammed. If the body answer rightly, it is suffered to rest in peace: if not, they beat it with iron maces, then press the earth on the corpse, which is knawed and stung by ninety nine dragons, which some explain allegorically, of the stings of conscience.

As to the souls of the faithful, when they are separated from the body by the angel of death, they believe that those of the prophets are admitted into paradise immediately: that the souls of believers are lodged with Adam in the lowest heaven; but that those of the wicked are confined in a dungeon under a great rock, to be there tormented till the general resurrection. In these points, however, they are by no means unanimous.

That the resurrection will be general, and extend to angels, genii, men, and animals, is the received opinion of the Mohammedans, and supported by the authority of the koran.*

Mankind, say they, at the resurrection will be distinguished into three classes; those who go on foot, those who ride, and those who creep. The first class will consist of those believers, whose good works have been few; the second of those who are more acceptable to God; whence Ali affirms that the pious, when they come forth from their sepulchres, shall find ready prepared for them white-winged camels, with saddles of gold. The third class will be composed of infidels, whom God will cause to make their appearance with their faces on the ground. When all are assembled together, they will wait in their ranks and orders for the judgment a very considerable time. At length God will come in the clouds, surrounded by angels, and will produce the books wherein every man's actions are written. Some say, that he will judge all creatures in the space of half a day, and others less. At this tribunal, every action, thought, and word, will be weighed in balances held by the angel Gabriel, of so vast a size, that its two scales are capacious enough to contain both heaven and earth. The trials being over, all must pass the bridge at *Sirat*, which is laid over the middle of hell, and is described to be finer than a hair, and sharper than the edge of a sabre. The wicked will miss their footing, and fall headlong into hell fire.†

In the koran it is said that hell has seven gates, for the mussulmans, the christians, the jews, the sabians, the magicians, the pagans, and for hypocrites of all religions. Here they will suffer a variety of torments, which shall be eternal, except to those who have embraced the true religion, who will be delivered thence after they have expiated their crimes by their sufferings.‡ The righteous, after having surmounted the difficulties of their passage, will en-

* Sale's Koran, p. 96, 97. † Ibid. p. 90—112.
‡ D'Ohosson's Hist. of the Ottoman Empire, vol. i. p. 109.

ter paradise, which they describe to be a most glorious and delicious place, inhabited by beautiful women or *houris*, abounding with rivers of milk, wine, and honey, &c. Here the faithful will enjoy the most exquisite delights, in a state of eternal beatitude, where the degree of felicity is proportioned to the sincerity of their faith, and the nature and number of their good works. Some of their philosophers, however, understand these descriptions allegorically.

The last great point of faith relates to God's absolute decrees. The doctrine which they call orthodox is, that whatever comes to pass in the world, whether it be good or bad, proceeds entirely from the divine will, and is irrevocably fixed, and recorded from all eternity in the *preserved table*; and that God hath secretly predetermined, not only the adverse and prosperous fortune of every person in the world; but also his obedience or disobedience, and consequently his everlasting happiness or misery after death; which fate or predestination, it is impossible by any foresight or wisdom to avoid. Notwithstanding this, some doctors of the Mohammedan law assert, that whoever denies free-will, and attributes human actions to the sole influence of the Deity, sins against religion; and, if he persist in his errour, becomes an infidel. They assert, that in every circumstance of life, the divine assistance ought first to be implored, through the intercession of the prophet: then every one should reflect, deliberate, and use that aid which prudence and experience may suggest. After these means have been employed, then, they say, that human events may be attributed to the decrees of heaven; to which mankind ought ever to submit with the most unlimited resignation.

It is certain that Mohammed made great use of the doctrine of predestination, or rather *fate*, for the advancement of his designs; encouraging his followers to fight without fear, and even desperately, for the propagation of their faith, by representing to them that all their caution would not avert their inevitable destiny, or prolong their lives: for not only the time, but the manner and circumstances of their death, have been unalterably fixed from all eternity. Hence the rigid mussulman deems every attempt to change the common order of things, rebellion against the established laws of God; and views the plague, which is common in those parts, ravaging his country, and destroying thousands and ten thousands in the streets, without exerting one effort to check its deadly effects.*

Of the four practical duties required by the koran, prayer is the first. Mahomet used to

* White's Bampton Lecture, p. 84.

call prayer, the *pillar of religion, and the key of paradise.* Hence he obliged his followers to pray, five times every twenty four hours, and always to wash before prayers.

The giving of alms is commanded jointly with prayer; the former being held of great efficacy in causing the latter to prevail with God.*

Fasting is another duty enjoined as of the utmost importance. They are obliged to fast the whole month of Ramadan, from day-light to sun-set; and the reason given is, because at that time the koran was sent down from heaven.

The pilgrimage to Mecca is so necessary a point of practice, that, according to a tradition of Mohammed, he who dies without performing it, may as well die a jew or a christian: they also practise circumcision as a divine institution; and keep their sabbath on a Friday.

The negative precepts of the koran are, to abstain from usury, gambling, drinking of wine, eating of blood, and swine's flesh.

The Mohammedans are no less divided in sentiment, than the Christians. The first division is into the followers of Abubekir and Ali; each of whom claimed the succession after Mohammed's death, as Caliph or vicar of the prophet; just as the pope pretends to be the successor of St. Peter. The adherents to the former are called *Somnites;* because they adhered to the *Somna* or traditions of the sayings of the prophet, in the same manner, as the Rabbins adhere to the Jewish Mishna. On the other hand the *Schiites,* who adhere to Ali, reject these traditions, as the Karaites do those of the Jews. Between these parties subsists the greatest animosity, each charging the other with corrupting their religion, and anathematizing each other as the vilest heretics. These are divided into a variety of inferiour sects, differing chiefly on the doctrines of fate and free-will; on the nature and duration of future rewards and punishments, and on certain rites and ceremonies; but the christian reader would be little interested by particulars. The followers of Ali are chiefly to be found in Persia; and the subjects of the great mogul are, in a great measure, neuter.

These principles are all professedly derived from the Koran, or Mohammedan bible, repeatedly referred to above. This book has been extolled as the standard of eloquence among the Arabians; and many learned christian writers have admitted that it contains eloquent passages, but it has been asserted, that "most of these are evidently borrowed from the writings of Moses and the prophets, and are written in a style similar to that of the Hebrew scriptures," and that

* Sale's Koran, p. 114—120.

"the commentators on the koran, not less numerous than those of christianity, have been equally successful with the latter, in darkening the text, they have attempted to explain."

This account, which would already be too long, were it not respecting the faith of an hundred and forty millions of the present race of mankind, shall be concluded with a brief summary of mussulman theology, in the form of a creed, said to be extracted from a catechism lately published at Constantinople. "I believe in the books which have been delivered from heaven to the prophets. In this manner was the koran given to Mohammed, the pentateuch to Moses, the psalter to David, and the gospel to Jesus. I believe in the prophets, and the miracles which they performed. Adam was the first prophet, and Mohammed the last. I believe that for the space of fifty thousand years, the righteous shall repose under the shade of the terrestrial paradise, and the wicked shall be exposed naked to the burning rays of the sun. I believe in the bridge Siret, which passes over the bottomless pit of hell; it is as fine as a hair, and as sharp as a sabre. All must pass over it, and the wicked shall be thrown off. I believe in the water-pools of paradise. Each of the prophets has in paradise a bason for his own use; the water is whiter than milk, and sweeter than honey. On the ridges of the pools are vessels to drink out of it, and they are bordered with stars. I believe in heaven and hell. The inhabitants of the former know no want, and the houris who attend them are never afflicted with sickness. The floor of paradise is musk, the stones are silver, and the cement gold. The damned, on the contrary, are tormented by fire, and by voracious and poisonous animals."*

MANICHEANS, or **Manichees**, a denomination founded in the third century, by one Manes, or Manicheus. Being a Persian by birth, and educated among the magi, he attempted a coalition of their doctrine with the christian system; or rather, the explication of the one by the other; and in order to succeed in the enterprize, affirmed, that Christ had left the doctrine of salvation imperfect and unfinished: and that *he* was the *Paraclete*, or Comforter, whom the departing Saviour had promised to his disciples, to lead them into all truth. He rejected the old testament, the four gospels, and the acts of the apostles; said that the epistles of Paul were falsified in a variety of places, and wrote a gospel which he pretended was dictated to him by God himself, and distinguished it by the name of *Erteng*.

* Sale's Koran. Prideaux's Life of Mohammed. Adam's Religious World displayed, vol. i. p. 217.

Manes taught, that there are two principles from which all things proceed; the one, a most pure and subtle matter, called *light;* and the other, a gross and corrupt substance, called *darkness.* Each of these is subject to the dominion of an eternal, superintending Being. He, who presides over the light, is called God; he, who rules the darkness, bears the title of *Hyle,* or a *Demon.* The ruler of the light is supremely benevolent, good, and happy. The prince of darkness is in himself unhappy; and being desirous to render others partakers of his misery, evil and malignant. These two beings have each produced an immense multitude of creatures resembling themselves, and distributed them through their respective provinces.

The prince of darkness long knew not that light existed in the universe; and no sooner did he perceive it, by means of a war kindled in his dominions, than he endeavoured to subject it to his empire. The ruler of the light opposed his efforts, at first with no great success: for the prince of darkness seized upon a considerable portion of the celestial elements, even of the light itself, and mingled them in the mass of corrupt matter. The ruler of the light then employed the living spirit, who succeeded better; but he could not entirely disengage the pure particles of the celestial matter from the corrupt mass, through which they had been dispersed. The prince of darkness after his defeat produced the first parents of the human race. These consist of a body formed out of the corrupt matter of the kingdom of darkness; and of two souls, one of which is sensitive and lustful, and is attributed to the evil principle; the other is rational and immortal; a particle of that divine light which was carried away by the army of darkness, and immersed into the mass of malignant matter.

Mankind being thus formed, God created the earth out of the mass of matter by that living spirit, who had vanquished the prince of darkness; in order to furnish a dwelling for the human race; to deliver by degrees the captive souls from their corporeal prisons; and to extract the celestial elements from the gross substance, in which they were involved. In order to this design, God produced two beings of eminent dignity from his own essence—Christ, and the Holy Ghost. The former is supposed to be that glorious intelligence which the Persians called *Mythras;* the brightness of the eternal light, subsisting in and by himself, endowed with life, enriched with infinite wisdom, and having his residence in the sun. The latter, also a luminous, animated substance, diffused throughout the atmosphere, which surrounds this terrestrial globe. This genial principle warms and illuminates the minds of men, also renders the earth fruitful, and draws forth gradually from its bosom the latent particles of celestial fire, which it wafts up on high to their primitive station.

After the supreme Being had for a long time admonished the captive souls, by the ministry of the angels and holy prophets, he directed Christ to descend upon earth, in order to hasten the return of those imprisoned spirits to their celestial country. In obedience to this command Christ appeared among the Jews, clothed with the shadowy *form* of a human body, and not with the real substance. He taught mortals how to disengage the rational soul from the corrupt body, to conquer the violence of malignant matter; and demonstrated his divine mission by stupendous miracles. On the other hand, the prince of darkness used every method to inflame the Jews against this divine messenger, and incited them at length to put him to death upon an ignominious cross; which punishment however, he suffered not in reality, but only in appearance, and in the opinion of men. When Christ had fulfilled the purposes of his mission, he returned to his throne in the sun, and appointed a certain number of chosen apostles to propagate his doctrines through the world. But before his departure, he promised that at a certain period he would send a messenger, superiour to all others in eminence and dignity, whom he called the *Paraclete*, or *Comforter*, who should add many things to the precepts he had delivered, and dispel the errours under which his servants laboured. This comforter is Manes, who, by order of the Most High, declared to mortals the *whole* doctrine of salvation, without concealing any of its truths under the veil of metaphor.

Those souls, who believe Jesus to be the Son of God, renounce the worship of the God of the Jews, who is the prince of darkness, obey the laws delivered by Christ, as they are enlarged and illustrated by Manes, and combat with persevering fortitude the lusts and appetites of a corrupt nature, derive from this faith and obedience the inestimable advantage of being gradually purified from the contagion of matter. The total purification of souls cannot indeed be accomplished during this life. Hence it is that the souls of men after death must pass through two states more of probation and trial, by water and fire, before they can ascend to the regions of light. They ascend, therefore, first into the moon, which consists of benign and salutary water; whence, after a lustration of fifteen days, they proceed to the sun, whose purifying fire removes entirely their corruption. The bodies, composed of matter, which they have left behind them, return to their first state, and enter into their original mass. On the other hand, those souls, who have neglected the salutary work of their purification, pass after death into the bodies of animals of different kinds, where they remain till they have expiated their guilt, and accomplished their salvation. When the greatest part of the captive souls are restored to liberty and to the regions of light, then a devouring fire shall break forth at the divine command, from the caverns in which it is at present confined, and shall destroy the frame of the world. After this tremendous event, the prince and powers of darkness shall be forced to return to their primitive abode of anguish and misery, in which they shall dwell forever: for, to prevent their renewing this war in the regions of light, God shall surround the mansions of darkness with an invincible guard, composed of those souls who have not finished their purifications. These set in array, like a military band, shall fully prevent any of their wretched inhabitants from coming forth again to the light.

To support their fundamental doctrine of two principles, the Manicheans argue thus: If we depend only on one almighty Cause, infinitely good, we cannot account for the existence of natural and moral evil: for it is impossible, that the first man could derive the faculty of doing ill from a good principle, for evil cannot proceed but from a bad cause; therefore the free-will of Adam was derived from two opposite principles. He depended on the good principle for his power to persevere in innocence; but his power to deviate from virtue owed its rise to an evil principle. Hence it is argued, there are two contrary principles; the one, the source of good; the other, the fountain of all vice and misery.

Manes enjoined his followers to mortify and afflict the body, which he looked upon as essentially corrupt; and to divest themselves of all the passions and instincts of nature: but he did not impose this severe manner of living without distinction. He divided his disciples into two classes; one of which comprehended perfect christians, under the name of the *elect;* the other the imperfect and feeble, under the title of *hearers.* The elect were obliged to an entire abstinence from flesh, eggs, milk, fish, wine, all intoxicating drink, and wedlock; and to live in a state of the sharpest penury, nourishing their emaciated bodies with only bread, herbs, pulse, and melons. The discipline of the hearers was milder: they were allowed to possess houses, lands, and wealth; to feed upon flesh, and to enter into the bonds of conjugal life; but under conditions of moderation and temperance.

The general assembly of the

Manicheans was headed by a president, who was considered as the representative of Jesus Christ. To him were joined twelve rulers, who were designed to represent the twelve apostles; and these were followed by seventy two bishops—the successors of the seventy two disciples. These bishops had presbyters and deacons under them; and all members of these orders were chosen out of the class of the elect.

The Manicheans observed the Lord's day, but fasted upon it. They likewise celebrated Easter, and had a regular church discipline and censors. They read the scriptures; they baptized in the name of the Father, Son, and Holy Ghost, and partook of the Lord's supper.

The doctrine of Manes differs from that of the Gnostics in this respect: instead of supposing evil to have originated ultimately from inferiour and subordinate beings, he held the doctrine of two original independent principles; the one immaterial, and supremely good; the other material, and the source of all evil; but actuated by a soul, or something of the nature of intelligence. This sect concealed themselves under various names during the fourth century; in the sixth, they revived and spread much in Persia: in the twelfth, they were again revived under one Constantine, an Armenian, with many refinements and improvements, and subsisted down to the fifteenth century.*

MARCELLIANS, a denomination in the fourth century; so called from Marcellus, bishop of Ancyra; he taught, that the Son and Holy Spirit are emanations from the Father; which, after the economy of redemption was finished, should return, and be absorbed again into the divine essence.†

MARCIONITES, a sect in the second century; so called from Marcion, successor of Cerdo, who made several additions to his doctrines. He taught men to believe in a God superiour to the creator; namely, the supreme God, the Father, invisible, inaccessible, and perfectly good. The creator, who was the God of the Jews, made this lower and visible world. The supreme God had also a world of his making; but perfect, immaterial, and invisible. For he supposed if a *good* God had made this world, there would have been neither sin nor misery; but all men would have been holy and happy. He taught that Jesus was the Son of the good God, who took the exteriour form of a man; and, without being born, he showed himself at once in

* Mosheim, vol. i. p. 239—245. Bayle's Hist. Dict. vol. iv. p. 2,487—2,489. Priestley's Eccles. Hist. vol. i. p. 518. Jortin's Remarks, vol. ii. p. 263.

† Mosheim, vol. i. p. 424, New Ed.

Galilee as a man grown, and assumed the character of a saviour.

According to this doctrine, Christ had the appearance of a human body, but not the reality. They founded this opinion on angels appearing, under the old testament, in bodily forms, and on Phil. ii. 6—8; *being in the* form *of God*, he emptied himself, and *took the* form *of a servant*—the appearance, not the reality. Marcion acknowledged, that the prophets had promised a saviour to the Jews, but pretended that this deliverer was not the Son of God. Hence he believed that there are two Christs; one, who appeared in the time of Tiberius, for the salvation of all nations; another, the restorer of the Jewish state, who is yet to come. He supposed, that the souls of the virtuous would enjoy eternal happiness; but he denied the resurrection of the body.

Marcion altogether rejected the old testament, and received but eleven books of the new; and of the gospels only Luke, and that with many alterations: he also rejected all the parts of the new testament which contain quotations from the old. The manners of this people were inoffensive and in some respects austere. They censured marriage, and praised virginity. They believed in a kind of necessity, and their zeal is charged with intemperance, in rashly offering themselves to martyrdom.*

MARCOSIANS, a branch of Gnostics in the second century; whose leaders were Marc and Colobarsus. The former is charged, with being a magician and an astrologer. He seems to have been fond of mysteries. He spoke highly of Jesus Christ, but symbolized in many points with the *Gnostics* and *Valentinians*.†

MARONITES, certain eastern christians who inhabit Maronia, near Mount Libanus, in Syria. This denomination retained the opinions of the Monothelites till the twelfth century, when they were re-admitted, in the year 1182, to the communion of the church of Rome. As to their peculiar tenets before their reconciliation, they observed the Saturday as well as the Sunday-sabbath. They held that all souls were created together, at the beginning; and that those of good men do not enter into heaven, till after the resurrection. They added other opinions, which were similar to those of the *Greek* church.‡

MARTINISTS, a sect which sprang up at Moscow, about the end of the reign of Catherine II. They received their name from one Martin, a Frenchman, who appears to

* Lardner's Works, vol. ix. p. 369—393.

† Mosheim, vol. i. p. 188. Lardner's Heretics, p. 172—184.

‡ Broughton, vol. ii. p. 51. Mosheim, vol. ii. p. 37.

have entertained opinions similar to those of the famous Jacob Behmen, and introduced the doctrines of the mystics into the cold regions of the North. They are constantly in search of mysteries, and new discoveries in revelation and nature. In their writings, they make use of a number of mystical signs or hieroglyphics, particularly the picture of an heart, which they fill with symbolical figures, expressive of the spiritual state of the supposed possessor. They have numbers of such pictures filled with hieroglyphics expressive of the passions, talents, virtues and vices of men, from the most abandoned to the most righteous.

They pretend to visions and discoveries both in physics and metaphysics; by which, they say, they arrive at the most exalted spiritual knowledge. This denomination are not numerous at the present day; but these mystical religionists are, in general, men who have the character of being learned, and whose chief object seems to be, to support this character by pretensions to great acquirements in hidden sciences; to which, they say, others can never attain, till they arrive at the same degree of spiritual and physical knowledge with themselves.

The Martinists profess a warm regard for the word of God, which according to them contains not only the way of deliverance to fallen man, but also the whole secrets of nature. Their mode of interpreting scripture is, to represent the most simple texts as full of some mystical meaning, which they call the spiritual sense.* See *New Jerusalem Church.*

*MARTYRS, those witnesses for the truth, who have sealed their testimony with their lives, in distinction from the *confessors*; who, though they suffered in the cause of religion, were not called to "resist unto blood."†

MASSALIANS, or *Euchites*, certain monks in the fourth century, who derived their name from a Hebrew word signifying *prayer*, it being their distinguishing tenet, that a man is literally to *pray without ceasing*. Hereupon they shunned society--avoided social religion and public ordinances, and retired into the woods, that they might wait solely and continually on prayer. They imagined that two souls resided in man; the one good, the other evil: and taught that it was impossible to expel the evil demon, otherwise than by constant prayer and singing of hymns; and that when this malignant spirit was cast out, the pure mind returned to God, and was again united to the divine essence, whence it had been separated. They boasted of extraordinary revelations, and a-

* Pinkerton's Greek Church, p. 273, 274. † Scotch Theol. Dict.

dopted many opinions of the Manichean system. They were a kind of Mystics.*

MATERIALISTS, or PHYSICAL NECESSARIANS, certain philosophers in the christian church, who admitting the maxim, *Ex nihilo nihil fit* (from nothing can arise nothing) had recourse to a supposed internal matter, as a kind of *substratum* for the creation of material beings. In modern language, Materialists are those who, denying the existence of spirit, conceive the soul of man to be material; or that thought is the result of corporeal organization. Of this class was the late Dr. Joseph Priestley, who considers man as consisting only of matter, disposed in a certain manner. At death the parts of this material substance are so disarranged, that the powers of perception and thought, which depend upon this arrangement, cease. At the resurrection they will be rearranged in the same, or in a similar manner, as before; and, consequently, the powers of perception and thought will be restored. Death with its concomitant putrefaction and dispersion of parts, is only a decomposition. What is decomposed may be recomposed by the being, who first composed it: so that, in the most proper sense of the word, the same body which dies shall rise again, not with every thing adventitious and extraneous, as what we receive by nutrition; but with the same stamina, or those particles which really belonged to the germ of the organical body. But the following particulars contain a farther developement of Dr. Priestley's system:

I. That man is no more than what we now see of him. The corporeal and mental faculties, inhering in the same substance, grow, ripen, and decay together; and whenever the system is dissolved, it continues in a state of dissolution, till it shall please that almighty Being, who called it into existence, to restore it to life again. For if the mental principle were, in its own nature, immaterial and immortal, all its peculiar faculties would be so too; whereas we see that every faculty of the mind is liable to be impaired, and even to become extinct, before death. Since, therefore, all the faculties of the mind, separately taken, appear to be mortal, the substance, or principle in which they exist, says Dr. Priestley, must be pronounced mortal too.

This system (it is added) gives a real value to the doctrine of the resurrection, which is peculiar to revelation; on this alone the sacred writers build our hope of future life: and represent all the rewards of virtue, and all the punishments of vice, as taking place at that awful day, and not before. See 1 Cor. xv. 16—32.

Farther, the scriptures, which speak of the state of man at death, expressly exclude any

* Mosheim, vol. i. p. 350, 351. Formey's Eccles. Hist. vol. i. p. 82.

trace of sense, thought, or enjoyment. See Psalm vi. 5. Job xiv. 10, &c.

II. That there is some fixed law of nature respecting the will, as well as the other powers of the mind, and every thing else in the constitution of nature; and, consequently, that it is never determined without some real or apparent cause foreign to itself; i. e. without some motive of choice: or, that motives influence us in some definite and invariable manner; so that every volition, or choice, is constantly regulated and determined by what precedes it: and this constant determination of mind according to the motives presented to it, is what is meant by its *necessary determination*. The term *necessary* being not here opposed to *voluntary*, but to contingent. This fact being admitted, there will be a necessary connexion between all things past, present, and to come, in the way of proper cause and effect, as much in the intellectual as in the natural world: so that, according to the established laws of nature, no event could have been otherwise than it *has been*, *is*, or *is to be*. Thus the will, in all determinations, is governed by the state of mind—this state of mind is in every instance determined by the Deity; and there is a continued chain of causes and effects, of motives and actions, inseparably connected, and originating from the condition, in which we are brought into existence by the Author of our being.

It is universally acknowledged, that there can be no effect without an adequate cause. This is even the foundation, on which the only proper argument for the being of a God rests. And the Necessarian asserts, that if, in any given state of mind, with respect both to dispositions and motives, two different determinations, or volitions, be possible, it can be on no other principle, than that one of them should come under the description of an effect without a cause; just as if the beam of a balance might incline either way, though loaded with equal weights. And if any thing whatever, even a thought in the mind of man, could arise without an adequate cause, any thing else, the mind itself, or the whole universe, might likewise exist without an adequate cause.

The scheme of philosophical necessity, therefore, implies a chain of causes and effects established by infinite wisdom, and terminating in the greatest good of the whole universe; evils of all kinds, natural and moral, being admitted, as far as they contribute to that end, or are in the nature of things inseparable from it. Vice is productive not of good, but of evil to *us*, both here and hereafter, though good may result from it to the whole system: and, according to the fixed laws of nature, our present and future happiness necessarily depend, on our cultivating good dispositions. By our being liable to punishment for our actions, is meant, on this hypothesis, that it is wise and good in the supreme Being, to appoint that certain sufferings should follow certain actions, provided they be voluntary, though necessary ones: a course of voluntary actions and sufferings being calculated to promote the greatest ultimate good.

Dr. Priestley distinguishes this scheme of philosophical necessity from the Calvinistic doctrine of predestination, in the following particulars:—

I. No Necessarian supposes, that any of the human race will suffer eternally; but that future punishments will answer the same purpose as temporal ones are found to do; all of which tend to good, and are evidently admitted for that purpose.

II. The Necessarian believes, that his own dispositions and actions are the necessary and sole means of his present and future happiness; so that, in the most proper sense of the words, it depends entirely *on himself*, whether he be virtuous or vicious, happy or miserable.

III. The Calvinistic system entirely excludes the popular notion of free-will; viz. the liberty or power of doing what we please, virtuous or vicious, as belonging to every person, in every situation; which is perfectly consistent with the doctrine of philosophical necessity, and indeed results from it.

IV. The Necessarian rejects original sin, the deity and atonement of Christ, divine influences, and other points of Calvinism. He believes nothing of the actions of any man being necessarily sinful: but, on the contrary, thinks that the very worst of men are capable of benevolent intentions in many things they do; and likewise that very good men are capable of falling from virtue, and consequently of sinking into final perdition. Upon these principles also, all late repentance, and especially after long and confirmed habits of vice, is altogether and necessarily impracticable and ineffectual.

In short, the three doctrines of Materialism, Philosophical Necessity, and Socinianism, are considered as essential parts of one system. The scheme of necessity is the immediate result of the materiality of man; for mechanism is the undoubted consequence of materialism: and that man is wholly material, is eminently subservient to the *mere* humanity of Christ. For if no man have a soul distinct from his body, Christ, (who in all other respects appeared as a man) could not have a soul which had existed before his body: and the doctrine of the pre-existence of souls, (of which the pre-existence of Christ is a branch,) will be effectually overturned.* See *Necessarians* and *Socinians.*

*MELATONI, the disciples of Melato, who believing the deity to be corporeal, supposed the creation of Adam in the "image of God," to refer to his bodily form.†

MELCHITES, the Syrian, Egyptian, and other eastern christians in the Levant, who (though not Greeks) follow the doctrines of the Greek church, except in some points which relate to ceremonies and ecclesiastical discipline. They were called *Melchites,* i. e. Royalists, by their adversaries, by way of reproach, on account of their implicit submission to the edict of the emperour Marcion, in favour of the council of Chalcedon.‡

MELCHIZEDECKIANS, a denomination which arose about the beginning of the third century. They affirmed that Melchizedec was not a man, but a heavenly power superiour to Jesus Christ: for Melchizedec, they said, was the intercessor and mediator of the angels, as Jesus Christ was for men; and his priesthood was only a copy of that of the former. See *Hieracites* and *Theodotians.*

It may be remarked here that the Hutchinsonians believe that Melchizedec was no other than Jesus Christ himself.

MELETIANS, the followers of Meletius, an Egyptian bishop, who, being deposed for sacrificing to idols, affected great severity against apostates, and like the Novatians, refused to re-admit them on their repentance.§

MENANDRIANS, a denomination in the first century, from Menander, a supposed disciple of Simon Magus. He pretended to be one of the *aions* sent from the *pleroma,* or celestial regions, to succour the souls that lay groaning under oppression; and to support them against the demons that hold the reins of empire in this sublunary world.‖

*MENDAI, or MENDÆANS, otherwise called *Christians of St. John,* or *Hemero Baptists,* which see. "These ambiguous christians (says Mosheim) dwell in Persia and Arabia, and principally at Bassora, and their religion consists in bodily washings, performed frequently and with great solemnity."¶

*MENDICANTS, or *Begging Friars:* several religious

* Priestley's Disquisitions on Matter and Spirit, vol. i p. 4—163; vol. ii. on Philosophical Necessity, p. 8—193. History of Early Opinions, vol. i p. 211, 212. Correspondence between Priestley and Price, p. 118—359. Crombie's Essay on Philosophical Necessity.

† Ross' View of Religions, p. 211.

‡ Mosheim's Eccles. Hist. vol. ii. p. 31. Collier's Hist. Dict. vol. ii.

§ Mosheim, vol. i. p. 384, 385, new ed.

‖ Mosheim, vol. i. p. 116. Formey's Eccles. Hist. vol. i. p. 21.

¶ Mosheim, vol. iv. p. 266, 267, new ed.

orders in popish countries, who, having no settled revenues, are supported by charitable contributions.*

MENNONITES, a society of baptists in Holland: so called from Menno Simonis, of Friesland, who lived in the sixteenth century. He was originally a Romish priest, but joined a party of the Anabaptists, and becoming their leader, reduced the system to consistency and moderation. The Mennonites maintain that practical piety is the essence of religion, and that the surest mark of the true church is the sanctity of its members. They plead for universal toleration in religion; and debar none from their assemblies who lead pious lives, and own the scriptures for the word of God. They teach that infants are not the proper subjects of baptism; and that the ministers of the gospel ought not to receive salaries. They object to the terms *person* and *trinity*, as not consistent with the simplicity of the gospel. They deny the lawfulness of repelling force by force, and consider war in all its shapes as unchristian and unjust; they also teach that it is unlawful to take an oath on any occasion; and are extremely averse to the infliction of capital punishments.

In their private meetings every one has the liberty to speak, to expound the scriptures, and to pray. They assemble (or used to do so) twice every year from all parts of Holland, at Rynsbourg, a village two leagues from Leyden, at which time they receive the communion, sitting at a table in the manner of the independents; but in their form of discipline they are said more to resemble the presbyterians.

The ancient Mennonites professed a contempt of erudition and science; and excluded all from their communion, who deviated in the least from the most rigorous rules of simplicity and gravity; but this primitive austerity is greatly diminished in their most considerable societies. Those, who adhere to their ancient discipline, are called Flemings, or Flandrians. The whole sect were formerly called *Waterlandians*, from the district in which they lived.

The Mennonites in Pennsylvania do not baptize by immersion, though they administer the ordinance to none but adult persons. Their common method is this: The person to be baptized kneeling, the minister holds his hands over him, into which the deacon pours water, and through which it runs on the head of the baptized; after which, follow imposition of hands and prayer.†

* Buck's Theological Dictionary.

† Mosheim's Eccles. Hist. vol. iv. p. 151—162. Dict. Arts and Sciences, vol. iii. p. 2,037. Edwards' Hist. of the Amer. Baptists, vol. i. p. 94.

MEN OF UNDERSTANDING. This title distinguished a sect, which appeared in Flanders and Brussels in the year 1511. They owed their origin to an illiterate man, named Egidius Cantor, and to William of Hildenison, a Carmelite monk. They pretended to be honoured with celestial visions; and declared the approach of a new revelation more perfect than that of the gospel. They held that the resurrection was accomplished in the person of Jesus, and no other was to be expected; that the inward man was not defiled by the outward actions, whatever they were; and that the pains of hell were to have an end.

This denomination seems to have been a branch of the brethren and sisters of the Free Spirit; and their system embraced some peculiarities both of the *Mystics* and *Universalists.**

METHODISTS, a name given in the seventeenth century to a new species of polemic doctors, who distinguished themselves by new and ingenious *methods* of defending the Roman Catholic church against the attacks of the protestants.† The same name, and for the same reason, had been applied to certain ancient physicians, who were celebrated for their skill and ingenuity.

Of late years the term has been applied to ministers and private christians, both in and out of the establishment, who have been remarkable for their zeal and activity in promoting their views of religion. More correctly taken, however, it applies to a large body of religious persons, neither strict churchmen nor regular dissenters, of whose rise and history the following is a brief abstract.

This denomination was founded in the year 1729, by Messrs. John and Charles Wesley, and Mr. Morgan. In November of that year, the former being then fellow of Lincoln college, he began to spend some evenings in reading the Greek testament with his brother, Mr. Morgan, commoner of Christ-Church, and Mr. Kirkham, of Merton college. Not long afterwards two or three pupils of Mr. John Wesley and one of Mr. Charles Wesley's obtained leave to attend these meetings. They then began to visit the sick, and the prisoners who were confined in the castle. Two years after they were joined by Mr. Ingham, Mr. Broughton, and Mr. Hervey; and in 1735, by the celebrated George Whitfield, then in his eighteenth year. At this time their number in Oxford amounted to about fourteen. They obtained their name, it is said, from the exact regularity of their lives, or the correct *method* in which they disposed of their time.

In October 1735, Messrs. John and Charles Wesley, Mr. Ingham, and Mr. Delamotte,

* Mosheim, vol. iii. p. 276

† Ibid. vol. iv. p. 307.

embarked for Georgia, in order to preach the gospel to the Indians. They were at first favourably received, but in a short time lost the affection of the people; and on account of some differences with the storekeeper, Mr. Wesley was obliged to return to England. He was, however, soon succeeded by Mr. Whitfield, whose repeated labours in this country are well known.

On Mr. Whitfield's return to England in 1741, he declared his full assent to the doctrines of Calvin; Mr. Wesley, on the contrary, professed those of Arminius, and had written in favour of *universal redemption* and *perfection*, and very strongly against *election*.

The doctrines of the *Calvinists* and *Arminians* may be seen under these articles. The leading principles common to both are said to be "*Salvation by faith only in Jesus Christ, perceptible conversion*, and *an assurance of reconciliation with God*:" but whether they both mean exactly the same things by these terms, may well be questioned. The Calvinists, when speaking of justification by faith alone, for instance, do not mean that we are justified by it as an act of our own, but *as having respect to the righteousness of Christ*. The imputation of faith, therefore, with them, is the same thing as the imputation of Christ's righteousness. But Mr. Wesley's views on this subject are as follows: "All I teach (says he) respects either the nature and condition of justification, the nature and condition of salvation, the nature of justification and saving faith, or the author of faith and salvation.

I. "The nature of *justification*: That justification, of which the articles and homilies speak, signifies present forgiveness, pardon of sin, and consequently acceptance with God. Rom. iii. 25. I believe the *condition* of this is faith: Rom. iv. 5. &c. I mean not only that without faith we cannot be justified; but also that as soon as any one has true faith, in that moment he is justified. Good works follow this faith, (Luke vi. 43.) but cannot go before it.

II. "By *salvation* I mean, not barely, according to the vulgar notion, deliverance from sin; but the renewal of our souls after the image of God, in righteousness and true holiness. This implies all holy and heavenly temper—all holiness of conversation.

III. "*Faith* is a divine, supernatural *evidence*, or conviction (ελεγχος) of things not seen—as being either passed, future, or spiritual. Justifying faith implies a sure trust and confidence that Christ loved me and gave himself for me. And the moment a penitent sinner believes this, God pardons and absolves him. And as soon as his pardon or justification is *witnessed* to him by the Holy Ghost, he is saved.*

IV. "The *author* of faith and salvation is God alone. He it is that works in us both to will and to do. He is the sole giver of every good gift; and the sole author of every good work. There is no more of power than of merit in man; but as all merit is in the Son of God, in what he hath done and suffered for us, so all power is in the Spirit of God. And therefore every man, in order to believe unto salvation, must receive the Holy Ghost."†

On no subject were Mr. Wesley's sentiments more excepted against by religious persons, than on that of *perfection.* This he explained to mean, "such a degree of the love of God and the love of man; such a degree of the love of justice, truth, holiness, and purity, as will remove from the heart every contrary disposition towards God or man; and that this should be our state of mind in every situation, and in every circumstance, of life." Even this perfection, however, at its greatest height, would not include absolute freedom from errour or mistake, nor from (sinless) infirmities or temptations; nor does it imply perfection in *degree,* so as not to admit of continual increase or growth in grace.‡

As to the *societies* formed by Mr. Wesley, the only condition required of members, is "a desire to be saved from their sins;" and these are formed into small companies, or *classes,* of from twelve to twenty persons; one of whom is styled the class-leader, whose office it is to examine, to superintend, and to exhort. He usually meets his class once a week, and once a week he usually meets the minister and stewards to make his report. Several congregations connected, within the compass of ten or fifteen miles, form a circuit, to which two or three preachers are appointed, one of whom is called the superintendent; and once in the quarter the preachers meet and examine all the classes. Several circuits form a district, all the preachers of which meet annually and send minutes of their proceedings to the conference. The conference is an annual meeting of the preachers at some one of their principal places in rotation. This is their supreme court, from which lies no appeal.

The public worship of the Methodists is much like that of the dissenters; but at a few of their principal places they adopt the service of the church of

* This "witness of the Spirit" is differently understood. Some seem to consider it as a mere persuasion that the person is converted. Others think it necessary, that persuasion should be founded upon evidence. To prove this they allege John iii. 14.

† Farther appeal to men of reason and religion.

‡ Sermon on Perfection.

England. Once a quarter *watch-nights* are held,* and also *love-feasts*, both of which are confined to members of their society. The former are meetings for prayer and exhortation, usually continued till midnight. The latter are friendly meetings, at which, besides social worship, the members eat together a small piece of cake or bun, in token of brotherly communion, and drink water; on these occasions something is collected for the poor, and the whole concluded with prayer. These meetings are formed on the model of the ancient *Agapæ*, or 'feasts of charity,' mentioned by St. Jude, ver. 12.

The zeal of both Messrs. Whitfield and Wesley was very great, and their labours were abundant. They were both professed members of the church of England, though neither of them confined himself, in all respects, within its rules. The former was most distinguished for his powerful eloquence, which arrested the attention and overawed the mind: the latter, for cool, persuasive reasoning, and for a kind of legislative wisdom, which he exercised in forming his numerous followers into societies, and establishing such a connexion and subordination among them, as to give a greater stability to his denomination.

Since the death of Mr. Wesley, his people have been divided with respect to discipline. He himself had always professed a strong attachment to the church of England, and exhorted the societies under his care to attend her service, and receive the Lord's supper, from the regular clergy. But some of the societies petitioned to have preaching in their own chapels during church hours, and the Lord's supper administered by the travelling preachers. This request he generally refused; but where it could be conveniently done, sent some of the clergymen who officiated at the new chapel in London, to perform these solemn services. At the first conference after his death, which was held at Manchester, the preachers published a declaration, in which they said, that they would "take up the *plan* as Mr. Wesley had left it." This was by no means satisfactory to many of the preachers and people, who thought that religious liberty ought to be extended to all the societies, which desired it. In order to favour this change, several respectable preachers came forward, and by the writings which they circulated through the connexion, paved the way for a pacification; by which it was stipulated, that in every place where a three-fold majority of class-leaders, stewards, and trustees,

* One of the watch-nights is generally held on the night immediately preceding the new year's day; when the infant year is ushered in with songs of gladness, praise, and thanksgiving. See Nightingale's Methodism, p. 217.

desired it, the people should have preaching in church hours, and the sacraments of baptism and the Lord's supper administered to them.

The spirit of inquiry did not stop here; for it appeared to them agreeable both to reason and the custom of the primitive church, that the people should have a voice in the temporal concerns of the societies, vote in the election of church officers, and give their suffrages in spiritual concerns. The subject produced a variety of arguments on both sides of the question. At a conference held at Leeds in 1797, there were delegates from many societies in various parts, who were instructed to request, that the people might have a voice *in the formation of their own laws, the choice of their own officers, and the distribution of their own property*. The preachers proceeded to discuss two motions: Shall delegates from the societies be admitted into the conference? Shall circuit-stewards be admitted into the district meetings? Both these motions were negatived, and consequently all hopes of accommodation between the parties were given up. From hence a plan was proposed of a NEW CONNEXION. A regular meeting was formed, and Mr. William Thom being chosen president, and Mr. Alexander Kilham, secretary, the meeting proceeded to arrange the plan for supplying the congregations which adhered to them, with preachers. The president and secretary were also desired to draw up rules of church-government, that they might be circulated through the societies for their approbation. The plan, being drawn up and printed, was examined by select committees through the connexion, and, with a few alterations, was accepted by their conference of preachers and delegates.

The preachers and people are incorporated in all meetings for business, not by temporary concession, but by the essential principles of their constitution; for the private members choose the class-leaders, the leaders' meeting nominates the stewards, and the society confirms or rejects the nomination. The quarterly meetings are composed of the general stewards and representatives, chosen by the different societies of the circuits, and the fourth quarterly meeting of the year appoints the preacher and delegate of every circuit, that shall attend the general conference. For a further account of their principles and discipline, the reader is referred to a pamphlet, entitled, "*General rules of the united societies of Methodists in the New Connexion.*"

The Calvinistic Methodists are not incorporated into a body as the Arminians are; but are chiefly under the direction or influence of their ministers or patrons. There are many congregations in London and elsewhere, called Methodists, though they are in neither of the above connexions. Some of these are supplied by a variety of ministers; and others, bordering more on the congregational plan, have a resident minister.

A distinct connexion, upon Mr. Whitfield's plan, was instituted and patronized by the late Lady Huntingdon, and this still subsists.

By the minutes of the conference in July 1814, it appears, that the numbers in the societies, continuing the connexion of Mr. Wesley, are as follow; and these, it must be remembered, form at most but a moiety of their public congregations.

Great Britain	173,885
Ireland	29,388
France	14
Gibraltar	65
Sierra Leone	96
Nova Scotia, Quebec, and Newfoundland	1,570
West Indies	17,002
United States	214,327
Total	436,347

Travelling Preachers, not included in the preceding account.

Great Britain	685
Ireland	114
Foreign Missionaries	56
United States	678
	437,880

The New Connexion have about twenty circuits, forty preachers, and seven thousand members; nor do they seem likely to increase, the parent society having conceded some points which occasioned the separation. Their discipline borders on that of the Independents.

There seems to be no method of estimating the numbers of the *Calvinistic* Methodists with any tolerable accuracy; but it is probable that in England, they are at least equal to the Arminian, and in Wales, considerably more numerous.*

MILLENNARIANS, or Chiliasts, a name given to all who believe that the saints will literally reign on earth with Christ a *thousand years* after the first resurrection, before the end of the world. The former appellation is of Latin original, the latter of Greek, and both are of the same import.

The ancient Millennarians held that, after the coming of antichrist, and the destruction which will follow, there shall be a first resurrection of the just alone—that all who shall be found upon earth, both good and bad, shall continue alive;—that Jesus Christ will then descend from heaven in his glory—that the city of Jerusalem will be rebuilt, in the manner described, Rev. xxi. and

* See Miles' Chronol. History of Methodism. Gillies' Life of Whitfield. Coke's Life of Wesley. Wesley's Sermons. Benson's Apology. Buck's Theolog. Dict.

Ezek. xxxvi. Here they suppose the Lord Jesus will fix the seat of his empire, and reign a thousand years with the saints, patriarchs, and prophets, who will enjoy perfect and uninterrupted felicity, in a second paradise, more glorious than that of Eden. This opinion is adopted in the epistle of Barnabas, by Papias, Irenæus, Justin Martyr, and many more of the ancient fathers; and is illustrated and confirmed by many learned moderns, from whom we shall subjoin an abstract of their opinions.

Dr. *Thomas Burnet* and Mr. *Whiston* concur in asserting that the earth will not be entirely consumed; but that the matter of which it consists will be purified, by the action of fire; from these materials, as from a second chaos, there will, by the will of God, arise a new creation: "new heavens and a new earth." The earth, and the atmosphere, will then be so restored as to resemble what they were in the paradisaical state; and consequently, to render it a most delightful abode for man. In proof of this hypothesis they urge the following texts:—Matt. xiii. 41—43. Luke xvii. 29, 30. Acts iii. 21. Heb. i. 11, 12. 2 Pet. iii. 13, &c. They suppose that the earth, thus beautiful and improved, shall be inhabited by those who inherit the first resurrection, and who shall here enjoy a very considerable degree of happiness, though not equal to that which is to succeed the general judgment, which shall open when the thousand years, mentioned in Rev. xx. 4—6. shall be expired.

Though Mr. *Fleming* does not entirely agree with the above, he interprets Rev. xx. 6. as referring to a proper resurrection, of which, he supposes, the event recorded in Matt. xxvii. 52, was a pledge. He conjectures that the most eminent saints of the old testament times then arose, and ascended with Christ to heaven; agreeably to this, he apprehends that the saints who are to be subjects of the first resurrection, after appearing to some of the inhabitants of this earth, which may be the mean of reviving religion among them, will ascend to heaven in triumph. To this peculiar privilege of the martyrs, and some other eminent saints, St. Paul is supposed to refer, Phil. iii. 11.

Mr. *Ray* agrees that there will be a renovation of the earth; and though he does not suppose that the same animals shall be raised again, yet he thinks that other animals, as well as vegetables, will be produced in higher degrees of beauty and perfection than ever before.

Dr. *Cotton Mather* supposed that the conflagration will take place at Christ's second personal coming; that after this great event God will create 'new heavens, and a new earth.'

The raised saints will inhabit the *new heavens,* attending on our Saviour there, and receiving immense rewards for their services and sufferings for his sake. The new earth will be a paradise, and inhabited by those who shall be caught up to meet the Lord, and be with him in safety, while they see the earth flaming under them. They shall then return to the *new earth,* possess it, and people it with an offspring who shall be sinless and immortal. The risen saints who shall inhabit the new heavens, and "neither marry nor be given in marriage," will be sent down from time to time to the new earth, to be teachers and rulers, and have power over nations; and "*the will of God be done on earth as it is in heaven.*" This dispensation will continue for one thousand years. There will also be a translation from the new earth to the new heavens, either successively during the thousand years, or all at once, after the termination of that period.

Mr. Kett, in a late publication, entitled, *History the Interpreter of Prophecy,* has advanced a new plan, of which the following is an imperfect sketch. He supposes, that the *antichrist* (or the many *antichrists*) spoken of in the new testament, means *a power, a person,* or *a succession of persons,* who were to arise in the world, and either deceitfully arrogate to themselves the place and office of Christ, or exercise a direct enmity to him and his religion:—that there appear to be three great forms of antichrist; viz. Popery, Mohammedanism, and Infidelity, which were to prevail a certain time for the trial and punishment of the corrupted church of Christ—that at the present period, the Infidel form of antichrist is begun, and will continue to prevail while the Papal and Mohammedan decline—that the rise, progress, and establishment of the Infidel power is predicted by *the little horn of the beast* in the visions of Daniel, and the *second beast and his image* in the revelation of St. John.—Mr. Kett supposes, that when the Infidel power shall have reached its summit of dominion; when the Jews are collected into their own land; when the church, purified by tribulation, shall be made ready to receive her Lord, Christ shall personally appear, and finish the reign of antichrist in all its various forms: the just shall be raised from the dead, and a new kingdom of peace and everlasting happiness be established under the immediate government of the Redeemer, agreeably to the description in Dan. ii. 35. Rev. xx. 4—6. and other passages. When this glorious period of the millennium shall commence, the New Jerusalem will be separated from the world as the garden of Eden, but the gates of entrance shall stand open: the world will continue a state of probation to all but those who arose from the dead; it will, however, be enlightened by the communication of those blessed instructors. At the expiration of the thousand years, Satan will be loosed, to deceive the nations without the city: but as soon as he shall attempt to disturb the peace of the saints, fire will descend out of heaven, and devour the incorrigible sinners. The final judgment, the resurrection of the wicked, the destruction of the world, the everlasting punishment of Satan and his followers, and the admission of the saints into eternal felicity in the heavens, will immediately succeed.

Dr. Gill, bishop Newton, and many other eminent divines, adopt the literal interpretation of the prophecies: but others of equal learning and piety, incline to a figurative interpretation of these scriptures, as will be seen in the following instances:

Dr. *Whitby* supposes the millennium to refer entirely to the prosperous state of the christian church after the fall of antichrist, and the conversion of the Jews—that then shall begin a glorious and undisturbed reign of Christ over the Jew and Gentile, to continue a thousand years—and as John the Baptist was Elias, because he *came in the spirit and power of Elias;* so shall this be the church of the martyrs, and those, "who have not received the mark of the beast," because the spirit and purity of the times of the primitive martyrs shall return. He argues, that it would be a degradation to the glorified saints to dwell upon earth; and that it is contrary to the genius of the christian religion to suppose it built on temporal promises.

Mr. *Worthington's* scheme is, that the gospel, being intended to restore the ruins of the fall, will gradually meliorate the world, till, by a train of natural consequences, under the influence of divine providence and grace, it is restored to a paradisaical state. He supposes that this plan is already advanced through some important stages, among which he reckons (with Dr. Sherlock) the amendment of the earth's natural state at the deluge to have been a considerable one. He considers all improvements in learning and arts, as well as the propagation of the gospel among the heathen nations, as the process of this scheme: but he apprehends much greater advances are to be made about the year of Christ 2,000, when the millennium will commence; which shall be, according to him, such a glorious state as Dr. Whitby supposes; but with this additional circumstance, that, after some interruption from the last effects of wickedness by Gog and Magog, this shall terminate in the still nobler state of the *new heaven* and the *new earth* spoken of in Rev. xxi. and xxii. when he supposes that all natural and moral evil, and death itself, shall be banished from the earth: but good men shall continue in the highest state of rectitude, and in the greatest imaginable degree of terrestrial felicity, till the final coming of Christ and universal judgment close this delightful scene, perhaps several thousand years afterwards. Indeed, he seems to apprehend that the consummation of all things will not happen till about the year of the world 25,920, the end of the great year, as the Platonics called it, when the equinoxes shall have revolved.

Mr. *Lowman* agrees with Dr. Whitby in supposing the scripture description of the millennium to be figurative, representing the happy state of the church on its deliverance from the persecution and corruption of the third period. He supposed the book of the Revelation, after the fifth chapter, to be a prophetic representation of the most remarkable events which were to befal the christian church from that time to the end. He divides the remainder into seven periods; the first, represented by the *seals*, shows the state of the church under the heathen Roman emperours from the year 95 to 323: —the second, that of the *trumpets*, relates to what was to happen in the christian church, from 337 to 750, when the Mohammedan conquests ceased in the West:—the third represents the state of the church and world in the time of the last head of the Roman government, i. e. under the popes, for 1,260 years; viz. from 756 to 2,016: each of the *vials* which are poured out, he reckons to denote some great judgment upon the papal kingdom; the sixth and seventh vials he supposes are yet to come, and that the seventh will complete the final destruction of Rome—the fourth is that of *a thousand years*, or the *millennium*, in which the church will be in a most prosperous state, A. D. 2,000 to 3,000; so that the seventh chiliad is to be a kind of sabbath—the fifth is the renewed invasion of the enemies of the church for a short time not defined, but which is to end in their final extirpation and ruin, (chap. xx. 7—10.)—the sixth is the general resurrection and final judgment; (chap. xx. 11—15.) these terminate in the seventh grand period, in which the saints are represented as fixed in a state of everlasting triumph and happiness in the heavenly world. chap. xxi. 1—5.

Dr. *Bellamy* supposes that the millennium will be a glorious scene of Christ's spiritual reign on earth, when universal peace shall prevail; wars, famines, and all desolating judgments be at an end; industry shall flourish, and all luxury, intemperance, and extravagance, be banished. Then this globe will be able to sustain with food and raiment a number of inhabitants immensely greater than ever dwelt upon it at one time: and if all those shall, as the scripture asserts, "know the Lord, from the least to the greatest," for one thousand years together, it will naturally come to pass, that there will be more saved in that thousand years, than ever before dwelt upon the face of the earth, from the foundation of the world.

Some understand the thousand years in the Revelation, (agreeably to other prophetical numbers in that book,) a day for a year, which would extend the period of the millennium, (as the scripture year contains 360 days) to 360,000 years; in which there might possibly be millions saved to one which has been lost.*

All the above systems respecting the millennium admit the eternity of future punishment. The plan of the late Mr. *Winchester* terminates in the universal restoration of all intelligent creatures.

This author supposes that, as an introduction to the millennium, the power and empire of the Turks shall be weakened, to make way for the return of the Jews to their own land, which event is expressly foretold in Ezek. xxxix. 25—28; and many other passages; that after their return, their enemies shall come against them in vast numbers, called by the names Gog and Magog, Ezek. xxxvii. 1—7.—that they shall take and plunder the city of Jerusalem, and bring the Jews to the brink of destruction—that at the height of their triumph, Christ, the manifested Jehovah, shall appear in the clouds of heaven, according to Zech. xiv. 14.—that his appearance shall effect the conversion of the Jews, who shall receive him as the true Messiah; *They shall look on him whom they have pierced.* Zech. xii. 10; Rev. i. 7. The dead saints shall then be raised, the living saints changed, and both caught up to meet the Lord in the air, and descend with him to reign on earth, when the glorious millennium shall commence. In that period the Jews shall be again acknowledged as the people of God; the twelve tribes settled in their own land, under the government of the Saviour, and be a holy and happy people; Jerusalem shall be rebuilt in greater splendour than ever; all nations shall yearly repair to this city to worship the Lord. (Zec. xiv. 16—20.) There shall be a glorious temple erected, (Ez. xl. 41, 42.) in which the Lord Jesus shall hold his court: from thence he shall send his saints through the whole earth, to instruct and bless mankind. At this blessed period satan shall be bound; the curse shall be removed from the earth;

* To this period Dr. Priestley inclines in his Theological Institutes: and Mr. Towers, in his "Illustrations of Prophecy."

the obstructions which hinder the success of the gospel removed; all be united in one religion; wars, famines, earthquakes, tempests, and pestilence shall cease; the inhabitants of the world be more numerous than ever, and all kinds of spiritual and temporal blessings be the portion of mankind. At the end of the millennium, Satan shall be loosed to deceive the nations of the earth; a mighty army, with this great apostate at their head, shall march in a hostile manner against the camp of the saints; but fire shall immediately descend from heaven to devour them. This army is described by the Gog and Magog of St. John, which our author supposes different from the Gog and Magog mentioned by Ezekiel. This destruction will be immediately followed by the resurrection of all the dead, and the day of judgment. After this the Lord, with all the redeemed, shall ascend to heaven; and the conflagration shall take place, by which the earth shall be reduced to a globe of fire, and be the final stage of punishment; where the wicked shall endure the pangs of the *second death*, and be tormented for *ages of ages* after the day of judgment. At length the renovation of the heavens and earth shall take place, according to various prophetic passages, particularly Isaiah lxv. 17. 2 Pet. iii. 13; Rev. xxi. 1, 2. After the new heavens and earth are prepared, as a new stage for the wonders of God's redeeming love, the holy city, or New Jerusalem, shall descend as the residence of the saints, during those ages, in which the great work of redeeming lost sinners is carried on. The saints shall reign with Christ, and be kings and priests, till all fallen intelligences are restored, sin and misery cease, and holiness and happiness be absolutely universal and complete, as is expressed in Rev. xxi. 1.* See *Universalists.*

***MODALISTS.** See *Pre-existents* and *Sabellians.*

MOHAMMEDANS. See *Mahometans.*

MOLINISTS, the followers of Lewis Molina, a Spanish Jesuit, professor of divinity in the university of Ebora, in Portugal. In the year 1598, he published a book, showing that the operations of divine grace were entirely consistent with the freedom of the human will; and introduced an hypothesis to remove the difficulties attending the doctrines of predestination and liberty. He asserted,

* Broughton's Hist. Lib. vol. ii. p. 93, 94. Doddridge's Lectures, p. 581—590. Burnet's Theory, p. 209. Whiston's Theory, p. 288. Fleming's Christology, p. 29—38. Ray's Discourses, p. 407—415. Whitby's Annotations, vol. ii. p. 740. Worthington on the Extent of Redemption. Lowman on Revelations, p. 243. Mather's Life, p. 141—143. Bellamy on the Millennium, p. 65—68. Encyclopedia, vol. i. p. 290—309; vol. ii. p. 299—306; vol. xii. p. 29. Kett's Hist. of Prophecy. Winchester's Lectures on Prophecy, 2 vols. 8vo.

that the decree of predestination to eternal glory was founded on a previous knowledge and consideration of the merits of the elect; that the grace, from whose operations these merits are derived, is not efficacious by its own intrinsic power only, but also by the consent of our own will, and because it is administered in those circumstances, in which the Deity foresees that it will be efficacious. This kind of prescience, (*scientia media,*) is that foreknowledge of future contingents, which arises from a perfect acquaintance with the nature and faculties of rational beings, of the circumstances in which they shall be placed, of the objects that shall be presented to them, and of the influence which these circumstances and objects must have on their actions.*

***MOLOKANS**, an obscure sect of Russian dissenters, so called from eating milk on their fast days, which are usually on Saturday. They have a tradition of certain miracles of Christ not recorded in the gospels, and are said to use certain religious pictures peculiar to themselves.†

***MONKS**, (*monachi,*) certain persons who secluded themselves from the world to make the stricter profession of religion; they were distinguished anciently into three classes. *Solataries* are those which lived alone, and remote from town and from human society. *Cœnobites* lived in community with others in monasteries and convents. *Sarabaites* were strolling monks, who lived without any fixed rule or settled residence; whence the Mendicants, or begging friars, which are divided into Capuchins and Franciscans.

Monks are distinguished by their habits, as black, white, grey, &c. or by the saint whom they take for their patron or model, as Benedictines, Bernardines, Franciscans, &c. Before the reformation, and in Popish countries since, these Monks have been extremely numerous.‡

MONARCHIANS, so called from believing one person only in the godhead. See *Patripassians.*

MONOPHYSITES maintained, that the divine and human natures of Christ were so united, as to form only *one nature*, yet without any change, confusion, or mixture of the two natures. They flourished in the fifth century.§

MONOTHELITES, a denomination so called, from teaching, that two natures in Christ's person had but *one will.* Their founder was Theodore, bishop of Pharan, in Arabia, in the seventh century; who maintained the following positions: (1.) That in Christ there were two distinct natures, which were so united, (though without the least mixture or

* Mosheim, vol. i. p. 475, 476.
‡ Scotch Theol. Dict.
† Pinkerton's Greek Ch. p. 334.
§ Mosheim, vol. i. p. 420.

confusion,) as to form by their union only one person.—(2.) That the soul of Christ was endowed with a will, or faculty of volition, which is still retained after its union with the divine nature.—(3.) That this faculty of volition in the soul of Christ was not absolutely inactive, but that it co-operated with the divine will.—(4.) That therefore in a certain sense there was in Christ but *one will*, and one manner of operation.*

MONTANISTS, a denomination which arose in the second century; so called from Montanus, who pretended to be the Paraclete, or Comforter: whom Christ at his departure promised to send his disciples, to lead them into all truth; which promise, other christians understand of the Holy Ghost. He declared that he was sent with a divine commission, to give to the moral precepts delivered by Christ and his apostles the finishing touch that was to bring them to perfection. He was of opinion, that Christ and his apostles made, in their precepts, many allowances for the infirmities of those among whom they lived, and that this condescending indulgence rendered their system of moral laws imperfect and incomplete. He therefore inculcated the necessity of multiplying fasts; prohibited second marriages as unlawful; maintained that the church should refuse absolution to those who had fallen into the commission of enormous sins; and condemned all care of the body, especially all nicety of dress, and all female ornaments. He also gave it as his opinion, that philosophy, arts, and whatever savoured of polite literature, should be banished from the christian church. He looked upon those christians as guilty of a heinous transgression, who saved their lives by flight from the persecuting sword; or who ransomed themselves by money from the hands of their cruel and mercenary judges.

It seems extraordinary, that Montanus should assume to himself the name of the *Paraclete;* but it appears probable, he did this under the persuasion of the holy spirit eminently residing in him, and it is certain that both himself and the prophetesses connected with him, Priscilla and Maximilla, affected extacies, and to be under a sacred violence of the spirit's influences. It was probably the appearance of these sacred influences, and their extraordinary zeal, which drew Tertullian, the Latin father, from the bosom of the church into their communion. It does not appear, that the visions and revelations of this denomination were intended to supersede the scripture, or introduce false doctrines; for they related chiefly to matters of ecclesiastical discipline, and some enlargements on the subjects of sacred

* Mosheim, vol. ii. p. 36.

prophecy. On all the grand points of doctrine, at least during Tertullian's time, they seem to harmonize with the orthodoxy of the Roman Catholic church.

This denomination had separate assemblies. They were first called *Cataphrygians*, from the place where they had their principal abode; they were also styled *Pepuzians*, from Pepuza, the village where their leader resided.*

MORAVIANS. See *United Brethren.*

MUGGLETONIANS, a denomination, which arose in England about the year 1657; so called from their leader, Ludowick Muggleton, a journeyman taylor, who, with his associate, Reeves, set up for great prophets, and declared that their message was wholly spiritual; and that whoever despised or rejected it, committed the unpardonable sin against the Holy Ghost. They asserted, that they were the Lord's two last witnesses spoken of Rev. xi. 3, &c. who should appear a little before the coming of Christ, and the end of the world. Reeves was to act the part of Moses, and Muggleton to be his *mouth.* Among other things, they denied the doctrine of the trinity; and affirmed that God the father came down from heaven and suffered in a human form; and that Elijah was taken up in a whirlwind to heaven, for the purpose of representing him while he remained on earth.†

*MUSSELMANS, true believers, i. e. in the mission of Mahomet. See *Mahometans.*

MYSTICS. This is a name not confined to any particular division of christians; but has been generally given to those, who maintain that the scriptures have a *mystical sense,* which must be sought after; and who, laying but little stress on outward forms, profess to aspire after a pure and sublime devotion—an infused and passive contemplation, through a silent and inward attention to the operations of the spirit of God upon the mind. They are said to derive their origin from Dionysius, the Areopagite, who was converted to christianity in the first century, by the preaching of Paul at Athens. To support this idea, they attributed to this great man various treatises, which others ascribe to a Grecian Mystic of much later date, who is supposed to have written under his venerable name.

Mysticism is, however, of a much earlier date, and subsisted both in the East and among the Jews, assuming a variety of forms according to the genius and temper of its disciples. In the christian church this denomination appeared in the third

* Mosheim's Eccles. Hist. vol. i. p. 192, 193. Formey's Eccles. Hist. vol. i. p. 48. Priestley's Eccles. Hist. vol. i. p. 254.

† Dictionary of Arts and Sciences, vol. iii. p. 2,149. Reeves and Muggleton's Spiritual Treatise, p. 3—23.

century, increased in the fourth, and in the fifth spread into the eastern provinces. In the year 824, the supposed works of Dionysius kindled the flame of Mysticism in the western provinces. In the twelfth century, they took the lead in expounding the scriptures; in the thirteenth, they were the most formidable antagonists of the schoolmen; towards the close of the fourteenth, they propagated their sentiments in almost every part of Europe; in the fifteenth and sixteenth, many persons of distinguished merit embraced their tenets; and in the seventeenth, the radical principle of Mysticism was adopted by the Behmenists, Bourignonists, Quietists, and Quakers.

The ancient Mystics were distinguished by their professing pure, sublime, and perfect devotion, with a disinterested love of God; and by their aspiring to a state of passive contemplation.

The first principles of these sentiments have been supposed to proceed from the well known doctrine of the Platonic school, (which was adopted by Origen and his disciples,) that the divine nature was diffused through all human souls, or in other words, that the faculty of reason, from which proceeds the health and vigour of the mind, was an emanation from God into the human soul, and comprehended in it the principles and elements of all truth, human and divine. They denied, that men could by labour or study, excite this celestial flame in their own breast; and therefore disapproved of the attempts of those who, by abstract reasonings, endeavoured to discover the hidden nature of truth. On the contrary, they maintained, that silence, tranquillity, repose, and solitude, accompanied with such acts of mortification as might tend to extenuate and exhaust the body, were the means by which the hidden and internal word was excited, and of instructing men in the knowledge of divine things. "They, who behold with a noble contempt all human affairs, who turn away their eyes from terrestrial vanities, and shut all the avenues of the outward senses against the contagious influence of an outward world, must necessarily return to God, when the spirit is thus disengaged from the impediments which prevent this happy union; and in this blessed frame they not only enjoy inexpressible raptures from their communion with the supreme Being, but also are invested with the inestimable privilege of contemplating truth undisguised, in its native purity, while others behold it in a vitiated and delusive form. The apostle tells us, that "*the spirit makes intercession for us.* Now if the Spirit pray in us, we must resign ourselves to its impulses, by remaining in a state of mere inaction."

As the late Rev. William Law, who was born in 1687, makes a distinguished figure among the modern Mystics, a brief account of the outlines of his system may be acceptable.—He supposed that the material world was the region which originally belonged to the fallen angels. At length the light and spirit of God entered into the chaos, and turned the angels' ruined kingdom into a paradise on earth. God then created man, and placed him there. He was made in the image of the triune God,* a living mirror of the divine nature, formed to enjoy communion with the Father, Son, and Holy Ghost, and to live on earth as the angels do in heaven. He was endowed with immortality, so that the elements of this outward world could not have any power of acting on his body: but by his fall he changed the light, life, and spirit of God, for the light, life, and spirit of the world. He died the very day of his transgression to all the influences and operations of the Spirit of God upon him, as we die to the influences of this world when the soul leaves the body; and all the influences and operations of the elements of this life were open in him, as they are in any animal, at his birth into this world: he became an earthly creature, subject to the dominion of this outward world, and stood only in the highest rank of animals. But the goodness of God would not leave man in this condition: redemption from it was immediately granted; and the bruiser of the serpent brought the life, light, and spirit of heaven, once more into the human nature. All men, in consequence of the redemption of Christ, have in them the first spark, or seed, of the divine life, as a treasure hid in the centre of our souls, to bring forth, by degrees, a new birth of that life which was lost in paradise. No son of Adam can be lost, except by turning away from the Saviour within him. The only religion, which can save us, must be that which can raise the light, life, and spirit of God in our souls. Nothing can enter into the vegetable kingdom, till it have the vegetable life in it, or be a member of the animal kingdom, till it have the animal life. Thus all nature joins with the gospel in affirming, that no man can enter into the kingdom of heaven, till the heavenly life is born in him. Nothing can be our righteousness or recovery, but the divine nature of Jesus Christ derived from our souls.†

The excellent Fenelon, archbishop of Cambray, held an eminent rank among the Mystics. See *Quietists*.

* "Nature (says Mr. Law) is the manifestation of the holy trinity in a triune life of *fire, light*, and *spirit*."

† Mosheim's Eccles. Hist. vol. i. p. 222, 223. Dictionary of Arts and Sci-

N

NAZARENES, a name originally given to christians in general, on account of Jesus Christ's being of the city of Nazareth; but was afterwards restrained to a denomination in the first and second centuries, which blended christianity and judaism together. They held that Christ was born of a virgin, and was also in a certain manner united to the divine nature. They refused to abandon the ceremonies prescribed by the law of Moses; but were far from attempting to impose the observance of these ceremonies upon gentile christians. They rejected those additions that were made to the Mosaic institutions by the pharisees and doctors of the law; but admitted the scriptures both of the old and new testament. They also used a spurious gospel which was called indiscriminately, "The gospel of the Nazarenes or Hebrews;"* and which is supposed by some to be the gospel St. Paul refers to in Gal. i. 6. But many think that St. Paul only referred to the gospel which he preached, and that the gospel of the Nazarenes was a Hebrew or Syriac version of St. Matthew.†

NECESSARIANS, or NECESSITARIANS; an appellation given to those who maintain, that moral agents act from *necessity*. Some suppose this necessity to be mechanical, and others moral. Mechanical necessity follows materialism: moral necessity results from the presumption, that there is a power existing distinct from matter. Dr. Priestley's scheme of mechanical, or philosophical necessity, has been delineated under the article *Materialists*, on account of its connexion with the doctrine of Materialism.

The following is a sketch of the sentiments of some of the most celebrated advocates for *moral* necessity.

Mr. Leibnitz, an eminent German philosopher, who was born in 1646, is a distinguished writer on this subject. He attempted to give Calvinism a more pleasing and philosophical aspect. He considered all the worlds which compose the universe as one system, whose greatest possible perfection is the ultimate end of creating goodness. As he laid down this great end as the supreme object of God's government,

ences, vol iii. p. 217. Encyclopedia, vol. xii. p. 598. Hist. of Religion, vol. iv. article Mystics. Law's Life, p. 1. Law's Appeal, p. 4—139.—Spirit of Prayer, p. 61—68. Spirit of Love, p. 52.—Christian Regeneration, p. 1—39. Letters, &c.

* Mosheim, vol. i. p. 173. Broughton, vol. ii. p. 155.

† Buck's Theolog. Dict.

and the scope to which all his dispensations were directed, he concluded that it must be accomplished: and hence the doctrine of necessity, to fulfil the purposes of predestination; a necessity physical and mechanical in the motions of material and inanimate things; but moral and spiritual in the voluntary determinations of intelligent beings, in consequence of propellent motives which produce their effects with certainty, though those effects are contingent, and by no means the offspring of an absolute and blind fatality.

Mr. Leibnitz observes, that if it be said, that the world might have been without sin and misery, such a world would not have been the best; for all things are linked together in each possible world. The universe, whatever it may be, is all of a piece, like an ocean: the least motion produces its effect to any distance, though the effect becomes less sensible in proportion to the distance. God having settled every thing beforehand, having foreseen all good and evil actions, &c. every thing did ideally contribute before its existence to his creating plan; so that no alteration can be made in the universe, any more than in a number, without destroying its essence, or its numerical individuality: and therefore, if the least evil which happens in the world were wanting, it would not be that world which, all things duly considered, the all-wise Creator has chosen and accounted the best. Colours are heightened by shadows, and a dissonance well placed, renders harmony more beautiful. Does any one sufficiently prize the happiness of health, who has never been sick? Is it not generally necessary, that a little evil should render a good more sensible, and consequently greater?

President Edwards' scheme of moral necessity is as follows: That the will is in every case necessarily determined by the strongest motives, and that this moral necessity may be as absolute as natural necessity; i. e. a moral effect may be as perfectly connected with its moral cause, as a naturally necessary effect is with its natural cause. He rejects the notion of liberty, as implying any self-determining power in the will, any indifference or contingency; and defines liberty to be the power, opportunity, and advantage, which any one has to do as he pleases. This liberty is supposed to be consistent with moral certainty, or necessity. He supports his scheme by the connexion between cause and effect, by God's certain foreknowledge of the volitions of moral agents, which is supposed to be inconsistent with such a contingence of those volitions as excludes all necessity. He shows that God's moral excellence is necessary, yet virtuous and praise-worthy; that the acts of the will of the human soul of Christ are necessarily holy, yet virtuous, praiseworthy, and rewardable; and that the moral inability of sinners, consisting in depravity of heart, instead of excusing, constitutes their guilt.

Lord Kaims has the following hypothesis:—That, comparing together the moral and material world, every thing is as much the result of established laws in the one as in the other. There is nothing in the whole universe which can properly be called contingent; but every motion in the material, and every determination and action in the moral world, are directed by immutable laws: so that, while those laws remain in force, not the smallest link in the chain of causes and effects can be broken, nor any one thing be otherwise than it is. That, as man must act with consciousness and spontaneity, it is necessary that he should have some sense of things possible and contingent. Hence the Deity has wisely implanted a *delusive* sense of liberty in the mind of man, which fits him to fulfil the ends of action to better advantage than he could do, if he *knew* the necessity which really attends him.

Lord Kaims observes that, in the material world, it is found that the representations of external objects and their qualities, conveyed by the senses, differ sometimes from what philosophy discovers these objects and their qualities to be. Were men endowed with a microscopic eye, the bodies which surround him would appear as different, from what they do at present, as if he were transported into another world. His ideas, upon that supposition, would be more agreeable to strict truth, but they would be far less serviceable in common life. Analogous to this in the moral world, the Deity has implanted in mankind the *delusive* notion of the power of being indifferent, that they may be led to the proper exercise of that activity for which they were designed.

The Baron de Montesquieu, in his Persian Letters, observes, that as God makes his creatures act just according to his own will, he knows every thing he thinks fit to know. But though it is in his power to see every thing, yet he does not always make use of that power: he generally leaves his creatures at liberty to act or not to act, that they may have room to be guilty or innocent. In this view he renounces his right of acting upon his creatures, and directing their resolutions: but when he chooses to know any thing, he always does know it; because he need only will that it shall happen as he sees it, and direct the resolutions of his creatures according to his will. Thus he fetches the things which shall happen, from among those which are merely possible, in fixing by his decrees the future determinations of the minds of his creatures, and depriving them of the power of acting or not acting, which he has bestowed upon them.

President Edwards makes the following distinction between his and Lord Kaims' ideas of necessity :—(1) Lord Kaims supposes such a necessity with respect to men's actions, as is inconsistent with liberty. Pres. Edwards thinks, that the moral necessity he defends is not inconsistent with the utmost liberty which can be conceived.——(2.) Kaims supposes, that the terms *unavoidable*, *impossible*, &c. are equally applicable to the case of moral and natural necessity. Edwards maintains, that such a necessity, as attends the acts of the will, may with more propriety be called *certainty*, it being no other than the certain connexion between the subject and predicate of the proposition which affirms their existence.—(3.) Kaims supposes, that if mankind could clearly see the real necessity of their actions, they would not appear to themselves or others praise-worthy, culpable, or accountable for them. Edwards asserts, that moral necessity is perfectly consistent with praise and blame, rewards and punishments. Lastly, Lord Kaims agrees with President Edwards in supposing that praise or blame rests ultimately on the disposition or frame of mind.

As, in the account of Dr. Priestley's sentiments, the manner, in which he distinguishes philosophical necessity from the Calvinistic doctrine of predestination, is inserted; perhaps those, who are fond of speculating on this subject, will be gratified by viewing, on the other hand, the following discrimination made by Dr. Emmons, of Franklin, Mass. between the Calvinistic idea of necessity and Dr. Priestley's.

It has long been a subject of controversy between Arminians and Calvinists, whether moral agents can act of necessity. Upon this subject, Dr. P. labours to prove the doctrine of necessity from the general principle, that no effect can exist without a cause. "Every volition (he argues) must be an effect, every effect must have a cause, every cause must necessarily produce its effect: therefore every volition, as well as every other effect, must be necessary." But though he agrees with the Calvinists in their first principles and general mode of reasoning, yet in one point he differs from them totally: for he thinks that motives, which are the cause of volitions, must operate mechanically, which, they suppose, totally destroys the freedom of the will. He is constrained to maintain the mechanical operation of motives, by his maintaining the materiality of the soul. "Every thing (he says) belonging to the doctrine of materialism is, in fact, an argument for the doctrine of necessity; and consequently the doctrine of necessity is a direct inference from materialism.*

"Whether man is a necessary or a free agent, is a question, that has been debated by writers of the first eminence. Hobbes, Collins, Hume, Leibnitz, Kaims, Hartley, Priestley, Edwards, Crombie, Toplady, and Belsham, have written on the side of Necessity: while Clarke, King, Law, Reid, Butler, Price, Bryant, Wollaston, Horsley, Beattie, Gregory, and Butterworth, have written against it. To state all their arguments in this place would take up too much room; suffice it to say, that the Anti-necessarians suppose that the doctrine of Necessity charges God as the *author of sin;* that it takes away the freedom of the will, renders man unaccountable, makes sin to be no evil, and morality or virtue no good; precludes the use of means, and is of the most gloomy tendency. The Necessarians deny these to be legitimate consequences; and observe, that the Deity acts no more immorally in decreeing vicious actions, than in permitting those irregularities, he could so easily have prevented. The difficulty is the same on each hypothesis. All necessity, say they, does not take away freedom. The actions of a man may be, at one and the same time, free and necessary. It was infallibly certain, that Judas would betray Christ, yet he did it voluntarily. Jesus Christ necessarily became man and died; yet he acted freely. That necessity does not render actions less morally good, is evident; for if necessary virtue be neither moral nor praiseworthy, it will follow that God himself is not a moral being, because a necessary one; and the obedience of Christ cannot be good, because it was necessary. That it is not a gloomy doctrine they allege, because nothing can be more consolatory than to believe that all things are under the direction of an all-wise Being; that his kingdom ruleth over all, and that he doth all things well."†

The texts of scripture referred to in favour of *necessity* are chiefly the following. Job xxiii. 13, 14.—xxxiv. 29. Prov. xvi. 4. Isaiah xlv. 7. Matthew x. 29, 30.—xviii. 7. Luke xxiv. 16. John vi. 37. Acts xiii. 48. Ephesians i. 11.—1 Thess. ii. 12. &c.

NEGROES, (The) natives of Africa, universally believe in a supreme Being, and have some ideas of a future state. They address the Almighty Being by a *fetiche*, or charm, which is considered as a subordinate,

* Mosheim's Eccles. Hist. vol. v. p. 24. Leibnitz's Essay on the Goodness of God, the Free-will of Man, &c. Letters between Clarke and Leibnitz. Edwards on the Will, p. 17—213. Kaims' Essays, p. 114—155—Montesquieu's Persian Letters, p. 134—136.

† Buck's Theological Dict.

mediatorial deity. They ascribe evil in general, and all their misfortunes to the devil, whom they so fear as to tremble at the mention of his name.*

The word *fetiche*, in a strict sense, signifies whatever represents their divinities; but the precise ideas of the Negroes concerning their lesser gods, are not well adjusted by authors, or even among the most sensible of themselves.——At Cape Coast, there is a public guardian fetiche, the highest in power and dignity. This is a peninsular rock, which projects into the sea from the bottom of the cliff on which the castle is built, making a sort of covert for landing. Besides this superiour fetiche, every separate canton, or district, has its peculiar fetiche, inferiour to that of Cape Coast. A mountain, a tree, a large rock, fish, or peculiar fowl, is raised to this high distinction, and the honour of being the national divinity. Among trees the palm has the pre-eminence, this being always deified; and in particular that species of it called *assoanum*; because it is the most beautiful and numerous. They pay profound adoration to these fetiches, and have great confidence in their power. But the fetiche of one province is despised in another.

The fetiches of Whidah may be divided into three classes; the *serpent*, *tall trees*, and the *sea*. The serpent is the most celebrated, the others being subordinate to the power of this deity. This snake has a large round head, beautiful piercing eyes, a short, pointed tongue, resembling a dart: its pace slow and solemn, except when it seizes on its prey, then very rapid; its tail sharp and short, its skin of an elegant smoothness, adorned with beautiful colours, upon a light grey ground: it is amazingly familiar and tame. Rich offerings are made to this deity; priests, and priestesses appointed for its service; it is invoked in extremely wet, dry, or barren seasons; and, in a word, on all the great difficulties and occurrences of life.

The ideas the Negroes entertain of a future state are various. Some maintain, that immediately upon the death of any person, he is removed into another world, where he assumes the very character in which he lived in this, and supports himself by the offerings and sacrifices his friends make after his departure. It is said, that the great body of Negroes do not entertain any ideas of future rewards and punishments annexed to the good or evil actions of this life. A few, however, have some notion of a future state, which consists in being wafted away to a famous river, situated in a distant inland country, called Bosmanque. Here their god interrogates them concerning the life

* Middleton's Geography, vol. i. p. 320.

they have led; whether they have religiously kept the holy days dedicated to fetiche, abstained from all meats, and inviolably kept their oaths? If they can answer truly in the affirmative, they are conveyed over the river to a land abounding in every luxury and human delight. If, on the contrary, the departed has sinned against any of the above capital points of their religion, then their god plunges him into a river, where he is buried in eternal oblivion. Others believe in a kind of metempsychosis, where they shall be transported to the land of white men, altered to that complexion, and endowed with a soul similar to theirs. But this is the doctrine only of those who think highly of the intellectual faculties of the white men.*

The Negroes, who inhabit the kingdom of Benin, acknowledge a supreme Being, whom they call *Orisa*; but think it needless to worship him, because, being infinitely good, they are sure he will not hurt them. On the contrary, they are very careful in paying their devotions to the devil, whom they consider as the cause of all their calamities. They do not think of any other remedy for their most common diseases, but that of applying to a sorcerer to drive them away. Such of them as believe in the devil paint his image *white*.†

The Negroes in Loango are said to acknowledge a supreme Deity, called *Zambi*, who is considered as the great cause of whatever is good and beautiful in the world. By his name they swear their most sacred oaths, the violation of which they think would be immediately followed with sickness. Him they love, but without worshipping him; and reserve their worship for a malignant deity, (or devil) called, *Zambi-an-hi*, whom they greatly fear, as is above stated. In order to appease him they abstain from some dish or other, and in order to please him they spoil their fruit-trees.—They think the soul survives the body, but have no distinct notions of its future residence and fate.

The celebrated traveller, Mungo Park, has given the following sketch of the religion of these pagans.

"The belief of one God, and of a future state of rewards and punishments, is entire and universal among the Africans. It is remarkable, however, that (except on the appearance of a new moon) the pagan natives do not think it necessary to offer up prayers and supplications to the Almighty. They represent the Deity indeed as the creator and preserver of all things; but, in general, they consider him as a being so remote, and of so exalted a nature, that it is idle to imagine the

* Modern Universal History, vol. xvii. p. 133—137.

† Kaims, vol. iv. p. 142.

feeble supplications of wretched mortals can reverse the decrees, or change the purposes of unerring wisdom. If they be asked for what reason then do they offer up a prayer on the appearance of the new moon? the answer is, that custom has made it necessary; they do it, because their fathers did it before them. The concerns of the world, they believe, are committed by the Almighty to the superintendance and direction of subordinate spirits, over whom they suppose certain magical ceremonies have great influence. A white fowl, suspended from the branch of a particular tree, a snake's head, or a few handfuls of fruit, are offerings, which the Negroes often present, to deprecate the wrath, or to conciliate the favour of these tutelary agents. But it is not often that they make their religious opinions the subject of conversation; when interrogated in particular concerning their idea of a future state, they express themselves with great reverence; but endeavour to shorten the discussion, by observing that no man knows any thing about it.*

NEONOMIANS, from νεος *new*, and νομος *law*, the advocates of a *new law*, the condition whereof is imperfect, though sincere and persevering obedience.

Neonomianism is supposed to be an essential part of the Arminian system. "The new covenant of grace, which, through the medium of Christ's death, the Father made with men, consists, according to this system, not in our being justified by faith, as it apprehends the righteousness of Christ; but in this, that God, abrogating the exaction of perfect legal obedience, imputes, or accepts of faith itself, and the imperfect obedience of faith, instead of the perfect obedience of the law, and graciously accounts them worthy of the reward of eternal life." This opinion was condemned at the synod of Dort,† and has been canvassed between the Calvinists and Arminians on various occasions.‡

Towards the end of the seventeenth century, a controversy was agitated among the English dissenters; in which the one side, who were partial to the writings of Dr. Crisp, were charged with *Antinomianism;* and the other, who favoured those of Mr. Baxter, were accused of *Neonomianism.* Dr. Daniel Williams, who was a principal writer in opposition to the former, gives the following as a summary of his faith in reference to these subjects:—"1. God has eternally *elected* a certain definite number of men, whom he will infallibly save. 2. These very elect are not personally justified, until they receive Christ, and yield up themselves to him; but they remain condemned whilst unconverted.—3. By the

* Park's Travels, p. 309.

† Acta Synodi, p. 253.

‡ See Edwards on the Will, Lond. edit. p. 220.

ministry of the gospel there is a serious offer of pardon and glory, upon the *terms* of the gospel, to all that hear it: and God thereby requires them to comply.—4. Ministers ought to use these and other gospel benefits as motives, assuring men that, if they believe they shall be justified; if they repent, their 'sins shall be blotted out:' but whilst they neglect these duties, they cannot have a personal interest in the benefits.—5. It is by the power of the spirit of Christ freely exerted, and not by the power of free-will, that the gospel becomes effectual for conversion.—6. When a man believes, yet is not that faith, much less any other work, the matter of that righteousness for which a sinner is justified; it is the imputed righteousness of Christ alone, which gives the believer a right to these and all saving blessings. By both this and the fifth head, it appears, that all boasting is excluded, and we are saved by free grace.—7. Faith alone receives the Lord Jesus and his righteousness; and the subject of this faith is a convinced, penitent soul; hence we are justified by faith alone, and yet the impenitent are not forgiven.—8. God has freely promised, that all whom he predestinated to salvation shall not only savingly believe, but that he by his power will preserve them from a total, or a final apostasy.—9. Yet the believer, whilst he lives in this world, is to pass the time of his sojourning here with fear, because his warfare is not accomplished; and it is true, that if he 'draw back,' God 'will have no pleasure in him.'—10. The *moral law* is so in force still, that every *precept* constitutes duty, even to the believer; every *breach* thereof is deserving of death. This law binds death by its *curse* on every unbeliever: and the *righteousness*, by which we are justified before God, is a righteousness adequate to that law, which is Christ's alone: and this is so imputed to the believer, as that God deals judicially with him according thereto.—11. Yet such is the grace of the gospel, that it promiseth in and by Christ, a freedom from the curse, forgiveness of sin, and eternal life, to every sincere believer; which promise God will certainly perform, notwithstanding the threatening of the law."*

Dr. Williams maintains the conditionality of the covenant of grace; but admits with Dr. Owen, who also uses the term *condition*, that "Christ undertook, that those who were to be taken into this covenant should receive grace enabling them to comply with the *terms* of it, fulfil its *conditions*, and yield the obedience which God required therein.†

On this subject Dr. Williams further says, "The question is not whether the first, (viz. re-

* Gospel Truth stated, p. 312, 313.

† Ibid. p. 70.

generating) grace, by which we are enabled to perform the condition, be absolutely given. This I affirm; though that [grace] be dispensed ordinarily in a due use of means.*

The following objection, among others, was made by several ministers in 1692 against Dr. Williams' Work, above quoted: "To supply the room of the moral law, vacated by him, he turns the gospel into a *new law*, in keeping of which we shall be justified for the sake of Christ's righteousness;† making qualifications and acts of ours a disposing subordinate righteousness, whereby we become capable of being justified by Christ's righteousness.‡

To this he answers: "The difference is not, (1.) Whether the gospel be a *new law* in the Socinian, Popish, or Arminian sense? This I deny. Nor (2.) is faith, or any other grace or acts of ours, any atonement for sin, satisfaction to justice, meriting qualification, or any part of that righteousness, for which we are justified at the bar of God? This I deny in places innumerable. Nor (3.) whether the gospel be a law more *new* than is implied in the first promise to fallen Adam, proposed to Cain, and obeyed by Abel, to the differencing him from his unbelieving brother? This I deny. (4.) Nor whether the gospel be a law that *allows sin*, when it accepts such graces as *true*, though short of perfection, to be the *conditions* of our personal interest in the benefits *purchased by Christ?* This I deny. (5.) Nor whether the gospel be a law, the promises whereof entitle the performers of its conditions to the benefits as of *debt?* This I deny.

"The difference is:—(1.) Is the gospel a law in this sense? viz. God in Christ thereby *commandeth* sinners to repent of sin, and receive Christ by a true operative faith, *promising* that thereupon they shall be united to him, justified by his righteousness, pardoned, and adopted; and that, persevering in faith and true holiness, they shall be finally saved; also threatening, that if any shall die impenitent rejecters of his grace, they shall perish without relief, and endure sorer punishments, than if these offers had not been made to them? (2.) Hath the gospel a *sanction?* i. e. doth Christ therein enforce his commands of faith, repentance, and perseverance, by the foresaid promises and threatenings, as motives to our obedience? Both these I affirm, and they deny; saying, the gospel in the largest sense is an absolute promise, without precepts and condition. (4.) Do the gospel *promises* of benefits to certain graces, and its *threats*, that those benefits shall be withheld, and the contrary evils inflicted for the neglect of such graces, render those graces the

* Gospel Truth stated, p. 61. † Ibid. p. 44—210. ‡ Ibid. p. 54—143.

condition of our personal title to those benefits? This they deny, and I affirm, &c."*

It does not appear to have been a question in this controversy, whether God *commands* sinners to repent and believe in Christ, nor whether he *promises* life to believers, and *threatens* death to unbelievers; but whether it be the *gospel*, under the form of a new law, that thus commands or threatens, or the moral law on its behalf; and whether its *promises* to believing render such believing a *condition* of the things promised.—In *another controversy*, however, about forty years afterwards, it became a question whether God did by his word (call it law or gospel) command unregenerate sinners to repent and believe in Chirst, or to do any thing else which is spiritually good. Of those who took the affirmative side of this question, some attempted to maintain it on the ground of the gospel's being a *new law*, consisting of commands, promises, and comminations, the terms or conditions of which were repentance, faith, and sincere obedience. But those who first engaged in the controversy, though they allowed the *encouragement* to repent and believe to arise merely from the grace of the gospel, yet considered the formal obligation to do so as arising from the moral law, which, requiring supreme love to God, requires acquiescence in any revelation which he shall at any time make known.†

NESTORIANS, a denomination which arose in the fifth century, from Nestorius, bishop of Constantinople. They maintain that the union of Christ's divinity with his humanity, is a union of will, operation, and benevolence; for the divine Word is perfect in his nature and person. The human nature, united to him is likewise perfect humanity in his nature and person; neither of them is changed, or undergoes any alteration. Therefore, there are two persons in Jesus Christ, and two natures, united by one operation and will. They conceived that, as there were two distinct natures in Christ, the divine and human, though both were united, as they express it, under one *aspect*, yet properly, it was the human nature *only* which obeyed and suffered, which was born and died. They therefore object to calling the virgin Mary *the mother of God*, so warmly contended for by the church of Rome; but which is equally objected to by protestants.

In the Nestorian controversy, the contending parties seem to have been all of one opinion as to the doctrine of the trinity,

* Gospel Truth, p. 256—258.

† Williams' Gospel Truth stated and vindicated. Chauncey's Neonomianism Unmasked. Maurice's Modern Question Affirmed and Proved. Witsius' Irenicum.

in opposition to the Arians: and held the co-equality of the three divine persons. The Nestorians are a branch of the Greek Church, and reside chiefly in Mesopotamia, Syria, and the Levant. Many also reside in India, where they are called the *Syrian Christians,* which see.*

*NETOVTSCHINS, a sect of Russian dissenters, said to be very ignorant, and much divided in opinion; they go under the general name of *Spasova Soglasia,* or the Union for Salvation. They believe that Antichrist is already come, (in the person of the pope perhaps,) and has put an end to every thing holy in the Church.†

NEW JERUSALEM CHURCH, a society founded by Emanuel Swedenborg, son of Jasper, a Lutheran bishop of West-Gothia. He was born at Stockholm in the year 1689, and died in London in 1772. He early enjoyed all the advantages of a liberal education, having studied with great attention in the academy of Upsal, and in the universities of England, Holland, France, and Germany. His progress in the sciences was rapid and extensive; and at an early period in life he distinguished himself by various publications in Latin on philosophical subjects. His studies led him to refer natural phenomena to spiritual agency, and to suppose that there is a close connexion between the two worlds of matter and spirit. Hence his system teaches us to consider all the visible universe, with every thing that it contains, as a theatre and representation of the invisible world, from which it first derived its existence, and by connexion with which it continually subsists.

Swedenborg's great genius and learning, accompanied with the purity of his character, attracted the public notice. Hence he received various literary and political honours. All these, however, he considered of small importance, compared with the distinguished privilege of having, as he declared, his spiritual sight opened, to converse with spirits and angels in the spiritual world. He first began to receive his revelations in London. He asserts that on a certain night, a man appeared to him in the midst of a strong shining light, and said, "I am God the Lord, the Creator, and Redeemer; I have chosen thee to explain to men the interiour and spiritual sense of the sacred writings. I will dictate to thee what thou oughtest to write." He affirms that after this period, his spiritual sight was so opened, that he could see in the most clear and distinct manner, what passed in the spiritual world, and converse with an-

* Priestley's History of Early Opinions, vol. iv. p. 252. Jortin's Remarks on Eccles Hist. vol. iv p 278. Mosheim, vol. ii. p. 70, 71. new edition.

† Pinkerton's Greek Church, p. 332.

gels and spirits in the same manner as with men. Accordingly, in his treatise concerning heaven and hell, he relates the wonders which he saw in the invisible worlds; and gives an account of various, and heretofore unknown particulars, relating to the peace, the happiness, the light, the order of heaven; together with the forms, the functions, the habitations, and even the garments of the heavenly inhabitants. He relates his conversation with angels, and describes the condition of Jews, Gentiles, Mahometans, and Christians of every denomination, in the other world.

Swedenborg called the principles which he delivered, "The Heavenly Doctrines of the New Jerusalem;" for, according to his system, the New Jerusalem signifies the new church upon earth, which is now about to be established by the Lord, and which is particularly described, as to its glory and excellency, in Rev. xxi. and many other parts of the sacred word. The holy city, or New Jerusalem, he interprets as descriptive of a new dispensation of heavenly truth, breaking through, and dissipating the darkness, which at this day prevails on the earth.

The following extract contains the general outlines of Swedenborg's theological system.—1. That the sacred scripture contains three distinct senses, called *celestial*, *spiritual*, and *natural*; and that in each sense it is divine truth, accommodated respectively to the angels of the three heavens, and also to men on earth.—2. That there is a correspondence or analogy between all things in heaven and all things in man; and that this science of correspondence is a key to the spiritual or internal sense of the sacred scriptures, every page of which is written by correspondences; that is, by such things in the natural world as correspond unto, and signify things in the spiritual world.*—3. That there is a divine trinity of Father, Son, and Holy Ghost, or in other words, of the all-begetting divinity, [*divinum a quo,*] the divine human, and the divine proceeding, or operation; but that this trinity consisteth not of three distinct persons, but is united as body, soul, and operation in man, in the one person of the Lord Jesus Christ, who therefore is the God of heaven, and alone to be worshipped; being Creator from eternity, Redeemer in time, and Regenerator to eternity.—4. That redemption consisteth not in the vicarious sacrifice of the

* Correspondence, in a philosophical sense, is a kind of analogy that one thing bears to another, or the relation subsisting between the essence of a thing and its form, or between the cause and its effect; thus the whole natural world corresponds to the spiritual world; the body of a man with all its parts, corresponds to his soul, and the literal sense of the word corresponds to the spiritual.

Redeemer, and an atonement to appease the divine wrath; but in a real subjugation of the powers of darkness; in a restoration of order in the spiritual world; in checking the overgrown influences of wicked spirits on the souls of men, and opening a nearer and clearer communication with the heavenly and angelic powers; in making salvation, which is regeneration, possible for all who believe on the incarnate God and keep his commandments. —5. That there is an universal *influx* from God into the souls of men. The soul, upon receiving this influx from God, transmits it through the perceptive faculties of the mind to the body. The Lord with all his divine wisdom, consequently with all the essence of faith and charity, enters by influx into every man, but is received by every man according to his state and form. Hence it is that good *influxes* from God are changed by the evil nature of their recipients into their opposites; good into evil, and truth into falsehood.—6. That we are placed in this world, subject to the influences of two most opposite principles, of good from the Lord and his holy angels, of evil from hell or evil spirits. While we live in this world our spirits have their abode in the spiritual world, where we are kept in a kind of spiritual equilibrium by the continual action of those contrary powers; in consequence of which we are at perfect liberty to turn to either as we please; that without this *free-will* in spiritual things, regeneration cannot be effected. If we submit to God, we receive real life from him; if not, we receive that life from hell which is called in scripture *spiritual death.*—7. That heaven and hell are not arbitrary appointments of God. Heaven is a state arising from the good affections of the heart, and a correspondence of the words and actions, grounded on sincere love to God and man: and hell is the necessary consequence of an evil and thoughtless life, enslaved by the vile affections of self-love, and the love of the world, without being brought under the regulations of heavenly love, by a right submission of the will, the understanding, and actions, to the truth and spirit of heaven.—8. That there is an intermediate state for departed souls, which is called *the world of spirits;* and that very few pass directly to either heaven or hell. This is a state of purification to the good; but to bad spirits it is a state of separation of all the extraneous good from the radical evil which constitutes the essence of their natures.—9. That throughout heaven, such as are of like dispositions and qualities are consociated into particular fellowships, and such as differ in these respects are separated; so that every society in heaven consists of similar members.—10. That man immediately on his decease rises again in a spiritual body, which was inclosed in his material body; and that in this spiritual body he lives as a man to eternity, either in heaven or in hell, according to the quality of his past life.—11. That those passages in the sacred scripture, generally supposed to signify the destruction of the world by fire, &c. commonly called *the last judgment*, must be understood, according to the abovementioned science of correspondences, which teaches, that by the end of the world, (or consummation of the age,) is not signified the destruction of the material world, but the end, or consummation, of the present christian church, both among Roman Catholics and Protestants of every description* and denomination: that this consummation, which consists in the total falsification of the divine truth, and adulteration of the divine good of the word, has actually taken place; and, together with the establishment of a new church in place of the former, is described in the Revelations, in the internal sense of that book, in which the new church is meant, as to its internals, by the new earth; also by the *New Jerusalem descending from God out of heaven.*†

It is a leading doctrine of Swedenborg in his explanation of the other books of scripture, that one of the principal uses for which the word is given, is, that it might be a medium of communication between the Lord and man; also that earth might be thereby conjoined with heaven, or human minds with angelic minds; which is effected by the correspondences of natural things with spiritual, according to which the word is written; and that in order to its being divine, it could not be written otherwise: that hence, in many parts of the letter, the word is clothed with the appearances of truths accommodated to the apprehen-

* An ingenious author, who has embraced the doctrines of the New Jerusalem church, thus explains this subject: "It may be expedient to observe that there is a *last judgment*, both particular and general, as it relates to an individual of the church, or to the church itself collectively considered. The last judgment, as it relates to an individual, takes place with every one when he dies; for then he passeth into another state of existence, in which, when he cometh into the full exercise of the life which he had procured to himself in the body, he is judged either to *death* or to *life*; i. e. to *hell* or to *heaven*. The last judgment, as it relates to the church collectively considered, takes place when there is no longer any genuine love and faith in it, whereby it ceaseth to be a church. See Notes on Swedenborg's Doctrine concerning the Lord, by Mr. Hill.

† The Rev. Mr Hargrave, minister of the New Jerusalem Church in Baltimore, observes, that the end of the world signifies the end of the churches, both as to life and doctrines; and the last judgment means an examination and condemnation of all those false principles which have brought the church to an end, See his Sermon preached at Philadelphia in 1802.

sions of the simple and unlearned; as, when evil passions are attributed to the Lord, and where it is said that he withholdeth his mercy from man, forsakes him, casts into hell, doeth evil, &c.: whereas such things do not at all belong to the Lord; but they are said in the same manner as we speak of the sun's rising and setting, and other natural phenomena, according to the appearance of things, or as they appear to the outward senses. To the taking up such appearances of truth from the letter of scripture, and making this or that point of faith derived from them the essential of the church, instead of explaining them by doctrines drawn from the genuine truths, which in other parts of the word are left naked, Swedenborg ascribes the various dissensions and heresies that have arisen in the church. These he says, could not be prevented consistently with the preservation of man's free agency, both with respect to the exertion of his will, and of his understanding. But yet, he observes, every one, in whatever heresy he may be with respect to the understanding, may still be reformed and saved, provided *he shuns evils as sins*, and does not confirm heretical falses in himself; for by *shunning evils as sins* the will is reformed; and by the will the understanding, which then first emerges out of darkness into light; that the word, in its lowest sense, is thus made the medium of salvation to those who are obedient to its precepts; while this sense serves to guard its internal sanctities from being violated by the wicked and profane, and is represented by the cherubim placed at the gates of Eden, and the flaming sword turning every way to guard the tree of life.

His doctrine respecting differences of opinion in the church is summed up in these words: "There are three essentials of the church; an acknowledgment of the Lord's divinity, an acknowledgment of the holiness of the word, and the life which is charity. Conformable to his life i. e. to his charity, is every man's *real faith*. From the word he hath the knowledge of what his life ought to be, and from the Lord he hath reformation and salvation. If these three had been held as essentials of the church, intellectual dissensions would not have divided it, but would only have varied it as the light varieth colours in beautiful objects, and as various jewels constitute the beauty of a kingly crown."

The moral doctrines of the New Jerusalem church are comprised under general heads, collected from Swedenborg's writings, and prefixed to some proposals published in England for the organization and establishment of a society. Under those general heads it is proposed to promote marriages on the principles of the new church; which are, that true conjugal love consists in the most perfect and intimate union of minds, which constitutes one life, as the will and understanding are united in one; that this love exists only with those who are in a state of regeneration; that after the decease of conjugal partners of this description they meet, and all the mere natural loves being separated, the mental union is perfected, and they are exalted into the wisdom and happiness of the angelic life.

Swedenborg founded his doctrines on the spiritual sense of the word of God, which he declared was revealed to him immediately from the Lord out of heaven. As his language is peculiar, his reasoning cannot be abridged so as to be rendered intelligible to the generality of readers. Those who are desirous of farther information are referred to the authorities cited below.

The receivers of the doctrines of the New Jerusalem church are numerous in England, and in some parts of Germany. There are also a considerable number of them in Sweden, Russia, and France, and in all the countries of Europe. They are also to be found in many of the countries of the East. In most of the United States, there are many readers, and some receivers of the doctrines, particularly in the cities of Baltimore, Philadelphia, and New York. Churches have been erected in Baltimore and Philadelphia, and meetings of the receivers of the doctrines are held in many places. They have three places of worship in London; and likewise several chapels in other parts of the country. They use a liturgy formed on the model of that of the church of England, and as similar as the difference of doctrines will admit. Some of the ministers of the establishment are converts to Swedenborg's testimony.*

NEW PLATONICS: See *Ammonians*.

NICOLAITANS, a sect that arose in the first century, and boasts its origin from Nicolas, one of the seven first deacons of Jerusalem, but is very severely censured by the Lord Jesus Christ himself, in the book of Revelation, chap. ii. 6. "The DEEDS of the Nicolaitans which I hate." By this expression it should seem that their heresy was rather practical than theo-

* Summary View of Swedenborg's Doctrines, p. 12—90. Swedenborg on the New Jerusalem, p. 28—34. On the Lord, p. 88. On Influx, p. 28, 29. On Heaven and Hell, p. 2—5. On the Doctrine of Life, p. 116. On Divine Providence, Note 259. Arcana Cœlestia, p. 47, 48. Apocalypse Revealed, vol. i p. 37. Aphorisms of Wisdom, p. 52—54. Hindmarsh's Defence of the New Church, p. 281—362. Dialogues on Swedenborg's Theological Writings, p. 11—37. See also Dr. Priestley's Letters to the New Jerusalem Church in Birmingham. The Christian Observer for June 1806. Barruel's Hist. of Jacobinism, vol. iv.

retical; and they stand charged in history with sensuality and profaneness: particularly, with allowing a community of wives. Whether Nicolas himself countenanced such conduct, or whether they abused his name to sanction it, is not now easily to be ascertained; but the latter seems very probable. The Nicolaitans of the second century were Gnostics; but there seems some doubt whether they were the same sect.*

NOETIANS, a denomination in the third century, the followers of Noetius, who affirmed that the supreme God, whom he called the Father, and considered as absolutely indivisible, united himself to the man Christ, whom he called the Son, and was born and crucified with him. See *Patripassiani.*†

*NOMINALISTS, a party of the schoolmen, who followed the doctrine of Aristotle, with respect to universal ideas, in opposition to the *Realists*, which see.

NON-CONFORMISTS, dissenters from the church of England; but the term applies more particularly to those ministers who were ejected from their livings by the act of uniformity in 1662: the number of whom was nearly 2000. These men were driven from their houses, from the society of their friends, and exposed to the greatest difficulties. Their troubles were greatly augmented by the conventicle act, whereby they were prohibited from meeting for any exercise of religion (above five in number) in any other manner than allowed by the liturgy and practice of the church of England. For the first offence the penalty was three month's imprisonment, or paying five pounds; for the second offence six month's imprisonment, or ten pounds; and for the third offence, to be banished to some of the American plantations, for seven years, or pay one hundred pounds; and in case they return, to suffer death without benefit of clergy. For a detailed account of the sufferings of the Nonconformists at this period the reader is referred to Neal's History of the Puritans, and Brooks' Lives of the Puritans.

For the the grounds of Nonconformity, see *Dissenters* and *Puritans.*‡

*NONJURORS, the remains of the ancient episcopal church of Scotland, who at the revolution of 1688 adhered to the banished family of the Stuarts, and refused to take the oaths of allegiance to king William. But at the death of the last pretender in 1788, the denomination became extinct, and the laws

* Dupin's Church Hist. vol. i. p. 30. Mosheim, vol. i. p. 143, 144. New Ed:

† Mosheim, vol i. p. 246, 247. Broughton, vol. ii. p. 172.

‡ See Palmer's Nonconformists' Memorial, preface, p. vi. vii. Buck's Theolog. Dict.

against them have been since repealed. The episcopal church of Scotland is now considered as a branch of that of England, and is governed by eight bishops, one of whom is styled *Primate.**

NOVATIANS, a denomination in the third century, who derive their name from their founders, Novat and Novatian; the first a priest of the church of Carthage, the other of that of Rome.

This denomination laid it down for a fundamental tenet, that the church of Christ ought to be free from every stain; and taught, that he, who had once fallen into any moral offence, could not again become a member of it, though they did not refuse him the hopes of eternal life. Hence they looked upon every society which readmitted those to their communion who, after baptism had fallen into heinous crimes, as unworthy the title of a christian church. They separated from the church of Rome, because she admitted to communion those who had fallen off in time of persecution, to which they objected from Heb. vi. 1—8. They likewise obliged such as came over to them from the general body of christians to submit to baptism a second time, as a necessary preparation for entering into their society.

This denomination also condemned second marriages, and denied communion forever to such as practised them. They assumed to themselves (as is pretended) the title of *Cathari*, or puritans.†

*__NOVOJENTZI__, a party of the "old believers" among the Russian dissenters, or Raskoliniks, who recommended marriage very strongly, in opposition to those who prefer celibacy.‡

*__NUNS__, religious women in the primitive and Roman church, who devote themselves, under a solemn vow, to celibacy and a recluse life. See *Monks*.

O

*__ŒCONOMISTS__, a party of French philosophers, who ingratiated themselves both with the king (Louis XV) and the people, under pretence of promoting œconomy in the

* Skinner's Eccles. of Scotland—Primitive truths and order vindicated—Adam's Religious World displayed, vol. ii. p. 399, &c. and Evans' Sketch, 13th ed. p. 158.

† Formey's Eccles. Hist. vol. i. p. 61. Mosheim's Eccles. Hist. vol. i. p. 250, 251. Hist. of Religion, vol. iv. Broughton's Hist. Lib. vol. ii. p. 173.

‡ Pinkerton's Greek Church, p. 333.

state, while their main object, according to the Abbé Barruel, was to subvert christianity, by circulating the writings of Voltaire, Diderot, and other infidels.

OPHIANS, Ophites, or Serpentarians, seems to be the name of several sects, so called from their reverence, and in many cases worship, of the serpent. Mr. Bryant thinks this almost universally prevailed in the heathen world, and names many countries which adopted it, particularly Egypt.* The cause seems to have had its origin in the opinion, that the serpent was "more subtle than any other beast of the field." It is not difficult to account, therefore, for the serpent's being an early emblem of wisdom.

There were also Ophites who were a sort of mongrel christians, and perhaps revered the serpent as a type of Christ,† as the brazen serpent is still considered. (John iii. 14, 15.) The Ophites are considered by many authors, as a kind of Gnostics.

*ORATORY, priests of the. There were two religious congregations which assumed this name; the one founded in Italy by Philip de Neri in 1548; who also founded an hospital for pilgrims to Rome so large that in the year 1600, it lodged successively 470,000 persons. The other, called "the oratory of Jesus," was founded in France, and its chief object was "neither learning nor theology;"—but to cultivate "the virtues of the ecclesiastical life."‡

ORIENTAL PHILOSOPHY. The oriental philosophers endeavoured to explain the nature and origin of all things, by the principle of emanation from an eternal fountain of being. The formation of this philosophy into a regular system has been attributed to Zoroaster, an ancient Persian philosopher, who adopted the principle, generally held by the ancients, that "from nothing nothing can be produced." He supposed spirit and matter, light and darkness, to be emanations from one eternal source.

The active and passive principles he conceived to be perpetually at variance; the former tending to produce good, the latter, evil: but that through the intervention of the supreme Being the contest would at last terminate in favour of the good principle. According to Zoroaster, various orders of spiritual beings, gods, or demons, have proceeded from the Deity, which are more or less perfect, as they are at a greater or less distance, in the course of emanation, from the eternal fountain of intelligence; among those, the human soul is a particle of divine light, which will return to its source and partake of its immortality: and matter

* Holwell's Mytholog. Dict. p. 303.
‡ Scotch Theolog. Dict.
† Lardner's Heretics, p. 352.

is the last, or most distant emanation from the first source of being, which, on account of its distance from the fountain of light, becomes opaque and inert, and whilst it remains in that state is the cause of evil: but, being gradually refined, it will at last return to the fountain from whence it flowed.*

ORIGENISTS, a denomination in the third century, who derived their opinions from Origen, a very learned presbyter of Alexandria, and a man of uncommon abilities, who interpreted the divine truths of religion according to the tenour of the Platonic philosophy. He pretended that many evils arise from adhering to the literal and external part of scripture; and that the true meaning of the sacred writers was to be sought in a mysterious and hidden sense.

The peculiar tenets ascribed to Origen, are the following:

I. A pre-existent state of human souls, prior to the Mosaic creation, and perhaps from eternity; which souls were clothed with ethereal bodies suited to their original dignity. See *Platonists*.

II. That souls were condemned to animate mortal bodies, in order to expiate faults they had committed in a pre-existent state; for no other supposition appeared to him sufficient to account for their residence in these gross material bodies. See John ix. 2, 3.

III. That the soul of Christ was created before the beginning of the world, and united to the divine word in a state of pristine glory. See Phil. ii. 5—7. This text, he thought, must be understood of Christ's human soul, because it is unusual to propound the Deity as an example of humility in scripture. Though the humanity of Christ was so God-like, he emptied himself of this fulness of life and glory, *to take upon him the form of a servant.* It was this Messiah, who conversed with the patriarchs under a human form: it was he, who appeared to Moses upon the holy mount: it was he, who spoke to the prophets under a visible appearance: and it is he, who will at last come in triumph upon the clouds, to restore the universe to its primitive splendour and felicity. See *Pre-existents.*

IV. That at the resurrection mankind will be again clothed with ethereal bodies. For the elements of our terrestrial composition are such as most fatally entangle us in vice, passion, and misery. The purer the vehicle the soul is united with, the more perfect is her life and operations. Besides, the supreme goodness, who made all things, assures us, he made all things good at first; and therefore his recovery of us to our lost happiness (which is the design of the gospel) must restore us to far better

* Enfield.

bodies and happier habitations; which is evident from 1 Cor. xv. 42. 2 Cor. v. 1. and other texts of scripture.

V. That after long periods of time, the damned shall be released from their torments, and restored to a new state of probation. For the Deity has such reserves in his gracious providence, as will vindicate his sovereign goodness and wisdom from all disparagement. Though sin has extinguished, or silenced the divine life, yet it has not destroyed the faculties of reason and understanding, consideration and memory, which will serve the life which is most powerful. If, therefore, the vigorous attraction of the sensual nature be abated by a ceaseless pain, these powers may resume the seeds of a better life and nature. As in the material system there is a gravitation of the less bodies towards the greater, there must of necessity be something analogous to this in the intellectual system: and since created spirits are emanations from God, and as self-existent power must needs subject all beings to itself, the Deity could not but impress upon the souls of men a central tendency towards himself—an essential principle of re-union to their great original.

VI. That the earth after its conflagration shall become habitable again, and be the mansion of men and other animals, and that in eternal vicissitudes. Heb. i. 10—12, where speaking both of the heavens and earth, the inspired writer says, "as a vesture shalt thou change them, and they shall be changed," &c. *The fashion of the world passes away* like a turning scene, to exhibit a fresh and new representation of things; and if only the present dress and appearance of things go off, the substance is supposed to remain entire.* See *Millenarians.*

Origen is also charged with Arianism. See *Arians.*

*ORTHODOX, sound in the faith; a term generally applied by the established church in every age and country to its own creed; and denied to all doctrinal dissenters from it.

OSIANDRIANS, a denomination among the Lutherans, founded in 1550, by Andrew Osiander, a celebrated German divine, of high Calvinistic principles, similar to Crisp, Hussey, and others, charged with leaning to Antinomianism. One of his positions was—that believers being made partakers of Christ's divine righteousness by faith, God can behold no sin in them, though in themselves the chief of sinners.†

OSSENIANS, or Ossens. See *Helcesaites.*

* Mosheim's Eccles. Hist. vol. i. p. 219—225. Cudworth's Intellectual System, vol. ii p. 818. Cheyne's Philosophical Principles of Religion, p. 47—84. Travels of Cyrus, p 235—238.

† Mosheim, vol. iv. p. 10.

P

*PAGANS, heathens, and particularly those who worship idols. The term came into use after the establishment of christianity; the cities and great towns affording the first converts, the heathens were called Pagans, (from *Pagus*, a Village,) because they were then found chiefly in remote country places; but we use the term commonly for all who do not receive the Jewish, Christian, or Mahometan religions. The Pagans may be divided into the following classes—

I. The Greeks and Romans, and others who admit their refined system of mythology.

II. The more ancient nations, as the Chaldeans, Phenicians, Sabians, &c.

III. The Chinese, Hindoos, Japanese, &c.

IV. The Barbarians, as the Indians of North and South America, and the Negroes of Africa.

The objects of worship among the Pagans are various and diverse, as 1. The heavenly bodies, and particularly the Sun and Moon. 2. Imaginary beings, as Demons, Genii, &c. 3. The spirits of departed princes, heroes, and philosophers: or, lastly, almost every object of the animate and inanimate creation. The more refined, indeed considered animals or images as only the representations of their gods, who were supposed to reside in them; or as the medium of their worship. But the vulgar, the multitude, looked no farther than the material images: "and it must be remarked, that however high they might look, if not to the great Supreme, they were equally idolaters, whether they worshipped the sun, or Apollo, or a departed ghost; or an ox, a tree, or a stone."

The rites of Paganism were as various as the objects of their worship. In general they had some idea of the necessity of an atonement for their sins, and that "without shedding of blood there is no remission;" in many cases, and on all emergencies, they were apprehensive that the sacrifice must be of equal dignity with the sinner; and hence among many nations both ancient and modern, from the worshippers of Moloch, to the South-sea Islanders, the practice (sometimes carried to great enormity) of human sacrifices, which have stained the altars of almost all the nations upon the earth.*

The peculiarities of many nations have been already noticed in these pages, and others are to follow. See the articles Celts, Chinese, Druids, Gaurs, Grecians, Egyptians, Hindoos,

* Adam's Religious World displayed—Stillingfleet's Original Sacræ.

Japanese, Indians, Magians, Negroes, Sabians, Samans, or Schamans, &c. &c.

*PANTHEISTS, a sort of philosophical atheists, who considered the universe as an immense animal, "whose body nature is, and God the soul." This was the system of Orpheus and other early Greeks, and seems to have been the original of the doctrine of two co-eternal principles in the *Oriental Philosophy*, which see. From this, sprung the opinions of the Gnostics and Manicheans, and in modern times, of Spinosa and Tho. Hobbes.* See *Spinosists.*

PAPISTS, those who receive the Pope *(Papia)* of Rome as the head of their church. See *Roman Catholics.*

PARMENIANITES. See *Donatists.*

PASAGINIANS, a denomition which arose in the twelfth century, called also *The Circumcised.* Their distinguishing tenets were 1. That the observation of the law of Moses, in every thing, except the offering of sacrifices, was obligatory upon christians. 2. That Christ was no more than the *first and purest creature of God,* which was the doctrine of the semi-arians. They had the utmost aversion to the church of Rome.†

PASSALORYNCHITES, a branch of the Montanists, who held, that, in order to be saved, it was necessary to observe a perpetual silence; wherefore they are said (no doubt in ridicule) to have kept their finger constantly upon their mouth, and dared not open it even to say their prayers: and from this circumstance arose the name of this denomination.

*PATRIARCHAL RELIGION, (The) was natural religion in its first and purest state after the fall: but it was not natural religion only; since we know that to the ancient patriarchs were made many divine revelations by the prophets, as Enoch and Noah; by angels, as in the case of Sodom; and by the Son of God himself. See *Pre-existents.* The patriarchs were the heads of numerous families, among whom they reigned as princes, and officiated as priests. See Acts ii. 29; vii. 8, 9. Heb. vii. 4. The same term in Ecclesiastical History is applied to Primates or Archbishops.

PATRICIANS, the followers of Patricius, in the second century, who taught that the substance of the flesh is not the work of God, but of an evil being, on which account it is pretended, they bore such hatred to their own bodies, as sometimes to kill themselves.‡ See *Marcionites.*

PATRIPASSIANI, or PATRIPASSIANS, a sect which arose in the latter part of the second century, and received their name from the following

* Cudworth's Intellectual System.

† Broughton, vol. ii. p. 248.

‡ Mosheim, vol. ii. p. 456.

principle:—They believed but one person in the Deity, (the Father,) and yet admitted that our Saviour was divine; hence their doctrine strongly implied the incarnation and sufferings of the Father. Praxeas was esteemed the founder of this sect, and is called a Sabellian; but Lardner thinks he was rather in the in-dwelling scheme. See *Pre-existents*.* Of the same sentiment seem to have been the *Noetians* and *Monarchians*.

PAULIANS, or PAULIANISTS, the followers of Paul of Samosata, bishop of Antioch, in the third century, who taught that the Son and the Holy Ghost exist in God, in the same manner as the faculties of reason and activity do in man: that Christ was born a mere man; but that the reason, or wisdom of the Father descended into him, and wrought miracles; and that, on this account Christ might, though improperly, be called God.†

PAULICIANS, a sect of Gnostics formed in the seventh century by two brothers, Paul and John, of Jerusalem, from the former of whom they derive their name.

The tenets attributed to this sect are:—1. That the inferiour and visible world is not the production of the supreme Being.—2. That the evil principle was engendered by darkness and fire, not self-originated nor eternal.—3. That though Christ was the Son of Mary, yet he brought from heaven his human nature, i. e. perhaps his human soul.—4. That he was clothed with an ethereal, and impassible body, and did not *really* expire on the cross.—5. That the bread and wine which Christ is said to have administered to his disciples at his last supper, is to be figuratively taken.—6. They rejected the old testament, and epistles of St. Peter.‡

Such is the account given by Mosheim and other ecclesiastical historians; but very different is the character given of them by Mr. Milner. He supposes the Paulicians took their name from the apostle himself, whose writings they particularly studied. The founder of the sect was, according to him, one Constantine, who assumed the name of Sylvanus. The errours charged upon them he considers as the calumnies of their adversaries, except as to the sacrament: and that their moral character was irreproachable. It is agreed on all hands that they refused to worship the virgin Mary and the cross; and Mr. Milner adds, that they rejected image worship and acknowledged one mediator only. They had no hierarchy, but their ministers claimed a perfect equality; and they were not distinguished by any sacerdotal vestments. Their founder suffered martyrdom, and the

* Lardner's Heretics, p. 414, 415.

† Mosheim, vol. i. p. 248.

‡ Mosheim, vol. ii. p. 175, 176.

denomination were for an hundred and fifty years the subjects of a cruel persecution.*

PEDO- or PÆDO-BAPTISTS, all who practise *infant baptism*. They believe that baptism is to be administered to believers and their children, and that the infants of christian parents belong to the visible church of Christ.

That the visible church is one and the same body, both under the law and gospel; for the Gentiles are grafted into the same stock from which the unbelieving Jews were broken off: Rom. xi. 17. That the Gentiles should be fellow-heirs of the same body, and partakers of the promise in Christ by the gospel. Matt. xxi. 43. Eph. ii. 11, &c.

The covenant made with Abraham was the covenant of grace; for God preached before the gospel unto Abraham, that *the blessing of Abraham might come on the gentiles through Jesus Christ.* Gal. iii. 8—14. Christians, being the spiritual seed of Abraham, are under the same covenant, and entitled to the same privileges, which they may justly claim also for their infants. Acts ii. 39.

I. Baptism is now used in the room of circumcision. For 1. Circumcision was appointed to be the token of the covenant of grace: it was a sign and seal of the righteousness of faith, the same thing which is signified by christian baptism.—2. Circumcision was appointed to be the sacred *symbol* of initiation into the visible church. So baptism is a *seal* of initiation into the visible church.—3. The same inward grace is signified both by circumcision and baptism. Rom. ii. 28, 29. To be a Jew *inwardly*, by being circumcised with the circumcision of the heart, and to be a christian *inwardly*, by being washed with the washing of regeneration, (Titus iii. 5.) is one and the same thing. Baptism is also called the circumcision of Christ. Col. ii. 11.

II. Infant baptism, they say, was the approved practice of the apostles. For the scriptures give us an account of the baptism of whole *households;* as the gaoler and his household, Lydia and her household, and the household of Stephanas: and some of these, it is presumed, must have contained children.

The Pedobaptists also conclude that sprinkling was the practice of the apostles, because such great numbers were converted and baptized, where the circumstances, shortness of time, and situation of place, render it unlikely that they were baptized by immersion.

III. The Pedobaptists practise baptism by *affusion*, or *sprinkling*, which, they think scriptural, from the import of the original word, which, they say, signifies *washing*, and is used in scripture for washing things which were not dipped

* Milner's Church Hist. vol. iii. p. 206, 207.

in water. (Luke xi. 38.) The influences of the spirit, represented in baptism, are often expressed by pouring, or sprinkling; as the renewing of the Holy Ghost, which he has *poured out*, or *shed*, on us abundantly. Acts x. 45. Titus iii. 6.

IV. Among the Pedobaptists, some assert farther, that the baptism of Christ by John is not an example for christian imitation. They say, Christ was not baptized to manifest his *repentance;* neither did he submit to baptism as an *example* to the Jews; nor was his baptism a token of being *washed from sin.* But his baptism was a conformity to the law of *priestly consecrations;* for it answered to the washing of the high priest at his admission to the priesthood.

That the *baptism of John* was not *christian baptism* they conclude, because:—1. The grand design of John's baptism was the *manifestation* of Christ; but christian baptism is used for different purposes.—2. John's baptism began and ended under the legal dispensation. The gospel kingdom did not begin till Christ rose from the dead. John's baptism was completed before the death of Christ, and consequently fell short of new testament times; for "where a testament is, there must also of necessity be the death of the testator." Heb. ix. 16, 17.—3. The Holy Trinity was not named in John's baptism. This is plain, because there is an account that *some were baptized by John, and yet had not heard of the Holy Ghost.* (Acts xix. 2, 5.) The consequence inferred is, *John's* baptism was *not christian* baptism.*

Some Pedobaptists, however, take a more simple view of this subject. Considering baptism as an act of religious worship, they represent adult baptism as an act of self-dedication, and the baptism of their children as the dedication of their offspring to the Lord. And they observe that many baptists, on the birth of their children, dedicate them to God in the same manner, except only that they omit the use of water. As to *immersion,* they admit that it was frequently and perhaps generally, practised in the apostolic times; but they suppose the mode no more essential in this than in the sister ordinance of the Lord's supper; and this they consider equally valid under the different forms in which it is administered and received, whether sitting, stand-

* Clarke's Scripture Ground of the Baptism of Infants. Parson's Infant Baptism vindicated. Bostwick's Vindication of Infant Baptism. Lathrop's Sprinkling a Scripture Mode. Cleveland on Infant Baptism. Fish's Japheth dwelling in the Tents of Shem. Lewis' Covenant Interest of the Children of Believers. Towgood's Baptism of Infants a Reasonable service. Strong's Demonstration of Infant Baptism. Glass' Dissertation on Infant Baptism. Allen's Essay on outward Christian Baptism. Fish's and Crane's Baptism of Jesus Christ not to be imitated by christians. Edwards' Candid Reasons.

ing, or kneeling—and whether the elements consist of unleavened bread, and wine lowered by water, as in the primitive church; or, as with us, leavened bread, and wine of various sorts, according to circumstances—or whether the time be in the morning, at noon, in the afternoon, or evening.

PELAGIANS, a denomination in the fifth century, so called from Pelagius, a monk, who looked upon the doctrines which were commonly received concerning the original corruption of human nature, and the necessity of divine grace to enlighten the understanding and purify the heart, as prejudicial to the progress of holiness and virtue, and tending to establish mankind in a presumptuous and fatal security. He maintained the following doctrines:—1. That the sin of our first parents was imputed to them only, and not to their posterity; and that we derive no corruption from their fall, but are born as pure as Adam when he came out of the hands of his Creator.—2. That mankind, therefore, are capable of repentance and amendment, and of arriving to the highest degrees of piety and virtue, by the use of their natural faculties and powers; that, indeed, external grace is necessary to excite their endeavours, but that they have no need of the internal succours of the divine spirit.—3. That Adam was by nature mortal; and, whether he had sinned or not, would certainly have died.—4. That the grace of God is given in proportion to our merits.—5. That mankind may arrive at a state of perfection in this life.—6. That the law qualified men for the kingdom of heaven, and was founded upon equal promises with the gospel.*

PELEW ISLANDS. The inhabitants of these islands believe in one God, in the unlimited extent of his government, in the most important moral distinctions, and religious duties as taught by the light of nature, in the immortality of the soul, and in future rewards and punishments. They have very few forms of religion, little ceremony in their worship, and no houses or temples devoted to this purpose.†

*PENITENTS, certain religious societies of both sexes among the Roman Catholics. The male penitents are distinguished by the colour of their garments, white, black, blue, &c. The black penitents (called the brethren of mercy, instituted 1488,) attended criminals to their execution. The female penitents are chiefly reformed courtezans, as the penitents of St. Magdalen, at Paris and Marseilles, the converts of the name of Jesus at Seville, &c.‡

* Mosheim, vol. i. p. 412. Milner's Church Hist. vol. ii. p. 390, &c.
† Delano's Voyages, published 1817, p. 71.
‡ Buck's Theolog. Dict.

PEPUZIANS. See *Montanists.*

***PEREMAZANOFTSCHINS,** re-anointers, a sect which separated from the Russian church of Votka about 1770. They are very numerous at Moscow, and agree in almost every thing with the *Starrobredsi,* except that they reanoint all who join them from other communions.*

***PERFECTIONISTS,** those who hold it possible to attain perfection in the present life. See *Methodists.*

***PERSEES,** a sect in India descended from the ancient Persians, who worshipped fire. See *Gaurs* and *Magians.*

PETROBRUSSIANS, a denomination which was formed about the year 1110 in Languedoc and Provence, by Peter de Bruys, who taught the following doctrines:—1. That no persons were to be baptized before they came to the full use of their reason.—2. That it was an idle superstition to build churches for the service of God, who will accept of a sincere worship wherever it is offered: and that such churches had no peculiar sanctity attached to them.—3. That the crucifixes deserved the same fate—4. That the real body and blood of Christ were not exhibited in the eucharist, but were only represented in that holy ordinance by their figures and symbols.—5. That the oblations, prayers, and good works of the living, could be in no respect advantageous to the dead.†—6. That crucifixes and other instruments of superstition should be destroyed.

Peter de Bruys (says Dr. Haweis) "inveighed against the vices and superstitions of the times, and boldly attacked the tyranny and abuses of Rome as antichristian. The enraged clergy stirred up the populace, and he was burnt alive, not judicially, but in a tumult raised by the priests."‡

PHARISEES, the most celebrated of all the Jewish sects, which is supposed to have subsisted above a century before the appearance of our Saviour. They separated themselves, not only from the Gentiles, but from all other Jews; but their separation consisted chiefly in certain distinctions respecting food and religious ceremonies; and does not appear to have interrupted the uniformity of religious worship, in which the Jews of every sect united.§ The dissensions between the schools of Hillel and Shammai, a little before the christian era, increased the number and power of the Pharisees: Hillel and Shammai were two great and eminent teachers in the Jewish schools. Hillel was born an hundred and twelve years before Christ. Having acquired

* Pinkerton's Greek Church, p. 303.
† Mosheim, vol. ii. p, 446, 447. ‡ Haweis' Church Hist. vol. ii. p. 224.
§ Percy's Key to the New Testament.

a profound knowledge of the most difficult points of the law, he became master of the chief school in Jerusalem, and laid the foundation of the Talmud. Shammai, one of the disciples of Hillel, deserted his school, and formed a college, in which he taught doctrines contrary to his master. He rejected the oral law, and followed the written law only in its literal sense. See *Karaites*. These schools long disturbed the Jewish church by violent contests; the party of Hillel was at last victorious.*

When our Saviour Jesus Christ appeared in Judea, the Pharisees were in great credit among the people, because of the opinion of their learning, sanctity, and exact observance of the law. They fasted often, made long prayers, paid tythes scrupulously, and distributed much alms. They wore large rolls of parchment on their foreheads and wrists, on which were written certain words of the law; they affected to have fringes and borders at the corners and hems of their garments, broader than those of the other Jews, as a badge of distinction, and as denoting them to be greater observers of the law than others.

This denomination by their show of piety had rendered themselves extremely popular among the multitude; and the great, who feared their artifice, were obliged to court their favour. Hence they obtained the highest offices both in the state and priesthood, and had great weight both in public and private affairs. It appears from the frequent mention, which is made by the evangelists, of the Scribes and Pharisees in conjunction, that the greater number of Jewish teachers, (for they were the scribes,) were at that time of this sect.

The principal doctrines of the Pharisees are as follow:—That the oral law, which they suppose God delivered to Moses by an angel on Mount Sinai, and which was preserved by tradition, is of equal authority with the written law:—That by observing both these laws, a man may not only obtain justification with God, but perform meritorious works of supererogation:—That fasting, almsgiving, ablutions, and confessions, are sufficient atonements for sin:—That thoughts and desires are not sinful, unless they are carried into action. This denomination acknowledged the immortality of the soul, future rewards and punishments, the existence of good and evil angels, and the *resurrection* of the body.

According to Josephus, the Pharisees maintained only a *Pythagorean* resurrection, that is of the soul, by its transmigration into another body, and being born anew with it. From this resurrection, he says, they excluded all who were notoriously wicked; being of opinion

* Encyclopedia, vol. xvii. p. 104.

that the souls of such persons were transmitted into a state of everlasting woe. As to lesser crimes, they held they were punished in the body, which the souls of those who committed them were next sent into.

There seems indeed to have been entertained amongst the Jews in our Saviour's time a notion of the pre-existence of souls. How else could the disciples ask concerning the blind man, "Who did sin, this man or his parents, that he was born blind?" (John ix. 2.) And when they told Christ that "some said he was Elias, Jeremias, or one of the prophets," (Matt. xvi. 14.) the meaning seems to be, that they thought he was come into the world with the soul of Elias, or some other of the old prophets, transmigrated into him.

It does not appear, however, that these notions were at all peculiar to the Pharisees; and still less, that in them consisted their doctrine of the resurrection. It is a well-known fact, that the resurrection of the body was commonly believed among the Jews, even in the most degenerate period of their history. This is manifest from the story of the *seven brethren*, who, with their mother, were put to death by Antiochus Epiphanes in one day; (2 Mac. vii. xii. 43, 44.) to which story the writer of the epistle to the Hebrews, in chap. xi. 35. clearly alludes, saying, "others were tortured, not accepting deliverance, *that they might obtain a better resurrection.*" And when Martha, the sister of Lazarus, was told that her brother should rise again, she answered, "I *know* that he shall rise again in the resurrection at the last day; (John xi. 23, 24.) which implies, that this doctrine was at that time a well-known and acknowledged truth. Luke also says expressly, that *the Pharisees confess the resurrection.* (Acts xxiii. 8.) And Paul, speaking before Felix of his hope towards God, says, "Which they themselves [the Pharisees] *also allow, that there shall be a resurrection both of the just and unjust.* (Acts xxiv. 15.) If the doctrine of the resurrection, as held by the Pharisees, had been nothing more than the Pythagorean transmigration, it is beyond all credibility that such testimony would have been borne of it.

The peculiar manners of this sect are strongly marked in the writings of the evangelists, and confirmed by the testimony of the Jewish authors. According to the latter, they fasted the second and fifth days of the week, and put thorns at the bottom of their robes, that they might prick their legs as they walked. They lay upon boards covered with flint-stones, and tied thick cords about their waists. They paid tythes as the law prescribed, and gave the thirtieth and fiftieth part of their fruits; adding voluntary sacrifices to those which were commanded. They were very exact in performing their vows.—The Talmudic books mention several distinct classes of Pharisees, among whom were the *Truncated* Pharisee, who, that he might appear in profound meditation, as if destitute of feet, scarcely lifted them from the ground; and the *Mortar* Pharisee, who, that his contemplations might not be disturbed, wore a deep cap in the shape of a mortar, which would only permit him to look upon the ground at his feet. Thus did they study to captivate the admiration of the vulgar: and under the veil of singular piety, they often disguised the most licentious manners.*

PHILADELPHIAN SOCIETY, the followers of Jane Leadley, who, towards the conclusion of the seventeenth century, by her visions, predictions, and doctrines, gained a considerable number of disciples, among whom were some persons of learning. This woman was of opinion that all dissensions among christians would cease, and the kingdom of the Redeemer become glorious, if all who bear the name of Jesus, without regarding the forms of doctrine and discipline, which distinguish particular communions, would join in committing their souls to the guidance of the Holy Spirit, by his divine impulses and suggestions. She went further, and declared that she had a divine commission to proclaim the near approach of this glorious event. This assertion she delivered with the utmost confidence, that the Philadelphian Society was the true kingdom of Christ, in which alone the divine Spirit resided and reigned. She also maintained the doctrine of universal salvation. See *Leadley* and *Universalists*.†

***PHILIPISTS**; the followers of Philip Melancthon, the amiable reformer, were sometimes so called.

***PHILISTINES**, an ancient nation situated on the borders of Canaan, remarkable for their idolatry, and particularly for the worship of Dagon, whose image however could not stand before the ark. See 1 Sam. chap. v.

***PHILOPONISTS**. See *Tritheists*.

***PHILOSOPHISTS**, another name for the sect of the *Illuminati*, and particularly for the infidel triumvirate, who plotted the ruin of christianity,—Voltaire, Diderot, and D' Alembert. The former being weary, as he said, of hearing that twelve men propagated christianity through the world, was determined to show that far less were sufficient to overturn it. The private watch-word of the party was, *Ecrasez l' infame*, "Crush the wretch"—meaning Christ, the great object of their hatred and aversion.‡

* Calmet's Dict. Stackhouse's Hist. of the Bible, vol. v. p. 122—413.
† Mosheim, vol. v. p. 66, 67.
‡ See Barruel's Memoirs of Jacobinism.

PHOTINIANS, the followers of Photinus, bishop of Sirmium, in the fourth century. He taught that Jesus Christ was conceived of the Holy Ghost and born of the Virgin Mary:—that a certain divine emanation, or ray of divinity (which he called the *Word*) descended upon this extraordinary man:—that, on account of the union of the divine Word with his human nature, Jesus was called the Son of God, and even God himself. They also taught that the Holy Ghost was not a distinct person, but a celestial virtue proceeding from the Deity.*

***PHRYGIANS**, or Cataphrygians, a small party of Montanists, who resided in Phrygia. See *Montanists*.

PICARDS, the Adamites of the fifteenth century, a set who went naked in their religious assemblies. It is generally believed that such a sect existed also in the primitive Church; but Lardner refuses to believe it, because they are not mentioned by any writer earlier than Epiphanius, and by him only from uncertain report.†

PIETISTS, a denomination in the seventeenth century, which owed its origin to the pious and learned Spener, who formed private societies at Frankfort, in order to promote vital and practical religion; and published a book, entitled, "Pious desires," which greatly promoted this object. His followers laid it down as an essential maxim, that none should be admitted into the ministry but such as had received a proper education, and were distinguished by the wisdom and sanctity of their manners, and had hearts filled with divine love. Hence they proposed an alteration of the schools of divinity, which consisted in the following points:—1. That the systematical theology which reigned in the academies, and was composed of intricate and disputable doctrines, and obscure and unusual forms of expression, should be totally abolished.—2. That polemical divinity, which comprehended the controversies subsisting between christians of different communions, should be less eagerly studied, and less frequently treated, though not entirely neglected.—3. That all mixture of philosophy and human learning, with divine wisdom, was to be most carefully avoided.—4. That, on the contrary, all those who were designed for the ministry should be accustomed from their early youth to the perusal and study of the holy scriptures, and be taught a plain system of theology, drawn from this unerring source of truth.—5. That the whole course of their education was to be so directed as to render them useful in life, by the practical power of their doctrine, and the commanding influence of their example.‡

* Mosheim, vol. i. p. 346. Broughton, vol. ii. p. 441.
† Lardner's Heretics, p. 168. ‡ Mosheim, vol. iv. p. 454—460.

But it was not on preachers only, but on all their members, that exemplary piety and practical religion were enjoined. Like the society of *Friends*, and others, they renounced all vain amusements, and attended meetings of devotion.

*PILGRIMS, in ecclesiastical history, are certain persons who undertook, from religious motives, long and painful journies to the holy land, Rome, or the shrines of certain saints. The former became so numerous in the middle ages that, on their account chiefly, the holy war was undertaken. See *Crusaders*.

PLATONISTS. The Platonic philosophy is denominated from Plato, who was born about two hundred and sixty seven years before Christ. He founded the old academy on the opinions of Heraclitus, Pythagoras, and Socrates; and by adding the information he had acquired to their discoveries, he established a sect of philosophers, who were esteemed more perfect than any who had before appeared in the world.

The outlines of Plato's philosophical system were as follow: —That there is one God, eternal, immutable, and immaterial; perfect in wisdom and goodness; omniscient, and omnipresent. That this all-perfect Being formed the universe out of a mass of eternally preexisting matter, to which he gave form and arrangement. That there is in matter a necessary, but blind and refractory force, which resists the will of the supreme Artificer; so that he cannot perfectly execute his designs: and this is the cause of the mixture of good and evil, which is found in the material world. That the soul of man was derived by emanation from God; but that this emanation was not immediate, but through the intervention of the soul of the world, which was itself debased by some material admixture. That the relation which the human soul, in its original constitution, bears to matter, is the source of moral evil. That when God formed the universe, he separated from the soul of the world inferiour souls, equal in number to the stars, and assigned to each its proper celestial abode. That these souls were sent down to earth to be imprisoned in mortal bodies; hence arose the depravity and misery to which human nature is liable. That the soul is immortal: and by disengaging itself from all animal passions, and rising above sensible objects to the contemplation of the world of intelligence, it may be prepared to return to its original habitation. That matter never suffers annihilation: but that the world will remain forever; and that by the action of its animating principle, it accomplishes certain periods, within which every thing returns to its ancient place and state.

This periodical revolution of nature is called the Platonic, or great year.*

The Platonic system makes the perfection of morality to consist in living in conformity to the will of God, the only author of true felicity; and teaches that our highest good consists in the contemplation and knowledge of the supreme Being, whom he emphatically styles the *good*.† The end of this knowledge is to make men resemble the Deity, as much as is compatible with human nature. This likeness consists in the possession and practice of all the moral virtues.‡

After the death of Plato many of his disciples deviated from his doctrines. His school was then divided into the old, the middle, and the new academy. The old academy strictly adhered to his tenets. The middle academy partially receded from his system, without entirely deserting it. The new academy, founded by Carneades, an African, almost entirely relinquished the original doctrines of Plato, and verged towards the sceptical philosophy.

PLOTINISTS, the disciples of Plotinus, a celebrated platonic philosopher, the disciple of Ammonius, who founded the sect of the Academists, the popular philosophy during the first ages of christianity. See *Academics* and *Ammonians*.

***PNEUMATOMACHIANS.** See *Macedonians*.

***POLYTHEISTS**, those who worship many gods. See *Pagans*.

***POMORYANS**, certain Russian sectaries, who believe that antichrist is already come; reigns in the world unseen, that is, spiritually; and has put an end in the church to every thing that is holy. They are zealous in opposing the innovations of Nikon, with regard to the church books; prefer a life of celibacy and solitude, and rebaptize their converts from other sects.§ See *Russian church*.

***POPERY**, the system of the Papists, or *Roman Catholics*, which see.

***POPOFTCHINS**, the great body of the Russian dissenters, including all those sects which admit the ordination of the

* Enfield's Hist. of Philosophy, vol. i. p. 227, 228.

† Plato believed that in the divine nature there are two, and probably *three hypostases.*—The first he considered as self-existent, calling him, by way of eminence, the *Being* (το ον) or (το εν) the *One.* The only attribute which he acknowledged in this person was goodness; and therefore he frequently styles him the (το ἀγαθον,) the *good.* The second he considered as (νους) the *mind*, or (λογος) the wisdom or reason of the former, and the (δημιουργος) maker of the world. The third he always speaks of as (ψυχη) the *soul* of the world. He taught that the second is a necessary emanation from the first and the third from the second, or perhaps from both; comparing these emanations to those of light and heat from the sun. Encyclopedia, vol. xviii. p. 43.

‡ Dacier's Plato, vol. I. p. 7, 8.

§ Pinkerton's Greek Church, p. 330.

mother church, but differ from each other in certain particulars of little moment. Most of their ministers are bred up in the establishment.*

PRE-ADAMITES, a denomination given to the inhabitants of the earth, conceived by some people to have lived before Adam.

Isaac de la Pereyra, a French Protestant, in 1655, published a book to evince the realityof Pre-Adamites, by which he gained a considerable number of proselytes to the opinion; but the answer of Demarets, professor of theology at Groningen, published the following year, put a stop to its progress, though Pereyra wrote a reply.

To support their principal tenet advocated by Pereyra, that *there must have been men before Adam*, his followers reason thus:

1. They argue from Rom. v. 12—14. The apostle says, "sin was in the world *till the law*;" meaning the law given to Adam: But sin, it is evident, was not imputed, though it might have been committed, before his time; for "*sin is not imputed where there is no law.*"—2. The election of the Jews is supposed to be a consequence of the same system: it began at Adam, who is called their father, or founder. God is also their Father, having espoused the judaical church. The gentiles are only adopted children, as being Pre-Adamites.—3. Men,† i. e. the gentiles, are said to be made by the word of God. (Gen. i. 26, 27.) Adam, the founder of the Jewish nation, (whose history alone Moses wrote,) is introduced in the second chapter as the workmanship of God's own hands, and as created apart from other men.—4. Cain, having killed his brother, was afraid of being killed himself! By whom?—He married! Yet what wife could he get?—He built a town! What workmen did he employ? The answer to all these questions is in one word, Pre-Adamites.—5. The deluge only overflowed the country inhabited by Adam's posterity, to punish them for joining in marriage with the Pre-Adamites, and following their evil courses.—6. The improvements in arts, sciences, &c. could not make such advances towards perfection, as it is represented they did between Adam and Moses, unless they had been cultivated before.—Lastly: the histories of the Chaldeans, Egyptians, and Chinese, whose chronology (as founded on astronomical calculations) is supposed infallible, demonstrate the existence of men before Adam.‡

PREDESTINARIANS, a

* Pinkerton's Greek church, p. 293.

† Observe, the plural number is here used, in contradistinction to the founder of the Jewish nation, who is called Adam, in the singular.

‡ Herbelot's Biblioth. Orient. p. 36. Picart's Religious Ceremonies. Blount's Oracles of Reason. Basnage's History of the Jews. Origines Sacræ, b. i.

name given in the ninth century to the followers of Godeschalus, a German monk, whose sentiments were as follow:—1. That the Deity predestinated a certain number to salvation, before the world was formed.—2. That he predestinated the wicked to eternal punishment in consequence of their sins, which were eternally foreseen. —3. That Christ came not to save all men individually, and that none shall perish for whom he shed his blood.—4. That since the fall, mankind can exercise free-will only to do that which is evil.* The term Predestinarian has since been applied to all doctrinal Calvinists, who hold, for substance, the same opinions. See *Calvinists.*

PRE-EXISTENTS, a name which may not improperly be applied to those who hold the doctrine of Christ's pre-existence. This name comprehends two classes: the Arians, who defend Christ's pre-existence, but deny that he is a divine person: and others on the Calvinistic side, who assert both his divinity, and that his intelligent, created soul, was produced into being, and united by an ineffable union to the second person of the trinity, before the heavens and the earth were created.

Under the article *Arians*, the reader has been presented with a view of the system of Arius and his immediate followers. The sentiments of the celebrated Dr. Richard Price will be brought to view under the article *Unitarians*. In this place a short sketch will be given of the hypothesis, which was maintained by Dr. Samuel Clarke.

This learned man held, that there is one supreme cause and original of all things; one simple, uncompounded, undivided, intelligent agent, or person; and that from the beginning there existed with the first and supreme cause, (the Father,) a second person, called the Word, or Son, who derived his being, attributes, and powers, from the Father. He is therefore called the Son of God, and the only-begotten;† for generation, when applied to God, is only a figurative word, signifying immediate derivation of being and life from him.

To prove that Jesus Christ was generated (or produced) before the world was created, the doctor adduces the following considerations: The Father made the world by the operation of the Son. (John i. 3—10. 1 Cor. viii. 6. Eph. iii. 9. &c.)

That all Christ's authority, power, knowledge, and glory, are the Father's, communicated

* Mosheim's Eccles. Hist. vol. i. p. 159. Eccles. Hist. of France, p. 63. Baxter's Church History, chap. x. p. 263.

† Dr. Clarke waves calling Christ a creature, as the ancient Arians did; and principally on that foundation, denies the charge of Arianism.

to him, Dr. Clarke endeavours to prove by a variety of scriptures. The Son, before his incarnation, was with and in the form of God, and had glory with the Father. (John i. 2; xvii. 5. Phil. ii. 5.) The Son, before his incarnation, made visible appearances, and spake and acted in the name and authority of the invisible Father.

Dr. Clarke calls Christ a *divine person,* solely on account of the power and knowledge which were communicated to him by the Father. He indeed owns that Christ is an object of religious worship; but then he confines it to a limited sense: The worship paid to Christ terminates in the supreme God.*

The doctrine of the preexistence of Christ's human soul has been held by several divines; as Mr. Fleming, Dr. Goodwin, and many others who profess to maintain the proper divinity of Christ. The following sketch of the hypothesis of the late pious and ingenious Dr. Watts is selected from the rest.

He maintained one supreme God, dwelling in the human nature of Christ, which he supposed to have existed the first of all creatures; and speaks of the divine *logos* as the wisdom of God, and the Holy Spirit as the divine power, which, he says, is a scriptural person; i. e. spoken of figuratively in scripture, under personal characters.†

In order to prove that Christ's human soul existed previous to his incarnation, the following arguments are adduced.

I. Christ is represented as his Father's messenger, or angel, being distinct from and sent by his Father, long before his incarnation, to perform actions which seem to be too low for the dignity of pure godhead. The appearances of Christ to the patriarchs are described like the appearances of an angel, or man, really distinct from God; yet such a one, in whom Jehovah had a peculiar indwelling, or with whom the divine nature had a personal union.

II. Christ, when he came into the world, is said, in several passages of scripture, to have divested himself of some glory, which he had before his incarnation. Now, if there had existed, before his incarnation, nothing but his divine nature, this divine nature could not properly divest itself of any glory. *I have glorified thee on earth; I have finished the work, which thou gavest me to do. And now, O Father, glorify thou me with thine own self, with the glory, which I had with thee before the world was.* See John xvii. 4, 5. *Ye know the grace*

* Clarke's Scripture Doctrine of the Trinity. Doddridge's Lect.

† Dr. Watts says, in his preface to the Glory of Christ, that true and proper deity is ascribed to the Father, Son, and Holy Spirit. The expression *Son of God,* he supposes, is a title appropriated exclusively to the humanity of Christ.

of our Lord Jesus Christ, that, though he was rich, yet, for our sakes, he became poor, that you, through his poverty, might be made rich. 2 Cor. viii. 9.

III. It seems needful that the soul of Christ should pre-exist, that it might have opportunity to give its previous actual consent to the great and painful undertaking of atonement for our sins. The divine nature is incapable of suffering.

IV. The covenant of redemption between the Father and the Son, is represented as being made before the foundation of the world. To suppose that the divine essence, which is the same in all the three personalities, should make a covenant with itself, seems highly inconsistent.

V. Christ is the angel to whom God was in a peculiar manner united, and who in this union made all the divine appearances related in the old testament. See Gen. iii. 8; xvii. 1; xxviii. 12, 13; xxxii. 24. Exod. iii. 2; and a variety of other passages.

VI. The Lord Jehovah, when he came down to visit men, carried some ensign of divine majesty; he was surrounded with some splendid appearance; such as often was seen at the door of the tabernacle, and fixed its abode between the cherubim. It was by the Jews called the *shekinah;* i. e. the habitation of God. Hence he is described as "dwelling in light, and clothed with light as with a garment." In the midst of this brightness there seems to have been sometimes a human form. It was probably of this glory that Christ divested himself when he was made flesh. With this he was covered at his transfiguration in the Mount, when "his garments were white as the light;" and at his ascension into heaven, when a bright cloud received him; and when he appeared to John, (Rev. i. 13;) and it was with this he prayed that his Father would glorify him.

VII. When the blessed God appeared in the form of a man, or angel, it is evident that the true God resided in this man, or angel; because he assumes the most exalted names and characters of godhead. And the spectators, and sacred historians, it is evident, considered him as true and proper God, and paid him the highest worship and obedience. He is properly styled *"the angel of God's presence"*—and *of the covenant.* Isaiah lxiii. Mal. iii, 1.

VIII. This same angel of the Lord was the particular God and King of the Israelites. It was he who made a covenant with the patriarchs, who appeared to Moses in the burning bush, who redeemed the Israelites from Egypt, who conducted them through the wilderness, who gave the law at Sinai, and transacted the affairs of the ancient church.

IX. The angels who have appeared since our blessed Saviour became incarnate, have never assumed the names, titles, characters, or worship, belonging to God. Hence we infer that the angel who, under the old testament, assumed such titles, and accepted such worship, was that angel in whom God resided, or who was united to the godhead in a peculiar manner; even the pre-existent soul of Christ himself.

X. Christ represents himself as one with the Father: John x. 30; xiv. 10, 11. There is, we may hence infer, such a peculiar union between God and the man Christ Jesus, both in his pre-existent and incarnate state, that he may properly be called *God-man* in one complex person.

Dr. Watts supposes that the doctrine of the pre-existence of the soul of Christ, explains several dark and difficult scriptures, and discovers many beauties and proprieties of expression in the word of God, which on any other plan lie unobserved. For instance; in Col. i. 15, &c. Christ is described as "the image of the invisible God, the first-born of every creature." His being the image of the invisible God, cannot refer merely to his divine nature; for that is as invisible in the Son, as in the Father: therefore it seems to refer to his pre-existent soul in union with the godhead. Again, the "godhead" is said to "dwell bodily in Christ," Col. ii. 9, and from hence this has been called the *indwelling* scheme.

"This system," says Dr. Price, speaking of Dr. Watts' sentiments, "differs from Arianism, in asserting the doctrine of Christ's consisting of two beings; one the self-existent Creator, and the other a creature, made into one person by an ineffable union and indwelling, which renders the same attributes and honours equally applicable to both."*

Mr. Evans observes, that, "Between the system of Sabellianism, and what is termed the indwelling scheme, there appears to be a considerable resemblance, if it be not precisely the same, differently explained. Dr. Watts," says he, "towards the close of his life became a Sabellian, and wrote several pieces in defence of it." To prove this assertion, Mr. Evans refers to Dr. Watts' Last Thoughts on the Trinity, in a pamphlet published by the Rev. Gabriel Watts of Chichester. It was printed by the Doctor in the year 1745. From this piece it appears, that Dr. Watts had discarded the common notion of the trinity. See *Sabellians*.

Under this denomination, the plan lately advanced by the Rev. Noah Worcester, in a work styled, "Bible News, relating to the living God, his only Son, and Holy Spirit,"

* Watts' Glory of Christ, p. 6—203. Johnson's Life of Christ, with notes by Palmer. Doddridge's Lectures, p. 385—403. Price's Sermons, p. 331. Fleming's Christology. Evans' Sketch.

may perhaps be inserted with propriety.

Mr. Worcester supposes, that the pre-existence of Christ is naturally implied in the numerous passages which speak of God's sending his Son into the world, and of God's giving his Son. The same idea is implied in all that Christ said of his coming forth from the Father, and coming down from heaven, and coming forth from God. Such representations naturally import that he had existed with the Father, with God, and in heaven, before he was sent, or before he came into the world.

Our author's theory respecting the metaphysical nature of our Saviour, is founded on the title *Son of God*, so frequently and so emphatically given to our Lord throughout the New Testament. He thinks that the language of scripture in which our Lord is styled God's "*own Son," the only begotten Son of God, the only begotten of the Father,* " must import that Jesus Christ is the Son of God in the most strict sense of the term, as truly as Isaac was the Son of Abraham. For in contradistinction to angels and men, and to all who may be called the Sons of God by creation and adoption, Christ is definitely called the Son of God. He, therefore, is not a created, intelligent being, but a being who properly derived his existence and nature from God. He is not a self-existent being, for it is impossible for God to beget or produce a self-existent son; but as Christ derived his existence and nature from the Father, he is as truly the image of the invisible God, as Seth was the likeness of Adam. He is therefore a person of divine dignity, constituted the Creator of the world, the angel of God's presence, or the medium by which God appeared or manifested himself to the ancient patriarchs. According to this plan, the Son of God became man, or the Son of man, by becoming the soul of a human body.

Mr. Worcester asserts, that it is plainly and abundantly represented in the scriptures, that the Son of God did really and personally suffer and die for us. And on this ground, both the love of God, and the love of his Son, are represented as having been manifested in an extraordinary manner. And if the Son of God be truly the Son of God, a derived intelligence, these representations may be strictly and affectingly true. For on this hypothesis, the Son of God may be the same intelligent Being as the soul of the man Christ Jesus, who suffered on the cross. If, on the other hand, according to the trinitarian system, the Son of God was the self-existent God, who became mysteriously united to a proper man, who had a true body and a reasonable soul; the self-existent God could not suffer in his divine nature: but altogether in his human nature, according to this theory, this man, and not the Son of God, endured the stripes by which we are healed. This theory, says our author, will not, I suspect, be found to admit, or support any thing more, than the shadow of the suffering and death of the Son of God; and as it respects the real character of the suffering Saviour, what is it better than Socinianism enveloped in mystery?

Mr. Worcester supposes, that the Holy Ghost is not a self-existent person; but that by the Holy Ghost is intended the fulness of God, or the efficient productive emanations of divine fulness.

Our ingenious author illustrates his ideas of the spirit by scripture metaphors. God, says he, is represented by the metaphor of the natural sun, "the Lord God is a sun;" then the rays of light and heat, which emanate or proceed from the sun, are an emblem of the Holy Spirit, which proceedeth from the Father. Like the rays of the sun, these divine emanations of the fulness of God, illuminate, quicken, invigorate and fructify.

In opposition to the trinitarian doctrine of three distinct, co-equal and co-eternal persons in one God, our author teaches, that the self-existent God is only one person. "If," says he, "God were three co-equal persons, it would be very natural to expect that we should find explicit evidence of this in the manner of giving the law, and in the prayers of saints. But when the law was given on Mount Sinai, God spake in the singular number—"I am the Lord thy God; thou shalt have no other gods before me." And in all the prayers throughout the bible, in which God is addressed, he is addressed as one individual person.

Christ addressed the Father not only as one person, but as the "Only True God." As the Son he addressed the Father, and in his prayer he hath these words; "And this is life eternal, that they might know *Thee*, the only true God, and Jesus Christ, whom *Thou* hast sent."

The following arguments are adduced as a specimen of Mr. Worcester's manner of arguing to defend his ideas respecting the Son of God.

"It is admitted by every sect of christians, that Jesus Christ was remarkable for humility, and as removed in the greatest degree from arrogance and ostentation. This being admitted, let the following brief summary be considered and the proper conclusions drawn.

"In two parables our Saviour represents himself as standing in the same relation to God that a king's son does to his father: 'The kingdom of heaven is like unto a certain king who made a marriage for his Son.' Matth. xxii. 2. In the parable of the vineyard, Mark xii. 6, he contrasts himself with former messengers of God in this manner: "Having yet, therefore one Son, his well beloved, he sent him also last unto them, saying, they will reverence my Son."

Christ spoke of it as a great display of God's love, that he was sent into the world. "God so loved the world, that he gave his only begotten Son, that whoever believeth on him should not perish, but have eternal life."

Now let it be asked, if Jesus were himself the Deity, what sense can be made of either of the foregoing passages? On the contrary, if he were but a man like Moses, where was his humility? But if he were indeed God's Son, with what force do these passages strike the mind!

Again, Jesus used unexampled familiarity in speaking of God, and to God as his Father, and in coupling himself with God: "My Father worketh hitherto, and I work." "I and my Father are one." "My Father is greater than I." "If a man love me, he will keep my words, and my Father will love him, and *we* will come unto him, and make our abode with him." "That they may be one, as thou, Father, art in me, and I in thee, that they may be one in us, even as we are one."

We may farther observe, that our Saviour had evidence that this familiar manner of saying my Father, was understood by the Jews, as claiming the dignity of God's own Son; for when he said, "My Father worketh hitherto, and I work," they were ready to stone him as a blasphemer, and affirmed according to the Greek, that he "made God his own Father." This they considered as such a manner of equalling himself with God, that he ought to be put to death. Yet while he knew the sense in which they understood him, he persisted in his claim, but assured them he was dependent on the Father, so dependent that he could do nothing of himself; and thus he received all his fulness, his life, and all his authority from the Father. On similar ground, they repeatedly accused, and he as repeatedly vindicated his claim, and justified himself.

Now what shall we say to these things? Shall we say that Christ was the supreme God, and thus render all the representations of God's love in sending his Son as perfectly unintelligible as the doctrine of the Trinity? Shall we say that Jesus was a mere man, and gave up all his claims to his being a pattern of humilty, and consider him as the most arrogant and vain-glorious teacher that ever appeared in human form? Shall we not rather admit his claims, and regard him as the Son of the living God?

Mr. Worcester asserts, that the precise difference between him and the Arians is, he supposes a Son from the uncreated essence of the Deity; the Arians a Son created out of nothing.*

PRESBYTERIANS, from the Greek πρεσβυτερος, a denomination of protestants: so called from their maintaining that the government of the church, appointed by the new testament, was by presbyters and ruling elders, associated for its government and discipline. The Presbyterians affirm, that there is no order in the church, as established by Christ and his apostles, superiour to that of presbyters—that all ministers, being embassadors, are equal by their commission; and the elder, or presbyter, and bishop, are the same in name and office, and the terms synonymous, for which they allege Acts xx. 28. Tit. i. 5—7. 1 Thes. v. 12. Heb. xiii. 7—17. and 1 Pet. v. 2, 3.

From the time of the reformation to that of the revolution, the Scotch church was torn with contentions respecting her form of church government; the court professing episcopacy, and the people presbyterianism, and each prevailed by turns: but on King William's accession, presbyterianism was finally settled to be the established religion, and has so continued ever since. Their form of church government is as follows:—

The *Kirk-session,* consisting of the minister and lay elders of the congregation, is the lowest ecclesiastical judicature. The next is the *Presbytery,* which consists of all the pastors within a certain district, and one ruling elder from each parish.

The *provincial Synods* (of which there are fifteen) meet twice in the year, and are composed of the members of the several presbyteries within the respective provinces.

From the Kirk-sessions appeal lies to the Presbyteries—from these to the Synod—and from them to the *General Assembly,* which meets annually, and is the highest ecclesiastical authority in the kingdom. This is composed of delegates from each presbytery, from every royal borough, and from each of the Scotch universities, and the king presides by a commission of his own appointment.

The Scotch ordain by the "laying on of the hands of the presbytery," before which persons may be licensed to preach as probationers, but cannot administer the sacraments. The clergy are maintained by the state, and nominated to livings by patrons, as in other estab lishments.

Of the presbyterians in England, some preserve their connexion with the Scotch Kirk, and others with the relief, &c. (See *Relief Kirk, Seceders, Burghers,* &c.) But those properly called the *English* pres-

* Bible News, second edition, p. 16, 26, 38, 57, 66, 143. Respectful Address to the Trinitarian clergy, p. 5. Manuscript of the Rev. Mr. Worcester.

byterians, have no connexion with the Scotch Kirk, though they preserve their forms of worship; nor do they adopt their creeds and catechisms, (which are confessedly Calvinistic,) but are avowed Arminians, and many of them Arians or Socinians.*

The Presbyterians are numerous in the United States of America; the majority of whom inhabit the middle and southern states. They had become a powerful and respectable body in New York before the commencement of the present century. They are now the most numerous religious denomination in this state. The doctrines of the Presbyterian churches in America are, generally, in strict conformity with the tenets of the Genevan school.†

PRIMINISTS, a party so called from Primianus, who became the head of the *Donatists*, which see.

PRISCILLIANISTS, a denomination in the fourth century, the followers of Priscillian, a Spaniard by birth, and bishop of Abila. He is said to have adopted the principal tenets of the Manicheans: it is more certain that he was cruelly persecuted, even unto death, for his opinions. This sect stands charged with practising in some instances dissimulation; but their morals were generally correct and austere.‡

PROCLIANITES, so called from Proculus, a philosopher of Phrygia, who appeared in 194, and put himself at the head of a band of Montanists, in order to spread the sentiments of that denomination.§ See *Montanists*.

PROTESTANTS, a name first given in Germany to those who adhered to the doctrine of Luther; because in 1529, they entered a solemn protest against a decree of the diet of Spires, (which prohibited all farther reformation,) declaring that they appealed to the emperour Charles V,‖ and to a general council. This name was afterwards given to the Calvinists, and has since become a common denomination for all who dissent from the Roman Catholic church, in whatever country they reside, or in whatever sects they have since been distributed.

Though some of the Protestants differ not more widely from the church of Rome, than they do from one another; they

* Collier's Hist. Dict. vol. ii. Scotch Theolog. Dict. Adam's Religious World displayed, vol. iii. p. 1.

† Wilson on the atonement.

‡ Mosheim, vol. i. p. 349. Priestley's Eccles. Hist. vol. ii. p. 411.

§ Broughton, vol. ii. p. 285.

‖ This was the second diet held at Spires on account of the religious disputes in Germany; it was held 1529, and revoked the decrees of the former diets, which were favourable to the reformation. "Every change in the doctrine, discipline, or worship of the established religion, was prohibited by this diet."

agree in professing to receive the scriptures as the supreme rule of their faith and practice.

Chillingworth, a learned divine of the church of England, addressing himself to a Roman Catholic writer, speaks of the religion of Protestants in the following terms:—"Know that when I say the religion of Protestants is in prudence to be preferred before yours; as, on the one side, I do not understand by your religion the doctrine of Bellarmine or Baronius, or any other private man amongst you, nor the doctrine of the Sorbonne, or of the Jesuits, or of the Dominicans, or of any other particular company among you; but that wherein you all agree or profess to agree, the doctrine of the council of Trent. On the other side, by the religion of Protestants I do not understand the doctrine of Luther, or Calvin, or Melancthon, nor the confession of Ausburg or Geneva, nor the catachism of Heidelberg, nor the articles of the church of England, no, nor the harmony of Protestant confessions; but that wherein they all agree, and which they all subscribe with a greater harmony, as a perfect rule of faith and action, that is, the Bible! The Bible, I say, the Bible only, is the religion of Protestants. Whatsoever else they believe besides it, and the plain irrefragable, indubitable consequences of it, well may they hold it as a matter of opinion, but as a matter of faith and religion, neither can they with coherence to their own grounds believe it themselves, nor require belief of it in others, without most high, and most schismatical presumption. I, for my part, after a long (and as I verily belive and hope) impartial search of the true way to happiness, do profess plainly, that I cannot find any rest for the sole of my foot, but upon this rock only. I see plainly, and with my own eyes, that there are popes against popes, and councils against councils; some fathers against other fathers, the same fathers against themselves; a consent of fathers of one age against a consent of fathers of another age; traditive interpretations of scripture are pretended, but there are few or none to be found; no tradition but that of scripture can derive itself from the fountain, but may be plainly proved either to have been brought in, in such an age after Christ, or that in such an age it was not in. In a word, there is no sufficient certainty, but of scripture only, for any considering man to build upon. This, therefore, and this only, I have reason to believe. This I will profess; according to this I will live; and for this, if there be occasion, I will not only willingly, but even gladly lose my life, though I should be sorry that christians should take it from me."

"Propose me any thing out of the book, and require whether I believe or no, and seem it never so incomprehensible to human reason, I will subscribe it with hand and heart, as knowing no demonstration can be stronger than this, *God hath said so, therefore it is true.* In other things I will take no man's liberty of judging from him; neither shall any man take mine from me. I will think no man the worse man, nor the worse christian; I will love no man the less for differing in opinion from me. And what measure I mete to others, I expect from them again. I am fully assured that God does not, and therefore men ought not to require any more of man than this: to believe the scripture to be God's word; to endeavour to find the true sense of it; and to live according to it."*

PSATYRIANS, a party of the Arians, in A. D. 360, who maintained that the Son was created.† See *Arians.*

PTOLEMAITES, a branch of the Valentinians, so called from Ptolemy, their leader, who differed from his master both in the number and nature of the *æons.*‡

PURITANS, *(Cathari.)* In the middle ages this term was applied to a branch of the Paulicians, (See *Catharist,*) who are charged with the tenets of the Manicheans; but whose principal crime, according to Milner, was their aversion to the church of Rome. (See *Paulicians.*) This able historian says, "They were a plain, unassuming, harmless, and industrious race of christians; condemning, by their doctrine and manners, the whole apparatus of the reigning idolatry and superstition; placing true religion in the faith and love of Christ, and retaining a supreme regard for the divine word."§

In England, the term Puritans was applied to those, who wished for a farther degree of reformation in the church than was adopted by Queen Elizabeth, and a *purer* form of discipline and worship. It was a common name given to all who, from conscientious motives, though on different grounds, disapproved of the established religion, from the *reformation* to the act of *uniformity* in 1662. From that time to the *revolution* in 1688, as many as refused to comply with the established worship, (among whom were about 2000 clergymen, and perhaps 500,000 people,) were denominated *Nonconformists.* From the passing of the act of *toleration* on the accession of William and Mary, the name of Nonconformists was changed to that of *Protestant Dissenters.* See *Dissenters.*

The greater part of the Pu-

* Mosheim, vol. iv. p. 71, 72. Adam's Religious World Displayed. Chillingworth's Religion of Protestants a safe way to heaven.

† Hist. of Religion, vol. iv. ‡ Mosheim, vol. i. p. 232.

§ Milner's Church Hist. vol. iii. p. 385.

ritans were Presbyterians.* Their objections to the English establishment consist principally in forms and ceremonies. Some, however, were Independents, and some Baptists. The objections of these were much more fundamental; disapproving of all national churches, and disavowing the authority of human legislation in matters of faith and worship.

The severe persecutions carried on against the puritans during the reigns of Elizabeth and the Stuarts, served to lay the foundation of a new empire in the western world. Thither, as into a wilderness, they fled from the face of their persecutors; and, being protected in the free exercise of their religion, continued to increase, till in about a century and a half, they became an independent nation. The different principles, however, on which they had originally divided from the church establishment at home, operated in a way that might have been expected, when they came to the possession of the civil power abroad. Those who formed the colony of *Massachusetts* having never relinquished the principle of a national church, and of the power of the civil magistrate in matters of faith and worship, were less tolerant than those who settled at *New Plymouth*, and at *Rhode Island and Providence Plantations.* The very men, (and they were good men too,) who had just escaped the persecutions of the English prelates, now, in their turn, persecuted others, who dissented from them, until, at length, the liberal system of toleration, established in the parent country at the revolution, extending to the colonies, in a good measure put an end to these cruel proceedings.

Neither the puritans, nor the nonconformists, appear to have disapproved of the doctrinal articles of the established church. At least the number who did so, was very small. It is said that while the great body of the clergy had, from the days of Archbishop Laud, favoured Arminianism, they were attached to the principles of the first re-

* The English church and the majority of the Puritans in Queen Elizabeth's reign, agreed that some religious establishment was necessary; and that the alliance between church and state was beneficial. "Both parties," says Mr. Neal, "agreed too well in asserting the necessity of an uniformity of public worship, and of calling in the sword of the magistrate for the support and defence of their several principles, which they made an ill use of in their turns, as they could grasp the power into their hands. The standard of uniformity, according to the bishops, was the Queen's supremacy, and the laws of the land; according to the Puritans, the decrees of provincial and national synods allowed and enforced by the civil magistrate; but neither party were for admitting that liberty of conscience, and freedom of profession, which is every man's right, as far as is consistent with the peace of the government under which he lives." See Neal's Hist. of the Puritans. See also Review of Brooks' Lives of the Puritans in Christian Observer 1815.

formers, and by their labours and sufferings the spirit of the reformation was kept alive. But after the revolution many of the Presbyterians veered towards Arminianism, then revived the Arian hypothesis, and by degrees settled in Socinianism. Some of the Independents, on the other hand, leaned to the Antinomian doctrines; but the rise of Methodism, in the latter part of the last century, greatly revived and encreased the dissenting interest.*

PYRRHONISTS, the disciples of Pyrrho, the sceptical philosopher. See *Sceptics.*

PYTHAGOREANS, the followers of Pythagoras, a celebrated Greek philosopher, who flourished about five hundred years before the christian era. His distinguishing doctrine was that of the *Metempsychosis,* which he learned among the philosophers of India. This doctrine refers to the transmigration of the human soul after death into the bodies of various animals, till it returns again to its own nature. This notion led to the total rejection of animal food, and inculcated a merciful treatment of the brute creation. The symbols of this philosopher were highly mysterious, and have never been completely developed.†

Q

QUAKERS. A small part of the American Quakers, during the revolutionary war, thought themselves at liberty to accept offices under government, or to bear arms. Among this party was the distinguished military character General Green, who died 1786, to whom congress decreed a monument. The ancient Quakers expelled from their assemblies the free or fighting Quakers, as they style themselves, and they were obliged to form a separate congregation, which still exists in Philadelphia. They differ from others of their denomination only in being less rigid.‡ See *Friends.*

QUARTODECIMANI, a denomination in the second century; so called because they maintained that Easter day was always to be celebrated, conformably to the custom of the

* Neal's History of the Puritans, 2 vol. 8vo. Palmer's Nonconformists' Memorial. Brooks' Lives of the Puritans, 3 vol. and Bogue and Bennett's History of Dissenters, 4 vol. 8vo.

† Ency. Perthensis, in Pythagoras.

‡ Gregoire's Histoire Des Sectes Relig.

Jews, on the *fourteenth day of the moon* of March, whatever day of the month that happened to be.*

QUIETISTS, the followers of Michael de Molinus, a Spanish priest, who flourished in the seventeenth century. They were so called, from a kind of absolute *rest* and *inaction*, which the soul is supposed to be in, when arrived at that state of perfection, which they call the *unitive life.*

The principles maintained by this denomination, are as follow: That the whole of religion consists in the perfect calm and tranquillity of a mind removed from all external and finite things, and centered in God, and in such a pure love of the supreme Being, as is independent on all prospect of interest or reward.

For, say they, the primitive disciples of Christ were all of them inward and spiritual; and when Jesus Christ said to them, *It is expedient for you that I go away; for if I go not away, the Comforter will not come unto you;* he intended thereby, to draw them off from that, which was sensible, though very holy, and to prepare their hearts to receive the fulness of the holy spirit, which he looked upon, as the *one thing necessary.*

To prove, that our love to the Deity must be disinterested, they allege, that *the Lord hath made all things for himself,* as saith the scripture; and it is for his glory, that he wills our happiness. Our happiness is only a subordinate end, which he has made relative to the last and great end, which is his glory. To conform, therefore, to the great end of our creation, we must prefer God to ourselves, and not desire our own happiness, but for his glory; otherwise we shall go contrary to his order. As the perfections of the Deity are intrinsically amiable, it is our glory and perfection to go out of ourselves, to be lost and absorbed in the pure love of infinite beauty. See *Mystics.*

Madam Guion, a woman of fashion in France, born (1648) was a warm advocate of these principles. She asserted that the means of arriving at this perfect love, are prayer and the self-denial enjoined in the gospel. Prayer she defines to be the entire bent of the soul towards its divine origin.

Fenelon, the excellent archbishop of Cambray, also favoured these sentiments in a celebrated publication, entitled, "The Maxims of the Saints." Hence arose a controversy between him and Bossuet, bishop of Meaux. The tenets objected by Bossuet to Fenelon may be reduced to two: 1. That a person may attain an habitual state of divine love, in which he loves God purely for his own sake, and without the slightest regard to his own interest, even

* Broughton, vol. ii. p. 307.

in respect of his eternal happiness: 2. That in such a state it is lawful, and may even be considered as an heroic effort of conformity to the divine will, to consent to eternal reprobation, if God should require such a sacrifice; the party which makes such an act, conceiving at the moment, that such a sacrifice is possible.

It was objected to Fenelon, that his doctrine elevated charity beyond human power, at the expense of the fear of God, and the hope of divine favour.

On the habitual state of disinterested divine love, the attainment of which was said to be inculcated in Fenelon's writings, Fenelon himself uniformly declared his opinion that a permanent state of divine love, without hope, and without fear, was above the lot of man; and Bossuet himself allowed that there might be moments, when a soul, dedicated to the love of God, would be lost in heavenly contemplation, and love, and adore without being influenced either by hope or fear, or being sensible of either.

The controversy* between these great men was referred to the decision of the Roman Catholic church; and in 1699, the pope issued a brief, by which twenty three propositions, reducible to the two above mentioned, were extracted from Fenelon's "Maxims of the saints" and condemned. Fenelon submitted to the decision of the church. But his enemies were mortified by a bon mot of the pope, "that Fenelon was in fault for too great love of God; and his enemies equally in fault, for too little love of their neighbour."

QUINTILIANS, a branch of the Montanists, who derived their name from the prophetess Quintilia. Their distinguishing tenet was, that women ought to be admitted to perform the sacerdotal and episcopal functions; grounding their practice on Gal. iii. 28. They added that Philip, the deacon, had four daughters, who were prophetesses, and were doubtless of their sect. In their assemblies it was usual to see the virgins enter in white robes, personating prophetesses.† See *Montanists*.

R

***RABBINISTS**, those Jewish doctors, who admit the *Cabbala*, or traditions of the Elders. See *Cabbalists*.

***RACOVIANS**, a term sometimes applied to the Polish Uni-

* For a particular account of the controversy between Bossuet and Fenelon, see also Cambray on Pure Love, p. 131—138. Lady Guion's Life and Letters, p. 167. Cowper's Translation of Guion's Poems. Chev. Ranway's Life of Fenelon. Mosheim, vol. iv. p. 328. Butler's Life of Fenelon.

† Hist. of Religion, vol. iv. Broughton, vol. ii. p. 310.

tarians, on account of their seminary at Racow, and of their adopting the Racovian catechism. See *Socinians.*

RANTERS, a denomination in the year 1645, who set up the light of nature, under the name of *Christ in men.* With regard to the church, scripture, ministry, &c. their sentiments were the same with the Seekers.* See *Seekers.*

*RASKOLNIKS, or Schismatics, a general name for dissenters from the Russian established church; but they call themselves *Starovertsi*, or believers of the old faith, because they adhere to the old manuscript formularies of the Greek church, and reject the printed formularies of the patriarch *Nikon*, who in the seventeenth century revised the ancient forms, and (as they say) corrupted them, and then had them printed by authority, for the use of the Russian establishment. It appears, however, that there were dissenters in Russia long prior to this period, and within four hundred and fifty years after the introduction of christianity. These were called *Strigolniks*, (which see;) but the modern dissenters, (who partly arose out of these, in the time of Nikon,) are divided into two principal classes, the *Popoftchins*, and the *Bezpopoftchins.* The former are divided into the *Starobredsi*, *Diaconoftchins*, *Epefanoftchins*, and *Tschunaboltsi*, each of which is allowed a place in this Dictionary.

The *Bezpopoftschins* (who were omitted above) include no less than thirteen different sects, which either have no regular priests, or refuse to acknowledge those ordained in the established church.† See *Duhobortis*, *Pomoryans*, &c.

*REALISTS, a party of the schoolmen, who conceive that *universals* are realities, and have an existence—*a parte rei*; whereas the *nominalists* conceive of them only as ideas existing in the mind. Under the denomination of Realists were comprehended the Scotists and Thomists, and all other sects of schoolmen, except the followers of Ocham. Among school-divines the term has been used to distinguish the orthodox Trinitarians, from the sects accounted heretical.‡

*REFORMED CHURCH. All the churches are considered by protestants as more or less reformed, who have separated from the church of Rome, but the term is more frequently applied to the protestant churches on the Calvinistic plan, to distinguish them from Lutherans.§

*REFORMERS, a term usually applied to those great and illustrious men, who introduced the reformation from popery in the sixteenth century, as Luther, Calvin, Zuinglius, Melancthon,

* Calamy's Abridgment of Baxter's History, vol. i. p. 310.
† Pinkerton's Greek Church.
‡ Buck's theolog. Dict.
§ Ibid. in Church Reformed.

and many others, whose sentiments will be found under the denominations, which bear their respective names.

The *English* reformers were the prelates and other eminent divines, who introduced the reformation into this country, under the reigns of Henry VIII, and Edward VI; and again under that of Queen Elizabeth. Cranmer, Latimer and Ridley, who were put to death in the reign of Queen Mary, for their adherence to the protestant faith, held a distinguished rank among the instruments of the reformation in England. By them and Bishop Jewel, the homilies and articles of the church of England were drawn up. See *English Church*.

*REFUGEES, a term first applied to the protestants who fled from France, on the revocation of the edict of Nantz; See *Huguenots:* but has been more recently applied to the French, who fled their country at the time of the revolution in that kingdom.

RELIEF KIRK, a denomination of dissenters from the Scotch establishment, so far only as respects the right of patronage; their congregations claiming the privilege of choosing their own ministers. This schism in the Scotch church was formed in 1752, when Mr. Gillespie was deposed from his living for refusing to sanction the ordination of a preacher who was disagreeable to his congregation. This exclusion served only to make him popular, and being soon joined by several other ministers, who took part with him, they formed the "Presbytery of Relief;" and the denomination continued increasing, until, a few years since, they formed a synod, including about sixty congregations, and thirty-six thousand members.

*RELLYANS, the followers of Mr. James Relly, who maintained the doctrine of universal restoration, upon high Calvinistic principles. Mr. Relly first appeared as a preacher in connexion with Mr. Whitfield, and was very popular, but adopting the principles of universal salvation, he was of course separated from the connexion, and some of his admirers followed him; and even lately, a remnant of them assembled at Philadelphia Chapel, in Windmill street, near Finsbury square, London; and have therefore been called by Mr. Evans, Philadelphian universalists.

REMONSTRANTS; Arminians; so called from a remonstrance they addressed to the states general in 1610, in which they state their grievances, and pray for relief. In the last century, disputes ran very high in Holland between Calvinists and Arminians. Episcopius and Grotius were at the head of the party of the latter.

* Adams' Religious World displayed, vol. iii. p. 223.

In order to terminate this controversy, the famous synod of Dort was held, 1618. The most eminent divines of the united provinces, both of the Arminian and Genevan school: and deputies from many of the reformed churches in Europe were assembled on this occasion. This synod was succeeded by a severe persecution of the Arminians; their doctrines were condemned; and they driven from their churches and country into exile and poverty. The learned Grotius, who was condemned to perpetual imprisonment, escaped from his confinement, and took refuge in France. An account of the proceedings of the synod may be seen in a series of letters, written by John Hales, who was present on the occasion. The reader is also referred to an abridgment of Gerard Brandt's History of the Reformation in the low countries, 2 vols. 8vo.

RESTORATIONISTS. See *Universalists.*

RHINSBERGHERS, a party of Mennonites, said to be unitarians, who attend the general meetings of the sect twice a year at Rhinsberg, near Leyden. See *Collegiates.*

ROGEREENS, so called from John Rogers, their chief leader. They appeared in New England about 1677. Their distinguishing tenet was, that worship performed the first day of the week is a species of idolatry which they ought to oppose; and in consequence of this notion they used a variety of measures to disturb those who were assembled for public worship on the Lord's day.*

ROMAN CATHOLICS, or members of the CHURCH of ROME, otherwise called *Papists,* from the pope being admitted as the supreme head of the universal church, the successor of St. Peter, and the fountain of theological truth and ecclesiastical honours. He gives bulls for the installing bishops and archbishops.† He has power to convoke general councils; to grant dispensations and indulgences; to excommunicate offenders; and to canonize‡ those, whom the church deem

* Backus' Hist. vol. i. p. 473. There is still remaining a small company of the Rogereens in Groton, near New London. See Benedict's Hist. of the Baptists, vol. ii. p. 426.

† In some Roman Catholic states, the sovereign nominates persons to bishoprics, and great benefices; but bulls from Rome are necessary to enable them to enter into the exercise of their functions. See Vattel's Law of Nations.

‡ Canonization is a ceremony in the Romish church, by which persons deceased are ranked in the catalogue of saints.

The beatification of a saint is previous to his canonization. Before that can take place, attestations of virtues and miracles are necessary. These are examined, sometimes for several years, by the congregation of rites. Before a beatified person is canonized, the qualifications of the candidate are strictly examined into, in consistories held for that purpose. After this, the pope decrees the ceremony, and appoints the day.

worthy of that honour. His jurisdiction is not, like that of other bishops, confined to particular countries, but extends through the whole body of Roman Catholics in the christian world.* He keeps his court in great state at the palace of the vatican, and is attended by seventy cardinals, as his privy counsellors, in imitation of the seventy disciples of our Lord. The pope's authority in other kingdoms is merely spiritual, but in Italy he is a temporal sovereign; Lewis XVIII and the allies having lately restored him to his throne, and to those temporalities of which he was deprived by Buonaparte and the French Revolution. On resuming his government, pope Pious VII has restored the order of Jesuits and the inquisition; so that the Roman Catholic religion is now re-instated in its ancient splendour and authority.

The principal dogmas of this religion are as follow:—

I. That St. Peter was deputed by Christ to be his vicar, and the head of the catholic church; and the bishops of Rome, being his successors, have the same apostolical authority. For our Saviour declares in Matt. xvi. 18. "Thou art Peter, and upon this rock will I build my church;" by which *rock* they understand St. Peter himself, as the name signifies, and not his confession, as the protestants explain it. And a succession in the church being now supposed necessary under the new testament, as Aaron had his succession in the old, this succession can now be shown only in the chair of St. Peter at Rome: therefore the bishops of Rome are his true successors.

II. That the Roman Catholic church is the mother and mistress of all churches, and cannot possibly err in matters of faith: for the church has the Spirit of God to lead it into all truth; *The gates of hell shall not prevail against it.* Matt. xvi. 18; and Christ, who is himself *the Truth,* has promised to the pastors and teachers of the church to be *with them always, even to the end of the world.* Matt. xxviii. 20. A promise which the protestants apply to the faithful in general, and not to any particular communion.

III. That the scriptures are received upon the authority of the church; but are not sufficient to our faith without apostolical traditions, which are of equal authority with the scriptures. For St. Peter assures us that, in St. Paul's epistles, there *are some things hard to be understood, which they who are unlearned and unstable wrest, as they do also the other scriptures, to their own destruction.* 2 Pet. iii. 16. We are directed by St. Paul *to stand fast, and hold the traditions which we have been taught, whether by word or by epistle.* 2 Thess. ii. 15.

* This peculiarly distinguishes the bishop of Rome from other bishops.

IV. That seven sacraments were instituted by Jesus Christ; viz. *baptism, confirmation, eucharist, penance, extreme unction, orders,* and *matrimony;* and that they confer grace.—To prove that *confirmation,* or imposition of hands, is a sacrament, they argue from Acts viii. 17.—*Penance* is a sacrament, in which the sins we commit after baptism are forgiven; and which they think was instituted by Christ himself when he breathed upon his apostles after his resurrection. John xx. 22. In favour of *extreme unction,* or anointing the sick with oil, they argue from James v. 14, 15, the text as it is rendered in the vulgate: Is any sick among you? Let him call for the *priests* of the church, and let them pray over him, anointing him with oil, &c. The sacrament of *holy orders* is inferred from 1 Tim. iv. 14:—That *marriage* is a sacrament they think evident from Eph. v. 32: *This is a great mystery,* representing the conjunction of Christ and his church. Notwithstanding this, they enjoin celibacy upon the clergy, because they do not think it proper that those who, by their office and function, ought to be wholly devoted to God, should be diverted from those duties by the distraction of a married life. 1 Cor. vii. 32. 33.

V. That in the *mass,* or public service, there is offered unto God a true and propitiatory sacrifice for the quick and dead: and that in the sacrament of the eucharist, under the forms of bread and wine, is really and substantially present the body and blood, together with the soul and divinity of our Lord Jesus Christ; and that there is a conversion made of the whole substance of the bread into his body, and of the wine into his blood, which is called *transubstantiation;* according to our Lord's words to his apostles, *This is my body,* &c. Matt. xxvi. 26; wherefore it becomes with them an object of adoration. Farther, it is a matter of discipline, not of doctrine, in the Roman church, that the laity receive the eucharist in one kind; that is in bread only.

VI. That there is a *purgatory;* and that souls kept prisoners there do receive help by the suffrages of the faithful. For it is said in 1 Cor. iii. 15, *If any man's work shall be burned, he shall suffer loss; but he himself shall be saved, yet so as by fire;* which they understand of the flames of purgatory. They also believe that souls are released from purgatory by the prayers and alms which are offered for them, principally by the holy sacrifice of the mass. They call purgatory a middle state of souls, where those enter who depart this life in God's grace; yet not without some less stain, or guilt of punishment, which retards them from entering heaven.

VII. That the saints reigning with Christ, (and especially the blessed virgin,) are to be honoured and invoked, and that they do offer prayers unto God for us; and their relics to be had in veneration. These honours, however, are not divine, but relative; and redound to the divine glory. See Rev. v. 8; viii. 4, &c.

VIII. That the images of Christ, of the blessed virgin, (the mother of God,) and of other saints, ought to be retained in churches; and honour and veneration to be given to them, even as the images of cherubim were allowed in the most holy place.

IX. That the power of indulgences was left by Christ to the church, and that the use of them is very beneficial to christian people; according to St. Matt. xvi. 19. By indulgences they do not mean leave to commit sin, nor pardon for sins to come; but only releasing, by the power of the keys committed to the church, the debt of temporal punishment, which may remain due upon account of our sins, after the sins themselves, as to their guilt and eternal punishment, have been already remitted through repentance and confession; and by virtue of the merit of Christ and of all the saints.

The church of Rome receives the Apostles', the Nicene, and Athanasian creeds; with all other things delivered, defined, and declared by the canons, and general councils, and particularly by the council of Trent,* which was convened in opposition to the doctrines of Luther and Calvin; since which time no general council has been held.

The ceremonies of this church are numerous and splendid, as the sign of the cross, holy water, blessing of bells, incense and burning of wax tapers by day light with the most splendid vestments, and the most costly crucifixes of silver and gold, images and paintings, &c. They also observe a variety of holy days, as the festivals of Christ and of the saints, &c. The pope also grants a jubilee, i. e. a general indulgence, every twenty-fifth year, or oftener, upon special occasions.†

That this is the general doctrine of the Roman Catholic church will not be disputed, though there are many shades of difference according, to the

* This council was convoked by Paul III, and assembled in 1546, and continued by twenty-five sessions till the year 1563, under Julius III, and Pius VI, in order to correct, illustrate, and fill with perspicuity the doctrines of the church, to restore the vigour of its discipline, and to reform the lives of its ministers. The decrees of this council, together with the creed of pope Pius IV, contain a summary of the doctrines of the Roman Catholics.

† See pope Pius' Creed. Bossuet's Exposition of the Catholic Creed, p. 62—107. Challoner's True Principles of a Catholic. Gother's Papist misrepresented and represented. Grounds of the Catholic Doctrine. Explication of the Sacrifice of the Mass, p. 22—35. Roman Catholic principles. Brent's Council of Trent.

different degrees of light afforded in different countries or circumstances; but the great cardinal point of the catholic religion appears to be *implicit faith*, or a steadfast determination to believe whatever is taught by the church or the highest eccletiastical authorities. It is said that according to this principle a correct creed is not of so much importance as a disposition at all times to submit our faith to authority, and to believe as the church believes, without examination or demur.

But the political opinions of the Catholics have been considered of more importance to the welfare of protestant states, and in the general question of toleration. It has been said that the pope claims a dispensing power, as to oaths of allegiance, and a paramount authority beyond all temporal powers. That the jesuits and some other Catholic priests have taught this, and that some ambitious popes have acted upon this principle, can hardly be denied; but that these claims are now relinquished, and the right denied by intelligent Catholics, appears probable from the following circumstances.

In the year 1788, when the committee of English Catholics waited on Mr. Pitt respecting their application to parliament for a repeal of the penal laws,* he proposed several questions "on the existence and extent of the pope's dispensing power, which were transmitted to the universities of Paris, Louvain, Alcala, Douay, Salamanca, and Valledolid, and the following is said to be their unanimous reply.

"I. That the pope, or cardinals, or any body of men, or any individual of the church of Rome, *has not* any civil authority, power, jurisdiction, or pre-eminence, whatsoever, within the realm of England.

"II. That the pope, or cardinals, or any body of men, or any individual of the Church of Rome, *cannot* absolve or dispense his majesty's subjects jects from their oaths of allegiance, upon any pretext whatsoever.

"III. That there is *no* principle in the tenets of the Catholic faith, by which Catholics are justified in not keeping faith with heretics, or other persons differing from them in religious opinions, in any transaction either of a public or a private nature."

As to the persecution of heretics, it is admitted that formerly this was held to be lawful, not by Catholics only, but by all the sects in christendom; but that the Catholics *now* hold

* The Catholic claims have undergone a discussion in the house of Lords, the result of which has been more favourable to the hopes of that body, than any parliamentary proceeding which has yet taken place. On a motion for taking the subject into early consideraton in the next session of parliament, sixty nine voted for it, and seventy three against it, leaving a minority of only four. See Christian Observer, July 1816.

such opinion, they "most explicitly deny;" and it is in general denied by all sects and parties, except among the most ignorant and illiberal.

The number of Catholics in Great Britain is estimated at about eighty eight thousand; and in Ireland at about three millions to two of protestants. In the whole of christendom the same writer estimates their number at about eighty millions to sixty five millions of protestants.*

*ROSECRUCIANS, certain hermetical philosophers, who, in the fourteenth century, formed a secret society, pretending to the knowledge of the philosopher's stone, and other wonderful mysteries derived from the Egyptians, Chaldeans, and Magi. Among their most celebrated professors they reckon Jacob Behmen, the mystic, Dr. Robert Fludd, an English physician, and many others of eccentric genius and learning, who blended the mysteries of alchymy, chemistry, and theology, into one system. The term Rosecrucian is of chemical derivation, from *ros*, dew, and *crux*, the cross; because they considered dew as the chief solvent of gold, and the cross as an emblem of *lux*, the light, those letters being all formed out of the figure of a cross.† The Rosecrucians have been sometimes confounded with the *free masons*, who pretend also to mystic secrets.

*RUSSIAN CHURCH. The Russians, like other nations, were originally Pagans, and worshipped fire, (which they considered as the cause of thunder,) under the name of *perun*, and the earth under the name *volata*; at the same time, having some notions of a future state of rewards and punishments. Christianity was first professed by the Princess Olga, who was baptized at Constantinople. She recommended it to her grandson Vladimir, on whose baptism, in 988, it was adopted by the nation generally; and from that time the Greek church has been the established religion throughout Russia, and Greek literature greatly encouraged. During the middle ages, however, the doctrine of transubstantiation and some other popish peculiarities were covertly introduced; and, by the irruption of the Mongol Tartars, in the fifteenth century, a stop was put to learning and civilization for full two centuries; but on the accession of the present dynasty in 1613, civilization and christianity were restored, and schools established for the education of the clergy.

The Russian clergy are divided into regular and secular, the former are all monks, and the latter are the parochial

* Adam's Religious World displayed, p. 1, &c.—p. 54, 94. Butler's Address to protestants.

† Mosheim, vol. iv. p. 226. Ency. Perthensis.

clergy. The superiour clergy are called Archires, but the title of Metropolitan, or Bishop, is personal, and not properly attached to the see, as in the western church. Next after the Archires rank the *black* clergy, including the chiefs of monasteries and convents, and after them the Monks. The secular priests are called the *white* clergy, including the Protoires (or proto-popes) priests and deacons, together with the Readers and Sacristans. These amounted, in 1805, throughout the empire, to ninety eight thousand seven hundred and twenty six. The white clergy must be married before they can be ordained, but must not marry a second time: but are at liberty then to enter among the black clergy, and a way is thus opened for their accession to the higher orders. The whole empire is divided into thirty six dioccesses, (or eparchies,) in which are four hundred and eighty three cathedrals, and twenty six thousand five hundred and ninety eight churches.

The churches are divided into three parts; 1. the altar, where stands the holy table, crucifix, &c. which is separated from the body of the church by a large screen (ikonostes) on which are painted our Saviour, the Virgin, the Apostles, and other saints. Upon a platform before this are placed the readers and singers, and here the preacher generally stands behind a moveable desk. 2. The Nave or body of the church, which may be called the inner court: and 3. The Trapeza, or outer court: both these are designed for the congregation, but neither have any seats. The walls of the church are highly embellished with scripture paintings, ornamented with gold, silver, and precious stones, but no images.

The church service is contained in twenty volumes folio, in the Slavonian language, which is not well understood by the common people. Parts of the scriptures are read in the service; but few, even of the ecclesiastics, possess a complete bible.

The patriarch of Russia was formerly almost equal in authority with the Czar himself; but Peter the Great, on the death of the patriarch in 1700, abolished his office, and appointed an Exarch. In 1721 he abolished this office also, and appointed a "holy legislative synod" for the government of the church, at the head of which is always placed a layman of rank and eminence. The monastic life was once so prevalent in this country, that there were four hundred and seventy nine convents for men, and seventy four for women, in which there were about seventy thousand monks and nuns, &c: but this kind of life was so much discouraged by Peter the Great, and the Empress Catherine, that the religious are now reduced to about five thousand monks and one thousand seven hundred nuns; a great part of their revenues has also been alienated, and appropriated to the support of hospitals and houses for the poor. For the doctrines of this communion, see the *Greek Church:* and for the principles of dissenters from it, see *Raskolniks.**

S

SABBATARIANS, a denomination of christians, who keep the seventh day as the Sabbath, and are to be found principally, if not wholly among the baptists. The three following propositions contain a summary of the grounds of their practice. 1. That God has required the observance of the seventh, or last day in every week, to be observed by mankind universally for the weekly Sabbath. 2. That this command of God is perpetually binding on man till time shall be no more. 3. That this sacred rest of the seventh day Sabbath is not (by divine authority) changed from the seventh and last to the first day of the week, or that the scripture does no where require the observation of any other day of the week for the weekly Sabbath, but the seventh day only.

Many of the Sabbatarians observe the first day of the week also, in conformity to the general custom of christians, founded (as should seem) on the practice of the apostles. See Acts xx. 7. 1 Cor. xvi. 2. Rev. i. 10.

Some divines, however, conceive that the first day of the week was the original Sabbath; that it was changed at the giving of the law, and restored at the resurrection of Christ. The spirit of the command is supposed only to require a seventh day, however it is reckoned; and as the sun rises and sets at different hours in various climates, it seems impossible that all nations should observe the same precise time.†

There are two congregations of the Sabbatarians in London, one among the General Baptists, the other among the Particular Baptists; and a few are found in different parts of the kingdom. In America the Dunkers and Keithians may be reckoned of that class; and the Abyssinians, and some members of the Greek Church keep both the Sabbaths.‡

* Pinkerton's Present State of the Greek Church in Russia, 8vo. 1814.

† See Kennicot's Dissertation on Ca n and Abel, p. 184

‡ Doddridge's Lectures Evans' Sketch, 12th ed p. 201 Cornthwaite's Tracts, published about 1740. See also Chandler, Orton, Palmer, and Dr. Watts' Holiness of times and places.

*SABEANS, or Sabians, the ancient inhabitants of Arabia, who worshipped the hosts of heaven (in Heb. *Sabbaoth*) though at the same time they acknowledged a supreme Being, by whom they were created.* See *Zabians*.

A sect in Ecclesiastical History are called by the same name, whose creed is a compound of Judaism, Christianity, and Idolatry. See *Mendai*.

SABELLIANS, the disciples of Sabellius, an African bishop (or presbyter) in the third century. He maintained that the Divine Essence subsisted in one person only, namely, the Father; but that a certain energy, or ray of divinity, was united to the man Jesus, and formed the character of the Son of God; while a similar divine emanation—a celestial warmth—constituted the Holy Ghost. This they endeavoured to illustrate by comparing God the Father to the material Sun, the Word, or Son of God, to the light issuing therefrom, and the Holy Spirit to the heat emanating from the same source. His doctrine seems to differ from that of Noetus in this respect, that the latter taught it was the one person of the Deity which acted under the three relative characters, as Father, Son, and Holy Spirit; the Creator, Redeemer, and Sanctifier of mankind; whence his followers were reckoned *Patri-passians*: but not so the Sabellians, who preserved a sort of distinction between the sacred Three, tho' it was not personal. This system is called an economical or modal trinity, and its believers are called *Modalists*.†

Sabellius had many followers during the age in which he lived; and modifications of his doctrines have subsisted in various succeeding denominations. It is said to be found in the creed of many of the general baptists in the principality of Wales. The Swedenborgians have also been charged with Sabellianism.‡

SACOPHORI, i. e. persons who wear sackcloth, as certain christians affected to do in the fourth century, by way of penance and mortification.§

*SACRAMENTARIANS, a term applied at the time of the reformation to all who denied the *real* presence in the sacrament.

SADDUCEES, an ancient Jewish sect, said to be founded about three hundred years before Christ, by one *Sadock*, who is reported by tradition to have been the disciple of Antigonus Socho, president of the Sanhedrim of Jerusalem. This celebrated teacher inculcated a pure and disinterested principle of obedience to God, independent

* Ency. Perthensis.

† Mosheim, vol. i. p. 244. Waterland on the Trinity, p. 385.

‡ Adam's Religious World displayed.

§ History of Religion, vol. iv. Art. Sacophor.

of rewards and punishments, from which some of his disciples inferred that none were to be expected; and hence the sect degenerated into infidelity; and denied the being of angels and spirits, and, consequently, a future state. Acts xxiii. 8.

It has been said that they rejected all the sacred writings but those of Moses; and it is probable that some did so, but that this was not universally the case.* It is certain, indeed, that they rejected the traditions of the elders, and paid little attention to any religious forms. To make amends for this, however, they were very strict in administering justice between man and man; so much so, that some have derived the denomination from the Hebrew word for justice, which is צדק. In their philosophy they were Epicureans or Materialists; but did not admit of a resurrection: and were so far from Necessarians, that they were great advocates for the doctrine of free-will, and totally rejected that of divine influences.† The history of the Sadducees may be traced down to the middle ages, and there are still said to be some remains of this sect in Africa. See *Jews*.

SAMARITANS, the inhabitants of Samaria, but chiefly the Cuthites, whom the kings of Assyria sent from beyond the Euphrates to people that country after they had carried away captive the children of Israel. The Samaritans, being a mixed multitude, at first worshipped Jehovah in connexion with their former idols, (2 Kings xvii. 24—33.) until a Jewish priest was sent to instruct them. At length Alexander the Great permitted them to build a temple on mount Gerizim, in opposition to that of Jerusalem. John iv. 20. Sanballat, the governour, made Menasses, the son of Juddua, high priest, and from this time they maintained, that this was the place where men ought to worship. This created an enmity between the two nations, which has never subsided to this day.

When Menasses was made high priest, he taught the Samaritans to worship the true God only according to the Mosaic institutions; and from this period they renounced idolatry and were considered a sect of the Jewish religion.

The Samaritans receive only the pentateuch, (or five books of Moses,) and their copy differs materially from that of the Jews in some chronological dates; it has also some repetitions and elucidatory passages, but the most material difference is that in Deut. xxvii. 12, 13. they have transposed the names Ebal and Gerizim to

* Prideaux's Connection. Anno. 107. Basnage's Hist. lib. 2, cap. 5. Scaliger Elench Triher, cap. 16.

† Prideaux's Connect Anno. 446. Lamy and Beausobre's Introduct. Calmet's Dict. vol. ii. new ed. Stackhouse's Hist. of the Bible, 8vo. vol. v. p. 118.

favour their schismatic temple; it is also written in the Samaritan character, which some suppose to be the ancient Hebrew, but on this the learned are much divided.

The Samaritans have been, like the Jews, dispersed in various countries; but for a long time their chief residence has been Naplouse, the ancient Sichem. As late as 1808, we learn from authentic documents,* that they still continue at Naplouse. They inhabit old deserted houses in a bad part of the city; and live in the most abject poverty. Those whose condition is most tolerable are in the service of the chief of the country, which employment just affords them bread. The others endeavour to gain it by industry; many of them keep shop, and live by petty commerce.

The Samaritans, like the Jews of the East, eat only of the flesh of animals, killed by one of their own sect, and with certain formalities. They are separated from the Jews, Turks and Christians, and form no alliances with them. If they are forced in their employment to touch a stranger, or his garment, they purify themselves as soon as possible. The dead are considered as impure, and they cause them to be buried by the Turks and Christians. They consider themselves to be true Israelites of the tribe of Joseph; and say that their law is written in the true Hebrew language. They have a priest of the race of Levi, but no iman or grand pontiff. They say, that they have not had any priests of the race of Aaron for one hundred and fifty years past.

The Samaritans celebrate the first day of the passover at midnight; a sheep is killed in the synagogue, roasted and eaten there. Since the year 1788 they have not been able to repair to mount Gerizim for worship; but have offered their sacrifices in the city Naplouse, which, they say, "is comprised in the chosen place." According to their account, there are no Samaritans in the East, excepting at Naplouse and Jaffa. These amount to two hundred persons, men, women, and children, composing thirty families. These are extremely exact in their observance of the ceremonies prescibed by Moses; and have preserved their pentateuch with the utmost care.†

***SAMMANS**, Schamans, or Shamans, (as the first letter is

* The celebrated Gregoire applied to the Consul of Aleppo for information respecting the Samaritans of Naplouse, who obtained from the chief of the synagogue an answer in Arabic, which was translated into the French by Corances, senior consul of France.

† Calmet's Dictionary, vol. ii. new ed. vol. iv. 239—468; vol. v. 310. Stackhouse's Hist of the Bible. Gregoire's Histoire Des Sectes Religieuses. Tom. ii. p. 325, 326, &c.

differently pronounced,) were originally worshippers of the heavens, (in Heb. *Shemim,*) and the heavenly bodies. Such were the ancient Chaldeans, Syrians, and Canaanites, whose idol was *Baal-Samen*, or *El-Samen*, the Lord or God of heaven, by which they meant the sun; and they had a city and temple, called *Beth-Shemesh*, the city or temple of the sun, whose Hebrew name is *Shemesh*.

From these Sammans seem to have sprung the Sammanes, an ancient sect of philosophers in India, from whom Dr. Priestley thinks the Hindoo religion was originally derived. "The Sammanians (or Sammans) being persecuted by the Bramins, and driven by them out of India Proper, are thought to have taken refuge in Pegu, Siam, and other countries beyond the Ganges; and it is supposed that the religion of those countries was derived from their principles. The religion of the Lamas in Tibet is also said to be a reformed Schamanism. See *Thibetians*. And from the same source this author, with great probability, derives the modern *Schamans* of Siberia.

"The people are at present described as wholly illiterate; but their predecessors are said to have written many books on philosophy and religion. They believe in one God, the maker of all things; but they think that he pays no attention to the affairs of men, leaving the government of the world to inferiour beings, to whom, therefore, all their devotions are addressed. Both the celestial bodies, and all terrestrial objects of considerable magnitude, are objects of worship to them; though some of them only believe that mountains, and great bodies of water, are the habitation of the gods, and not themselves animated. They have, however, a great variety of subordinate deities, whom they invoke for different purposes, viz. one for health, another for their cattle, another when they travel, another for the women, another for their children, another for their reindeer, &c. &c. thinking that particular spirits preside over and have the care of them. But though they have goddesses, as well as gods, they do not believe that they are married. These spirits, they suppose, appear to their priests in the form of bears, serpents, or owls; and on this account they have a particular respect for those animals.

"Besides these deities of a nature superiour to man, the Siberians worship the *manes* of their ancestors, and especially of the settlers of colonies, whom they regard as demi-gods.

"They not only suppose that there are superiour beings of very different dispositions, some friendly and others unfriendly to men, but think the best disposed of them are sometimes partial, obstinate, and vindictive: and over the malevolent deities they place one of much superiour power, whom they call *Scaitan*. But though he is very wicked, they think it possible to appease him, and therefore much of their worship is addressed to him.

"They have no temples, but perform their religious rites in the open air, on eminences, or the banks of rivers. In some places their religious ceremonies are performed at any hour of the day indifferently; but generally during the night, by the light of a fire, kindled for the purpose.

"They have idols of stone or wood, having some rude resemblance of the human form, and they pretend to feed them, smearing their faces with blood and grease. By way of incensing them, they make a smoke with burning flesh, blood, or boughs of fir and wormwood before them. But when misfortunes befall them, they load them with abuse, sometimes dash them against the ground, throw them into the water, or beat them with rods.

"Man they believe to be compounded of soul and body; and that immediately after death the soul passes into another state of existence; which, however, most of them think to be at least but a very uncomfortable one, and therefore they have a great dread of death."*

*SAMOKRESTSCHENTSI, or self-baptizers, a small sect in Russia, who separated from the church. They baptize themselves, under an idea that no other persons are sufficiently pure to perform the rite for them.†

SANDEMANIANS. This denomination arose in Scotland about the year 1728, and was originally called Glassites, (see that term above,) but afterwards Sandemanians from the following circumstance.

Soon after the year 1755, Mr. Robert Sandeman, an elder in one of these churches in Scotland, published a series of letters addressed to Mr. James Hervey, occasioned by his Theron and Arpasio, in which he endeavours to show that his notion of faith is contradictory to the scripture account of it; and would only serve to lead men, professedly holding the doctrines called Calvinistic, to establish their own righteousness upon their frames, feelings, and acts of faith. The leading sentiments which Mr. Sandeman endeavours to prove in these letters, are as follow:

I. That justifying faith is no more than a simple belief of the truth, or the divine testimony passively received.

II. That this divine testimony carries in itself sufficient

* Holwell's Mythological Dict. p. 383. Priestley's Institutions of Moses and the Hindoos, p. 105. and Tooke's Russia, (from whom he quotes,) Introduction.

† Pinkerton's Greek Church, p. 334.

ground of hope, and occasion of joy, to every one, who believes it, without any thing wrought in us, or done by us, to give it a particular direction to ourselves.

To support this system, the Sandemanians allege, that faith is called *receiving the love of the truth;* and the apostle often speaks of faith and truth to the same purpose, as in John xvi. 13. *The spirit of truth;* 2 Cor. iv. 13. *The spirit of faith;* Acts vi. 7. *Obedient to the faith;* 1 Pet. i. 22. *In obeying the truth;* and divers other passages. The scriptures consider faith, not as a work of ours, nor as any action exerted by the human mind; but set it in direct opposition to every work, whether of body or mind. See Rom. iv. 4, 5. This contrast excludes every idea of activity in the mind, from the matter of justification; so that we cannot speak of preparatory works of any sort, without making the gospel a law of works. Rom. iii. 27. *Where is boasting then? It is excluded,* &c. Now boasting cannot be excluded, if any thing, done by us, sets us in a more probable way of obtaining the salvation, which is of grace, whether it be called by the names of a law work, serious exercise of seeking souls, or labouring to obtain an interest in Christ, &c.

Every doctrine, then, which teaches us to do, or endeavour, any thing towards our acceptance with God, stands opposed to the doctrine of the apostles, which, instead of directing us what to do, sets before us all, that the most disquieted conscience can require in order to acceptance with God, as already done and finished by Jesus Christ.

Some of "the popular preachers," as they were called, had taught that it was of the essence of faith, to believe that Christ is ours: but Mr. Sandeman contended, that that which is believed in true faith is the truth, and what would have been the truth, though we had never believed it. They invited sinners to repent and believe in Christ in order to forgiveness; but he maintained, that the gospel contained no offer but that of evidence; but that it was merely a record or testimony to be credited. They had taught that though acceptance with God (which included the forgiveness of sins) was merely on account of the imputed righteousness of Christ; yet that no one was forgiven, or accepted of God, till he repented of his sin, and received Christ by faith; but he insists that there is acceptance with God for sinners, while such, before "any act, exercise, or exertion of their minds whatsoever;" and that, "a passive belief of this quiets the guilty conscience, begets hope, and so lays the foundation for love."

The authors, to whom Mr. Sandeman refers under the title of "popular preachers," are Flavel, Boston, Guthrie, the

Erskines, &c. These he has treated with great acrimony and contempt. Yet some of the writers, who have vindicated these ministers from his invectives, have acknowledged that he has pointed out many blemishes in their writings. Others have endeavoured to show, that Mr. Sandeman's notion of faith, by excluding all concurrence of the will with the gospel plan of salvation, confounds the faith of devils with that of christians, and is calculated to deceive the souls of men. It has also been observed, that though Mr. Sandeman admits of the acts of faith and love, as fruits of believing the truth, yet "all his godliness consisting (as he acknowledges,) in love to that which first relieved him," it amounts to nothing but self-love.

The principal practices in which this denomination differ from the generality of other christians are as follow:

They administer the Lord's supper every Sabbath; for they look upon the christian Sabbath as designed for the celebration of divine ordinances, which are summarily comprised in Acts ii. 42. They make weekly collections before the Lord's supper, for the support of the poor, and defraying other expenses.

In the interval between their morning and afternoon service, they have their love feasts, of which every member is required to partake, to testify they are all brethren of one family. They allege, that these love feasts were not laid aside by St. Paul's writing to the Corinthians; but enjoined to be observed in a right manner, and the abuses of them corrected; and they continued in practice while the primitive profession of brotherly love remained among the ancient christians; and as *charity never faileth*, (1 Cor. xiii. 8,) so neither should any of the duties or expressions of it be allowed to fail.

At their love feasts, and on the admission of a new member, and on other occasions, they use the kiss of charity, or the saluting each other with an holy kiss, a duty this denomination believe expressly enjoined, Rom. xvi. 16; and in 1 Cor. xvi. 20. They also practise washing each other's feet; for which usage they allege John xiii. 14, 15.

They hold to community of goods, so far as that every one is to consider all that he has in his possession and power liable to the calls of the poor and of the church; and maintain the unlawfulness of laying up treasures on earth, by setting them apart for any distant, future, or uncertain use.

They allow of public and private diversions so far as they are not connected with circumstances really sinful; but apprehending a lot to be sacred, disapprove of lotteries, playing at cards, dice, &c.

They have a plurality of elders, pastors or bishops, in each church. In the choice of these elders, want of learning and engagement in trade are no sufficient objections, if qualified according to the instructions given by Paul to Timothy and Titus; but second marriages disqualify for the office.

Their discipline is very strict, and they think themselves obliged to separate from the communion and worship of all such religious societies, as appear to them not to profess the simple truth for their only ground of hope, and who do not walk in obedience to it. Moreover, in their church proceedings, they are not governed by majorities, and esteem unanimity to be absolutely necessary. With excommunicated members they hold it unlawful either to eat or drink.*

Mr. Sandeman came to New England, and settled a society at Boston, Danbury, &c. He died in America 1772.

SATANIANS, so called, it is said, because they taught that since Satan, or the devil, was extremely powerful, and full of mischief, it was wise to pay him some respect, in order to conciliate him. They are supposed to have been a branch of the Messalians, about the year 390. They possessed no goods, lived by begging, and lay in the streets. It is reported they called themselves patriarchs, prophets, and angels.†

SATURNIANS, an obscure sect which arose about the year 115, and derived their name from Saturninus of Antioch, one of the Gnostic chiefs, whose notions coincided with those of Basilides and other Gnostics. See *Basilidians*.‡

*SCHAITES, or SCHIITES, those Mahometans which consider Ali Taleb as the true Iman. See *Mahometans*.

*SCHAMANISM. See *Sammans*.

SCEPTICS. This sect derive their name from the Greek verb σκεπτομαι, *to consider*, from their leading character, which is, to hesitate and call in question the truth of every opinion, and maintain that every thing is uncertain.

The original design of the sceptic philosophy was to compare external phenomena with mental conceptions, in order to discover their inconsistency, and the consequent uncertainty of all reasoning from appearances:—to cure that restlessness which attends the unsuccessful search after truth, and by means of an universal suspension of judgment to establish mental tranquillity. Its fundamental principle is, that to every argument, an argu-

* Glasse's Testimony of the King of Martyrs. Sandeman's Letters on Theron and Arpasio, vol. i. p. 16. vol. ii. p. 38. Bellamy's Nature and Glory of the Gospel, London edition. See the notes, p. 65—126. Backus' Discourse on Faith and its Influence, p. 7—30. Fuller on Sandemanianism. Scotch Theol. Dict. &c.

† Broughton's Hist. Lib. vol. i. p. 369.

‡ Mosheim, vol. i. p. 176. Lardner's Heretics, p. 71.

ment of equal weight may be applied.*

The sceptic does not deny that he can see, hear, or feel; but he maintains that the inferences which philosophers have drawn from the reports of the senses are doubtful; and that any general conclusion, deduced from appearances, may be overturned by reasonings equally plausible with those by which it is supported.

Pyrrho, a Greek philosopher of Peloponnesus, (about 300 years before Christ,) was the founder of this sect, but it obtained no great popularity till the time of the Roman Emperors. His object was rather to destroy other systems, than to establish a new one. He asserted nothing positively; even on the point of morals he doubted, because he could not certainly discriminate between good and evil, or indifferent.

Many of his early followers chose to shelter themselves under the name of Academics, who (especially the disciples of Carneades) were much inclined to scepticism; only they did admit certain degrees of probability, which the others rejected. The Academics allowed that nothing (except mathematical science) could be known with certainty; but the Pyrrhonists were not certain even of this: and so fond were they of doubting, that they even *doubted* their only position, that *every thing was doubtful*. In the common business of life, however, it is said, they were too wise to act upon this principle.

The celebrated Mons. Bayle, author of the Historical and Critical Dictionary, who was born in 1647, has been considered as one of the most powerful advocates for scepticism among the moderns. He was educated a protestant, and early in life gave proofs of superiour genius. But while he attended the Jesuits' college at Toulouse, the reading of controversial books, and the conversation of a popish priest, led him to embrace the Roman catholic religion, which in eighteen months after he renounced, and then became a sceptic, without any fixed system of opinions.

Mr. Hume, the English historian, makes a distinguished figure also among the modern sceptics. The chief aim of his philosophical writings is to introduce doubt in every branch of physics, metaphysics, history, ethics, and theology. "There is," says this celebrated author, "a species of scepticism, antecedent to study and philosophy, which is much inculcated by Des Cartes and others, as a sovereign preservative against error and precipitate judgment. It recommends an universal doubt, not only of our former principles and opinions, but also of our very faculties; of

* Gale's Court of the Gentiles. Enfield's Hist. of Philosophy, vol. i. p. 489.

whose veracity we must assure ourselves by a chain of reasoning, deduced from some original principles, which cannot be fallacious or deceitful."*

SCHEWENKFELDIANS, a denomination so called from Gasper Schewenkfeldt, a Silesian knight in the sixteenth century. He differed from Luther in the three following points. 1. On the doctrine of the eucharist; Schewenkfeldt inverted the words of Christ, *This is my body;* and insisted on their being thus understood: *My body is this,* i. e. such as this bread, which is broken and consumed; a true and real food, which nourisheth, satisfieth, and delighteth the soul. *My blood is this;* its effects are like those of wine, which strengthens and refreshes the heart. 2. He denied that the *external* word, which is the holy scriptures, was endowed with the power of healing, illuminating, and renewing the mind: and he ascribed this power to the *internal* word, which, according to his opinion, was Christ himself. 3. He would not allow Christ's human nature, in its exalted state, to be called a creature, or a created substance; as this appeared to him infinitely below its dignity, after it had been united to the divine essence.†

***SCHOOLMEN,** a sect of men in the twelfth, thirteenth, and fourteenth centuries, who were versed in the subtilties of academical disputation. The philosophy and metaphysics of Aristotle principally contributed to the formation of the scholastic theology. Thomas Aquinas, who flourished in the thirteenth century, was eminently distinguished among the schoolmen. His writings on theology are held in high estimation by the Roman catholic church, and his authority has always been great in their schools. He was canonized by pope John XXII, in the year 1323. He founded the sect of the Thomists.‡ See that article.

SCOTCH BAPTISTS. It does not appear that there were any Baptist churches in Scotland till the year 1783, (except one,) of which some traces remain in a book, entitled, "A confession of the several congregations of churches of Christ in London, which are commonly, though unjustly, called Anabaptists, printed in 1653."

In 1786, all the Baptist churches in Scotland were agreed in their religious sentiments and practices, but of late years various classes of this denomination have sprung up in this part of the united kingdom, who have no connexion with the original societies, nor indeed with one another, but have formed themselves into separ-

* Hume's Essays, vol. iv. p. 210. † Mosheim, vol. iv. p. 32.
‡ Buck's Theological Dict. Knox's Essays, vol. i. p. 281.

ate and distinct parties. In 1809, there were fifteen Baptist churches in Scotland; and their nnmber of late years have considerably increased. In England and Wales there are a few churches, and smaller societies who are of the same faith and order with the majority of their brethren in Scotland, and consequently distinct from the two great bodies, known by the names of General and Particular Baptist.

Many of the Scotch Baptists, among whom is a church in Edinburgh, formed in the year 1765, have adopted some of the peculiar sentiments of Mr. Sandeman. Like him, they reject every doctrine, how much soever it may be qualified, and refined, which makes a sinner's acceptance with God in any respect to depend upon his own virtuous actions, his good dispositions, his devotional exercises, or his endeavours to prepare and qualify himself for being made a partaker of Christ, they suppose faith signifies simply believing or giving credit to the divine record. They have also adopted many of the usages of the Sandemanians, as observing the love feasts, the kiss of charity, and partaking of the Lord's supper every first day of the week, &c.

The Scotch Baptists reject creeds, liturgies, and confessions of faith, and acknowledge no standard of faith and practice among Christians, except divine revelation itself, and think themselves justified by this one consideration, that while there is a perfect and infallible standard, by which, if it be really followed, neither churches nor individuals can be led astray; it is equally unreasonable and dangerous to couple with it one, which, in the nature of things, must be imperfect. Aside from the erroneous doctrines contained in confessions of faith, they disapprove of them, because they are used as standards or tests in addition to the word of God, and consequently are engines to cramp, or circumscribe, all further advancement in the knowledge of divine truth, yet they are by no means satisfied with a general acknowledgment that the bible is the word of God, and an infallible standard. They maintain that the sense in which a man understands the scriptures, constitutes his faith; and therefore they have no communion with those who do not profess agreement with them in their sense of scripture, with respect to every thing they deem essential to their faith and order.

The teachers among the Scotch Baptists are ranked among their brethren, without attempting to form themselves into a separate class; and the official character which they sustain, gives them no pre-eminence whatever in a worldly point of view. Their churches, like most of those of the other Baptists, maintain close communion. The discipline and government of their churches are strictly congregational.*

*SCOTISTS, the followers of Duns Scotus, a Cordelier, who maintained the immaculate conception of the Virgin Mary, in opposition to Aquinas and the Thomists.†

SECEDERS, a numerous body of Presbyterians in Scotland, who adhere to the doctrine and discipline of their ancestors, and maintain the binding obligation of the Scotch covenant, and of the solemn league and covenant of the three nations.‡ They always have declared that they did not secede from the principles of the church of Scotland, as they are represented in her confession of faith, catechisms, longer and shorter, directory for worship, and form of presbyterian government; but only from her present judicatories, who, they suppose, have departed from her true principles. A sermon preached by Mr. Ebenezer Erskine, of Stirling, at the opening of the synod of Perth and Stirling, gave rise to this party. In this discourse he boldly testified against what he supposed corruptions in the national church; for which freedom the synod voted him censurable, and ordered him to be rebuked at their bar. He, and three other ministers, protested against this sentence, and appealed to the next assembly. The assembly approved of the proceedings of the synod, and ordered Mr. Erskine to be rebuked at their bar. He refused to submit to the rebuke; whence he and his brethren were suspended from the ministry, after which they seceded from the national church. They were joined by others; and the ministers and their elders who declared their secession from the national church, did in 1736 constitute themselves into an ecclesiastical court, which they called the Associate Presbytery.

In 1745, the seceding ministers were become so numerous, that they were erected into three different presbyteries, under one synod. In 1747, through a difference in civil matters, they were divided into burghers and anti-burghers. Of these two classes, the latter are the most rigid in their sentiments, and associate therefore the least with any other body of christians.§

* Adam's Religious World displayed, vol. iii. p. 233. Sketch of the Church order, and Social Religious Practices of the original Baptist Church in Edinburgh.

† Mosheim, vol. iii. p. 360, new ed.

‡ The national covenant in Scotland is an engagement which was entered into by all ranks of persons soon after the Reformation. The solemn league and covenant is an oath, which in 1643 was taken by persons of all ranks in the three kingdoms; it was intended to bring about an uniformity in doctrine, discipline, and worship.

§ Marshal's Catechism. Evans' Sketch, p. 78. Brown's rise and progress of the Secession. Scotch Theolog. Dict.

Both classes of the Seceders, and the Relief Kirk, including, in 1811, about three hundred ministers in Scotland, are strict Presbyterians, notwithstanding their secession or dissent from the Scotch establishment.

SECUNDIANS, the followers of Secundus, a disciple of Valentine. See *Valentinians.*

SEEKERS, a denomination which arose in the year 1645. They derived their name from their maintaining that the true church, ministry, scripture, and ordinances were lost, for which they were *seeking*. They taught that the scriptures were obscure and doubtful—that present miracles were necessary to warrant faith—that the ministry of modern times is without authority—and their worship vain and useless.*

*SEEKS, a religious sect at Patna in India, being a sort of Hindoo deists—differing from both the Mahometans and the worshippers of Brahma. Mr. Wilkins describes them as a very harmless people, founded by one Naneek Sak, about four centuries ago. He wrote a book of his principles in verse, inculcating the doctrines of one supreme omnipresent Being, and of a future state of rewards and punishments. It enjoins all the moral virtues, particularly philanthropy and hospitality. They have a kind of chapel, in which the priests chant their liturgy, with drums and cymbals, the people joining in responses. They have a kind of love feast connected with their worship, consisting of sweetmeats and sugarplumbs. Their language is a mixture of the Persian, Arabic, and Sanscrit, grafted on the Moorish tongue. The term Seeks, (from a word signifying *learn thou,)* intimates that they are inquirers after truth . They are often confounded with the nation of *Seiks*, in Lahore.†

SELEUCIANS, disciples of Seleucus, a philosopher of Galatia, who, about the year 380, adopted the sentiments of Hermogenes. See *Hermogeneans.*

SEMBIANI, so called from Sembianus, their leader, who, it is said, condemned all use of wine as evil in itself—pretended that wine was a production of satan and the earth; denied the resurrection, and rejected most of the books of the old testament.‡

SEMI-ARIANS, so called because they held the opinions of the Arians in part only, allowing to Christ the highest rank next to God the Father. The orthodox contended that the Son was ὁμοουσιος, of the *same* substance with the Father; the Semi-arians that he was

* Calamy's Abridgment of Baxter's History, vol. i. p. 110.

† Asiatic Researches. Ency. Perthen. Broughton, vol. ii. p. 559.

‡ History of Religion, vol. iv.

ὁμοιουσιος, of the *like* substance with the Father; the latter say that the Son was begotten by the *will* of the Father; the former, by necessary and eternal generation.*

*SEMI-JUDAIZERS, the followers of Francis David, a Hungarian, superintendant of the Socinian churches in Transylvania, and who opposed with great zeal the worship of Jesus Christ, which, it appears, was in some sense as strongly defended by Socinus; and David, in consequence of tenaciously adhering to his own opinions, was thrown into prison, where he died at an advanced age. His sect, however, did not die with him, and Socinus wrote against them under the name of Semi-Judaizers. It is remarkable, that though Socinus urged the worship of Christ, not as God, but as Mediator, he acknowledges a stronger degree of faith, in those who pray immediately to God, *without* a Mediator.†

SEMI-PELAGIANS, a branch of the Pelagians in the fifth century. The monk Cassian was the leader of this denomination. In order to accommodate the difference between Augustin and Pelagius, he maintained the following doctrines :—1. That God did not dispense his grace to one more than to another, in consequence of the decree of predestination; but was willing to save all men, if they complied with the terms of his gospel.—2. That Christ died for all men.—3. That the grace purchased by Christ, and necessary to salvation, was offered to all men.—4. That man, before he received grace, was capable of faith and holy desires.—5. That man, born free, was consequently capable of resisting the influences of grace, or of complying with its suggestions.

The Pelagians and Semi-Pelagians differ in this respect: the former assert that there is no necessity for inward grace; but the latter maintain that no persons can advance in virtue without the assistance of divine grace: though they subject this inward grace to the freedom of the will.‡ See *Pelagians.*

SEPARATES. This appellation was given about the year 1740 to a number of people, whose zeal was produced by the instrumentality of the celebrated George Whitfield, and other itinerant preachers. Soon after these reformers, who were at first called New Lights, and afterwards Separates, were organized into distinct societies, they were joined by Shubal Stearns, a native of Boston, who, becoming a preacher, laboured among them until 1751, when he embraced the sentiments of the Baptists, as many others of the Pedobaptist Separates did about this time. He

* Mosheim, vol. i. p. 420, new ed. † Ibid. vol. iv. p. 525—7.
‡ Mosheim, vol. i. p. 426. Stackhouse's Body of Divinity, p. 150.

was ordained the same year he was baptized, in Tolland, Connecticut; but afterwards removed from New England, and settled in North Carolina.

Mr. Stearns, and most of the Separates, had strong faith in the immediate teachings of the Spirit. They believed that to those who sought him earnestly, God often gave evident tokens of his will. That such indications of the divine pleasure, partaking of the nature of inspiration, were above, though not contrary to reason; and that following these, and leaning in every step upon the same wisdom and power by which they were first actuated, they would inevitably be led to the accomplishment of the two great objects of a christian's life, the glory of God, and the salvation of men.*

SERVERIANS, a small party of Gnostics, in the second century; so called from Serverus, who is said to have taught that the world was made by principalities and powers; and that the devil is the son of the great prince of the principalities.†

SERVERITES, a party of the Monophysites, called after Serverus, a monk of Palestine; the same (or nearly so,) as the *Angelites*, in the fifth century.

SERVETIANS, a name which in the sixteenth century distinguished the followers of Michael Servetus, a very learned and ingenious Spaniard. He is said to have taught that "the Deity, before the creation of the world, had produced within himself two personal representations, or manners of existence, which were to be the medium of intercourse between him and mortals, and by whom consequently he was to reveal his will, and display his mercy and beneficence to the children of men:—that these two representatives were the Word and the Holy Ghost—that the former was united to the man Christ, who was born of the Virgin Mary by an omnipotent act of the divine will; and that on this account Christ might be properly called God—that the Holy Spirit directed the course, and animated the whole system of nature; and more especially produced in the minds of men wise counsels, virtuous propensities, and divine feelings—and finally, that these two representations were, after the destruction of this globe, to be absorbed into the substance of the Deity, whence they had been formed."

Servetus denied infant baptism, and maintained, that no man ought to be punished as a criminal for any point of doctrine. This was not the opinion of the age, nor of the reformers. For it is asserted, that when Servetus had escaped from his prison at Vienne, and was travelling through Swit-

* Benedict's Hist. of the Baptists, vol. ii. p. 87.

† Broughton, vol. i. p. 340. Hearn's Ductor Histor. vol. ii. p. 101.

zerland in order to seek refuge in Italy, Calvin caused him to be apprehended at Geneva in the year 1553, and had an accusation of blasphemy brought against him before the council. The issue of this accusation was fatal to Servetus, who, adhering resolutely to the opinions he had embraced, was, by a public sentence of the court, declared an obstinate heretic, and condemned to the flames. Persecution for opinions was strongly supported by the habits of the sixteenth century; and all the reformers, as well as Calvin, were advocates for persecution, when applied to others.*

SETHIANS, so called because they paid high honours to Seth, whom, it is said, they looked upon to be Jesus Christ; but here (as Lardner remarks) must be some mistake, because they said Christ was descended from Seth in a miraculous way, i. e. by being born of a virgin. Perhaps they considered Seth as the promised seed: Gen. iii. 15. and iv. 20. and might suppose the pre-existent soul of Christ had animated the patriarch. They had several apocryphal books in addition to the scriptures. This denomination appeared in Egypt about the year one hundred and ninety, and continued above two hundred years.†

SHAKERS. In the account these people give of themselves, they mention the Quakers in the time of Oliver Cromwell, and the French Prophets at a later date, as being the first who had a peculiar testimony from the Lord to deliver to the christian world. But they complain that the former degenerated, "losing the desire of love and power with which they first set out," and the latter being of short continuance, "their extraordinary communications" have long ago ceased. This testimony was revived in the persons of "James Wardley, a taylor by trade, and Jane his wife, who wrought at the same occupation."—"And the work under them began at Bolton and Manchester in Lancashire, about the year 1747." They had belonged to the society of Quakers, but receiving the spirit of the French prophets, and a farther degree of light and power, by which they were separated from that community, they continued for several years disconnected from every denomination. During this time their testimony, according to what they declare they saw by vision and revelation from God, was, "that the second appearance of Christ was at hand, and that the church was rising in her full and transcendent glory, which would affect the final downfall of Antichrist." From the shaking of their bodies in religious exer-

* Mosheim, vol. iv. p. 172, 173. Memoirs of Literature, vol. iv. p. 199. Erskine's Sketches of Eccles. History, vol. ii. p. 277.

† Broughton, vol. ii. p. 390. Lardner's Heretics, p 333. &c.

cises they are called Shakers, or Shaking Quakers. This name they acknowledge to be proper. For say they, "The work which God promised to accomplish in the latter day, was eminently marked out by the prophets to be a work of Shaking; and hence the name (though by the world intended for derision) was very properly applied to the people; who were both the subjects and instruments of the work of God in the latter day."

The work went on under Wardley, till the year 1770, when a new impulse was given to the society by Anne Leese, who became a distinguished leader of this denomination. This woman declared herself "*the Elect Lady*," *the woman spoken of in Rev.* xii. and *the mother of all the elect.*" To such as addressed her with the customary titles used by the world, she would reply, "*I am Anne, the Word*," signifying, that in her dwelt the word. She was received and acknowledged, by the Shakers, "as the first mother, or spiritual parent in the line of the female, and the second heir in the covenant of life, according to the present display of the gospel." Hence among believers, she has been distinguished by no other name or title than that of mother. Her followers assert, that she was the instrument to introduce the glory of the latter day.

The manner of worship, of this denomination and the exercises used in their public assemblies are shaking and trembling, singing and dancing, leaping and shouting; and, according to their account, "prophesying or speaking with new tongues; and they exhibit such supernatural effects of the power of God, as appear to the blind spectators of this world like the most unaccountable confusion. But such," say they, "as were in the work, knew perfectly what these things meant, and felt therein the greatest possible order and harmony, it being to them the gift and work of God for the time then present; and which bore the strongest evidence, that the world was actually come to an end, (at least to those who were the subjects of it,) and the day of judgment commenced."

In 1774, Anne Leese, and a number of her followers, who complained of being persecuted in Manchester, set sail from Liverpool for New York. Being joined by others, they settled at Nisqueunia near Albany; where they have spread their opinions, and increased to a considerable number. The persevering efforts of this society multiplied the converts to their doctrines. Anne Leese, and her elders, used to delight in missionary journeys, being out for two or three years, and returning with wonderful accounts of their success.

Anne Leese died in 1784,*

* This denomination appears to suppose, that the divinity dwelt in Anne

James Whilacher succeeded this elect lady, but dying in 1787, John Hocknell, the last of the European band, took the lead, and he died 1799, in the seventy sixth year of his age. Joseph Meacham, and Lucy Wright, were the next administrators of this spiritual kingdom.

It appears from a work of the Shakers, published at Albany 1810, entitled, "The Testimony of Christ's second appearance," &c. that in the delineation of their doctrines this denomination are exceedingly mystical and obscure; it is much easier to pronounce negatively rather than positively concerning them. They are neither Trinitarians nor Satisfactionists. They deny also the imputation of Adam's sin to his posterity; the doctrine of election and reprobation, as well as the eternity of future punishments. And in their chapter on the resurrection, the resuscitation of the body is denied very positively, and at great length. They reject the celebration of water baptism and the Lord's supper.

The tenets, on which the Shakers most dwell, are those of human depravity, and of the miraculous effusion of the Holy Spirit. Their leading practical tenet is the abolition of *marriage*, or indeed the total separation of the sexes. The essence of their argument is, that the resurrection spoken of in the new testament means nothing more than conversion; our Saviour declares that in the resurrection *they neither marry, nor are given in marriage*, therefore on the conversion or the resurrection of the individual, marriage ceases. To speak more plainly, the single must continue single, and the married must separate. Every passage in the gospel and in the epistles is interpreted according to this hypothesis. In particular they endeavour to support their opinion from 1 Cor. vii.

This denomination asserts, that the day of judgment is past, and consider their testimony as a new dispensation, which they call *Christ's second appearance*. In which they are not to be guided so much by the scriptures, as by the influences of the Holy Spirit. They pretend to have the power imparted to them of working miracles; and have related several instances of supernatural cases, attested by witnesses, &c. "by which," say they, "the most stubborn unbelievers were confounded, and the faith of others strengthened."

They maintain that it is unlawful to take oaths, game, or use compliments to each other. They practise a community of goods; and have no persons regularly educated for the ministry. In their chapter upon public worship, they vindicate their music and dancing as

Leese, as truly as in Christ; and that in her, his second coming to judge the world was verified.

leading parts of worship, especially alluding to the return of the prodigal, while the elder son, disliking music and dancing, represents the natural man condemning their soul-reviving practices.*

SIMONIANS, the supposed followers of Simon Magus, whose history is recorded in Acts viii. 9—24. He is said to have been the founder of the Gnostics, but this is denied by others, who consider him as a total apostate from christianity, and refuse him even the honour of being a heretic.† See *Gnostics*.

*SIMONISTS, a name given to persons who purchase holy orders, in allusion to the crime of Simon Magus, just referred to.

SINTOOS, the ancient idolaters of Japan. See *Japanese*.

SOCIETY OF THE VICTIMS. On the 23d of June, 1804, an imperial decree was issued for the suppression of those associations, known under the names of *Fathers of the Faith*, adorers of Jesus or Pacanaristes. This decree was provoked by a report of Portalis, minister of worship; a report extremely well written, printed, but not published. It has been translated into German, and therein speaks of a secret society of Victims, concerning which society the following account has been given by Gregoire, in his learned work, styled, "Histoire Des Sectes Religeuses."

Catherine de Bar was born at Lorraine in 1619. She established, in the year 1657, at Rambervillers, a new religious order, for persons of her own sex, which spread rapidly in France. She adopted the rule of St. Benedict, but with some modifications, which she explained in a work, entitled, "The true spirit of the perpetual religious worshippers of the most holy sacrament of the altar." The proper character of these nuns was that of being *Victims*, to expiate the sins committed against Jesus Christ in the celebration of the eucharist. Each day one of the Religious remains in her retreat from mattins until vespers. Her office is to be the expiatory Victim. When the sisters go to their dining room, the Victim is the last to leave the choir. She appears with a cord about her neck, and a torch in her hands. When they have all taken their places, she reminds them that they are all *Victims*, immolated for the sake of Jesus Christ; she then bows herself, returns to the choir dur-

* See the Testimony of Christ's second appearance, containing a general statement of all things pertaining to the faith and practice of the church of God in the latter day. This work in the United States is called the Shakers' Bible, because it contains a full account of their faith and practices. Evans' Sketch of Religious Denominations, edit. 13.

† Mosheim's Eccles. Hist. vol. i. p. 115 Dupin's Church Hist. vol. i. p. 29. Formey's Eccles. Hist. vol. i. p. 21. Calmet's Dictionary, vol. ii.

ing dinner, and remains there until after vespers, like a victim separated from the flock, and destined for sacrifice.

Regnauld, a curate of Vaux, author of a work, entitled, "The Mystery of Iniquity," makes mention of a work, entitled, "Les Galarics," published in 1754, a species of mysticism in favour of convulsions. In the fourth galeric of Elias, the author asserts, "The victims are of the greatest importance. They are devoted for every crime, and each of them bears different parts in the sacrifice of Jesus Christ. This character will make them known to the Gentiles. The despair of the victims will expiate presumptuous confidence, as the sacrifice of Jesus Christ on the cross has represented and expiated the sins into which mankind had fallen. They must bear to be culpable in the eyes of men, that they may complete what is wanting in the passion of our Saviour. They must bear the burdens of the anger of God and men. They must be found amid the abodes of infamy, among robbers and murderers. Besides these public victims, there must be secret ones, delivered up to the horrible states of passion, despair, and distraction."

Such probably were the ideas of the lady when on the eve of founding the order of the Victims. She had lived in Lorraine, where the houses of the Benedictines of the holy sacrament were numerous. She relates that at the age of nine years, having experienced in a sensible manner the protection of the blessed virgin, she consecrated herself to her service.

Madam Brohon, who was born at Paris, early devoted herself to the cultivation of letters. The Abbe la Porte, author of the "Literary History of French Women," written in 1769, says, "It is now fifteen years since much mention was made of the mind, the graces, and talents of Madam Brohon, though she was then but eighteen years old. He proceeds to give an analysis of a work of hers, entitled, "The Charms of Ingenuity." It is a tale of about twenty eight pages. Bossy, the editor of the Mercury, has praised it.

Her life having been preserved, as she asserts, by a miracle of the blessed father Fourier, she determined to take the monastic vows. She repented having written romances, and consulted the Abbe Clement, who directed her for some time, and whose virtues she highly extolled.

The penitent devoted herself to retirement, for the space of fourteen years. At last she returned to Paris, and there died, the eighteenth of September, 1778, being upwards of forty years old.

From the time she quitted her literary career her active spirit exercised itself on ascetic subjects. Many of her works have been anonymously published by her admirers. Such as "Edifying Instructions on the fasting of Jesus Christ in the desert;" and, "The Manuel of the Victims of Jesus, or Extracts from the instructions which the Lord has given to his first victims." This last work appeared in 1799, a volume in octavo of four hundred pages.

In 1774, writing to Beaumont, archbishop of Paris, she predicted that God was about to execute his judgments on the nations, to punish a tenth part of the earth, and to choose a new people; but first he would establish those victims, who would constantly immolate themselves to him. The Abbe de Garry would be their director. France, which had been the first christian kingdom, and which had distinguished itself by the purity of its faith, and its piety towards the holy virgin, would be the cradle of this new people, if its perversity did not deprive it of this benefit. If France rejected the Victims, God would take away its provinces; he would raise up a strange prince to devastate and enslave it. She pretended to foresee that the Spanish nation was to be the instrument of God's vengeance. Great calamities would then fall upon the capital; the clergy, secular as well as regular, would be humbled; the sanctuaries would be abolished, in order to punish those who ought to have been their ornaments and glory. This was published in 1791.

In a letter to Lewis XV, then sick, Madam Brohon introduces the Almighty as a Mediator, and demands in his name Madam Victoire to be one of the victims. Sophia du Castelle, the daughter of a Notary de Peronne, a novitiate of the Benedictines de Gomer Fontaire, was also to be one of the victims. The number was fixed at twelve to represent the apostolic college with the same attributes. The college of Victims was composed of an equal number of men and women. The latter would have the honour of beginning the new mission; 1. as an effect of the love of Jesus Christ for his holy mother; 2. in order to reward the fidelity of the women to Jesus Christ in the course of his mortal life and passion; 3. in order to humble the masculine sex, who abuse their authority; and to provoke their jealousy when they see the zeal of feeble women. The male victims would be clothed with the sacerdotal garments. The women, however, would not be subordinate to them; they acknowledge no superiour but the bishops; but they would preserve a great respect for the body of pastors, united to the Pope, the head of the true church, who would receive an augmentation of power over faithful souls. Some auxiliaries would form a body for reserve out of which the successors of the Victims would be chosen.

The Victims, according to their own account, are predicted in the bible; without them an essential part of the Messiah would fail. They will be established near Jesus Christ, to fulfil the same functions for him that he has fulfilled for his Father. There are, say they, some faithful souls, who have grace enough to ensure their own salvation; but not enough to immolate themselves to divert the plague which menaces the human species. The Victims are consecrated to do it by taking upon themselves the general anathema. They are the centre and recipients of grace, the fountain from which it is distributed over the whole earth. They boasted of being advanced in glory above the monastic life, and having the same privileges as the angels, who would mourn if any thing was wanting to complete their felicity. They asserted, that "they were very dear to the Saviour; that the precious blood which flowed from his side is the adorable ink with which their names are written;" and that "himself and the holy virgin have declared themselves the father and mother of the Victims, with the promise of refusing them nothing."

"The sacrifice of the mass will continue during the glorious reign of the Redeemer. Then there will be no more monasteries. The Victims will be the vine and body of the church. Enoch and Elias will preside."

The greatest crimes are committed between six o'clock in the evening and two in the morning; the Victims pass that time in prayer, and recite matins at midnight.

Each Victim has suspended to her neck a silver medal, on which is engraven the sacred hearts of Jesus and Mary, to which they owe a perfect devotion.

Madam Brohon, being the first Victim, it will not be found surprising that she was adorned with extraordinary graces by Jesus, who was her common confessor. She declares, that he said to her one day, as he showed her the wounds on his side, "Seek me no more on the cross, I have yielded to thee my place, I shall no more be crucified, my Victims will be instead of me."

In 1792, a consultation of many of the professors and doctors of the Sorbonne was printed on the following works: "Edifying Instructions," and "Edifying Reflections." They reproached Madam Brohon, the author, with various impieties, and the most reprehensible ideas.*

SOCINIANS, a denomination which appeared in the sixteenth century, followers of Lelius Socinus, and Faustus Socinus, his nephew, who propagated his uncle's sentiments in

* Gregoire's Histoire Des Sectes Religeuses, vol. ii. p. 1, 2, 3, 4, &c.

a public manner after his death.

Their principal tenets are—1. That the holy scriptures are to be understood and explained in such a manner as to render them conformable to the dictates of right reason, and sound philosophy.—2. That Jesus Christ, who was conceived by the Holy Ghost, born of the Virgin Mary, was the true Messiah, and the chief of the prophets. That in order to qualify him for his extraordinary office, before he commenced his ministry, he was taken up to heaven* and instructed fully in the object of his mission, after which he returned to the earth to promulgate among mankind a new rule of life, more excellent than any under which they had formerly lived; to propagate divine truth by his ministry, and to confirm it by his death; in reward for which he is raised to dominion and glory.—3. That those who believe and obey the voice of this divine teacher (which is in the power of every one) shall at the last day be raised from the dead, and made eternally happy; while, on the other hand, the wicked and disobedient shall be sorely tormented, and afterwards annihilated.

Such were the religious tenets of Socinus and his immediate followers. Those of the present day, who maintain the mere humanity of Christ, differ from Socinus in many things; particularly as to the miraculous conception, and in not paying religious worship to Jesus Christ, which was a point that Faustus Socinus vehemently insisted on. See *Humanitarians*.†

Socinus allowed that the title of *God* might be given to Christ; because he had a real divine power and dominion bestowed upon him, to qualify him to take care of the concerns of christians, and to hear and answer their prayers, though he was originally no more than a human creature.

There were some among the early Socinians who disapproved of the worship paid to Christ; and at present, it is agreed among all Unitarians, that the Supreme God in one person is the only object of religious worship. See *Unitarians*.

Socinus was a strict Pelagian in his sentiments respecting hu-

* Socinus, and some of his followers, entertained a notion of Christ's having been, in some unknown time of his life, taken up personally into heaven, and sent down again to the earth, which was the way, in which they solved these expressions concerning him: John iii. 13, *No man hath ascended up to heaven, but he that came down from heaven, even the Son of man which is in heaven.* Thus Moses, who was the type of Christ, before the promulgation of the law, ascended to God upon Mount Sinai. So Christ, before he entered on the office assigned him by the Father, was, in consequence of the divine counsel and agency, translated into heaven, that he might see the things he had to announce to the world, in the name of God himself.

† The terms, Socinians and Humanitarians, are used to denote all Unitarians who deny the pre-existence of Christ. See Yates' Sequel, p. 8.

man nature, and the divine decrees. See *Pelagians.*

The Socinians differ from the Arians in the following particulars.

The Socinians assert, that Christ was simply a man, and consequently had no existence before his birth and appearance in this world. The Arians maintain that Christ was a super-angelic being, united to a human body: that, though he was himself created, he was the creator of all other things under God, and the instrument of all the divine communications to the patriarchs.

The Socinians say that the Holy Ghost is the power and wisdom of God, which is God. The Arians suppose, that the Holy Spirit is the creature of the Son, and subservient to him in the work of redemption.

The Socinians flourished greatly in Poland about the year 1551, and J. Siemienius, Palatine of Podolia, built purposely for their use the city of Racon. A famous catechism was published by them, called the Racovian catechism; but it never obtained among this denomination the authority of a public confession, or rule of faith. Their most able writers are known by the title of the Fratres Poloni, or Polonian Brethren. Their writings were republished together, in the year 1656, in one great collection, consisting of six volumes in folio, under the title of Bibliotheca Fratrum. An account of these authors may be seen in Dr. Toulmin's Life of Socinus.*

SOLDINS, the followers of Soldin, a Greek priest, about the middle of the fifth century, who, in the mass, it is said, offered gold, incense and myrrh, in memory of the like offerings made by the Magi.†

*SOMNITES, orthodox *Mahometans*, which see.

*SOUL-SLEEPERS, a term sometimes applied to Materialists, because they admit no intermediate state between death and the resurrection.

SOUTHCOTTIANS, the followers of Joanna Southcott, who was born in 1750. In 1792, she assumed the character of a prophetess, and the number of people, who have joined with her from that period to the time of her death, as believing her to be divinely inspired, is considerable. She declared that she was the woman in the wilderness, spoken of Rev. xii. 6; and having first excited the feelings of her adherents, gave them sealed passports, which were called her seals, and which were to protect them from the judgments of the present and future world. She next called upon them to sign their names for

* For an account of the Socinian divisions, see Biddelians, Budneians, and Farvonians.

† Broughton, vol. ii. p. 560.

Christ's glorious and peaceable kingdom to come upon the earth, and for satan's to be destroyed. *The sealed of the Lord, Elect, Precious, &c.* were then written on a piece of paper; and Joanna affixed her signature. Each of the seals being then signed, the impression of the seal of the prophetess was made on the outside, with wax. Her followers placed implicit confidence in her certificates; and it is said, that some who were actually dying, ordered these seals to be buried with them as a passport to heaven.

Her predictions were delivered both in prose and verse, and contained, besides some personal threatenings, denunciations of judgments on the surrounding nations, and a promise of the speedy approach of the millennium. The whole purport of her predictions was, she said, to warn the world at large that the second coming of Christ is nigh at hand; and to show from the fall, that the promise, which was made to the woman at first, must be accomplished at last, and in h r sex too, before man's complete redemption can take place.

In the course of Joanna's mission, as she called it, the desire of increasing her followers* induced her to itinerate through different parts of England, particularly at Bristol, Leeds, &c. She met with followers in most directions, especially at Leeds, where her cause greatly flourished. Having satisfied herself with being an itinerant, Joanna finally settled near the metropolis. Her leading chapel was in Duke-street, St. George's Fields, in the vicinity of the Obelisk; where her high priest, Mr. W. Tozer, presided, and where the liturgy of the church of England was read, preparatory to the sermonic elucidation of her prognostications. They had a choir of singers, her poetry supplying them with hymns. Anxious to be regarded as within the acknowledged pale of the christian church, notwithstanding their eccentricities, the sacrament was regularly administered among them, and they even affected to consider themselves in the character of members of the establishment.

Joanna continued to gain proselytes, to whom she made the most magnificent promises of wonderful events, which would shortly be accomplished in her person; but her death, which took place in 1814, disappointed their raised expectations, and exposed them to the derision and contempt of the enemies of the pretended prophetess. Those, who wish for a more detailed account of this woman, are referred to the statement of the life, predic-

* She asserted, that her followers were to make up the sealed number of one hundred and forty-four thousand to stand with the Lamb on Mount Zion.

tions, and death of the Exeter prophetess; see also Hughson's History of Religious Impostures, and Carpenter's Missionary Magazine.

SOUTH-SEA ISLANDERS are the inhabitants of the Society, Friendly, Sandwich, and some other Islands; of none of which have we so much or so correct knowledge as that of Otaheite, (or rather *Taheite,*) to which therefore the following account principally, but not exclusively, refers.

They in general acknowledge an almighty Creator of the universe, who executed the various parts of the creation by subordinate powerful beings. They acknowledge a something within them, which sees, hears, smells, tastes, and feels, which they call *eteehee;* and they believe that after the dissolution of the body, it hovers about the corpse, and at last retires into the wooden representations of human bodies, erected near the burying places. They expect a future happy life in the sun, where they shall feast on bread-fruit, and meat which requires no dressing: and they direct their prayers to the supreme divinity, or *Eatooa-Rahai.*

The name *Eatooa* admits a very great latitude in its interpretation. Each of the islands has a tutelar deity, which is always the divinity, to whom the high priest of the isle addresses his prayer, at the grand morai of the prince. The great deity, or *Eatooa-Rahai,* they consider as the primary cause of all divine and human beings; and suppose the inferiour deities, and even mankind, are descended from him and a female deity, for which reason they call him the great procreating stem. They imagine a co-existing material substance necessary, which they called *O-te-pa-pa.* These procreated *O-hee-naa,* the goddess of the moon; the gods of the stars, (whom they call the children of the sun and moon;) of the seas, and of the winds. But the sea is under the direction of thirteen divinities, who have all their peculiar employment. Their supreme god lives in the sun, and is thought to be the cause of earthquakes. They have one inferiour genius, of a malignant disposition, residing near the morai, or burying places, and in or near the chest including the heads of their deceased friends, each of which is called the house of the evil genius. The people think that when a priest invocates this evil genius he will kill, by a sudden death, the person on whom they intend to bring down his vengeance.—They have another inferiour divinity, who had the same power of killing men, with this difference, that he is worshipped only by hissing. This is called *Tee-hee,* which, they say, is the being that hears, smells, tastes, and feels within us, and after death exists separately from the body, but lives near burying places, and hovers round the dead. These *Tee-hees* are likewise feared: because, according to their belief, they creep during the night into houses, and eat the hearts and entrails of people sleeping therein, and cause their death.

These islanders honour their divinities by prayers, by setting apart certain days for religious worship, by consecrating certain persons and places for that purpose, and by offering human sacrifices, which are generally either prisoners of war, or condemned malefactors.* They prepare those oblations on their morais.

The deities of Otaheite are nearly as numerous as the persons of the inhabitants. Every family has its *Tee*, or guardian spirit, whom they set up and worship at the morai: but they have a great god, or gods of a superiour order, denominated Fwhanow Po, or born of night. The general name for deity, in all its ramifications, is *Eatooa*. Three are held supreme in celestial dignity, which are called, *Tane, te Medooa*, the Father; *Oromattow, Tooa tee te Myde*, God in the Son; *Taroa, Mannoo te Hooa*, the Bird, the Spirit. To these they only address their prayers in times of very great distress, supposing them to be too highly exalted to be troubled with matters of less moment than the illness of a chief, storms, devastation, war, or any great calamnity.—For general worship they have a kind of *dii penates*, or household gods. Each family has its guardian spirit, who is supposed to be one of their departed relatives, who, for his superiour excellence, has been exalted to an *Eatooa*. They suppose this spirit can inflict sickness, or remove it, and preserve them from a malignant deity, who is always employed in mischief. Some of the Otaheitans are very devout, and not only are the whattas, or offering places of the morais, commonly loaded with fruits and animals, but there are few houses where you do not meet with a small place of the same sort near them. They imagine that their punctual performance of religious offices prepares for them every temporal blessing. They believe that the animating and powerful influence of the divine Spirit is every where diffused; and that sudden deaths, and all accidents, are effected by the immediate action of some divinity; and they have some notion of a *metempsychosis*, or transmigration of the soul, and that it returns eventually into reunion with the supreme Deity.

The missionaries, who have for several years resided at Otaheite, have found the inhabitants to be cannibals, and that they not only sacrifice their enemies, but eat them; besides which they have a horrid custom of destroying their infants,

* Foster's Geographical Observations, p. 333, 334.

which, with their wars, has much depopulated them. However, as Christianity has obtained influence among them, these evils have, in some degree, disappeared.

From recent intelligence, it appears that many of the inhabitants of these islands have embraced the christian religion. It is said, that the majority of the people of Eimeo have renounced heathenism, and it is supposed there are upwards of one thousand people in that island who are professedly the worshippers of the true God. They are distinguished from their countrymen by the name of "Bure Atua," or Praying People. The missionaries at Eimeo have printed the Bible in the Taheitean language, and the number of christians is increasing rapidly in Eimeo, and Otaheite.* See *Appendix*.

SPINOSISTS, the followers of Benedict Spinosa, a celebrated Portuguese Jew, who died at the Hague in 1677. He was the great champion of the *Pantheists*, (which see,) and his writings had the more weight because his character was moral, and his language, both in speaking and writing, decorous and inoffensive: so much so, that he had many advocates, who thought him unjustly accused of such principles. In his *Ethics*, however, a posthumous work, he throws off the mask, and avows his opinion, that the *Deity* is only another name for the universe, "producing a series of *necessary* movements or acts, in consequence of its own intrinsic, immutable, and irresistible energy." It is said that he was seduced into this opinion by the Cartesian philosophy.*

STANCARIANS, disciples of Francis Stancarus, Hebrew Professor at Koningsburgh, in the sixteenth century, who taught that Jesus Christ was mediator in quality of a mere man only, and not as God in the form of man.†

*STAROBREDSI, or *Old Ceremonialists*, a numerous sect of Russian Dissenters, who strongly objected to the innovations of Nikon, but do not object to the ordinations of the Mother Church. In 1735 the two churches of Staradubofsk and Vetka amounted to 80,000 members; but the latter has since been scattered by persecution throughout all Russia and Siberia; and many fled into Poland about 1764, where this sect is now supposed to amount to several hundred thousands.‡

*STAROVERTSI, *believers of the old Faith;* the name assumed by the Russian Dissenters, generally called *Rascolniks*, which see.

STOICS, a sect of heathen

* American Baptist Magazine, 1817. Bayle's Dictionary in Spinosa, vol. iv. p. 338. new edit.

† Mosheim, vol. iv. p. 338. ‡ Pinkerton's Greek Church, p. 298, &c.

philosophers, of which Zeno, who flourished about three hundred and fifty years before Christ, was the founder. They received their denomination from a portico at Athens, in which Zeno delivered his lectures. Their distinguishing tenets were—That God is underived, incorruptible, and eternal; possessed of infinite wisdom and goodness; the efficient cause of all the qualities and forms of things; and the constant preserver and governour of the world. That *matter* is also underived and eternal, and by the powerful energy of the Deity impressed with motion and form. That though God and matter subsisted from eternity, the present regular frame of nature had a beginning, and will have an end. That the element of fire will, at last, by an universal conflagration, reduce the world to its pristine state. That at this period all material forms will be lost in one chaotic mass; and all animated nature be reunited to the Deity. That from this chaotic state, however, the world will again emerge by the energy of the efficient principle; and gods, and men, and all forms of regulated nature, be renewed and dissolved, in endless succession. That after the revolution of the great year all things will be restored, and the race of men will return to life. Some imagined that each individual would return to its former body, while others supposed that similar souls would be placed in similar bodies.

Those among the Stoics, who maintained the existence of the soul after death, supposed it to be removed into the celestial regions of the gods, where it remains until, at the general conflagration, all souls, both human and divine, shall be absorbed in the Deity. But many imagined that, before they were admitted among the divinities, they must purge away their inherent vices and imperfections, by a temporary residence in some aerial regions between the earth and the planets. According to the general doctrine of the Stoics all things are subject to a blind irresistible fatality, even the gods themselves; though some explained this fate as meaning only the irresistible decrees of divine providence.* It was the object of this philosophy to divest men of their passions and affections; they taught, therefore, that a wise man might be happy in the midst of torture, and that all external things were to him

* Dr. Priestley observes, that "It is not easy to say what the heathen philosophers, and others thought of fate, and the relation the gods bore to it. Sometimes they seem to have thought that they directed fate; at other times that fate was a power independent of them, and that controuled them. Seneca seems to have thought that fate was nothing more than the will of the gods themselves." See Priestley's Heathen Philosophy, p. 244.

indifferent. Their virtues all arose from, and centred in themselves, and self-approbation was their great reward.*

*STRIGOLNIKS, the most ancient sect of Russian Dissenters. They appeared in Novogorod, and were founded by a half-christian Jew, named Horie, who attempted, after the manner of the Ebionites, to blend the laws of Moses with the doctrines of the gospel. They were at first inconsiderable; but, by the absurd system of persecution, were rendered very numerous, and dispersed very extensively.†

STYLITES, so called by the Greeks, and *Sancti Columnarii*, or *Pillar Saints*, by the Latins. They stood motionless upon the top of pillars, expressly raised for this exercise of their patience; and remained there for several years, amidst the admiration and applause of the populace.

The inventor of this discipline was Simeon, a Syrian, who, in order to climb as near to heaven as possible, passed thirty-seven years of his life upon five pillars, of six, twelve, twenty two, thirty six, and forty cubits high; and thus acquired a most shining reputation, and attracted the veneration of all about him. Many of the inhabitants of Syria followed his example, though not with the same degree of austerity: and this practice, which was begun in the fifth, continued in vogue till the twelfth century.‡

SUBLAPSARIANS, an appellation given to those Calvinists, who suppose, that the decree of predestination regards man as *fallen*, by an abuse of that freedom which Adam had, into a state, in which all must have perished but for the election of grace.§

SUFIS, or SOUFFEES, a sect of modern philosophers in Persia, who are so called, either from the Greek word for a sage, or from the woollen mantle which they used to wear in some provinces of Persia. Their fundamental tenets are: That nothing exists absolutely but God; that the human soul is an emanation from his essence; and though divided for a time from its heavenly source, will be finally re-united with it; that the highest possible happiness will arise from its re-union; and that the chief good of mankind consists in as perfect a union with the eternal spirit, as the incumbrances of a mortal frame will allow: that, for this purpose, they should break off all connexion with extrinsic objects, and pass through life without attachments, as a

* Enfield, vol. i. p. 282. Mosheim, vol. i. p. 35, new edition.
† Pinkerton's Greek Church, p. 280, &c.
‡ Mosheim, vol. i. p. 391. History of Don Ignatius, vol. i. p. 31.
§ Doddridge's Lectures, p. 460.

swimmer in the ocean strikes freely without the impediments of clothes: that, if mere earthly charms have power to influence the soul, the idea of celestial beauty must overwhelm it in ecstatic light. They maintain also that, for want of apt words to express the divine perfections and the ardour of devotion, we must borrow such expressions, as approach the nearest to our ideas, and speak of beauty and love in a transcendent and mystical sense; that, like a reed torn from its native bank, like wax separated from its delicious honey, the soul of man bewails its disunion with melancholy music, and sheds burning tears, like the lighted taper, waiting passionately for the moment of its extinction; as a disengagement from earthly trammels, and the means of returning to its only beloved. This theology prevails also among the learned Mussulmans, who avow it without reserve.*

SUPRALAPSARIANS, a title given to those Calvinists, who suppose that God, in the decree of election, viewed his people merely as *creatures*, (or rather as to be created,) and not as *fallen* creatures, as is supposed by the Sublapsarians just mentioned.

The Supralapsarians consider the divine glory to be the great object of the divine decrees, whether in the salvation of the elect or the punishment of the wicked. Eph. i. 5, 6. Prov. xvi. 4. They conceive that St. Paul reasons on this principle when speaking of Jacob and Esau—the one elected, and the other not—when as yet they had "done neither good nor evil." That the one was chosen and the other rejected on the same principle of *sovereignty*, as the potter appoints "one vessel to honour and another to dishonour;" and that he has forbidden our farther inquiry by the question, "Who art thou, O man, that repliest against God?" See Rom. xi. throughout. Finally, they consider this principle to harmonize best with the case of the *elect angels*, who, not being permitted to sin, could be elected only as pure creatures.

Sublapsarians on the other hand observe, that the elect are chosen "*out* of the world," John xvii. 9—that they are called "vessels of mercy," Rom. ix. 23; and that our election in Christ Jesus is essentially connected with the decree of predestination to adoption, sanctification, and redemption.

Calvinists, however, are much divided on this question. Among the Supralapsarians rank Beza, Twisse, and Dr. Gill; among the Sublapsarians Calvin himself, Bp. Davenant, most of the

* Middleton's Geography, vol. i. p. 69, &c.

English Reformers, and Mr. Toplady.*

*SWEDENBORGIANS. See *New Jerusalem Church.*

SYNCRETISTS, the followers of Calixtus. See *Calixtins.*

SYNERGISTS, (so called from the Greek συνεργεια, i. e. *co-operation,*) a name given to those in the sixteenth century, who affirmed that man co-operates with divine grace in the accomplishment of his salvation.† See *Arminians.*

SYRIAN CHRISTIANS, remains of the Eastern churches in India, recently visited and described by Dr. Buchanan. When the Portuguese arrived in India, they were surprised to find more than a hundred christian churches who knew nothing of the Pope, but boasted a succession of regular bishops derived from the Patriarch of Antioch, and continued for one thousand three hundred years. When the Roman Catholics acquired sufficient power, they began to persecute; and established the Inquisition at Goa,‡ as the cruel instrument of their power; an institution which subsisted lately under the protection of the British government. At the Roman Catholic Synod of Diamper, the Syrian clergy were accused of the following sins and heresies: "That they had married wives; that they owned but two sacraments, baptism and the Lord's supper; that they neither invoked saints, nor worshipped images, nor believed in purgatory: and that they had no other orders in the church, than bishop, priest, and deacon." These tenets they were required to abjure, and to admit the authority of the pope. Many of the churches on the sea-coast compromised matters by acknowledging the pope, and admitting their liturgy to be purged of what they called its errours; but still insisted on worshipping in their own Syriac language, which they continue to this day, and are called Syro-Roman churches. The number of these churches is estimated at ninety thousand.

The churches in the interiour, however, were not so docile. They concealed their books, fled to the mountains, and sought the protection of the native princes. These Dr. Buchanan visited, under the sanction of the Rajah of Travancore, in whose dominions they reside. Dr. Buchanan describes the faith of these christians as comprehending the doctrines of the trinity, the atonement, and regeneration.

* Gill's Body of Divinity, vol. i. p. 299. Doddridge's Lectures, p. 460.

† Mosheim, vol. iv. p. 338. new ed.

‡ The inquisition of Goa has been abolished by an order of the Prince Regent of Portugal. It is said, however, that the Archbishop retains all the power that was lodged in the court of the inquisition. See Mr. Newell's Journal in the Panoplist, May, 1815.

More particularly, they believe "that, in the appointed time, through the disposition of the Father and Holy Ghost, the Son appeared on earth for the salvation of mankind; that he was born of the virgin Mary, through the means of the Holy Ghost, and was incarnate God and man."*

Dr. Buchanan does not state the number of these christians; he mentions forty five churches under the archbishop of Cranganore (where the apostle Thomas is reported to have landed) beside sixty four Syro-Roman churches, under the apostolic vicar.† And in another place the Dr. states that besides the Syrians, there are upwards of two hundred thousand christians who speak the Malabar language.‡

Dr. Kerr, the senior chaplain of Madras, was sent by the government of that presidency, in 1806, to investigate the state of the Syrian and other christians in Malabar and Travancore. In his official report he observes, "It has been believed that the Syrian christians, who have not conformed to the church of Rome, held the tenets of Nestorius, and that they were obliged to leave their own country in consequence of persecution. However, it appears that the creed they now hold denies that doctrine, and seems to coincide with the Athanasian creed, without its damnatory clauses. Their number is calculated by Dr. Kerr at seventy or eighty thousand.

Many of the Syrian churches are destitute of the bible, and there is a consequent defect of christian knowledge among them. The late Dr. Buchanan, who was deeply interested in the fate of these christians, whom he had visited, was assiduously engaged in preparing for the press a Syriac copy of the scriptures. This excellent man died suddenly on the ninth of February, 1815, at the village of Broxbourue, whither he had retired to superintend the printing of an edition of the Syriac bible.§ This edition, begun by him, is continued since his death by the British and Foreign Bible Society.

* Buchanan's Researches, p. 117.

† Ibid. p. 125, 126

‡ Christian Observer, 1815, 1816.

§ Such was the prevalence of mind over body, of principle over the languor of disease and decrepitude, that, till almost the hour of his death, Dr. Buchanan was employed rarely less than nine hours daily, in preparing for the press a Syrian copy of the scriptures.

T

TABORITES, a denomination in the fifteenth century; so called from a mountain well known in sacred history. They not only insisted on reducing the religion of Jesus to its primitive simplicity, but required also that the system of ecclesiastical government should be reformed in the same manner; the authority of the pope destroyed, and the form of divine worship changed. They maintained the lawfulness of defending religion by the sword; and some of them are said to have expected Christ's personal appearance among them. After some time, however, they became more calm and rational, and relinquished many opinions, which they found to be inconsistent with the spirit and genius of the gospel; and thus new modelled were the same with those Bohemian brethren, who joined Luther and his successors at the time of the reformation.*

*TALMUDISTS, those Jewish doctors who admit the authority of the Talmuds; which are collections of Jewish traditions and allegorical expositions. See *Cabbalists*.

TANQUELINIANS, a numerous sect, so called from Tanquelinus in the twelfth century. He is charged with slighting the external worship of God, and the holy sacraments; with holding clandestine assemblies to propagate his opinions: and above all with abusing the clergy of the Roman Catholic church.

TATIANITES, a denomination in the second century; so called from Tatian, a disciple of Justin Martyr. They are, however, more frequently distinguished from other sects by names relative to the austerity of their manners. For they rejected with horror, all the comforts and conveniences of life. See *Encratites*.

*TEMPLARS, or KNIGHTS of the TEMPLE. See *Knights*.

THEODOSIANS. See *Angelites*. This is also the name of a numerous sect in Russia, which some years since separated from the *Pomoryans*, (which see,) partly on account of their not purifying by prayer the various articles they purchase of unbelievers: they are very strict in their religion, and inveigh bitterly against the national church as Antichrist.†

THEOPASCHITES, a denomination in the fifth century, (which derive their name from Θεος, *God*, and πασχω, *to suffer*,) the followers of Peter the fuller. His doctrine is said to have differed from that of the *Patripassians*, by implying the suffering of all the Holy Trinity.‡

* Mosheim, vol. iii. p. 260, 264.

† Pinkerton's Greek Church, p. 331.

‡ Mosheim's Eccles. Hist. vol. i. p. 417. Priestley's Hist. of Early Opinions, vol. iv. p. 262.

THEOPHILANTHROPISTS, (lovers of God and man,) a sect of deists, which made its appearance in France, amid the storm of the revolution. The celebrated Thomas Paine was one of their first apostles, and delivered a discourse before them, on the principles of this new scheme. In September 1796, a kind of catechism, or directory, for public or social worship, appeared at Paris, under the title of "*Manuel des Theanthrophiles;*" this breviary was received favourably by the public, and the congregations became very numerous. From this book the following particulars of their tenets are extracted:

"The temple most worthy of the Deity is the *universe*. Absorbed sometimes under the vault of heaven, in the contemplation of the beauties of nature, we render its Author the homage of adoration and gratitude. Nevertheless, we have temples constructed by the hands of men, which are more commodious for the purpose of assembling to hear the lessons of his wisdom. Certain moral inscriptions;—a simple altar, on which are deposited, as a token of gratitude for the benefits of the Creator, such fruits and flowers as the seasons afford;—and a tribune for the lecturers,—form the whole of the ornaments of these temples."

Of the inscriptions, the first is, "We believe in the existence of God, and in the immortality of the soul." This is "placed above the altar, to remind us of the two religious dogmas, which are the foundation of our moral precepts."—2. "Worship God; cherish your fellow-men; render yourselves useful to your country."—3. "Whatever tends to the preservation or perfection of man is good, whatever has a tendency to destroy or deteriorate him is evil."—4. "Children, honour your fathers and mothers; obey them with affection; comfort their declining years. Fathers and mothers, instruct your children."—5. "Wives, esteem your husbands, the chiefs of your houses. Husbands, love your wives; and render yourselves reciprocally happy."

"The assembly sits to hear lessons, or discourses, on morals, on principles of religion, of benevolence, and of universal salvation: principles equally remote from the severity of Stoicism, and the supineness of Epicurean indulgence. These lectures and discourses are diversified by hymns; and the assemblies are held on the first day of the week, and on the decades.

"Should we be asked what is the origin of our religion and worship? we reply: Open the most ancient books extant, and there examine what was the religion, what the worship, of the first human beings, whose actions are recorded in history.

It will be seen that their religion consisted of what is now called *natural religion,* because its object is the Author of nature; and he has engraven it upon the hearts of the first men, upon ours, and upon those of all the inhabitants of the earth. This religion, which consists in worshipping God, and loving our fellow-creatures, is what we express by the simple word *Theophilanthropy:* our religion is, consequently, that of our first parents; it is also yours, as well as ours; in a word, it is the universal religion. As to our worship, it is likewise that of our first fathers. Even in the most ancient writings it may be discovered; the exterior signs, by which they rendered their homage to the Creator, were of the utmost simplicity. They raised an altar of earth; they offered him, in token of their gratitude and submission, some of the productions which they had received from his liberal hand. Fathers inculcated the practice of virtue upon their children; and all endeavoured to stimulate each other, under the auspices of the Deity, to the performance of their duties. This simple worship has been professed by the sages of all nations, and they have transmitted it down to modern times, unimpaired and uninterrupted.

"To queries respecting our mission, we reply: We hold it of God himself; who, in giving us power to assist our fellow creatures, has likewise endued us with intelligence, for our mutual edification; and the love of good, to bring us together to virtue: of that God, in a word, who has given experience and wisdom to the aged to guide the young, and authority to parents to direct their children.

"Should the force of these reasons be insufficient to satisfy the inquirer, we forbear any farther discussion, rather than engage in a controversy tending to diminish the love of our neighbours. Our principles being the eternal truth, they will subsist, let who may pretend to support or to suppress them; nor can the efforts of the wicked ever prevail against them. Let us rest, therefore, firmly attached to them, without attacking or defending any religious system: remembering that such discussions have never been attended with good; but, on the contrary, have frequently dyed the earth with human blood. Let us lay aside systems, and apply ourselves to doing good, which is the only road to happiness."

The Theophilanthropists are now said to be nearly extinct; they arose, as already observed, out of the vortex of the revolution, which had engulphed all institutions, moral and divine; during that gloomy period, when the demagogues had forbidden the exercise of public worship, when the churches were converted into heathen temples, and when "Death is an eternal sleep," being inscribed upon the graves, had removed for a time the hope of immortality from the minds of men. When Buonaparte re-opened the churches, Theophilanthropy became neglected, and is now scarcely known otherwise than by its name.*

*THEOSOPHISTS, a sect of chemical philosophers, who pretended to derive their occult science from divine illumination, whence they have been called *Illuminati*, but most usually *Rosicrusians;* which see.

*THERAPEUTÆ, a sect of Jews, generally considered as a branch of the *Essenes*, which see. They affected extraordinary silence and decorum in their worship, and remarkable austerity in their manners. Some of the sect probably verged to Paganism, and others to Christianity; which has occasioned circumstances which the learned have found great difficulty in reconciling.†

THIBETIANS. The GRAND LAMA is at once the High Priest and the visible object of adoration, to this nation, to the hordes of wandering Tartars, and to the prodigious population of China. He resides at Patoli, a vast palace on a mountain near the banks of the Burampooter, about seven miles from Lahassa. The foot of the mountain is surrounded by twenty thousand Lamas, in attendance on their Sovereign Pontiff, who is considered as the vicegerent of the Deity on earth; and the more remote Tartars are said to regard him absolutely as the Deity himself, and call him *God, the everlasting Father of heaven.* They believe him to be immortal, and endowed with all knowledge and virtue. Every year they come up from different parts to worship, and make rich offerings at his shrine. Even the emperor of China, who is a Mantchou Tartar, does not fail in acknowledgments to him in his religious capacity; and entertains in the palace of Pekin an inferiour Lama, deputed as his nuncio from Thibet. The grand Lama is only to be seen in a secret place of his palace, amidst a great number of lamps, sitting cross-legged on a cushion, and decked all over with gold and precious stones; while, at a distance, the people prostrate themselves before him; it being not lawful for any so much as to kiss his feet. He returns not the least sign of respect, nor ever speaks even to the greatest princes; but only lays his hand upon their heads, and they are fully pursuaded that they thereby receive a full forgiveness of their sins.

The *Sunniasses*, or Indian pilgrims, often visit Thibet as a holy place; and the Lama

* Manuel of the Theophilanthropists. Evans' Sketch, p. 17. 13th Ed.
† Calmet's Dictionary, vol. ii.

entertains a body of two or three hundred in his pay. Besides his religious influence and authority, he is possessed of unlimited power throughout his dominions, which are very extensive. The inferior Lamas, who form the most numerous, as well as the most powerful body in the state, have the priesthood entirely in their hands; and besides, fill up many monastic orders, which are held in great veneration among them. The whole country, like Italy, abounds with priests; and they entirely subsist on the rich presents sent them from the utmost extent of Tartary, from the empire of the Great Mogul, and from almost all parts of the Indies.

The opinion of those, who are reputed the most orthodox among the Thibetians, is, that when the grand Lama seems to die, either of old age or infirmities, his soul, in fact, only quits a crazy habitation, to look for another, younger or better; and is discovered again in the body of some child, by certain tokens, known only to the Lamas, or priests, in which order he always appears.

Almost all the nations of the East, except the Mahometans, believe the *metempsychosis*, or transmigration of the soul, as the most important article of their faith; especially the inhabitants of Thibet and Ava, the Peguans, the Siamese, the greater part of the Chinese and Japanese, and the Moguls and Calmucks. According to their doctrine, the soul no sooner leaves her old habitation, than she enters a new one. The Dailai Lama, being a divine person, can find no better lodging than the body of his successor; or the *Foe*, residing in the Dailai Lama, which passes to his successor: and this being a god, to whom all things are known, the grand Lama is therefore acquainted with every thing which happened during his residence in his former body.

This religion, which was early adopted in a large part of the globe, is said to have been of three thousand years standing; and neither time, nor the influence of men, has had the power of shaking the authority of the grand Lama. This theocracy, which extends as fully to temporal as to spiritual concerns, is professed all over Thibet and Mongalia; is almost universal in Greater and Lesser Bucharia, and several provinces of Tartary; has some followers in the kingdom of Cassimere, in India, and is the predominant religion of China.*

It has been observed, "that the religion of Thibet is the counterpart of the Roman Catholic, since the inhabitants of that country use holy water and a singing service: they also offer

* Annual Register for 1780, p. 62.

alms, prayers, and sacrifices for the dead. They have a vast number of convents filled with monks and friars, amounting to thirty thousand; and confessors, chosen by their superiors. They use beads; wear the mitre and cap like the bishops; and their *Dailai Lama* is nearly the same among them as the sovereign pontiff is among the Romanists."* See *Chinese*.

*THOMISTS, the followers of St. Thomas Aquinas, in opposition to the celebrated Duns Scotus, in the fourteenth century, on the doctrines of grace, and on some metaphysical speculations.† See *Scotists*.

TRASKITES, the followers of Mr. J. Trask, 1634. His opinions were similar to the *Sabbatarians*;‡ which see.

TRIFORMIANI, a denomination which appeared about the year 408; so called from the Latin *tria forma*. They maintained that the divine nature was one and the same in the three persons together; but not complete in either separately.§

TRINITARIANS, a name applied to all who profess to believe the doctrine of the Trinity, in opposition to Arians, Socinians, and all Antitrinitarians. "The word Trinity," says Mr. Evans, "is not to be found in the bible, but is a scholastic term, derived from the Latin word *trinitas*, denoting threefold unity."

Theophilus of Antioch, a learned writer of the second century, is said to have been the first who made use of the word Trinity to express the distinction of what divines call *persons* in the godhead.||

Dr. Doddridge remarks, speaking of the ancient writers upon the Trinity, that "after the time of the celebrated council of Nice,¶ they ran into several subtleties of expression, in which one would imagine they studied rather to conceal than to explain their sentiments; yet they grew so warm upon the subject, as to anathematize, oppose, and murder each other on account of some unscriptural phrases, much to the dishonour of their common profession."

The following is a brief account of the opinions of a number of learned modern divines, concerning the doctrine of the Trinity.

* Payne's Epitome of History, vol. ii. p. 33. Guthrie's Geopraphy (ed. 1788) p 660. Raynal's Hist. of the Indians, vol. ii. p. 219.

† Mosheim, vol. iii. p. 365. ‡ Pagit's Heresiography, p. 135.

§ Hearne's Ductor Historicus, vol. ii. p. 170.

|| See Maclaine's Chronol Tables to Mosheim's Eccles. Hist.

¶ The first general Council, assembled by the Emperor Constantine at Nice, in the year 325, in which Arius was condemned, and certain measures agreed upon to calm the religious tumults that had long troubled the church. But the spirit of dissension and controversy triumphed both over the decrees of the Council, and the authority of the Emperor. See Mosheim's Eccles. Hist. vol. i. p. 403.

Dr. Waterland, Dr. Taylor, with the rest of the Athanasians, assert three proper distinct persons,* entirely equal and independent of each other; yet making but one and the same being.

Mr. Baxter seems, as some of the schoolmen did, to have thought the three divine persons, to be one and the same God, *understanding*, *willing*, and *beloved* by himself, or wisdom, power, and love, which he thinks illustrated by the three essential formalties, (as he calls them,) in the soul of man; viz. power, intellect, and will, and in the sun, motion, light and heat.

Mr. Howe seems to suppose, that there are three distinct, eternal spirits, or distinct, intelligent hypostaces, each having his own distinct, singular, intelligent nature, united in such an inexplicable manner, as that upon account of their perfect harmony, consent, affection, and self-consciousness, they may be called the one God, as properly as the different corporeal, sensitive, and intellectual natures united, may be called one man.

Dr. Thomas Burnet maintains, one self-existent and two dependent beings; but asserts, that the two latter are so united to, and inhabited by the former, that by virtue of that union, divine perfections may be ascribed, and divine worship paid to them.

Bishop Pearson, bishop Bull, and Dr. Owen, are of opinion, that, though God the Father is the fountain of the Deity, the whole divine nature is communicated from the Father to the Son, and from both to the Spirit; yet so as that the Father and Son are not separate, nor separable from the divinity; but do still exist in it, and are most intimately united to it.

Dr. Wallis thought the distinctions in the Trinity were only modal;† and thus states his doctrine, "a divine person is only a mode, a respect, or relation of God to his creatures. He beareth to his creatures these three relations, modes, or respects, that he is their creator, their redeemer, and their sanctifier. This is what we mean, and all we mean, when we say, God is three persons."‡ See *Sabellians*.

Dr. Clarke's scheme is, that there is a supreme Father and two subordinate, derived and dependent beings, the Son and

* According to Bishop Sherlock, "Father, Son, and Holy Ghost are as really distinct persons, as Peter, James, and John; each of whom is God. We must allow each person to be a God." These three "infinite minds are distinguished just as three created minds are, by self-consciousness. And by mutual consciousness each person of these has the whole wisdom, power, and goodness of the other two persons." Vindication of the Trinity. Obs. on the Vind. p. 19, 20. quoted by Mr. Worcester in his Trinitarian Review, No i. p. 8.

† This seems, says Dr Doddridge, to have been Archbishop Tillotson's opinion.

‡ Considerations on the Trinity, p. 7. quoted by Yates in his Reply to Wardlaw, p. 126.

Holy Spirit; but he waives calling Christ a creature, as the ancient Arians did; and principally on that account disclaims the charge of Arianism. See *Pre-existents.*

Dr. Watts maintained one supreme God, dwelling in the pre-existent human soul of Christ, whereby he is entitled to all divine honours. See *Pre-existents.*

Mr. Wardlaw maintains, that the three persons in the Godhead are distinct, but in using the term *persons*, he explicitly disavows all pretensions to understanding the nature of the distinction; and affirms, that by making use of it, he means no more than that in the unity of the Godhead there is a distinction, which, while he believes it to exist, he cannot pretend to explain or to comprehend.*

Dr. Jeremy Taylor observes, that, "he who goes about to speak of the mysteries of the Trinity, and does it by words and names of man's invention, talking of essences and existences, hypostases and personalities, priorities in co-equalities, &c. and unity in pluralities, may amuse himself, and build a tabernacle in his head, and talk something, he knows not what; but the good man that feels the power of the Father, and to whom the Son is become wisdom, sanctification, and redemption; in whose heart the love of the spirit of God is shed abroad—this man, though he understands nothing of what is unintelligible, yet he alone truly understands the christian doctrine of the Trinity."†

The limits of this work will not admit of giving a sketch of the various arguments, by which these statements are supported; some of them may be found under the articles *Arians, Anthanasians, Pre-existents,* &c.

TRITHEISTS, a denomination in the sixth century, whose chief was John Ascusnage, a Syrian philosopher, and at the same time a Monophysite. He imagined in the Deity three natures, or substances, absolutely equal, and joined together by no common essence: to which opinion his adversaries gave the name of Tritheism, or the worship of three gods. One of the defenders of this doctrine was John Philoponus, an Alexandrian philosopher and grammarian of the highest reputation; and hence he was considered by many as the author of this sect. This name has also been applied, by way of reproach, to certain Trinitarians.‡ See *Athanasians.*

* See Wardlaw's Reply to Yates.

† Doddridge's Lectures, p. 401—403. Baxter's Works. vol. ii. p 1. Howe's Works, vol. iii. Bull's Sermons, vol. iv. p 829. Pearson on the Creed, p. 154. Owen on the Hebrews, vol. i. Tillotson's Works. Jeremy Taylor on John vi. 17.

‡ Mosheim, vol. i. p. 473. Barclay's Dictionary, article *Tritheists.*

TSCHERNABOLTSI, a Russian sect which arose in 1775 among the old believers of Staradubofsk, from whom they differ in the three following points. First, they refuse to take an oath, because they say Christ forbids swearing of every kind. Secondly, they refuse to shave their beards. Thirdly, they refuse to pray for the emperor and imperial family, according to the form prescribed by the holy synod.*

*TSCHURSLVINIKS, the friends of union among the Raskolniks, who attempt to propagate their conciliatory principles among the different sects, and on this account are persecuted by the zealous men of all parties.†

*TUNKERS, a congregation of seventh-day baptists at Ephrata in Pennsylvania.‡ See *Dunkers.*

TURLUPINS, a sect which appeared about the year 1372, in Savoy and Dauphiny. They taught, that when a man is arrived at a certain state of perfection, he is freed from all subjection to the divine law; which we call Antinomianism. John Dabantonne was the author of this denomination. Some think they were called Turlupins because they usually abode in desolate places, exposed to wolves, *lupi.* They called themselves the *Fraternity of the poor;* but they were commonly called *Brethren of the free spirit;* which see.§

U & V

VALENTINIANS, a branch of the *Gnostics,* which sprang up in the second century; so called from their leader, Valentinus. His principles were, generally speaking, the same with those of the Gnostics, whose name he assumed; yet in many things he entertained opinions peculiar to himself. He placed, for instance, in the *pleroma* (so the Gnostics called the habitation of the Deity) thirty *aions,* of which the one half were male, and the other, female. To these he added four others, which were of neither sex; viz. Horus, (who guarded the borders of the pleroma,) Christ, the Holy Ghost, and Jesus. The youngest of the *aions,* called Sophia, (i. e. *wisdom,)* conceived an ardent desire of comprehending the nature of the supreme Being, and by the force of this propensity

* Pinkerton's Greek Church, p. 204. † Ibid. p. 334.
‡ Evans' Sketch, 13th edit. p. 257.
§ Broughton, vol. ii. p. 474. Dufresnoy's Chronological Tables, vol. ii. p. 243.

brought forth a daughter, named Achamoth. Achamoth being exiled from the pleroma, fell down into the rude and undigested mass of matter, to which she gave a certain arrangement; and by the assistance of Jesus, produced the Demiurge, the Lord and Creator of all things. This Demiurge separated the subtile, or animal matter, from that of the grosser, or mere terrestrial kind. Out of the former he created the heavens; and out of the latter, this terraqueous globe. He also made man, in whose composition the subtile and the grosser matter were united in equal portions; but Achamoth, the mother of Demiurge, added to them a spiritual and celestial substance—the immortal soul.

The Creator of this world, who was the God of the Jews, according to Valentinus, arrived by degrees to that pitch of arrogance, that he either imagined himself to be God alone, or at least was desirous that mankind should consider him as such. For this purpose he sent forth prophets to the Jewish nation, to whom he affected to be the supreme Being; and the other angels, who preside over different parts of the world, imitated his ambition. To correct this arrogance of Demiurge, and to teach mankind the true and supreme Deity, Christ appeared upon earth, composed of an animal and spiritual substance, and clothed moreover with an aerial body, which passed through the womb of Mary untainted. Jesus, one of the supreme *aions*, was substantially united to him when he was baptized in Jordan. The God of the Jews, when he perceived his empire shaken by this divine man, caused him to be apprehended and nailed to the cross. But before Christ submitted to this punishment, not only Jesus, the Son of God, but also the rational soul of Christ, ascended up on high; so that only the animal soul and the ethereal body suffered crucifixion. Those who abandoned false deities, and the God of the Jews, and, living according to the precepts of Christ, submit the animal and sensual soul to the discipline of reason, shall be finally happy. Their rational and sensual soul shall ascend to the seats of bliss, which border on the pleroma. And when all souls are purified thoroughly, and separated from matter, then a raging fire shall dissolve the frame of this corporeal world.

The Valentinians were divided into many branches.* See *Heracleonites*, *Ptolemites*, *Secundians*, &c.

VANISTS, so called from Sir Henry Vane, who was appointed governour of New England in the year 1636; and is said to have been at the head of the party there, who were charged with maintaining An-

* Mosheim, vol. i. p. 185—188.

tinomian tenets.* See *Antinomians.*

VAUDOIS. See *Waldenses.*

UBIQUITARIANS derived their name from maintaining that the body of Jesus Christ is *ubique*, every where, and in every place. Brentius is said to have first advanced this sentiment about the year 1560. The Ubiquitarians were not quite agreed among themselves; some holding that Christ, even during his mortal life, was every where, and others dating the ubiquity of his body from the time of his ascension.†

UCKEWALLISTS, a party of Mennonists, followers of Ucke-Walles, a native of Friesland, who published his sentiments in the year 1637. He entertained a favourable opinion of the eternal state of Judas, and the rest of Christ's murderers. To give an air of plausibility to this sentiment, he invented the following hypothesis: that the period of time, which extended from the birth of Christ to the descent of the Holy Ghost, was a time of darkness; during which the Jews were entirely destitute of divine light; and that, of consequence, the sins committed during this interval were in a great measure excusable.‡

VERSCHORISTS, the followers of Jacob Verschoor, a native of Flushing, who published his sentiments in the year 1680, much resembling those of the *Hattemists;* which see.§

UNITARIANS, a comprehensive term, including all who believe the Deity to subsist in *one person only*. The Socinians have claimed an exclusive right to this title, but unjustly, as Arians, Humanitarians, and all Anti-trinitarians have an equal right to the denomination.—Even some Trinitarians have claimed it: "but," it is evident, "this is to introduce a confusion of terms; since, as has been observed, Unitarian is not opposed to Tritheist or Polytheist: it does not denote a believer in *one God* only; but a believer in God in *one person* only, in opposition to the Trinitarians."

The chief article in the religious system of the class of Unitarian Socinians‖ is, that Christ was a mere man. But they consider him as the great instrument in the hands of God

* Calamy's Abridg. vol. i. p. 98.

† Broughton, Hist. Dict. vol. ii. p. 481.

‡ Mosheim, vol. v. p. 8.

§ Mosheim, vol. iv p. 552.

‖ Mr. Yates observes, that, "When our opponents call themselves Trinitarians, they do not mean to intimate, that they believe in three Gods; nor when we call ourselves Unitarians do we intend that term to signify that we believe in one God only. The former term was first in use, having been adopted by the Trinitarians themselves to express their belief, that there is a trinity of persons in the Godhead. The latter was invented as a correlative appellation to designate those who believe, that there is in the Godhead a unity of persons, that is, only one person. See Yates' Sequel, p. 15.

of reversing all the effects of the fall; as the object of all the prophecies from Moses to his own time; as the great bond of union to virtuous and good men, who, as Christians, make one body in a peculiar sense; as introduced into the world without a human father;* as having communications with God, and speaking and acting from God in such a manner as no other man ever did, and, therefore, having the *form of God*, and being the *Son of God* in a manner peculiar to himself: as the means of spreading divine and saving knowledge to all the world of mankind; as, under God, the head of all things to his church; and as the *Lord of life*, having power and authority from God to raise the dead, and judge the world at the last day. They suppose that the great object of the whole scheme of revelation was to teach men how to live *here*, so as to be happy *hereafter;* and that the particular doctrines there taught, as having a connexion with this great object, are those of the unity of God, his universal presence and inspection, his placability to repenting sinners, and the certainty of a life of retribution after death.

This denomination argue thus against the divinity and pre-existence of Christ:—The scriptures contain the clearest and most express declarations that there is but one true God, and forbid the worship of any other. Exod. xx. 3. Deut. vi. 4. Mark xii. 29. 1 Cor. viii. 6. Ephes. iv. 5. In the prophetic accounts which preceded the birth of Christ, he is spoken of as a man highly favoured of God, and gifted with extraordinary powers from him, and nothing more. He was foretold, Gen. xxii. 8. to be of *the seed of Abraham.* Deut. xviii. *A prophet like unto Moses.* Psal. cxxvii. 11. *Of the family of David, &c.* As a man, as a prophet, though of the highest order, the Jews constantly and uniformly looked for their Messiah. Christ never claimed any honour or respect on his own account, but such as belonged only to a prophet, an extraordinary messenger of God. He in the most decisive terms declares the Lord God to be one God, and the sole object of worship. He always prayed to him as his God and Father. He always spoke of himself as receiving his doctrine and power from him, and again and again disclaimed having any power of his own. John v. 19, 21, 30, &c. xiv. 10. He directed men to worship the Father, without the least intimation that himself or any other person whomsoever was the object of worship. Luke xi. 1, 2, Matt. iv. 10. John xvi. 23.

* Dr. Priestley, Evanson, Belsham, and others give up the miraculous conception, and with it the introductory chapters of Matthew and Luke. See *Humanitarians*.

Christ cannot be that God to whom prayer is to be offered, because he is the high priest of that God, to make intercession for us. Heb. vii. 25. The apostles speak the same language, representing the Father as the only true God, and Christ as a man, the servant of God, who raised him from the dead, and gave him all the power of which he is possessed, as a reward for his obedience. Acts ii. 22, 33. The apostle directed men to pray to God the Father only. Phil. iv. 20. Rom. xvi. 27, &c.

This denomination maintain that repentance and a good life are of themselves sufficient to recommend us to the divine favour; and that nothing is necessary to make us in all situations the objects of his favour, but such moral conduct as he has made us capable of; that Christ did nothing by his death, or in any other way, to render God merciful to sinners; but that God is, of his own accord, disposed to forgive men their sins, without any other condition than the sinner's repentance. Isaiah lv. 7. Ezek. xviii. 27. Above all, the beautiful and affecting parable of the prodigal son, (Luke xv.) is thought most decisive, that repentance is all our heavenly Father requires, to restore us to his favour.

The Unitarians of all ages have adopted the sentiments of Pelagius, with respect to human nature.*

The name of Unitarians is also claimed by all those christians who believe there is but one God, and that this one God is the Father only, and not a trinity, consisting of Father, Son, and Holy Ghost. They may or may not believe in Christ's pre-existence. The term is thus defined by the celebrated Dr. *Price*, and applied by him to what he calls a middle scheme between Athanasianism and Socinianism. His plan, and a few of the arguments he brings to support it, may therefore be inserted under this appellation.—It teaches, that Christ descended to this earth from a state of pre-existent dignity; that he was in the beginning with God, and that by him God made the world; and that by a humiliation of himself, which has no parallel, and by which he has exhibited an example of benevolence that passes knowledge, he took on him flesh and blood, and passed through human life, enduring all its sorrows, in order to bless and save a sinful race. By delivering himself up

* Priestley's Eccles. Hist. vol. i. p. 143. History of Early Opinions, vol. i. p. 10—51. vol. iii. p. 7—27. vol. iv. p. 67. Corruptions of Christianity, vol. i. p. 135. Disquisitions, vol. i. p. 376. Institutes, vol. ii. p. 281. Appeal, 19—47. Theological Repository, vol. iv. p. 20—436. Lindsey's View of the Unitarian Doctrine, &c. p. 355. Vindiciæ Priestleianæ, p. 223—227. Apology, p. 186. Answer to Robinson's Plea.

to death, he acquired the power of delivering us from death. By offering himself a sacrifice on the cross, he vindicated the honour of those laws which sinners had broken, and rendered the exercise of favour to them consistent with the holiness and wisdom of God's government; and by his resurrection from the dead, he proved the efficacy and acceptableness of his sacrifice. Christ not only declared, but obtained the availableness of repentance to pardon; and became by his interposition, not only the conveyer, but the author and means of our future immortality.* This was a service so great, that no meaner agent could be equal to it, and in consequence of it offers of full favour are made to all. No human being will be excluded from salvation, except through his own fault; and every truly virtuous man from the beginning to the end of time, let his country or religion be what it will, is made sure of being raised from death, and of being made happy forever. In all this the Supreme Deity is to be considered as the first cause; and Christ as his gift to fallen man, and as acting under that eternal and self-existent Being, compared with whom no other being is either great or good; and *of whom, and through whom, and to whom are all things.*

Our learned author argues in this manner to prove the preexistence of Christ. The history of our Saviour, as given in the new testament, and the events of his life and ministry, answer best to the opinion of the superiority of his nature. Of this kind are his introduction into the world by a miraculous conception; the annunciations from heaven at his baptism and transfiguration, proclaiming him the Son of God, and ordering all to hear him; his giving himself out as come from God to shed his blood for the remission of sins; his perfect innocence, and sinless example; the wisdom by which *he spake as never man spake;* his knowledge of the hearts of men; his intimation that he was greater than Abraham, Moses, David, or even angels; those miraculous powers by which, with a command over nature like that which first produced it, he ordered tempests to cease, and gave eyes to the blind, limbs to the maimed, reason to the frantic, health to the sick, and life to the dead; his surrender of himself to the enemies who took away his life, after demonstrating that it was his own consent, which gave them power over him; the signs which accompanied his sufferings and death; his resurrection from the dead, and triumphant ascension into heaven.

There are in the new testa-

* This author considers the destruction of being as the main circumstance in the punishment of the wicked.

ment express and direct declarations of the pre-existent dignity of Christ. John i. 1, compared with the 14th verse: John iii. 13; vi. 62; viii. 58; John xvii. 5. 2 Cor. viii. 9. Phil. ii. 5, and following verses. There remain to be quoted the texts which mention the creation of the world by Jesus Christ. In Heb. i. 2, we read that *God hath in these last days spoken to us by his Son, whom he hath appointed heir of all things, by whom also he made the worlds.* John i. 3—10. Col. i. 16.

The doctrine of God's forming the world by the agency of the Messiah gives a credibility to the doctrine of his interposition to save it, and his future agency in renewing it; because it leads us to conceive of him as standing in a particular relation to it, and having an interest in it.

The doctrine of Christ's simple humanity, when viewed in connexion with the scripture account of his exaltation, implies an inconsistency and improbability, which falls little short of an impossibility. The scriptures tell us that Christ, after his resurrection, became Lord of the dead and living; that he had all power given him in heaven and earth; that angels were made subject to him; that he is hereafter to raise the dead and judge the world, and finish the scheme of the divine moral government with respect to the earth, by conferring eternal happiness on all the virtuous, and punishing the wicked with everlasting destruction. Can it be believed that a mere man could be advanced at once so high as to be above angels, and to be qualified to rule and judge the world? Do not all things rise gradually, one acquisition laying the foundation for another, and perhaps for higher acquisitions? The power, in particular, which the scriptures teach us Christ possesses, of raising to life all who have died, and all who will die, is equivalent to the power of creating a world. How inconsistent is it to allow that he is to restore and renew this world, and yet to deny he might have been God's agent in originally forming it!

This plan coincides with the foregoing Unitarian system, in rejecting the trinity of the Godhead; the real divinity of Christ; his being a proper object of prayer; the imputation of Adam's sin to his posterity; and such a total corruption of our nature by original sin, as deprives us of free-will, and subjects us, before we have committed actual sin, to the displeasure of God and future punishment; and also in rejecting absolute predestination, particular redemption, invincible grace, and justification by faith alone. It differs from the foregoing in two respects:—(1.) In asserting Christ to have been more than any human being.—(2) In asserting that he took upon him human nature for a higher purpose than merely revealing to mankind the will of God, and instructing them in their duty, and in the doctrines of religion.*

The celebrated Dr. Priestley calls those *Philosophical Unitarians,* who, in the early ages of christianity, explained the doctrines concerning Christ according to the principles of the philosophy of those times. As the sun was supposed to emit rays and draw them into himself again, so the divine Being, of whom they imagined the sun to be an image, was supposed to emit a kind of efflux, or divine ray, to which they sometimes gave the name of *logos,* which might be attached to any particular substance or person, and then be drawn into the divine Being again. They supposed that the union between this divine *logos* and the man Christ Jesus was only temporary: for they held that this divine efflux, which, like a beam of light from the sun, went out of God, and was attached to the person of Christ, to enable him to work miracles while he was on earth, was drawn into God again when he ascended into heaven, and had no more occasion to exert a miraculous power. Some of them might go so far as to say, that since this ray was properly divine, and the divinity of the Father, Christ, who had this divine ray within him, might be called God, but not as a distinct person from the Father. They are, moreover, charged with saying, that the Father, being in Christ, suffered and died in him also; and from this they got the name of *Patripassians,* which denomination has been also applied to the *Sabellians, Monarchians,* and others; which see.†

UNITAS FRATRUM, i. e. the Unity of the Brethren; or FRATRES UNITATIS, the United Brethren, is the denomination of a society of christians, usually called *Moravians,* because they first arose as a distinct church in Moravia; and sometimes *Hernhutters,* from one of their first settlements in Hernhutt.

In their history, as given by Crantz, their historian, they are distinguished into ancient and modern. The former refers to them before their settlement in Upper Lusatia in 1772; the latter after it.

In an address on their behalf to the English privy council in 1715, they are called *The reformed episcopal churches, first settled in Bohemia, and since forced by the persecutions of their enemies to retire into the Greater Poland, and Polish Prussia.* In an address also from themselves to the church of England, in the time of Charles II. they claim to have

* Price's Sermons, p. 153—192. Price's Dissertations, p. 134.

† Priestley's History of Early Opinions, vol. iii. p. 376. vol. iv. p. 279. Priestley's Eccles. Hist. vol. i. p. 296, 297.

been "free for almost 700 years from the encroachments of the Romish see;" and speak of *Huss*, and *Jerome* of Prague, as their famous martyrs, by whose blood the church of Bohemia had been watered and enriched. By the Bohemian church, however, can only be meant the christians, who resided in that country; for Mr. Crantz places the beginning of the church of *The United Brethren* in the year 1457, and represents it as rising out of the scattered remains of the followers of Huss. "This people, in order to free themselves from the tyranny of Rome, had applied in 1450 for a re-union with the Greek church, of which they had been anciently a part, and their request was cheerfully granted; but on the taking of Constantinople by the Turks, about two years after, which put an end to the Greek empire, this proposed junction came to nothing. After this they resolved to establish a community among themselves, and to edify one another from the word of God. But as this would expose them in their own country to persecution, they obtained permission to withdraw to a part of the king's domain, on the boundary between Silesia and Moravia, to settle there, and regulate their worship according to their own conscience and judgment.

"In the year 1457, they assumed the above denomination of United Brethren, and bound themselves to a stricter church discipline, resolving to suffer all things for conscience's sake; and instead of defending themselves, as some had done, by force of arms, to oppose nothing but prayer and reasonable remonstrances to the rage of their enemies.

"From this period to the reformation they were severely persecuted, but still preserved their unity. A connexion was also formed between them and the Waldenses, who had for many centuries borne witness to the truth. They had several conferences with Luther, Calvin, and other reformers, and some attempts were made for an union. They approved of the Augsburg confession; but not agreeing in discipline, they still continued a distinct body.

"After various persecutions, distresses, and discouragements during the seventeenth century, they became in a manner extinct: but about the year 1720, a remarkable awakening took place among the posterity of the Brethren in Bohemia; and as no free toleration could be obtained for them in that country, they agreed to emigrate. Christian David, who had been very useful amongst them, applied on their behalf to Nicholas Lewis, Count Zinzendorf, who granted them permission to settle on his estates in Upper Lusatia. Thither, in 1722, a company of them repaired, and formed the settlement of *Hernhutt*. Within the first four or five years they had well nigh been broken up by religious dissensions, occasioned (it is said) by parties from among the Lutherans and the Reformed coming to settle with them. At length, by the exertions of Count Zinzendorf, the Unity was renewed, and in 1727 rules agreed to, by which divisions might in future be avoided. The Count, who from the first was friendly, now became united to them, and, in 1735, was chosen to be their bishop; having been the preceding year received into clerical orders by the Theological Faculty of Nubingen.

With respect to their *doctrinal* sentiments, they, as before observed, avow the Augsburg confession; and, in 1784, they published an Exposition of Christian doctrine in harmony with it. In a summary of the doctrine of Jesus Christ, published in 1797 for the instruction of their youth, they say nothing on the trinity, but merely quote passages of scripture which relate to it. Under the article of the Holy Spirit, however, they say, "He is very God with the Father and the Son." They appear to avoid the doctrine of unconditional election, and believe that "Jesus Christ died for all men, and hath purchased salvation for all."* Yet they say, "We do not become holy by our own power; but it is a work of the Father, Son, and Holy Spirit." There is no doctrine on which they seem to dwell with such delight, as that of the cross, or the love of Christ in laying down his life for sinners. This, they say, has been the preaching which the Lord hath mostly blessed to the conversion of the heathen.

The church of the United Brethren is *episcopal;* and the order of succession in their bishops, is traced with great exactness in their history: yet they allow to them no elevation of rank, or pre-eminent authority; their church having from its first establishment been governed by synods, consisting of deputies from all the congregations, and by other subordinate bodies, which they call *conferences*. The synods, which are generally held once in seven years, are called together by the elders, who were in the former synod appointed to superintend the whole Unity. In the first sitting, a president is chosen, and these elders lay down their office, but they do not withdraw from the assembly; for they, together with the bishops, lay elders, and those ministers who have the general care or inspection of several congregations in one province, have seats allowed in the synod. The other members are one or more deputies sent by each congregation, and such ministers or missionaries as are particularly called to attend. Women, approved by the congregations,

* Crantz's History of the Brethren, section 82.

are also admitted as hearers, and are called upon to give their advice in what relates to the ministerial labour among their own sex; but they have no vote in the synod.

In questions of importance, or of which the consequences cannot be foreseen, neither the majority of votes, nor the unanimous consent of all present can decide; but recourse is had to the *lot*. For this practice the brethren allege the examples of the ancient Jews, and of the apostles, (Acts i. 26.) the insufficiency of the human understanding, amidst the best and purest intentions, to decide for itself in what concerns the administration of Christ's kingdom; and their own confident reliance on the promise of the Lord Jesus, that he will approve himself the head and ruler of his church. The lot is never made use of, but after mature deliberation and fervent prayer; nor is any thing submitted to its decision which does not, after being thoroughly weighed, appear to the assembly eligible in itself.

In every synod, the inward and outward state of the Unity, and the concerns of the congregations and missions, are taken into consideration. If errors in doctrine, or deviations in practice have crept in, the synod endeavours to remove them, and by salutary regulations to prevent them for the future. It considers how many bishops are to be consecrated to fill up the vacancies occasioned by death; and every member of the synod gives a vote for such of the clergy as he thinks best qualified. Those who have the majority of votes are taken into the *lot*, and they who are approved are consecrated accordingly.

Towards the close of every synod a kind of executive board is chosen and called, "The Elders' Conference of the Unity," divided into committees or departments—(1.) The *missions'* department, which superintends all the concerns of the missions into heathen countries. —(2.) The *helpers'* department, which watches over the purity of doctrine, and the moral conduct of the different congregations.—(3.) The *servants'* department, to which the economical concerns of the Unity are committed.—(4.) The *overseers'* department, of which the business is to see that the constitution and discipline of the Brethren be every where maintained. No resolution, however, of any of these departments, has the smallest force, till it be laid before the assembly of the Elders' Conference, and have the approbation of that body.

Besides this general Conference of Elders, there is a Conference of Elders belonging to each congregation, which directs its affairs, and to which the bishops and all other ministers, as well as the lay members of the congregation, are subject. This body, which is called, "The Elders' Conference of the Congregation," consists,—(1.) Of the *minister*, as president, to whom the ordinary care of the congregation is committed—(2.) The *warden*, whose office it is to superintend all outward concerns of the congregation.—(3.) A *married* pair, who care particularly for the spiritual welfare of the married people.—(4) A *single* clergyman, to whose care the young men are more particularly committed.—And, (5.) Those *women* who assist in caring for the spiritual and temporal welfare of their own sex, and who in this conference have equal votes.

Episcopal consecration does not, in the opinion of the Brethren, confer any power to preside over one or more congregations; and a bishop can discharge no office but by the appointment of a synod, or of the Elders' Conference of the Unity. Presbyters amongst them can perform every function of the bishop, except ordination. Deacons are assistants to the presbyters, much in the same way as in the church of England; and deaconesses are retained for the purpose of privately admonishing their own sex, and visiting them in their sickness: but though they are solemnly blessed to this office, they are not permitted to teach in public, and far less to administer the ordinances. They have likewise *seniores civiles*, or lay elders, in contradistinction to spiritual elders, or bishops, who are appointed to watch over the constitution and discipline of the United Brethren; over the observance of the laws of the country in which congregations or missions are established, and over the privileges granted to the Brethren by the governments under which they live.

They have economies, or char-houses, where they live together in communities: the single men and single women, widows and widowers apart, each under the superintendance of elderly persons of their own class. In these houses every person who is able, and has not an independent support, labours in his or her own occupation, and contributes a stipulated sum for their maintenance. Their children are educated with peculiar care. In marriage they may only form a connexion with those of their own communion: the brother, who marries out of the congregation, is immediately dismissed from church-fellowship. Sometimes, however, a sister is by express license from the Elders' Conference permitted to marry a person of approved piety in another communion, yet still to join in their church ordinances as before. As all intercourse between the different sexes is carefully avoided, very few opportunities of forming particular attachments are found; and they usually refer their choice to the church rather than decide for themselves. And as the *lot* must be cast to sanction their union, each receives his partner as a divine appointment. They do not consider a literary course of education as at all necessary to the ministry, provided there be a thorough knowledge of the word of God, a solid christian experience, and a well regulated zeal to serve God and their neighbours. They consider the church of Christ as not confined to any particular denomination: and themselves, though united in one body or visible church, as spiritually joined in the bond of christian love to all who are taught of God, and belong to the universal church of Christ, however much they may differ in forms, which they deem not essentials.

Their public worship is very simple; their singing, accompanied by an organ, played very soft and solemn. On a Sunday morning they read a liturgy of their own church, after which a sermon is preached, and an exhortation given to the children. In the afternoon they have private meetings, and public worship in the evening. Previous to the sacrament, which is administered once a month, and on Maunday Thursday, every person intending to communicate, converses with one of the elders on the state of his soul. The celebration of the communion is preceded by a love-feast; and on Maunday Thursday by a solemn washing of each other's feet, after which the kiss of charity is bestowed. All the above-named ceremonies they consider as obligatory, and authorized in all ages of the church; quoting John xiii. 14. Romans xvi. 16. On Easter-Sunday they attend the chapel, or in some places the burial ground, where they read a peculiar liturgy, and call over the names of all their members, who died in the preceding year. And every morning in Easter-week they meet at seven o'clock to read the harmonies of the Gospel on the crucifixion, &c.

But the most distinguishing feature of this denomination is their earnest and unremitted labour in attempting to convert the heathen. They seem to have considered themselves within this last century as a church of missionaries. And though other denominations have of late emulated their zeal, yet they are said to be far behind them.* By the most indefatigable labour and sufferings they have sent the gospel to the four quarters of the earth.† For an account of

* Crantz's History of the United Brethren. Summary of the Doctrine of Jesus Christ. Haweis' Church Hist. vol. iii.

† The Moravians have missionaries established in the Danish West-India islands. Two Moravian missionaries formed the project; and were exceedingly desirous of selling themselves as slaves, that they might have an opportunity of preaching Christ to the negro slaves at St. Thomas'. They suppos-

their numerous missionary settlements, see *Appendix*.

UNIVERSALISTS. The sentiment which has procured its professors this appellation was embraced by Origen in the third century, and in more modern times by Chevalier Ramsay, Mr. Jer. White, Dr. Cheyne, Dr. Hartley, Dr. Newton, bishop of Bristol, and many others. The plan of Universal salvation, as exhibited by a late, learned divine (Dr. Chauncy of Boston, in America,) who, in his work entitled, "*The Salvation of all men,*" has made several additions to the sentiments of the above-mentioned authors, is as follows:

That the scheme of revelation has the happiness of all mankind lying at bottom, as its great and ultimate end; that it gradually tends to this end, and will not fail of its accomplishment when fully completed. Some in consequence of its operation, as conducted by the Son of God, will be disposed and enabled in this present state to make such improvements in virtue, the only rational preparative for happiness, as that they shall enter upon the enjoyment of it in the next state. Others who have proved incurable under the means, which have been used with them in this state, instead of being happy in the next, will be awfully miserable; not to continue so finally, but that they may be convinced of their folly, and recovered to a virtuous frame of mind: and this will be the effect of the future torments upon many, the consequence whereof will be their salvation, after being thus fitted for it. And there may be yet other states, before the scheme of God may be perfected, and mankind universally cured of their moral disorders; and in this way qualified for, and finally instated in, eternal happiness. But however many states some individuals of the human species may pass through, and of however long continuance they may be, the whole is intended to subserve the grand design of universal happiness, and will finally terminate in it; insomuch, that the Son of God, and Saviour of men, will not deliver up his trust into the hands of the Father, who committed it to him, till he has discharg-

ed, that a teacher, by becoming himself a slave, might be always among them, and hence able to instruct them, without interruption Upon being informed, that no white persons could, according to law, be admitted as slaves, they purposed to work at a trade for a livelihood, and arrived at St. Thomas', December 13, 1732. Their sufferings, in the beginning of the mission, were exceedingly great, but at length their labours were crowned with abundant success. To use the words of one of the Moravian society—"Many thousands are now gathered around the throne of the Lamb from that quarter, and about ten thousand, in our connexion, are at present belonging to his church here on earth." See Baptist Annual Register.

ed his obligations in virtue of it; having finally fixed all men in heaven, when God will be *all in all.* 1 Cor. xv. 28.

A few of the arguments made use of, in defence of this system, are as follow:*

I. Christ died not for a select number of men only, but for mankind *universally,* and without exception or limitation.

For the sacred writers are singularly emphatical in expressing this truth. They speak not only of Christ's "*dying for us,*" "*for our sins,*" "*for sinners,*" "*for the ungodly,*" "*for the unjust;*" but affirm, in yet more extensive terms, that "*he died for the world,*" for "*the whole world.*" See 1 Thess. v. 10. 1 Cor. xv. 3. Rom. v. 6, 8. 1 Pet. iii. 18. John i. 29; iii. 16, 17. 1 John ii. 2. Heb. ii. 9; and a variety of other passages.

If Christ died for all, it is far more reasonable to believe, that the whole human kind, in consequence of his death, will finally be saved, than that the greatest part of them should perish. More honour is hereby reflected on God; greater virtue is attributed to the blood of Christ shed on the cross; and instead of dying in vain, as to any real good, which will finally be the event, with respect to the greatest part of mankind, he will be made to die to the best and noblest purpose, even the eternal happiness of a whole world of intelligent and moral beings.

II. It is the purpose of God, according to his good pleasure, that mankind *universally,* in consequence of the death of his Son Jesus Christ, shall certainly and finally be saved.

The texts, which ascertain this, are those, which follow: First, Rom. v. 12, to the end. There Adam is considered as the source of damage to mankind universally; and Christ, on the other hand, as a like source of advantage to the same mankind; but with this observable difference, that the advantage on the side of Christ exceeds, overflows, abounds, beyond the damage on the side of Adam; and this to all mankind. The 15th, 16th, and 17th verses, are absolutely unintelligible upon any other interpretation.

Another text, to the purpose of our present argument, we meet with in Rom. viii. from the 19th to the 24th verse. On the one hand, it is affirmed of the creature, that is, of mankind in general, that they are subjected to vanity, that is, the imperfections and infelicities of a vain, mortal life, here on earth. On the other hand, it is positively affirmed of the creature, or mankind in gener-

* The learned author of the performance, whence these arguments are extracted, has illustrated the passages of scripture quoted, by critical notes on the original language, and by showing their analogy to other passages in the inspired writings. Those, who would form a just idea of the arguments, must consult the work itself.

al, that they were not subjected to this vanity, finally and forever, but in consequence of hope; not only that they should be delivered from this unhappy subjection, but instated in immortal glory.

Another text to this purpose occurs in Col. i. 19, 20. *For it pleased the Father, that in him should all fulness dwell; "and (having made peace through the blood of his cross) by him to reconcile all things unto himself; &c.* And in this Epistle, chapter ii. verse 9, the apostle (speaking of Christ) says, *In him dwelleth all the fulness of the Godhead bodily;* that is, he is the glorious person, in whom God has really lodged, and through whom he will actually communicate all the fulness, wherewith he intends this lapsed world shall be filled in order to its restoration. And Christ, having this fulness lodged in him, *ascended up far above all heavens, that he might fill all things.* Eph. iv. 10. And as the filling all things in this lapsed world, that they might be restored, was the final cause of the ascension of Christ up to heaven, all things must accordingly be filled in fact by him, sooner or later; the apostle therefore observes in the following verses, not only that he has imparted gifts in prosecution of the end of his exaltation, but that in order to the full accomplishment of it, he would go on to impart them, *until we all come to the unity of the faith, unto a perfect man, unto the measure of the stature of the fulness of Christ.* And it is declared in Ephes. i. 9, 10, that all things in heaven and earth shall be reduced from the state they were in, by means of the lapse, into a well subjected and subordinate whole by Christ. Another proof of the present proposition we find in 1 Tim. ii. 4. If God is able in consistency with men's make, as moral and intelligent agents, to effect their salvation, his desiring that they should be saved, and his eventually saving them, are convertible terms.

III. As a mean in order to men's being made meet for salvation, God will sooner or later, in this state or another, reduce them all under a willing and obedient subjection to his moral government.

The texts which confirm this proposition are numerous. The apostle says in 1 John iii. 8. *For this purpose the Son of God was manifested, that he might destroy the works of the devil.* Parallel to this passage, see John i. 29, Matt. i. 21, and Psa. viii. 5, 6, as explained and argued from Heb. ii. 6, 9. These words are applicable to Christ, in their strict and full sense. And if *all things,* without any limitation or exception, shall be brought under subjection to Christ, then the time must come, sooner or later, in this state or some other, when there shall be no rebels among the sons of Adam, no enemies against the moral government of God: for there is no way of reducing rebels, so as to destroy their character as such, but by making them willing and obedient subjects. That this scripture is thus to be understood is evident by a parallel passage in Phil. ii. 9—11. The next portion of scripture, in proof of the present proposition, we meet with in 1 Cor. chap. xv. from the 24th to the end of the 28th verse. Though the apostle, in this paragraph, turns our view to the end of the mediatory scheme, it is affirmed, that universal subjection to Christ shall first be effected, in a variety of as strong and extensive terms, as could well have been used: as, by "*putting down all rule, and all authority and power;*" by "*putting all enemies under his feet,*" &c. It is worthy of special notice, that, before Christ's delivery of the mediatorial kingdom to the Father, *the last enemy must be destroyed, which is death*—the *second death*—which those, who die wicked men, must suffer, before they can be reduced under willing subjection to Jesus Christ. For the *first death* cannot be called the *last enemy* with propriety and truth, because the *second death* is posterior to it, and has no existence till that has been so far destroyed, as to allow of a restoration to life.

The two periods, when the mediatory kingdom is in the hands of Jesus Christ, and when God, as king, will be immediately *all in all*, are certainly quite distinct from each other: and the reign of Christ, in his mediatorial kingdom, may be divided into two general periods. The one takes in this present state of existence, in which Christ reigns at the head of God's kingdom of grace. During this period a number of the sons of Adam will be fitted for a glorious immortality in the next state. The other period of Christ's reign is that which intervenes between the general resurrection and judgment, and the time when God shall be *all in all*. This state may contain a duration of so long continuance, as to answer to the scripture phrase, εις τους αἰῶνας των αἰώνων, *forever and ever*, or as it might more properly be rendered *for ages of ages*. During the whole of this state the righteous shall be happy, and the wicked, who are most obdurate, miserable, till they are reduced, as willing and obedient servants to Christ, which when accomplished, the grand period shall commence, when God shall be himself immediately *all in all*.*

IV. The scripture language concerning the reduced or restored in consequence of the mediatory interposition of Jesus Christ is such as leads us to conclude, that it is comprehensive of mankind universally. See Rev. v. 13. *And every crea-*

* Chauncy's Salvation of all men, p 12, 13, 20, 22, 81, 117, 123, &c.

ture which is in heaven, and on the earth, and under the earth, and such as are in the sea, and all that are in them, heard I, saying, blessing, and honour, and glory, and power, be unto him that sitteth upon the throne, and unto the lamb forever and ever.

This title also distinguishes those who embrace the sentiments of Mr. Relly, a modern preacher of *universal salvation* in England, and Mr. Murray in this country. See *Rellyans.*

This denomination build their scheme upon the following foundation; viz.—That Christ, as Mediator, was so united to mankind, that his actions were theirs, his obedience and sufferings theirs; and consequently he has as fully restored the whole human race to the divine favour, as if all had obeyed and suffered in their own persons. The divine law now has no demands upon them, nor condemning power over them. Their salvation solely depends upon their union with Christ, which God constituted and established before the world began; and by virtue of this union they will all be admitted to heaven at the last day.

They allege that the union of Christ and his church is a necessary consideration for the right explanation of the following passages of scripture; Eph. v. 30. 1 Cor. xii. 26; xii. 12. See also Col. i. 18. Ephes. i. 22, 23. Col. ii. 10. Rom. xii. 5. Heb. ii. 11. John xvii. 22, 23.

The scriptures affirm, that *by the offence of one, judgment came upon all men unto condemnation.* Rom. v. 8; iii. 25. It is evident hence, that in Adam's offence all have offended; which supposes such a union between Adam and his offspring, that his sin was their sin, and his ruin their ruin: and if this be granted, why should it be thought a thing incredible, that the like union, subsisting between Jesus and his seed, should render his condition theirs? especially as the apostle has stated the matter thus: Rom. v. 19.

To prove that the atonement was satisfactory for the whole human race, they allege that it is said, "Christ died for all;" that "he is the propitiation for our sins, and not for ours only, but for the sins of the whole world."

This denomination admit of no punishment for sin but what Christ suffered; but speak of a punishment, which is consequent upon sin, as darkness, distress, and misery, which they assert are ever attendant upon transgression. But, as *to know the true God and Jesus Christ is life eternal,* and as *all shall know him from the least to the greatest,* that knowledge, or belief, will consequently dispel or save from all the darkness, distress and fear, which is attendant upon guilt and unbelief; and being perfectly holy, we shall consequently be perfectly and eternally happy.

As the reader has been presented with a brief account of the arguments in favour of universal salvation, it is proper to give a sketch of the evidence brought on the opposite side of the question.

A few of the arguments alleged to support the eternity of future punishment are as follow:

The sacred scriptures expressly declare that the punishment of the finally impenitent shall be eternal. Matt. xxv. 46. *And these shall go away into everlasting punishment*, &c. See also Mark ix. 45, 46. Matt. xviii. 8, 9. 2 Thes. i. 9. 2 Pet. ii. 17. Jude 13. Rev. xiv. 11; xix. 3; xx. 10.

The texts concerning the sin against the Holy Spirit in particular, are a clear proof of endless punishment. *It shall not be forgiven him, neither in this world, nor in the world to come.* Matt. xii. 31, 32. See also Mark iii. 28, 29. Luke xii. 10. So long as the gospel rejects every idea of the salvation of men without forgiveness, so long will those texts confute the salvation of all men. The apostle says, 1 John v. 16, "If any man see his brother sin a sin which is not unto death, he shall ask, and he shall give him life for them that sin not unto death. There is a sin unto death: I do not say that he shall pray for it." It is evident the reason, why we are not to pray for those who sin unto death, is, because their salvation is impossible. It is said in Heb. vi. 4—6, "It is impossible for those who were once enlightened, and have tasted of the heavenly gift, &c. if they should fall away, to renew them again to repentance:" now since it is impossible to renew them to repentance, it is impossible that they can be saved. Of like import is chap. x. 26, 27.—The woe denounced by Christ on Judas also seems to afford a demonstrative proof of endless punishment: "Woe to that man by whom the Son of Man is betrayed; good were it for that man if he had never been born." Matt. xxvi. 24. Mark xiv. 21. But if Judas were finally to enjoy endless happiness, he would be an infinite gainer by his existence, let the duration of his previous misery be what it might. It was, therefore, on the supposition of his final salvation, not only good, but infinitely good, that he had been born; which is a direct contradiction to the declaration of our Saviour.

All the texts which declare that those who die impenitent shall perish, be cast away, rejected, &c. disprove universal salvation: as, 1 Cor. i. 18. 2 Pet. ii. 12, &c. With what truth or propriety can those be said to *perish*, be *cast away*, be *rejected*, *destroyed*, and *lost*, who shall finally be saved? So it is said in Heb. vi. 8, "That which beareth thorns and briers is rejected, and is nigh unto cursing, whose *end* is to be burned." How is it the end of any man to be burned, if all shall finally be saved? The figurative descriptions of the punishment of the wicked are strong, emphatical, and decisive of it, as hopeless of restitution, and of endless duration. It is set forth by *devouring fire*, by *eternal fire, everlasting burnings;* and, if possible, more strongly, by *the worm that dieth not, and the fire that is not quenched:* this must mean a punishment which hath not, and never shall have, an end. The scripture represents, that at the end of the world all things are brought to an end. 1 Pet. iv. 7. Then shall there be a fixed, unalterable state; and after that there can be no passing from hell to heaven. Rev. xxii. 11, 12. The last words determine this text to refer to the general judgment; for a period of ages of ages after the general judgment cannot be said to come quickly, and to be at hand. The representation in the parables of our Lord is, that after the general judgment the tares and chaff shall no more be mixed with the wheat, nor the good with the bad. Besides, the judgment is said to be *eternal* (αιωνιου;*) doubtless with respect to its endless and unchangeable consequences. But if the judgment be eternal with respect to its consequences, the punishment of the damned will be without end. The peculiar epithets and emphasis put upon the future judgment indicate it final. It is frequently styled the *last day;* and the great works appropriated to it are, the universal resurrection, and the general judgment and decision of the states of the whole moral world.—That the wicked will never be released from punishment, and pass from hell into the abodes of the blessed, is expressly asserted by our Saviour, Luke xvi. 26. All the texts which speak of the divine *vengeance, fury, wrath, indignation, fiery indignation,* &c. hold forth some other punishment than that which is merely disciplinary. See Deut. xxxii. 41. Rom. iii. 5, 6; ix. 22. 2 Thes. i. 8, &c. Besides the arguments drawn directly from texts of scripture, there is one from the general nature of the gospel. Those who die impenitent deserve an endless punishment: for if endless punishment be not the penalty threatened in the law, no account can be given of the penalty of the law. It cannot be the temporary punishment actually suffered by the damned, because then they would be finally saved without forgiveness. It cannot be a temporary punishment of less duration than that which is suffered by the damned, be-

* Dr Edwards, and the other advocates for the eternity of future punishment, assert that the Greek words αιων and αιώνιος strictly imply an endless duration. On the other hand, Dr. Chauncy has taken great pains to show that they mean a limited duration.

cause on that supposition they are punished more than they deserve. It cannot be a temporary punishment of longer duration than that which the scriptures abundantly declare the damned shall suffer, because no such punishment is threatened in the law or in any part of scripture: it must therefore be an endless punishment. The doctrine of the perpetuity of future punishment is also confirmed by the constitution of nature, which connects sin and misery together, and will finally make the wicked necessarily miserable as long as they have existence; unless this constitution be annihilated, or superseded by the grace of God, which he assures us never shall be the case.*

A new scheme of universal salvation has been advanced by the late Dr. Joseph Huntington, of America, in a posthumous work, entitled, "Calvinism Improved; or, The Gospel Illustrated as a System of Real Grace, issuing in the Salvation of all Men." The author of this performance supposes the atonement to be "a direct, true, and proper setting all our guilt to the account of Christ, as our federal head and sponsor; and alike placing his obedience to death to our account." "The Son of Man," says he, "is God's only object, as an elect head, in regard to our eternal salvation; and all human nature is one entire, elect object, in union with Christ, as a body with a head." Agreeably to this idea, Dr. Huntington maintains, that our sins are transferred to Christ, and his righteousness to us; that *he was a true and proper substitute for all mankind*, and has procured *unconditional, eternal salvation, for every individual;* that the gospel is all mere *news, good news*, and hath no threatenings in it: that law and gospel are diametrically opposite; that these two dispensations of God oppose each other from beginning to end. "The moral law," says he "every where speaks to man in his own personal character, the gospel in that of the Messiah. The law informs us what man in justice deserves, the gospel what the Son of God deserves." Accordingly Dr. Huntington understands all the threatenings in the word of God as the pure voice of law and justice. Thus he explains Matt. xxv. 46: "Mankind in this passage are considered in two characters: in their own personally; and then the voice of the righteous law is, *These shall go away into everlasting punishment; but* [in Christ] *the righteous* [by union of faith] *shall enter into life eternal.* The wicked character shall remain an everlasting object of shame, contempt, and condemnation, in the view of God and holy intelligences; the right-

* Edwards against Chauncy, p. 53—293. Johnson on everlasting punishment, p. 59—67.

eous character an eternal object of approbation, worthy of life eternal."

This author declares, that the whole tenor of divine revelation ascertains the salvation of all men. In support of this assertion he adduces various texts of scripture. But, as many of his general arguments in favour of universal salvation have been exhibited in the foregoing articles, our curious readers are referred to his posthumous publication;* especially as this does not appear to be so properly a new scheme, as a revival of Mr. Relly's, above-recited.

An answer to Dr. Huntington's "Calvinism Improved" has been published by the late Dr. Nathan Strong, minister of Hartford in Connecticut. In this work he endeavours to reconcile the doctrine of *eternal misery* with the *infinite benevolence of God.* Dr. Strong observes, that those who believe in eternal punishment, found their belief in consistence with the infinite benevolence of the Godhead. They suppose that benevolence is the sum of all his glorious perfections; that it is a comprehensive name for his whole moral rectitude; that there is no separation to be made between punitive justice and benevolence; that it is benevolence which moves him to punish both now and eternally; and that if he did not punish, he would not be an infinitely benevolent God. He states benevolence to be—(1.) A love of the greatest quantity of happiness.—(2.) That it is consistent with the existence of misery.—(3.) That it has regard to the greatest quantity of happiness in *society*, and not to the happiness of every individual. "Benevolence thus defined (says he) is that goodness, or holiness, which directs the supreme God in creating, governing, and rewarding. The good of the *whole*, or the greatest happiness of intellectual being, is the object of benevolence. We may be assured that the infinitely benevolent, all-wise, and all-powerful God, will eternally execute such a government as will produce the greatest possible portion of happiness in the universe.

In order to confute Dr. Huntington's plan of *universal* salvation, Dr. Strong attempts to prove—(1.) That the gospel contains threatenings of death, and impenitent sinners will be as much condemned by the gospel, as by the law.—(2.) That there is in no sense a contradiction, or opposition, between the law and the gospel. "Neither the law nor the gospel gives life or death independent of the moral temper and actions of men. The law itself hath the same power to give life as to give death. To the obedient and holy the law gives life. It gave life to Adam so long as he was a holy being,

* Huntington's Calvinism improved, p. 26—165.

and it now gives life to all those beings who have not sinned. To the disobedient, by means of their sin, it gives death; and as all men have become disobedient, they are under a sentence of condemnation. (See Rom. vii.) So it is with the gospel: there are conditions on which life is offered, "repentance towards God, and faith in our Lord Jesus Christ; and if there be not a compliance with these conditions, the gospel becomes a dispensation of death to sinners, as much as the law is; yea, of a much more awful death than the law threatened."

Dr. Strong next attempts to prove that Dr. Huntington's notions of the atonement of Christ are unscriptural and absurd. His own ideas on that subject are as follow:

"Christ, according to the will of the Father, and with his own choice, hath by obedience and sufferings made a display of certain moral truths, which the eternal misery of those, who were forgiven, was necessary for displaying; so that their misery is not now necessary for the good government of the universe. The reason that their eternal suffering was fit under the law was to make this display, the necessity of which hath now ceased, if God will be pleased to sanctify and forgive through Christ; but if he be not pleased to sanctify them through Christ, the necessity doth not cease. The meritorious cause on which he forgives, is the atoning sufferings of his Son. The moving cause in his own mind to provide the gospel-atonement, and pardon the sinner on account of it, was his own goodness and the general good.

"The atoning sufferings of Christ were necessary on the gospel scheme, for the same reason as the eternal misery of the sinner was under the law; viz. to make a display of God's moral character—of his righteousness, as King of the universe—of his sense of the turpitude of the sinner's principles and practice; and also the nature of benevolence in its high and infinite source, Godhead himself."*

The name of Hypothetical Universalists was given to those of the reformed church in France, who in the seventeenth century attempted to reconcile the doctrine of predestination, as it had been taught at Geneva, and confirmed at Dort, with the sentiments of those who represent the Deity as offering the display of his goodness and mercy to all mankind. Moses Amyrault, a man of distinguished ability and learning, who was professor of divinity in the university of Saumur, in 1634 exerted all his energy, in this attempt of reconciling

* Strong's Benevolence and Misery, p 152—266. Winchester's Universal Salvation. See also Fuller's Letters to Vidler.—Vidler's Letters to Fuller—and a Review of both in Scrutator's Letters, by Mr. Jerram.

the Calvinists and Arminians; and his writings made no small change in the doctrines commonly received among the reformed in France.

The doctrine of Amyrault may be summed up in the following propositions: "That God desires the happiness of all men, and that no mortal is excluded, by any divine decree, from the benefits that are procured by the death, suffering, and gospel of Christ: That, however, no one can be made a partaker of the blessings of the gospel, nor of the eternal salvation, unless he believe in Jesus Christ: That God refuses to none the power of believing, though he does not grant to all his assistance that they may improve this power to the attainment of everlasting salvation:—And, that many perish, through their own fault, and not from any want of goodness in God." See *Cameronians*.

The mitigated view of the doctrine of predestination was advocated by many of the reformed church in France. Those who embraced this doctrine were called Universalists, because they represented God as willing to show mercy to all mankind; and Hypothetical Universalists, because the condition of faith in Christ was necessary to render them the objects of this mercy.*

W

WAHABEES or WAHABITES, a sect of religionists founded by Abdoulwehhab, about a century ago. He received an orthodox education at Medina, but early formed the design of reforming the Mahometan religion. As his scheme of reform was not likely to gain ground in Mecca or Medina, where interest furnished obvious motives for maintaining the ancient rites and customs, he began his career among the wandering Bedouin Arabs of the Desert. The sword was the weapon he made use of to promulgate his religion.

With regard to the religious tenets of this sect, their founder, while acknowledging fully the authority of the Koran, professed obedience only to the literal text of this book; rejecting all additions of the Imans and doctors of law, and condemning various practices of the Mahometans, which he supposed had sullied the purity of the faith.

The period of the reform of Abdoulwehhab may be reckoned from 1747.

As his design was to receive only the texts of the Koran, he annulled many rites, and re-

* Mosheim, vol. v. p. 359. Willson on the atonement. p. 47.

nounced many opinions generally received by the Mahometans. For instance, every good mussulman believes, that after the death and burial of the prophet, his soul reunited itself to his body, and ascended to Paradise, mounted upon the mare of the angel Gabriel, named El Borak, the head and neck of which were of a fine form.

This event, indeed, is not an article of faith; but every mussulman, who did not believe it, would be looked upon as an infidel, and treated as such. Abdoulwehhab asserted, that the mortal remains of the prophet continued in the sepulchre the same as those of other men.

Among the mussulmans it is customary to inter those, who have obtained the reputation of being virtuous, or saints, in a private sepulchre, more or less ornamented after their death, and to build a chapel over it, where their protection is invoked for the supplicant, and God is supposed to befriend their intercession.

Already had the well-informed mussulmans begun to despise these superstitions secretly, though they seemed to respect them in the eyes of the people. But Abdoulwehhab declared boldly, that this species of worship rendered to the saints was a very grievous sin in the eyes of the Divinity, because it was giving him companions. In consequence of this his sectaries have destroyed the sepulchres, chapels, and temples, elevated to their honour.

In virtue of this principle Abdoulwehhab forbids veneration or devotion to the person of the prophet as a very great sin. This does not prevent him from acknowledging his mission; but he pretends he was no more than another man, before God made use of him to communicate his divine word to men, and, that when his mission was at an end, he became an ordinary man.

It is on this account that the reformer has forbidden his followers to visit the tomb of the prophet at Medina. When they speak of it, instead of making use of the form employed by other mussulmans, namely, "Our Lord Mahomet," or "Our Lord the Prophet of God," they only say Mahomet.

The grand doctrine of this sect is the *unity* of God. Their confession of faith is, "there is no other God than God; Mahomet is the Prophet of God." Their public criers made this profession of faith to be heard in all its extent, from the top of the minarets of Mecca, which they have not destroyed, as well as the temple, which was under their dominion. They call themselves mussulmans by way of eminence, and when they speak of Islamites, they understand only by that word the persons of their sect, which they look upon as the only orthodox. They esteem the Turks, and other Mahometans as schismatics; but they do not treat them as idolaters, or infidels.

Abdoulwehhab never offered himself as a prophet, as has been supposed. He only acted as a learned Sheik reformer, who was desirous of reducing the Mahometan religion to the primitive simplicity of the Koran.

The religious services of this sect are performed in the open sky, and not below the roofing of a mosque. They once gained possession of Mecca and Medina. The former was taken in 1802, the latter in 1804. After they had conquered Arabia, they became formidable neighbours to the Pacha of Egypt, who conducted the war against them with energy. By his strenuous exertions they were driven with loss from the Arabian coasts; Mecca, Medina, and Jedda were retaken and restored to the authority of the Porte and to the Mahometan worship. It does not, however, appear that this success is complete, or that its consequences will be permanent.*

WALDENSES, or VAUDOIS. The antiquity of this denomination can be traced back four hundred years before the time of Luther, and twenty before Peter Waldo. Many protestants suppose that Waldo derived his name from the Waldenses, whose doctrine he adopted, and who were known by the name of Waldenses, or Vaudois, before he or his immediate followers existed.

The learned Dr. Allix, in his history of the churches of Piedmont, gives this account: "That for three hundred years or more, the bishop of Rome attempted to reduce the church of Milan under his jurisdiction: and at last the interest of Rome grew too potent for the church of Milan, planted by one of the disciples; insomuch that the bishop and the people, rather than own their jurisdiction, retired to the vallies of Lucerne and Angrogne, and thence were called *Vallenses, Wallenses*, or *The People in the Valleys.*"† From a confession of their faith of nearly the above date, are extracted the following particulars.—(1.) That the scriptures teach that there is one God almighty, all-wise, and all-good, who made all things by his goodness; for he formed Adam in his own image and likeness: but that by the envy of the devil, sin entered into the world, and that we are sinners in and by Adam.—(2.) That Christ was promised to our fathers, who received the law; that so knowing by the law their unrighteousness and insufficiency, they might desire the coming of Christ, to satisfy for their sins, and accomplish

* Legh's Travels in Egypt, p. 45. Travels of Ali Bey, vol. ii. p. 44, 52, 118. Jackson's Journey from India, 1797. Dunbar's Essays.

† See Allix's History of the churches in Piedmont, and Perrin's History of the Waldenses.

the law by himself.—(3.) That Christ was born in the time appointed by God the Father; that is to say, in the time when all iniquity abounded, that he might show us grace and mercy as being faithful.—(4.) That Christ is our life, truth, peace, and righteousness; as also our pastor, advocate, and priest, who died for the salvation of all who believe, and is risen for our justification.—(5.) That there is no mediator and advocate with God the Father, save Jesus Christ.—(6.) That after this life there are only two places, the one for the saved, and the other for the damned. —(7.) That the feasts, the vigils of saints, the water which they call holy, as also to abstain from flesh on certain days, and the like, but especially the masses, are the inventions of men, and ought to be rejected. —(8.) That the sacraments are signs of the holy thing, visible forms of the invisible grace; and that it is good for the faithful to use those signs, or visible forms; but that they are not essential to salvation.—(9.) That there are no other sacraments but baptism and the Lord's supper.—(10.) That we ought to honour the secular powers by subjection, ready obedience, and paying of tribute.*

"The external history of the Waldenses," says Mr. Milner, "is little else than a series of persecution." In the thirteenth century, Pope Innocent III instituted a crusade against them, and they were pursued with unrelenting fury, and thousands were put to a cruel death. Their principles, however, continued unsubdued, and at the reformation their descendants were reckoned among the protestants, with whom they were in doctrine so congenial. But in the seventeenth century the flames of persecution were again rekindled by the cruelty of Louis XIV.

It affords much pleasure to hear from a clergyman of the church of England, who lately visited the Vales of Piedmont, that this people are by no means extinct, but preserve a pleasing vestige of their ancient piety and simplicity among all the calamities of the late war, and the miseries it has introduced.†

*WATERLANDIANS, a party of Mennonites, distinguished by their prudence and moderation, who, in their Confessions, adhered closely to the language of the scriptures; expressed their peculiarities with much caution and reserve, avoiding the language and conduct of the early Anabaptists.‡

*WELCH INDIANS, (or *Padoucas,*) a colony supposed to have emigrated from Wales in

* Perrin's History of the Waldenses, p. 226. Athenian Oracle, vol. i. p. 224. Milner's Church History, vol iii. ch. iv.

† Jones' Hist. of the Waldenses. Brief Memoir of the Waldenses, by a clergyman, 1815.

‡ Mosheim, vol. iv. p. 464. new ed.

the twelfth century, (three hundred years before Columbus,) under Prince Madoc; and whose descendants still reside on the borders of the Missouri far to the westward of the Missisippi.* Several accounts are to be found in Welch and other histories, and various letters have appeared at different times in the Gentleman's and Monthly Magazines. These accounts have been collected with additions and remarks, in three pamphlets, two by the late Dr. E. Williams, and one by the Rev. G. Burder, referred to below. They were much confirmed in conversations with Gen. Bowles, the Indian Chief, when in England; by Mr. Chesholm, from the Creek Indians, also in his visit to Philadelphia; and by Mr. Heckewelder, a Moravian gentleman at Bethlehem; an abstract of these and other accounts was printed in the Weekly Register, for December 26, 1798.

The substance of all the accounts is, that there is a nation of Indians of so much lighter complexion, as to indicate an European origin; that their language is Welch, at least radically so; that they have sacred books in that language, (which have been seen by native Britons,) though they have lost the art of reading; and that there are vestiges of the European arts among them, particularly remnants of earthen ware, &c. Several natives of Wales, and some descendants from that nation in America, have expressed a great desire to go in search of this very distant country, and to commence a mission among them, which indeed was the express object of Mr. Burder's pamphlet.†

*WESLEYANS, the followers of Messrs. John and Charles Wesley. See *Methodists*.

*WHITEFIELDITES, a term applied to those of the early Methodists who sided with Mr. Whitefield and the Calvinists. See *Methodists*.

WICKLIFFITES, a denomination which sprang up in England in the fourteenth century. They derived their name from John Wickliff, doctor and professor of divinity in the university of Oxford, a man of an enterprizing genius and extraordinary learning. He began with attacking the jurisdiction of the pope and the bishops, and declared that penance had no sort of merit in the sight of God, unless followed with a reformed life. He was a warm opposer of absolution; for he alleged that it belonged to God alone to forgive sins; but instead of acting as God's min-

* Mr. W. Owen fixes their situation between 37 and 43 degrees N. lat. and between 97 and 110 W. long. Gentleman's Magazine, 1791, vol. i p. 329.

† Burder's Welch Indians, 8vo. 1797. Dr. E. Williams' Enquiry into the truth of the discovery of America by Prince Madoc, and farther observations on ditto, 1792. Weekly Register, Nos. 4 and 38.

isters, the Romish clergy took upon them, he said, to forgive sins in their own name. He also taught that external confession was not necessary to salvation, exclaimed against indulgences, prayers to the saints, the celibacy of the clergy, the doctrine of transubstantiation, monastic vows, and other practices in the Roman Catholic church. He not only exhorted the laity to study the scriptures, but also translated them into English, in order to render the perusal of them more universal. The followers of Wickliff were also called *Lollards.**

WILHELMINIANS, in the thirteenth century, the disciples of Wilhelmina, a Bohemian woman who resided in the territory of Milan. She persuaded a large number that the Holy Ghost was become incarnate in her person for the salvation of a great part of mankind. According to her doctrine, none were saved by the blood of Jesus but true and pious christians; while the Jews, Saracens, and *un*worthy christians were to obtain salvation through the Holy Spirit which dwelt in her; and in consequence all which happened to Christ during his abode upon earth, was to be repeated in her person.†

WILKINSON, Jemima, an American female of some notoriety in the last century. It is said that she asserted, that in 1776, she was taken sick, and actually died, and her soul went to reside in heaven. Soon after, her body was re-animated with the spirit and power of Christ, upon which she set up as a public teacher; and declared she had an immediate revelation for all she delivered, and was arrived to a state of absolute perfection. It is also said she pretended to foretell future events, to discern the secrets of the heart, and to have the power of healing diseases; and if any persons, who had made application to her, were not healed, she attributed it to their want of faith. She acknowledged no other name but that of Universal Friend. She made some converts in New York,‡ and in Rhode Island; but chiefly in the Gennessee country.

An ingenious young gentleman, in his tour to the falls of Niagara, Montreal, and Quebec in 1812, was introduced to Jemima Wilkinson, and has given a very entertaining account of the interview. Among other things he says, "Her command of the contents of the bible, and her readiness in the use of scripture language was surprising." He supposed that "like most of the false pretenders to religious superiority, she made her claims to uncom-

* Mosheim, vol. iii. p. 166. Gilpin's Life of Wickliff, p. 67—73.

† Mosheim, vol iii. p. 131.

‡ The Duke de Rochefoucault, in his travels in America in 1796, met with Jemima Wilkinson in the state of New York, and describes her as a personable but artful woman.

mon inspiration with sincerity." He, however, describes her as an ambitious and selfish woman; whose mental powers were vigorous, who was acute and cunning, and must, he says, be skilled in human nature to have gained such an ascendency over so many minds. She amassed a large fortune by the donations of her followers, and lived in a luxurious and expensive manner."*

*WINCHESTERIANS, a name sometimes given to the admirers of Mr. Elhanan Winchester, who preached the doctrine of universal salvation both in England and America. See *Universalists.*

Y

*YOGEYS, (SANAISYS, or SUNASEES,) Hindoo Devotees, who practise a variety of self-tortures, and mortify the body in order to merit heavenly felicity, and obtain the immaterial nature of Brahma, the supreme. In the Mahabarat, a Yogey is thus defined: "The man who keepeth the outward accidents from entering the mind, and his eyes fixed in contemplation between his brows; who *maketh his breath pass equally through his nostrils;* . . . . . . keeping his head, his neck, and his body steady without motion, his eyes *fixed on the point of his nose,* looking at nothing else around," &c. he is a *Yogey*—and is forever blessed.

These Yogeys, as practices of self-devotion, cast themselves down on spikes stuck in bags of straw, walk on fire, pierce themselves with pins, and bore their tongues; but the most famous act of devotion is swinging by means of hooks drawn through their backs and sides, and fastened with ropes to trees, by which they will *spin* round very rapidly for half an hour or more. And some poor creatures, in order to be sure of going to heaven (as they suppose) cast themselves under the wheels of the chariot of Jaggernaut,† and are voluntarily crushed to death.‡

* See Extract from a Journal of a tour to Niagara Falls, in the spring and summer af 1812, in the Christian Disciple, September 1817.

† In the interior part of Hindostan an idol, called Jaggernaut, is worshipped by immense numbers, who make frequent pilgrimages to his temple in Orisa. On these occasions the idol is brought forth on a stupendous car or tower, about sixty feet in height, amidst the acclamations of hundreds of thousands of worshippers, who resort thither from various parts of India. Many of whom sacrifice themselves to this idol; numbers of pilgrims die on the road; and their bodies frequently remain unburied. See Buchanan's Researches, p. 105, 106, and his Apology for Christianity in India.

‡ Sketches relating to the Hindoos. Ward's account of the religion and manners of the Hindoos.

Z

ZABATHAI ZEVI, a celebrated Jewish impostor, who appeared at Smyrna about 1666, and pretending to be the Messiah, promised to deliver the Jews, and re-establish them in more than their pristine glory. Multitudes of his nation acknowledged him for their Messiah and king, and many of his followers pretended to visions and prophetic ecstacies. At length he fell into the hands of the Grand Seignor, who commanded him to be set as a mark for his archers, to prove whether he was invulnerable. To avoid this trial Zevi renounced his vainglorious pretensions; and saved his life by professing the Mahometan religion.

The denomination of Zabathaites is given to the followers of Zabathai Zevi. The sect he formed survived him; and he actually has yet, at Salonichi, partisans, who, outwardly professing Mahometanism, observe in secret the Judaic rites, marry among themselves, and all live in the same quarter of the city, without communicating with the mussulmans, except for the purpose of commerce, and in the mosques.*

Zabathai Zevi is said to have had many adherents among the Jews of England, Holland, Germany, and Poland, who have continued in small numbers to our days.

***ZABEANS,** a name given to the Chaldeans, Persians, and other ancient Idolaters, who worshipped the Host of Heaven, and pretended to the arts of Astrology and Necromancy.† See *Sabeans*.

ZACCHEANS, disciples of Zaccheus, a native of Palestine, who about the year 350 retired to a mountain near the city of Jerusalem, and there performed his devotions in secret; conceiving that prayer was only agreeable to God when performed secretly and in silence.‡

ZANZALIANS. See *Jacobites.*

***ZEALOTS,** or ZELOTS, the followers of Judas of Galilee, who (like many others) committed all manner of excesses, under pretence of zeal for God and his law.||

ZUINGLIANS, a branch of the ancient protestants; so called from Ulric Zuinglius, a divine of Switzerland, who received the doctor's cap at Basil in 1501. Possessing an uncommon share of penetration and acuteness of genius, he declaimed severely against indulgences, the mass, the celibacy of the clergy, and other doc-

* Scotch Theol. Dict. in Messiah. Gregoire's Histoire Des Sectes Religieuses.

† Calmet's Dict. ‡ Broughton, vol. ii. p. 516.

|| Josephus' Antiq. lib. 18. Stackhouse's Hist. of the Bible, vol. v. p. 130.

trines of the Roman church. He differed from Luther in supposing only a *figurative* presence of the body and blood of Christ in the eucharist; and simply considered it as a pious remembrance of Christ's death, and of the benefits it procured to mankind. He denied that either of the sacraments confers grace, and had some peculiar notions on the doctrines of original sin, grace, &c. He was also for removing out of the churches many things which Luther was disposed to treat with toleration and indulgence; such as images, altars, wax-tapers, and other ceremonies.

The religious tenets of this denomination were, in most other points, similar to those of the *Lutherans*.*

* Mosheim, vol. iv. p. 66—79. Milner, vol v. Cent. 16, chap. xii.

APPENDIX.

A BRIEF SKETCH

OF THE

STATE OF RELIGION THROUGHOUT THE WORLD,

BY MR. T. WILLIAMS.

NOTWITHSTANDING the most important articles comprised in the second and third parts of the former editions of this work are incorporated in the preceding DICTIONARY, the editor judged that the following *bird's-eye* view of all the religions and principal religious denominations now existing in the world, might glean up a few remaining particulars that had been passed over, and form an acceptable appendage to the work: and in order to make it useful, as well as entertaining, he has subjoined a miscellany of observations, not only on the population and ecclesiastical government of the various nations, but on the present state of vital and evangelical religion, and the exertions making for the propagation of the gospel throughout the world.

In so compressed a form it would be impossible to cite all the authorities he has made use of, which are in general the most modern, as well as authentic, he could procure ;* and on the state of religion, and the heathen, he has particularly consulted the transactions and reports of missionary and bible societies, and the most respectable periodical publications of a religious nature. It is but just to acknowledge, that for the first hint of these tables he is indebted to a tract of the great Dr. Carey of Serampore, (but then in England,) entitled, "An Enquiry into the obligations of christians to use means for the conversion of the heathen :" a tract which laid the foundation of the Baptist Mission Society, and was one considerable mean of calling the attention of other denominations to the work. It deserves to be added, that this excellent man, after pointing out the way to others, was himself one of the first to lead in the great work which he recommended.

* Principally Pinkerton's Geography, and sundry Voyages and Travels, &c.

Religious Denominations established or tolerated, the former printed in Italics.

Countries.	EUROPE.	Pop. in mill.
ENGLAND and WALES.	*Church of England*, or *Episcopalians*,* with a general toleration of all sects of Dissenters in religious worship; but which however are restrained, by the Corporation and Test Acts, from certain offices of trust and honour. It is difficult to estimate the number of Dissenters in this country. The Arminian Methodists (including the new Connexion) amount to more than 180,000 in Society, besides occasional hearers. The Calvinistic Methodists are probably equally numerous with the Arminian; and the Independents, Baptists, and Presbyterians, with a few other sects, may be reckoned equal to both classes of Methodists. The Roman Catholics are estimated at nearly 100,000; and the Friends are very numerous; so that the whole body of Dissenters must certainly exceed a Million, and make about one tenth of the population. All who are not Dissenters are generally considered Members of the Establishment; but if we farther deduct all who make no profession of religion, and who attend to no forms of worship, the number of real Churchmen must be still considerably reduced. For a man who neither believes the articles, nor attends the worship of the Establishment, has no more right to be called a Churchman than a Mahometan or a Chinese.	11

* It will be readily perceived, that the account of "the present state of religion," &c. in the countries mentioned, is placed *opposite to*, and *not after* the statement of their population and of the numerical strength of the different religious denominations.

Present State of Religion, &c.

EUROPE.

ENGLAND and Wales. Among the circumstances favourable to vital religion in this country may be reckoned the following. 1. The institution of bible societies, and particularly that great engine of benevolence, "The British and Foreign Bible Society," which, in ten years has been the mean, in whole or in part, at home and abroad, of printing and distributing 1,148,850 bibles and testaments. With this parent Society are connected more than four hundred Auxiliary and Branch Societies, in the British dominions only.

2. The general establishment of Free Schools for the education of the poor: as 1. Sunday Schools for children employed in manufactories and manual labour. 2. Daily Schools either for children of the Church of England, as Dr. Bell's; or for all denominations, as those of the British and Foreign School Society, whose influence promises to be as extensive as that of the Bible Society. 3. Schools for adults, whose education had been neglected till they came to years of maturity.*

3. Village preaching, by which the gospel is spreading in all the obscure and distant parts of the kingdom, where it had not usually been heard.

4. Societies for Foreign Missions, which now exist in almost every denomination of Christians, and extend to every quarter of the world.

* Among the other benevolent institutions in England which are mentioned by Mr. Williams, the "London Society for Promoting Christianity amongst the Jews," which he has not mentioned, holds a distinguished rank. A brief account of this institution is given under the article Jews. From the last report of the society it appears, that a great field of usefulness is opened to their labours in Poland and Russia, where there are vast numbers of Jews. The Committee have turned their attention to these countries, and propose to send missionaries among them. See Boston Recorder, May 7, 1817.

Countries.	*Religious Denominations, &c.*	Pop. in mill.
Scotland and the adjacent Isles.	The *Scotch Kirk*, or *Presbyterians;* the Protestant Dissenters from which are called Seceders, and are divided into Burghers, Anti-burghers, and the Relief Kirk, &c. It is remarkable that Episcopalians also, by crossing the Tweed, become Dissenters.	2
Ireland.	*Church of England*, with the like toleration as in England; and the like disabilities as to the Catholics, who form (says Mr. Butler) "two thirds of the population of Ireland." The Wesleyan Methodists have in their Societies above 29,000; (besides occasional hearers;) there is also a considerable number of Presbyterians (especially in the North) and other protestant dissenters; so that the established religion can hardly claim more than one fourth of the population.	5
Holland and the Netherlands.	The *Reformed Church*, or Calvinism, is the Established Religion of Holland, with a general toleration to all other sects; but though Calvinism must be considered as the established religion, a great part of the people are Arminians, under the forms and discipline of Calvin, as is also the case in Scotland. The Netherlanders are generally Catholics, with	

Present State of Religion, &c.

5. Benevolent institutions, adapted to meet and to relieve almost every species of human misery; and these supported in times and circumstances which bear very hard upon the class of persons, by whom they are chiefly maintained.

In *Wales*, it may be added, the children of the poor have derived great advantage from Circulating schools, which remain for a certain time to teach the children of a particular district, and then remove to instruct another.

SCOTLAND Partakes in all that has been said of England; and has been particularly benefited by the institution of Sabbath schools, which have been introduced in many parts of the country with great success.

IRELAND Is certainly far behind England in mental culture, and has been kept back by priestcraft and superstition. Now, however, the various denominations of Protestants are vying with each other in the propagation of evangelical doctrine through the country. The Sunday school, Hibernian, and other societies are displaying great zeal in teaching the rising generation to read the bible, not only in the English, but in the Irish language, where the former is not understood.

HOLLAND. Before the French invasion of Holland, there were reckoned 1579 ministers in the establishment, 90 of the Walloon Church, [or Protestant Church of the United Netherlands,] 800 Catholics, 53 Lutherans, 43 Arminians, and 312 Baptists. The French introduced their infidel philosophy, but it was not adapted to the people, who are generally grave and steady. There are

Countries.	*Religious Denominations, &c.*	Pop. in mill.
	a limited toleration to all other sects; but being now brought under the same government as Holland, will probably much increase the Protestant interest.	7
DENMARK and its Islands.	*Lutherans*, Calvinists, and Catholics; the latter with Mennonites (or Baptists) exist under some restraints and disabilities.	3
SWEDEN, Norway, and their dependencies.	*Lutherans*, Calvinists, Catholics, and Swedenborgians, (or New Jerusalem Church,) which are in Sweden numerous and respectable. The Catholics are under some restraints as to the publicity of their religious ceremonies. The recent union between Norway and Sweden will make no alteration in the state of religion, as they were both Protestant kingdoms.	4
PRUSSIA.	*Lutherans*, *Calvinists*, and *Catholics*, with a free toleration to others; which may partly be attributed to the infidel principles of Fred-	

also many pious christians, who have not only contributed freely of their property to the cause of religion; but several of the most useful missionaries in Africa have been from that country, as Vanderkemp, Kicherer, &c.

DENMARK. The Danes have formerly taken an active part in missions to the heathen, and have particularly countenanced the United Brethren in Greenland,* and in their West India islands. They had also the honour to patronize and foster the Baptist Mission at Serampore, when discountenanced by our East India Company. The king, it is said, has expressed a great desire for the instruction of his subjects, and the British system of education is intended to be introduced. The scriptures have been printed at Copenhagen in the Icelandic dialect, for the use of Iceland.

SWEDEN. A Bible Society has been formed at Stockholm, which has co-operated with that in London, in printing the scriptures in the Swedish language and that of Lapland.† The Stockholm Society is also active in the circulation of religious tracts in those languages. A Bible Society has been also formed at Abo in Finland, by the aid of the London Society, for the printing of the Finnish scriptures, to which the present emperor of Russia has contributed 5000 rix dollars.

PRUSSIA. Berlin is famous for an excellent seminary for the education of Protestant ministers; and several missionaries to the heathen have been furnished from that quarter to different societies in England. A Bible Society was formed at Ber-

* The Danish missionaries have made two different translations of the new testament, both of which have been printed in the Greenland language.

† In 1811, the British and Foreign Bible Society published a large edition of the new testament in the Laponese language.

Countries	Religious Denominations, &c.	Pop. in mill.
	eric the Great, and partly to the influence of Protestant principles in the country.	8
SAXONY	Is to be divided, which will give nearly a million of subjects to Prussia (included above) and leave about 1,200,000 subjects under the old government. The inhabitants are chiefly Lutherans or Calvinists.	1
POLAND.	*Catholics*, with toleration to Protestants under certain disabilities. The Lutherans are governed by a consistory, and the Calvinists by a principal and three seniors. This state is about being again formed into a distinct government, under the protection of Russia. Transylvania in 1787 contained 28,700 Socinians, usually called the Polish Brethren.	6
AUSTRIA, Hungary, and Bohemia.	The established religion of this great empire was the *Catholic*, but from the intermixture of Protestant states, contains a considerable number of Lutherans, Calvinists, and other Protestants of all denominations; and, by the new constitution, there is to be a perfect equality of rights and privileges among the Roman Catholic, Lutheran, and Calvinistic churches. In Hungary it was calculated in 1787, that the Catholics and Protestants were nearly equal; besides which this kingdom was stated to contain 223,000 Jews, 50,000 Gypsies, and a great number of Greek christians.	20
SWITZERLAND, Piedmont, &c.	Switzerland is divided into cantons: those of Berne, Zurich, &c. are Calvinists; Uri, Schweitz, &c. Catholic; some are composed	

lin in 1806, to which the king himself was both a contributor and patron.

SAXONY. Little is known of the religious state of Saxony, which has been wholly occupied with political events; but we should hope to find in the native country of Luther a considerable number of true Protestants.

POLAND. The plan of a Bible Society for this country is just formed under the auspices of the Emperor Alexander.

AUSTRIA. The establishment of Bible and Missionary Societies in various parts of Germany must greatly subserve the cause of christianity. On its being represented to the British and Foreign Bible Society in London, that there were upwards of a million of Protestants in Hungary, who were in great want of bibles, and too poor to purchase them, 500*l*. was given for the formation of a society in that country, for printing and circulating the scriptures in the Hungarian and Sclavonian dialects, which has been effected. Bible Societies have also been lately formed at Dresden and Hanover. The United Brethren have spread a sweet savour of evangelical religion throughout Bohemia, Moravia, and various other parts of Germany, from whence also they have sent missionaries to the remotest parts of the earth.

SWITZERLAND. The Canton of *Basle* has of late been remarkable for activity in promoting the circulation of the scriptures, and the cause of missions, so long

Countries.	*Religious Denominations, &c.*	Pop. in mill.
	of both religions, and the French introduced a considerable portion of infidelity. The Vallais, or inhabitants of the vallies of Piedmont, were formerly called Waldenses, of which there are still some remains; but a great part of the people were driven, by a long and cruel persecution, within the pale of the Roman church, in which they still continue.	4
France.	The Roman Catholic religion is declared to be that of the majority of the French people, and is supported by the state; but the state provides equally for the ministers of the reformed church, either of the Lutheran or Calvinistic profession, and superintends even the synagogue of the Jews. Difference of religion is no bar to the advancement of any French citizen to the highest offices of the state. The Protestants are very numerous in the south of France, but with a great number of infidels throughout the country.	24
Spain and Portugal.	*Catholics*, without toleration to any other denomination. The late Cortes showed a disposition to enlighten the people, and tolerate Protestants; but Ferdinand VII, since his return, has re-established the order of Jesuits, and the Inquisition;* and liberal men	

* The pope, however, has endeavoured to effect a reform in the inquisition. He has ordered, that the proceedings in ecclesiastical tribunals shall be regulated by the same principles as those which govern in civil and criminal cases. Every individual, of whatever religious persuasion he may be, will be admitted as a witness, if cited by the accused. Relations, domestics, and persons of infamous characters are to be excluded. The proceedings shall be public; and no witness shall ever be admitted to give hearsay evidence. In the Brief containing these orders, the pope says, "The way to render religion powerful, is to show that she is divine, and that she brings to mankind only consolation and blessings. The precept of our divine Master, *love one another*, ought to be the universal law." See Christian Observer, May 1816.

as they had any means left them. The modern *Waldenses*, who are a simple and pious people are divided into thirteen parishes with each a minister; they had formerly fifteen great schools, ninety smaller, and two Latin schools. Both the ministers and schools subsisted in great measure by charitable assistance from Holland, Switzerland, and even England; but the events of the late war have reduced them to much wretchedness and misery.

FRANCE. In the South of France the gospel is heard with eagerness, and evangelical ministers from other countries are received with open arms; the fullest liberty of conscience is allowed, and there is an university for the education of the Protestant clergy. Mr. Martin, a young minister from Bourdeaux, is now in England for the express purpose of learning the new system of education, with a view to introduce it into his native country.

SPAIN. The introduction of an English army into these countries had a tendency to weaken the prejudices of the people against Protestants as heretics, though there is little to recommend true religion in the general morals of soldiers. Some of the late Cortes were also favourable to a reformation of religion, and of the priests; which has been lately given as the true reason of their being so obnoxious to the present government, which is certainly under the influence of the church.

Countries.	*Religious Denominations, &c.*	Pop. in mill.
	have been made the objects of persecution. The Catholic clergy in Spain are estimated at 200,000, and in Portugal but little less. In Portugal the same bigotry and superstition prevails, but the assistance they have received from the English inclines them to somewhat more liberality; and English Protestants may live unmolested, though not beloved.	13
ITALY, including Naples and Sicily, Sardinia, &c.	*Rome* is the metropolis of the *Catholic* church, and the popedom. No toleration to Protestants can be expected here, though the pope shows some peculiar civilities to the English nation. There are nine or ten thousand Jews resident in Rome and its vicinity. The inhabitants of Naples and Sicily (about six millions) are also *Catholics;* but when under the government of Murat, (formerly one of Buonaparte's generals,) a degree of toleration prevailed, especially at *Naples,* which was favourable to the introduction of the gospel. In 1782 there were counted in Naples above 45,525 priests, 24,694 monks, 20,793 nuns; but the next year a decree passed to dissolve 466 convents, which must have greatly lessened them.	15
TURKEY in Europe, with the Isles of the Archipelago.	The empire is *Mahometan,* and toleration is purchased by the payment of a capitation tax. Of christians, those of the Greek church are far the most numerous, and are in some parts (as in Moldavia and Wallachia) admitted to places of trust and honour. The Greeks, in general, are subject to the patriarch of Constantinople in ecclesiastical matters; but there are some Armenians, Copts,	

ITALY. A Protestant congregation has been lately formed at Naples; the government has granted them one of the unoccupied churches for their worship, and there seems a great disposition to listen to evangelical preaching. It is said also, that the pope has complained of the Protestant worship's being tolerated at Venice.

TURKEY. It is hoped among the Greek, as well as Protestant christians, thinly scattered over this empire, may be found the seed of a future christian church, whenever it may please God to open a door for the gospel to enter this country.

Countries.	*Religious Denominations, &c.*	Pop in mill.
	Nestorians, &c. The Jews are very numerous, and subject to a chief of their own nation.	8
Russia in Europe.	The *Greek church* is the establishment in this country, with a free toleration to Raskolniks, or Dissenters, as well as to Catholics, Protestants, and Jews.* The church is governed, not by the patriarch of Constantinople, as formerly; but by a grand national council of ecclesiastics, in which the emperor has a layman of high rank as his representative. The church service is performed in the old Sclavonian language. [Pinkerton.]	33

ASIA.

Countries.	*Religious Denominations, &c.*	Pop in mill.
Russia in Asia, including Siberia, Kamschatka, &c.	The *Greek Church* is the established religion in all the civilized provinces; but with a general toleration throughout this vast empire. A great part of the inhabitants of the desert are Pagan Tartars of the Samman religion. Some attach great importance to the form of their whiskers; and the Altaians are so fond of military show, that they dress up their idol deity in the uniform of an officer of dragoons. The Kamschatkans have been converted to the Greek religion by a ten years' exemption from all taxes.	3

* The emperor Alexander has lately issued an Ukase at Petersburgh, by which peculiar privileges are granted to Jews who become converts to christianity. They are to form a society under the title of Jewish Christians; and are to be established as colonists upon the land of the crown, to form separate communities, and to enjoy a temporary exemption from taxes. Privileges, however, are continued to the Jews, independent of their conversion to christianity, though they are more fully to be enjoyed on that event. See Literary Panorama, 1817.

Russia in Europe. The emperor's patronage of Bible Societies* in Petersburgh, Moscow, &c. cannot but have a favourable aspect to the cause of true religion. Mr. Pinkerton, who has visited this country, gives a pleasing account of the orthodoxy of the Greek church, as to the main points of the christian religion, and mentions several denominations of Raskolniks, (or Dissenters,) who discover much of the life and power of religion.

ASIA.

Russia in Asia. The United Brethren have long had a missionary establishment at Sarepta, and the Russian government encouraged Protestant settlements on the banks of the Wolga. Some years since the Edinburgh Missionary Society also attempted a mission at Karass near Astracan: but all are broken up (at least for the present) by the calamitous effects of the war. The missionaries of both settlements have, however, in the mean time been usefully and honourably employed in translating the new testament; the one, (whose work is already in circulation,) into the Turkish language, and the other into that of the Kalmuck Tartars, many of whom have embraced christianity in the Greek church. A mission is also in contemplation to the Mogul, and Manjur Tartars, who reside in that part of Siberia, which borders on the Chinese empire.

* The Bible Society in Russia print the sacred scriptures in all the languages spoken in the Russian empire.

Countries.	*Religious Denominations, &c.*	Pop. in mill.
TURKEY in Asia.	*Mahometans* occupy Palestine, or the holy land, Syria, Mesopotamia, and other countries, the scene of scripture history : but there are also many Jews* and Christians, of various denominations, who are indulged, by paying for it, with living under the ecclesiastical government of their respective patriarchs, whether of Jerusalem or Antioch, Alexandria or Constantinople. The same may be said of the Nestorians, Armenians, and other reputed Sectaries.	10
ARABIA.	*Mahometans*, Sabeans, and Wahabees.	8
PERSIA.	*Mahometans*, of the sect of Ali ; (who differ from the Turks as to the true successour of Mahomet ;) also Sufis and Gaurs, or Guebres, the disciples of Zoroaster.	10
TARTARY.	*Mahometans*, Pagans, and worshippers of the Grand Lama. See *Shamans*.	6
CHINA.	*Pagans* of various sects, but chiefly worshippers of Foe. There are some Catholics, Greeks, and Jews among them, rather by connivance than legal toleration. The Russians have a church at Pekin, and the Jews a synagogue at Kai-song-fou. The Catholics notwithstanding the persecution they have met with, boast of 60,000 converts still in Pekin.	250
JAPAN.	*Pagans*, particularly Sintoos, Budsoes, and a	

* The London Society for promoting christianity amongst the Jews contemplate sending missionaries to those of that nation in Palestine. See Boston Recorder, Oct. 7, 1817.

Present State of Religion, &c.

Bible Societies have been formed, not only at Petersburgh and Moscow under royal patronage, but in the provinces of Esthonia and Livonia, for the express purpose of printing the new testament and religious tracts in those dialects.

TURKEY, Arabia, Persia, Tartary. No mission has yet been attempted to these countries, but the way is preparing by printing the scriptures in almost all the various languages of the East. A mission was attempted by the late Mr. Bloomfield at the Isle of Malta, with a view to introduce the gospel into the Greek Isles, and eventually into Turkey: but the pestilence which raged there, and the death of that missionary, have hitherto retarded the object. It is not, however, forgotten; Dr. Naudi has been attempting to excite attention to it among the christians residing on the borders of the Mediterranean; and mentions it as a promising circumstance, that there have been of late many conversions of Jews residing in those parts. A late decree in Persia has permitted the public reading of the scriptures. The new testament has been printed in Persian and Arabic.

CHINA. The Jesuits undertook a mission to this country in the sixteenth century, on the plan of blending the Catholic religion with that of Foe and the philosophy of Confucius; this however was disapproved by Pope Innocent X, and he enjoined a renuciation of their idolatries. In 1788 it was reported that the Catholics had, in the course of thirty years, made 27,000 converts in the province of Suschuen, and 30,000 in Nankin; but a storm of persecution gathered soon after this, and the name of christianity became peculiarly obnoxious in China. A Chinese edict has lately

Countries.	*Religious Denominations, &c.*	Pop. in mill.
	kind of moral philosophers. (See *Japanese.*) The celebrated Francis Xavier, and other Jesuits, commenced a mission here in 1549, and were followed by the Franciscans. Their success at first was rapid and extraordinary; but their imprudence (as is asserted) brought on a persecution which lasted forty years, and ended in their utter extermination.	25
THIBET, or Tibet.	The worship of the *Grand Lama* is the established religion, (See Thibetians,) mixed with various shades of Paganism.	2
INDIA beyond the Ganges, including the Birman empire, Malaya, Siam, &c.	The Birman and Siamese *Hindoos* are disciples, not of Brahma, but of Boodu; but the Malays are chiefly Mahometans. Some Dutch and Portuguese settlements exist in different parts of this extensive country. The Catholics boast of 300,000 converts in Tonquin, and 160,000 in Cochin-china.	20
HINDOOSTAN.	The native inhabitants are *Hindoos* (followers of Brahma) Mahometans and Persees; among whom, about fourteen millions are reckoned to be British subjects. The Afghans are supposed to be the descendants of the ten tribes of the Jews carried into captivity, to whom a mission is projected from this country. Under the article, 'Syrian Christians,' in the Dictionary, it is mentioned that there is a considerable body of professing christians in the interiour of the country. I would add, from the report of Dr. Kerr, the christians of St. Thomas are stated at 70 or	

been issued against the introduction of missionaries and their books into this country, yet Mr. Morrison* has been long employed at Canton and Macao, in translating the scriptures and instructing the natives, and has lately been joined by Mr. Milne; and though they may not penetrate directly into the interiour of China, there is no doubt but they will send in the scriptures by means of the natives, whose curiosity seems much excited.

INDIA. The American Baptists have a mission at Rangoon, a sea-port town in the Birman empire; consisting of Messrs. Judson and Haught. Messrs. Coleman and Wheelock were ordained in Boston, Sept. 10, 1817, to join the same mission.

The missionaries at Serampore have presented a press and Birman types to their brethren at Rangoon. Mr. Judson has published a catechism and religious tract in the Birman language. More missionaries are solicited for this station.

HINDOOSTAN. Almost all the existing Missionary Societies have made attempts to convert the Hindoos. The "Society for promoting Christian Knowledge" has missionaries at Trinchinopally, Tanjore, Madras, and Cuddalore. The Danes, while they had possessions in the East Indies, were active in this good work. The Baptists†

* Mr. Morrison has effected the important work of translating the new testament into the Chinese language. He has also translated the book of Genesis and the Psalms.

† The Baptist missionaries in the East Indies are eminently distinguished for their zealous and successful efforts to convert the heathen. "The labours of a Carey, a Marshman, and a Ward have excited the admiration of the Christian world. Under their

Countries.	*Religious Denominations, &c.*	Pop. in mill.
	80,000; the Syrian Catholics at 90,000, and the Roman Catholics (strictly so) at 35,000. For the use of the Syrian christians, a Malayan version of the New Testament has been lately printed at Bombay.*	100
	For the religion of the natives, see *Hindoos* and *Yogeys*.	

* The American Board of Commissioners for Foreign Missions have under their patronage at Bombay, Messrs. Newell and Hall, who have lately established a printing press. There are also under the same patronage, five or more missionaries in, or near Ceylon. In 1817, five missionaries were ordained by the same board, some of whom are to be sent to Bombay, and the others are to instruct the Indians in North America.

Contributions have been repeatedly made in America for the translation of the scriptures into the Eastern languages. See Dr. Holmes' discourse before the Society for Foreign Missions, 1813; and Boston Recorder, 1817.

have been particularly successful; besides the settlement at Serampore, they have missionaries at Cutwa, Goamalty, Dinagepore, Saddomahl, &c. in Bengal, and in other parts of India. Calcutta itself is not the seat of infidelity as formerly; but contains many hundred serious christians in all the ranks of society.

The Missionary Society of London has missionaries in Vizigapatam, Madras, Ganjam, Bellary, Chinsurah, Oodagerry, &c. The Society for missions to Africa and the East has also two or three missionaries, with native readers and catechists; and there are perhaps, among all the societies, nearly a hundred persons engaged in the instruction of a hundred millions of inhabitants.

The United Brethren had a mission in the neighbourhood of Tranquebar, and attempted one in the Nicobar Islands, but both have failed.

An Auxiliary Bible Society has been formed at Calcutta to co-operate with the society in London, and with the Baptist missionaries, in translating and printing the scriptures in every considerable language of the East; and great progress has been already made in this important work.*

superintendence, the sacred scriptures are translating into thirty three different languages. At the same time they have not less than twenty mission stations, which are occupied by more than fifty preachers, scattered over the different regions of the East, to the distance of four thousand miles. At most of these stations Christian churches are established, in which are united Hindoos and Mussulmans; Armenians and Europeans. Bramins also of every order have renounced Cast, and embraced the gospel of Christ." See Dr. Baldwin's Sermon, delivered at Philadelphia, May 7, 1817.

* Calcutta is the seat of the first Protestant Bishop's See in India; the diocess extending over all the territories of the company.

Countries.	*Religious Denominations, &c.*	Pop. in mill.
ASIATIC ISLES, Ceylon, Celebes, Borneo, Java, &c.	Pagans and Mahometans, with an intermixture of European settlers of various nations. The inhabitants of Amboyna, a Dutch settlement, were in 1796 more than 45,000, among whom were nearly 16,000 Protestants, and about 25 christian chapels. The native religion of *Ceylon* is the same as that of the Birmans; besides which, it is said to contain 100,000 Protestants, 50,000 Roman Catholics, and in the whole, about a million and a half of inhabitants.	20

AUSTRALASIA.

Under this term are comprehended the vast and innumerable islands of the South Sea.

NEW HOLLAND. Geographers are not yet agreed, whether to call this a continent or an island, or several adjacent islands; the whole length being 1960 miles, and its breadth 1680, which is nearly two thirds the size of Europe, besides the surrounding islands. The original inhabitants are savages of two or three races, and in the lowest state of barbarism. In 1770, Capt. Cook took possession of the eastern coast in the name of his Britannic Majesty, and called it New South Wales, and here a colony has been settled, at Sidney Cove, chiefly formed of convicts from Great Britain. Dr. Carey estimated the population at twelve millions; but I can find no authority to justify such a calculation; the coast is thinly peopled, and great part of the interiour perhaps uninhabited. Van Dieman's

Present State of Religion, &c.

ASIATIC ISLES. The Missionary Society has three missionaries at Batavia, the capital of the Isle of Java, under the protection of the British government; one of whom is invited to Amboyna, the chief of the Molucca Isles. Here many Chinese reside, and others trade, by whom it is expected christianity may be carried into the heart of China. The same Society has two or three missionaries in *Ceylon*, and the Baptists one. The Methodists have also very recently commenced a mission in this Island, and all have been favourably received. A Bible Society was formed at Columbo in this Island, 1812.

AUSTRALASIA.

NEW SOUTH WALES. At Sidney cove in 1809 the population amounted to between eight and nine thousand, and has been gradually increasing. The gospel is preached by Mr. Marsden, chaplain to the colony and schools, opened under his patronage. Several of the missionaries sent to the South Seas have occasionally resided and preached here; schools have been opened both for the Europeans and natives, and one of them has met with very encouraging success in his attempts to teach the latter, who prove far more docile than was expected.

Countries.	*Religious Denominations, &c.*	Pop. in mill.
	land, formerly supposed a part of New Holland, is found to be a separate island. On mature consideration I cannot rate the whole population at more than	4
New Zealand, New Guinea, New Britain and Ireland, &c.	New Zealand is the most considerable island in this neighbourhood, being about six hundred miles long, and a hundred and fifty broad. The others are inferiour islands, differing greatly in population, but the whole probably not exceeding	1
Polynesia. Pelew Isles, Ladrones, Carolines, Sandwich Isles.	After all that navigators have said, I dare not reckon the inhabitants of these islands at more than the preceding. Pinkerton remarks that navigators have overrated them at least ten to one.	
Marquesas, Society Is. &c.	This is proved to be the case with Capt. Cook; and it is not likely that either Forster or La Perouse was more accurate. Otaheite had been rated at 160,000; the missionaries found it to contain little more than 16,000. On the other hand Mr. Pinkerton, who makes this remark, has been quite as much mistaken in underrating the population of some other places, particularly the Cape. I take the population collectively at	1

AFRICA.

Countries.	*Religious Denominations, &c.*	Pop. in mill.
States of Barbary.	*Mahometans,* with a considerable number of Jews; but few christians, excepting what are in a state of slavery.	3

New Zealand. An island (600 miles in length by 150) has been lately made a missionary station, by the Church Society for missions to Africa and the East.

Otaheite. The first efforts of the London Missionary Society were directed to the islands in the South Pacific Ocean. The missionaries were called to endure many trials, and exposed to peculiar difficulties. But after the perseverance of more than twenty years, a permanent mission has been established at Otaheite. In 1812, Pomare, the king of this island, avowed himself a christian. Many have followed his example, and diligently attend the ordinances of religion. Schools have been established to instruct the natives, particularly their children. A christian church has been formed among the natives of Otaheite, and civilization may be expected to advance rapidly. Missionaries have also been sent to Eimeo and Tongataboo; and have converted many of the inhabitants of these Islands.*

AFRICA.

Barbary. Christianity can be expected to make no progress in these states while the system of piracy is tolerated and every christian made a slave:

* For a particular account of the labours of the missionaries in the South Sea islands the reader is referred to Brown's History of Missions.

Countries.	*Religious Denominations, &c.*	Pop. in mill.
N. Western Coast.	This district comprehends a great number of independent tribes or nations, as the Monselmines, Mongearts,* Foulahs, Jaloofs, Feloops, Mandangos, and many others as far interiour as the Great Desert. Most of these are *Pagans*, except the Foulahs, who are *Mahometans*, as are also the wandering inhabitants of the Desert. The Foulahs are a very powerful nation, and make war on their neighbours to procure slaves for the Europeans.	4
Nigritia, or Negroland, and the coast of Guinea,	Runs far across the continent on the north side of the great chain of mountains, and furnishes, as well as Guinea, a considerable portion of victims for the slave trade. Some of these parts are very populous, as they must be to furnish, as it is said they did, 100,000 slaves annually to the West Indies. The king of Benin, who possesses but a small part of this territory, is said to be able to raise an army of 100,000. Widah is also very populous, and Haussa has been said (falsely no doubt) to be more populous than London. The French have agreed to give up the slave trade north of Cape Formosa.	6
S. Western Coast.	This includes the kingdoms of Loango, Congo, Angola, and the extensive country of the Jagas, and many other tribes as far south as the Damaras. The Portuguese sent Catholic missions to some of these countries as	

* A Jew is not suffered to enter this country, under pain of being burnt alive.

but it is hoped the restoration of peace in Europe will lead to the suppression of this system of cruelty and violence.

N. WESTERN Coast.

Towards the end of the last century a company of benevolent persons, in this country, formed a settlement with a view to the civilization of Africa and the extermination of the slave trade: but the settlement was destroyed by some French ships and afterwards given up to our government. Mr. Nylander is chaplain of the colony; and in 1811 the Wesleyan Methodists sent out missionaries thither.

The Church Society for missions to Africa and the East have stations at Bashia and Canofee, (both on the Rio Pongos,) where they have erected churches and founded schools.

S. Western Coast.

In the fifteenth century some Portuguese missionaries persuaded the king of Congo and his subjects to receive the Roman Catholic religion; and they were followed by some others; but they soon revolted again to Paganism, and have not yet been visited by Protestant missionaries.

Countries.	*Religious Denominations, &c.*	Pop in mill.
	early as the fifteenth century; and some converts have been made to christianity, but in general this part of Africa is involved in Paganism. See *Negroes.*	3
Damara, Namaquas, and Corannas.	The Damaras, are divided into five tribes; those who reside near the coast are very poor, and many become servants to the Namaquas: farther inland some become rich in cattle, (the only riches of those countries,) and upon the death of such, the horns and bones of the animals they have consumed are laid upon their graves as trophies. They are naturally mild, and treat their prisoners with humanity. The Namaquas are known to have ten tribes, and the Corannas fifteen. [Campbell.]	1
COLONY of the Cape.	*Calvinists,* and chiefly Dutchmen; the settlement having been peopled from Holland; but general toleration prevails under certain restrictions. The population in 1810 was ascertained to exceed 81,000, of whom 50,000 were Hottentots or slaves.	
Boshesmens' Country, and Caffraria.	The Boshesmen, or Bushmen, are a wild nation with no settled abode, who traverse the country to the extent of eight or nine degrees of longitude, and plunder whenever they can find opportunity. The term Caffraria, or the land of Infidels, was probably given to this country by the Arabs, and it is certain they are in the rudest state of heathenism; but their country is far more populous than that of the Bushmen or the Corannas. These nations, with the inhabitants of the Cape may form a population of	

Present State of Religion, &c.

DAMARA, &c. The Missionary Society of London have two settlements in the Namaqua country, Pella, and Mr. Schmelin's station on the Orange river; also one among the Corannas, called Orlam Kraal, and more recently Bethesda.

CAPE. The United Brethren have long had two flourishing settlements in this colony—one at Groene (formerly Bavian's) Kloof—the other at Genadendal (Gnadenthall) or Grace Vale.

The Missionary Society of London have several settlements in these parts, viz. at Stellenbosh between the Moravian stations—at Tulbach or Rodesand, where Mr. Vos resides—at Zurbrak near Zwellendam—at Hooge Kraal in George Drosdy; and toward the east end of the Colony, at Bethelsdorp near Algoa bay, which was founded by Dr. Vanderkemp: but as this last has been found an inconvenient situation for a mission, a new settlement has been formed farther east (on a spot pointed out by the governor) and called Theopolis, which may at present be considered as the principal missionary Station of this society in South Africa. An Auxiliary Missionary Society exists here, and another in Graaf Reynet, which approaches the limit of the

Countries.	*Religious Denominations, &c.*	Pop. in mill.
Griquas, Bootchuanas, and other neighbouring nations.	These are numerous and powerful, the city Latakoo alone has about 8000 inhabitants; and the capital of Makquanas is three times as large. They are all *Pagans.* [Campbell.]	1
Eastern Coast.	Tambookies, Mambookies, and the inhabitants of the coast, as far as Delagoa Bay, are Pagans and Mahometans, mixed with some Portuguese christians, who of course are Catholics.	1
Interiour Coast.	As not more than half this quarter of the globe has been hitherto explored by Europeans, and even that very imperfectly, it is but reasonable to assign a considerable population to this great extent of unknown country, which is wholly *Pagan.*	4
Abyssinia.	*Christians* of the Abyssinian church, (which see.) They practise circumcision, and some other Jewish rites; but were converted to christianity between the fourth and sixth centuries, and still retain the name of christians.	3
Nubia.	A miserable country, and in some parts thinly peopled, chiefly with Mahometans. Senaar, however, one of its cities, is said to contain 100,000 persons, and Dongola about half as many.	$1\frac{1}{2}$

Colony toward Caffraria. Here resides Mr. Kicherer, the minister, and the three converted Hottentots, who visited England in 1803, and 1804; a great revival of religion has very recently taken place in all these stations; and several African preachers (one a Hottentot) have been appointed as itinerants to assist the European missionaries.

GRIQUAS. The same society have a mission at Claarwater, now called Griqua Town, where King Gika and his people profess great respect for Dr. Vanderkemp, who resided some time among them.

The king of Latakoo, on a visit from Mr. Campbell, expressed his willingness to receive missionaries, and promised to be a father to them. A mission is therefore immediately designed to Latakoo, and to Malapeetze, and Makoon's Kraal—stations farther to the east, where the inhabitants have expressed the same willingness to receive instruction.

ABYSSINIA. In the latter part of the last century the United Brethren sent missionaries into Egypt, with a hope of their penetrating into this country, which proved impracticable, and the door seems shut against the gospel, as much as in any pagan nation whatever.

Countries.	*Religious Denominations, &c.*	Pop. in mill.
EGYPT.	*Mahometans,* Jews and Copts. This country is known to be very populous. Cairo alone is reckoned to contain 300,000 inhabitants.	3
MADAGASCAR, & other Isles on the Eastern Coast.	*Pagans,* with some European strangers of different nations. The inhabitants, who are very numerous, bear the character of intelligence and hospitality.	4½
ISLANDS on the Western Coast.	Partly Pagans, and partly Catholics or Protestants, according to the European powers to whom they belong.	1

NORTH AMERICA.

WESTERN COAST & Indian tribes in the North.	The inhabitants are *Pagans* of various Indian tribes, thinly scattered over the continent, and much diminished by disease and war; yet it must be considered there are many tribes and countries yet unknown—I therefore take them at	½
SPANISH Dominions, including *Mexico.*	These nations being, by the power of Spain, and the arts of the Jesuits, reduced under Spanish dominion, of course profess the *Catholic* religion, and are in a great measure civilized.* The inhabitants in 1803 were estimated at six and a half millions, and supposing they were exaggerated, as some think, I cannot conceive they ought now (after ten years' increase) to be taken at less than	7

* The Gospels and Epistles have been translated both into the Mexican language; and into the Mextecan, the vulgar language of New Spain. Part of the Old Testament has also been translated into the Mexican language. See Appendix to Brown's History of Missions.

EGYPT. The gospel was introduced into Egypt before the close of the first century, but expelled again by Mahometanism during the seventh and eighth. There is, however, a considerable number of Copts in the country, who retain the name and many of the forms of christianity.

MADAGASCAR. Dr. Vanderkemp had long intended a mission to this island, and was about entering upon it at the time of his death. Mr. Milne has since visited it to make inquiries, and it will no doubt become a missionary station of great importance.

NORTH AMERICA.

SPANISH Dominions. The inhabitants of those provinces are Roman Catholics. The Spaniards consider the nations whom they have reduced as converts to christianity. There are said to be in New Mexico, thirty villages of christian Indians, who live in society and industry, professing the Catholic faith.

Countries.	*Religious Denominations, &c.*	Pop. in mill.
UNITED STATES.	Christians of all denominations, Infidels and Jews, with equal rights and complete liberty of conscience. The proportion may be judged of by the following estimates of the number of congregations of the different sects. In Massachusetts, Congregationalists 450, Baptists 125, Episcopalians 15, Friends 36, Presbyterians 6, Universalists 4, Catholics, Unitarians and Methodists each 1.—total 639. In Philadelphia only, Friends 5, Presbyterians 6, Episcopalians 3, Lutherans 3, Catholics 4; German Calvinists, Moravians, Baptists, Universalists, Methodists, and Jews, 1 each—total 27.* In New York the Presbyterians are most numerous, and the Baptists in Kentucky. The Catholics who are not numerous, reside chiefly in Maryland.† The population of the United States was taken in 1810 at 7,238,421; which, comparing it with preceding estimates, gives an increase of about a million and a quarter in ten years; we may, therefore, in 1815, (allowing for the war,) very safely estimate them at	8
BRITISH Dominions in America.	*Protestants* and *Catholics*, (the latter, strange as it may seem,) being the established religion in Canada, while the establishment in New Brunswick, Newfoundland, &c. is that of the Church of England. The coasts of *Labrador* and *West Greenland* are too thinly peopled to admit a distinct enumeration in this brief sketch.	$\frac{1}{2}$

* This statement was made in 1801, and is consequently at present incorrect.

† In 1801, the number of Catholics in Maryland was computed to amount to about 25,000.

Present State of Religion, &c.

UNITED STATES. Though there is no ecclesiastical establishment in the United States, it does not follow that there is no religion; indeed in most of the states every man is required to contribute to the support of public worship (where it is instituted) though he may choose the denomination he will support. Missionary Societies have been established at Boston, New York, and most of the capital towns; and many Bible Societies have been instituted. In many parts great revivals of religion have taken place, and it is hoped that true religion is, in general, on the increase rather than otherwise.

The United Brethren have long had missionaries among the Indians in the back settlements of Pennsylvania, North Carolina, Georgia, and among the Cherokees on the borders of Tennessee; and in 1803 the American General Assembly sent a mission to the same neighbourhood; but some of these have been interrupted, by the events of the late war.*

BRITISH Dominions. There are several missionary stations also in the back settlements of Canada, &c. supported by various American Societies, by some in England, and by the United Brethren. "The Soci-

* The zeal for the circulation of the scriptures is not less active and ardent in the Western Hemisphere, than on the old continent. In 1816, it is stated that there were 125 Bible Societies in the United States. A National Bible Society was established in New York the same year: and in 1817, the number of its auxiliaries amounted to 108. The missionary zeal is also active in the United States; and numerous societies have been instituted for evangelizing the heathens. For a particular account of the religious and benevolent institutions in America, see Christian Disciple, Panoplist, American Baptist Magazine, and Boston Recorder.

Countries.	*Religious Denominations, &c.*	Pop. in mill.

SOUTH AMERICA.

CARACCAS.	The inhabitants of this province, at the time of the invasion of Spain by the French, declared themselves independent; and are not willing to resign their independence, though the ancient family is restored. They are Catholics.	$1\frac{1}{2}$
NEW GRANADA.	*Catholics.*	$1\frac{1}{2}$
PERU.	*Catholics.*	2
CHILI.	*Catholics* and Pagans.	$1\frac{1}{2}$
PARAGUAY or Buenos Ayres.	*Catholics*—This province has also claimed independence, and maintained a civil war with the Caraccas.	2
BRAZIL.	*Catholics.*—On the conquest of Portugal by the French, the royal family removed and still resides in this settlement, which has thereby the honour to be the seat of royalty.	2
NATIVES in the interiour.	*Pagans.*—The population little known, but may be moderately estimated at	3
GUIANA.	What was called French and Dutch Guiana has been conquered by the British, and the establishment is Protestant; but the population is inconsiderable. The United Brethren have sent missionaries to Paramaribo, the	

ety for propagating the Gospel in Foreign Parts" employs chaplains in many towns of Canada, New Brunswick, and Newfoundland, but few of them preach to the heathen. The Methodists have also a number of missionaries in the same parts, and some considerable congregations.

The United Brethren have long established settlements in *West Greenland*, and on the coast of *Labrador*, which have given an evangelical *tint* (so to speak) to those inhospitable regions.

SOUTH AMERICA.

GUIANA. The United Brethren, who penetrate all the most desolate parts of the earth, have several settlements here* viz. at Paramaribo, Bombay,

* In the year 1812, the United Brethren had thirty three settlements among the heathen, in which they employed a hundred and fifty seven missionaries, under whose care were, according to an estimate of Mr. Latrobe, about twenty seven thousand four hundred converts. See Brown's History of Missions, vol. ii. p. 107.

Countries.	*Religious Denominations, &c.*	Pop. in mill.
	capital of Surinam in Guiana; the labours of the brethren have been instrumental in converting many of the negroes.	

WEST INDIES.

BAHAMA ISLES.	Numerous and fertile, and subject to England; but few inhabited, and the population very inconsiderable.	
CUBA.	Spanish *Catholics*, all the natives being extirpated, and the island cultivated by negroes. The capital, Havannah, was reckoned to contain 30,000 inhabitants many years since	½
JAMAICA.	*Church of England*, and Pagans, with a legal toleration, often impeded by the high church zeal of the colonial assembly, which is discouraged by the government at home. Kingston the capital has 50,000 inhabitants.	½
HAYTI,	Or St. Domingo, was formerly divided between the French and Spaniards, afterwards possessed by the French only; but is now an independent island, exhibiting the singular phenomenon of an empire of blacks and people of colour, regularly organized under a black emperor.*	½
PORTO RICO	Spanish *Catholics*.	¼
VIRGIN ISLES.	*Protestants*. A group of small islands formerly occupied by the Danes, but in the late war captured by the English. The principal are	

* The king of Hayti is about to change the religion of his kingdom, which was Roman Catholic, to the Episcopal communion.

Sommelsdyk, and Hope on the Corentyn. The Missionary Society of London have also missionaries at Demarara, Mahaica, and Essequebo, and the gospel has been attended with such success and advantages among the slaves, that some of the planters have encouraged it.

WEST INDIES.

BAHAMA. The Methodists have a promising interest here and have built a chapel which is well attended, both by the white and black inhabitants.*

JAMAICA. The Methodists have a considerable interest here, and the United Brethren two small settlements upon the island.

VIRGIN ISLES. The United Brethren have several settlements in these isles, which were commenced under the

* The Methodist missionaries in the West India islands have exerted themselves, and have been frequently successful in their attempts to christianize the negro slave population of these islands.

Countries.	*Religious Denominations, &c.*	Pop. in mill.
	St. Thomas and St. John's; but the population will not bear a distinct enumeration.	
LEEWARD ISLES.	These Isles being divided between the English, Dutch, and French, were partly Protestant and partly Catholic—but of late have been all under the British flag; Guadaloupe and Dominica (two of the most populous) are to be restored to France.	$\frac{1}{4}$
WINDWARD Isles.	Of these Barbadoes, which is an English and a Protestant settlement, has a population of more than 120,000 Under this group I also include Trinidad, the farthest of these islands toward South America.	$\frac{1}{2}$

Danish government, and are still continued. The Methodists also have several little societies at Tortola, and other of the Islands.

Leeward Isles. The Methodists have missionary stations in most of these islands, particularly at St. Eustatia, Antigua, and Dominica, where they are rapidly on the increase. The United Brethren have also an established and growing interest at Antigua.

Windward Isles. *Barbadoes* is but ill provided with religious instruction. The Methodists and United Brethren have however each a small society upon the island. The Missionary Society, and the Methodists, have each attempted to introduce the gospel at Trinidad, and at Tobago, but with no remarkable success.

APPENDIX

TO THE FOURTH AMERICAN EDITION.

As Mr. Williams has been very concise in his account of the religious denominations existing in the United States of America, the following brief sketch is added.

The Congregationalists are the predominant religious denomination in each of the New England states, Rhode Island excepted. It has been computed that there are in Massachusetts Proper 350 congregations; in Connecticut 212; in Maine 114; and in Rhode Island 8. The churches in New Hampshire and Vermont are chiefly Congregational.* They are divided into Calvinists of the old school, a large number of Hopkinsians, Arminians, Unitarians of different grades, &c.

The Congregationalists are not numerous in the Middle and Southern States; they have, however, a number of churches in New Jersey, and South Carolina.

The Baptists form the most numerous body, Congregationalists excepted, in New England. They have greatly increased of late, for it appears from the report of the General Convention of Baptists for Foreign Missions, assembled at Philadelphia, May 7, 1817, that the number of their churches, in the United States, was 2727, of their ministers 1935; that the number baptized last year amounted to 10,000, and the whole number of members in fellowship was 183,245. Their clergy are organized into Associations.† This body is generally composed of Calvinists or Hopkinsians. In the foregoing account none of the members of the Baptist congregations are included, but only those in actual communion.

There are also Arminian, or Free Will Baptists, Sabba-

* See General Repository, No. VI, and Boston Recorder, 1816.

† See proceedings of the General Convention at Philadelphia, 1817.

tarians, Haldamites, Mennonites, Dunkers, and Separates,* who, though differing from the Baptist Associations above-named, as well as from each other in many points, yet all agree in denying infant baptism. These denominations are not included in the preceding computation.

The Presbyterian churches, under the jurisdiction of the General Assembly, preponderate in the Middle States. In New York are Antiburgher Seceders, and other classes, who embrace the Presbyterian form of church government. The tenets of the Genevan school are generally maintained by this denomination; but some have adopted, at least in part, the Hopkinsian system.

The General Synod of the Reformed Dutch Church is a considerably powerful body of Presbyterians, not acting in concert with the General Assembly, nor with any other circle of Presbyterians; their churches are principally in New York and New Jersey. The General Synod of the Associate Reformed Church is another connexion of Presbyterians, not acting in concert with either of the bodies above-mentioned. The Presbyterians are also numerous in the Southern States; and have several large congregations in South Carolina, Virginia and Tennessee. It is computed that there are about eighty seven Episcopal churches in New England. Those in Massachusetts, New Hampshire, Vermont and Rhode Island were, in 1810, organized, and styled "The Eastern Diocess of the United States of America." Their Bishop is the Right Rev. Alexander V. Griswold. Connecticut, where there are many Episcopalians, forms another Diocess, under the superintendence of a bishop. There are also bishops in those of the Middle and Southern States, where there is a large number of Episcopalians.† A few of the Episcopal churches are Calvinistic; but it is understood, that they generally embrace Arminian sentiments.

The Roman Catholics have in the United States of America one archbishop in Baltimore, and bishops in Boston, Philadelphia, New York, Beardstown, Ken'y. and New Orleans.

* There is an Association of Separate Baptists.

† Boston Recorder, 1816.

Their number, including those in Louisiana and some Indian tribes, is said to amount to 140,000.*

The Friends, or Quakers, are a numerous denomination of Christians in the United States. There are thirteen collections of this people in New England. The celebrated William Penn, the founder of Pennsylvania, by his meekness and wisdom, did honour to this society, whose sentiments he embraced and defended. They have at present fifty four congregations in that state. This denomination have been eminently distinguished for their zealous and persevering efforts to procure the abolition of the slave trade. There are nearly one thousand congregations of Friends in this country.

The Methodists are a numerous and popular combination in the United States. The greatest part of this denomination are in the Middle and Southern States. There are, however, in Massachusetts twenty societies of this people, and eighteen in Maine. Those in this country are all, with a very small exception, Westleian, or Arminian Methodists.

The German Moravians are a numerous and respectable body of Christians in Pennsylvania. In the village of Bethlehem they have two large stone buildings, in which the different sexes are educated in habits of industry, being employed in various useful manufactures. They have also flourishing settlements in North Carolina; and one church in Rhode Island.

The German Lutherans have several places of worship in Pennsylvania and New York.

There are twelve societies of Universalists in New England—seven in Massachusetts, four in Maine, and one in New Hampshire. There is also a society of Universalists in Pennsylvania. One part of this denomination are disciples of Chauncy and the other of Murray in their sentiments. The Separates are said to have six churches in Connecticut.

There are two Sandemanian churches in New England; one in Danbury, Connecticut, and one in Portsmouth, New

* This statement was given by the Rev. Dr. Matignon, who now officiates at the Roman Catholic church in Boston.

Hampshire. There is also a small number of Sandemanians in Boston.

There is a considerable number of believers in the doctrines of Swedenborg in the United States. They have churches or temples, as they call them, in New York, Philadelphia, and Baltimore. There are also a few who embrace his sentiments in Massachusetts, Virginia, and Ohio. There are likewise Halcyons, who agree with the Swedenborgians, in maintaining *the sole divinity of Jesus Christ;* though they differ in other respects.*

There is in the United States a considerable number of the followers of Mr. Elias Smith, formerly a Baptist minister in the Warren Association. They call themselves Chrystians, and profess to found their opinions solely on the sacred scriptures. In many respects they are said to harmonize with the Free Will Baptists. Mr. Smith, in some of his publications, advocates the doctrine of the annihilation of the finally impenitent; but he is said to have frequently changed his opinions. Those who wish to know more of this denomination are referred to Smith's New Testament Dictionary, and Benedict's History of the Baptists.

It appears from the most authentic intelligence which could be obtained, that there are, in the United States, about three thousand Jews.

They have one synagogue in New York; two in Philadelphia; one in Charleston, South Carolina; and one in Virginia.

The numerous religious denominations in the United States all unite in approving and establishing Bible Societies. The Congregationalists, Baptists, Episcopalians, Presbyterians, Moravians, and Methodists have made energetic exertions to convert the heathens, both in our own and foreign countries. Sunday Schools have also been established; and various societies formed to promote the present and future welfare of mankind: for instance, the Peace Societies which have been honoured with the approbation of the Emperor

* See New Jerusalem Magazine, 1817.

Alexander and Prince Galitzin, President of the Russian Bible Society. A society has also been formed for the religious and moral improvement of seamen, and there are many other religious and benevolent institutions. It has been justly remarked, that "At no time since the days of the apostles have equal exertions been made for the advancement of Christian knowledge, piety and virtue, as are at this time, and have been for a few years past, both in Europe and in our own country."*

The diversity of sentiment among Christians has been exhibited in the preceding pages. The candid mind will not consider those various opinions as an argument against divine revelation. The truth of the sacred writings is attested by the strongest evidence, such as the miracles recorded in the New Testament; the accomplishment of the prophecies; the rapid spread of the gospel, notwithstanding the most violent opposition; the consistency of the several parts of the inspired pages with each other; the purity and perfection of the precepts of christianity; their agreement with the moral attributes and perfections of the Deity; and their benevolent tendency to promote the good of society, and advance our present and future happiness. Perhaps there may be as great a variety in the moral, as in the physical world.

From this diversity in mind, some may have a natural bias towards one religious system, and some to another. "The education of different persons," says Dr. Watts, "has a mighty influence to form their opinions, and to fix their practices; and this, it must be confessed, is not in a man's own choice; but depends on the providence of the great and blessed God, the Overruler of all things."

Notwithstanding the great variety of opinions which divide the christian world, the following articles are acceded to by all who profess to believe in divine revelation.

1. That there is one Supreme Being of infinite perfections.

* Christian Disciple, July, 1814.

The Manicheans may seem to be an exception to this article of belief, because they maintained the doctrine of two principles. But as they supposed the good principle would finally be victorious, and reign supreme, their evil principle may only be considered as a powerful demon.

2. That this Supreme Being is the object of religious worship.—This appears naturally to result from the preceding article; if we admit the being of a God, the propriety of worshipping him is obvious.

Trinitarians pray to one God in three persons; Unitarians address God in the person of the Father only. Roman Catholics pray to the Virgin Mary and other saints; but they profess to address them only as intercessors and mediators, and that one God is the ultimate object of their religious worship. The Swedenborgians address all their prayers to Jesus Christ, because they believe he is the Supreme and *only Deity*, made visible and accessible in a human form; and therefore to be alone worshipped.

3. That Jesus of Nazareth is the Messiah, (that is, the anointed of God,) to whom the prophecies of the old testament refer. All who profess to believe in divine revelation agree in this article, though their ideas respecting Christ's person, and the ends of his mission, are widely different.

4. That there will be a resurrection of the dead. The doctrine of a literal resurrection was indeed denied by some of the Gnostics, and is still by a few modern denominations; yet even these admit a resurrection of some kind, though they explain the term metaphorically.

5. That piety and virtue will be rewarded in a future state, and impiety and vice punished. This article includes the idea that piety and virtue are indispensably necessary to happiness. This point is universally acceded to; and therefore, upon every religious system now embraced, it is our duty and interest to be virtuous and pious.

The wretched state of the world at the time of our Saviour's appearance, which is exhibited in the Introduction to this work, evinces the necessity of the Christian dispensation.

The gross superstition of the Pagans, the degeneracy of the Jewish nation, the inconsistency of the ancient philosophers, and their uncertainty respecting a future state, elucidate the apostle's declaration, that "life and immortality are brought to light by the gospel."* It also appears from our Introduction, that it is highly unreasonable to consider the various opinions among Christians as an objection to the truth of divine revelation. At the time of Christ's appearance, there was a variety of modes in the pagan worship,† and a great diversity of philosophical opinions. The Jews were divided in their opinions at the time of our Saviour, and there are still some remains of the ancient sects.

The preceding work farther evinces, that the Pagan world still practise a variety of religious rites; and that the Mahometans are as much divided as the Christians. Neither are those who reject revelation better agreed among themselves; for it appears that the greatest infidels, which any age ever produced, were divided and unsettled in their philosophical opinions. Voltaire leaned to deism, and seemed for some time to have adopted it; but insensibly falling into Spinoza's system, he knew not what to believe. D'Alembert, involved in uncertainty respecting the being of a God, asserts that it is

* Cicero, famous throughout the learned world for his inquiries after truth, and investigations into the nature, moral faculties, and future expectations of man, gives us the sum of all the knowledge that could be acquired without revelation. In his Tusculan questions, lib. i. he gives us to understand, that whether the soul be mortal or immortal is a question which cannot be positively decided. He devoutly wished that the immortality of the soul could be proved to him. So that with all his knowledge, and after all his researches, he was not able to determine a fact, on which the happiness of the rational creature, for time and eternity, must depend. See Boudinot's Age of Revelation.

† According to Themistius, an ancient Greek orator and philosopher, there were more than three hundred sects of the Western philosophers, differing greatly on subjects of high importance. According to Varro, there were two hundred and eighty eight different opinions entertained by them concerning the *summum bonum*. or chief good; and three hundred opinions concerning God; or as Varro himself declares, three hundred Jupiters or supreme deities. See President Dwight's Sermon on the Nature of the Infidel Philosophy.

more rational to be skeptical than dogmatical on the subject. We find Diderot, after having decided against the deist, deciding in the same peremptory manner for or against the skeptic or the atheist; and Rousseau, that prodigy of inconsistency, sometimes declaring his certainty of the existence of a Deity, and writing the most sublime eulogies upon Christ, that human eloquence could devise; at other times a distinguished champion of skepticism and infidelity. Surely a difference of sentiment cannot reasonably be objected against Christians, when we find the most celebrated Infidels thus divided, and inconsistent with themselves and each other.

The differences among Christian denominations will appear still greater than they really are, unless we recollect that a large number of the ancient sects, which are described in the preceding work, are now extinct. It is also to be considered, that the opinions of several sects are nearly the same, though under different names, and some few modifications. Mr. Evans, in his "Sketch of the denominations of the Christian world," observes, that the most distinguished denominations, which attract our attention at the present day, may be included under the following threefold arrangement.

1. Opinions respecting the person of Christ. These include all the various grades of Trinitarians, Sabellians and Unitarians.

2. Opinions respecting the means and measure of God's favour. Under this head Calvinists, Baxterians, Arminians, and others are comprehended.

3. Opinions respecting church government, and the administration of ceremonies. These include the Roman Catholic, Greek, Episcopalian churches, and various denominations of Dissenters.

To these divisions Mr. Evans adds a few denominations, which cannot be classed with propriety under any of these three general heads.

From the foregoing view of the various religions of the different countries of the world, it appears, that the Christian religion is of very small extent, compared with the many and vast countries overspread with Paganism and Mahometanism. This great and painful truth is further evidenced by the calculations which have been made of the population of the world,* and the proportion of the principal religious denominations to each other.

In reviewing the history of the various denominations of Christians in past ages, humanity is deeply wounded by the intolerant spirit which has been so often exhibited by the dominant party. Till of late, attempting to suppress by persecution, what were deemed erroneous opinions, was judged lawful, not by Catholics only, but by the Reformers, by Episcopalians, and almost all the different denominations of Dissenters. But such is the happy progress of religious liberty and toleration, that at present, almost all sects and parties of Christians disclaim the right of using coercive measures in the sacred concerns of religion.

Though the ends to be answered by divine Providence, in permitting such a variety of opinions, cannot be fully comprehended; yet we may be assured, that they are under the direction of an all-perfect Being, who governs in infinite wisdom.

> "From seeming evil still educing good,
> And better thence again, and better still
> In infinite progression." THOMSON.

* Mr. Cummings, in his Geography, estimates the population of the world at eight hundred millions; and gives the following statement of the religious divisions of the inhabitants.

Of the four principal religious denominations,

Christians, - - - - - - - - - -	170,000,000.
Jews, - - - - - - - - - - - -	9,000,000.
Mahometans, - - - - - - - - -	140,000,000.
Pagans, - - - - - - - - - - - -	481,000,000.
Total,	800,000,000.

Subdivisions among christians may be thus:

Protestants, - - - - - - - - - -	50,000,000.
Greeks and Armenians, - - - - - -	30,000,000.
Catholics, - - - - - - - - - - - -	90,000,000.
Total,	170,000,000.

Hence it appears that about one fifth part only of the human race have yet embraced the Christian religion in any of its forms.

Why providence has suffered the Christian religion to be hitherto confined to so small a portion of the globe is also a mystery which we cannot fathom. But we are encouraged by many prophecies in the sacred scriptures to expect a period when the gospel shall be universally extended, and received with unanimity; when all superstition shall be abolished; the Jews and Gentiles unitedly become the subjects of Christ's universal empire, *and the knowledge of the Lord fill the earth, as the waters cover the sea.*